Cognitive Intelligence
and Big Data in Healthcare

Scrivener Publishing
100 Cummings Center, Suite 541J
Beverly, MA 01915-6106

Artificial Intelligence and Soft Computing for Industrial Transformation

Series Editor: Dr. S. Balamurugan (sbnbala@gmail.com)

Scope: Artificial Intelligence and Soft Computing Techniques play an impeccable role in industrial transformation. The topics to be covered in this book series include Artificial Intelligence, Machine Learning, Deep Learning, Neural Networks, Fuzzy Logic, Genetic Algorithms, Particle Swarm Optimization, Evolutionary Algorithms, Nature Inspired Algorithms, Simulated Annealing, Metaheuristics, Cuckoo Search, Firefly Optimization, Bio-inspired Algorithms, Ant Colony Optimization, Heuristic Search Techniques, Reinforcement Learning, Inductive Learning, Statistical Learning, Supervised and Unsupervised Learning, Association Learning and Clustering, Reasoning, Support Vector Machine, Differential Evolution Algorithms, Expert Systems, Neuro Fuzzy Hybrid Systems, Genetic Neuro Hybrid Systems, Genetic Fuzzy Hybrid Systems and other Hybridized Soft Computing Techniques and their applications for Industrial Transformation. The book series is aimed to provide comprehensive handbooks and reference books for the benefit of scientists, research scholars, students and industry professional working towards next generation industrial transformation.

Publishers at Scrivener
Martin Scrivener (martin@scrivenerpublishing.com)
Phillip Carmical (pcarmical@scrivenerpublishing.com)

Cognitive Intelligence and Big Data in Healthcare

Edited by

D. Sumathi
T. Poongodi
B. Balamurugan
and
Lakshmana Kumar Ramasamy

Scrivener
Publishing

WILEY

This edition first published 2022 by John Wiley & Sons, Inc., 111 River Street, Hoboken, NJ 07030, USA and Scrivener Publishing LLC, 100 Cummings Center, Suite 541J, Beverly, MA 01915, USA
© 2022 Scrivener Publishing LLC
For more information about Scrivener publications please visit www.scrivenerpublishing.com.

Wiley Global Headquarters
111 River Street, Hoboken, NJ 07030, USA

For details of our global editorial offices, customer services, and more information about Wiley products visit us at www.wiley.com.

Limit of Liability/Disclaimer of Warranty
While the publisher and authors have used their best efforts in preparing this work, they make no representations or warranties with respect to the accuracy or completeness of the contents of this work and specifically disclaim all warranties, including without limitation any implied warranties of merchantability or fitness for a particular purpose. No warranty may be created or extended by sales representatives, written sales materials, or promotional statements for this work. The fact that an organization, website, or product is referred to in this work as a citation and/or potential source of further information does not mean that the publisher and authors endorse the information or services the organization, website, or product may provide or recommendations it may make. This work is sold with the understanding that the publisher is not engaged in rendering professional services. The advice and strategies contained herein may not be suitable for your situation. You should consult with a specialist where appropriate. Neither the publisher nor authors shall be liable for any loss of profit or any other commercial damages, including but not limited to special, incidental, consequential, or other damages. Further, readers should be aware that websites listed in this work may have changed or disappeared between when this work was written and when it is read.

Library of Congress Cataloging-in-Publication Data

ISBN 978-1-119-76888-3

Cover image: Pixabay.Com
Cover design by Russell Richardson

Set in size of 11pt and Minion Pro by Manila Typesetting Company, Makati, Philippines

Printed in the USA

10 9 8 7 6 5 4 3 2 1

Contents

Preface

The introduction of new technologies into various domains, such as manufacturing, pharmaceuticals, healthcare and education, has contributed to their evolution. As health is the foremost factor affecting the quality of human life, it is necessary to understand how the human body is functioning by processing health data obtained from various sources more quickly. Since an enormous amount of data is generated during data processing, a cognitive computing system could be applied to provide responses to queries, thereby providing assistance in customizing intelligent recommendations. This decision-making process could be improved by the deployment of cognitive computing techniques in healthcare, especially so that bodily functions and machines can be associated. Therefore, cutting-edge techniques that could be integrated into healthcare must be investigated in order to provide intelligent services in various healthcare applications.

This book can be viewed as part of an initiative to provide diversified topics in healthcare sectors to show the range of recent innovative research, in addition to shedding light on future directions in this area. It will be a useful source of information for those involved in different areas of research and both graduate and postgraduate students interested in advanced technologies for the augmentation of healthcare services. A brief chapter-by-chapter description of the information covered in the book follows.

Chapter 1 discusses the evolution of various computational cognitive techniques in healthcare systems; and Chapter 2 deals with the metaheuristic algorithm of cognitive computing for classification of erythrocytes and leukocytes in healthcare informatics. Chapter 3 presents information about the convergence of big data and cognitive computing in healthcare. Chapter 4 deliberates on the intervention of IoT techniques deployed to prevent health problems; and the significance of cognitive computing in healthcare applications is analyzed in Chapter 5. A detailed overview of computational cognition and its techniques and potential in various healthcare systems is given in Chapter 6; and Chapter 7 discusses how to provide data security through the deployment of two-factor authentication.

Next, Chapter 8 highlights the benefits of data analytics for monitoring healthcare applications and its inferences through deployed models. Various investigations on optimistic approaches for the detection of Parkinson's disease are presented in Chapter 9; and Chapter 10 presents a holistic approach to big data analytics in healthcare. Chapter 11 provides a detailed view of the integration of big data and cognitive intelligence in healthcare; and a detailed case study is discussed in Chapter 12 in which the authors focus on the analysis, challenges and advancements of social media and how much of an impact it has on mental health. Chapter 13 highlights the management of chronic disease by considering the integration of artificial intelligence (AI), blockchain, and the internet of things (IoT). Finally, Chapter 14 sheds light on the research challenges and future prospects of deploying cognitive computing in the healthcare domain.

The editors thank the contributors for their splendid work and time.

The Editors:
D. Sumathi
T. Poongodi
B. Balamurugan
Lakshmana Kumar Ramasamy

1

Era of Computational Cognitive Techniques in Healthcare Systems

Deependra Rastogi[1]*, Varun Tiwari[2], Shobhit Kumar[3] and Prabhat Chandra Gupta[4]

[1]*School of Computing Science and Engineering, Galgotias University, Greater Noida, Uttar Pradesh, India*
[2]*Manipal University Jaipur, Rajasthan, India*
[3]*Graphic Era Hill University, Bhimtal, Uttarakhand, India*
[4]*School of Computing Science and Engineering, Galgotias University, Greater Noida, India*

Abstract

Biomedical informatics and behavioral medicine are developing in parallel with its own theories and methods in the field of science. The conjunction of research cognitive information science offers enormous challenges and opportunities in addressing community health glitches and supervision of disease prevention. Classification of the healthcare cognitive informatics system accumulates medical, communal, and individual statistics from diverse sources of healthcare to enhance the rendezvous of patients. This chapter provides comprehensive review on the preceding research linked to cognitive informatics and computing in healthcare division. The era of computational cognitive informatics and technique has been divided into three areas of computing and healthcare informatics such as tabulating era, programmable era, and cognitive computing. Tabulating era was completely nourished into machine-driven system and the figuring was principally achieved by tabulating machines, calculators, and vacuum systems. The programmable era was entirely meticulous by the user interface design such as mainframe, smart computer machines, and personal computer. The era evolved of cognitive computing from 2011, this era nourished to the formation of automated IT systems that can resolve difficulties deprived of the necessity for human assistance. The main emphasis and driver of this cognitive era was the swift exponential upsurge in the flow of unstructured data. This chapter deals with the significant role of cognitive informatics in terms of the emerging areas in healthcare as well as to explore the methods, algorithms, in the healthcare division.

Corresponding author: deependra.rastogi@galgotiasuniversity.edu.in

D. Sumathi, T. Poongodi, B. Balamurugan and Lakshmana Kumar Ramasamy (eds.)
Cognitive Intelligence and Big Data in Healthcare, (1–40) © 2022 Scrivener Publishing LLC

Keywords: Cognitive science, cognitive computing, cognitive intelligence, machine learning, natural language processing, deep learning, cognitive intelligence in healthcare

1.1   Introduction

The future of healthcare depends on giving patients a full understanding of the multiple variables impacting their health. Today's consumers want customized, open, integrated, and high-quality care in search of the same conveniences they get in other industries. Healthcare providers need new ways to tap into and interpret health knowledge in real time in order to deliver the experience empowered by customer demand. Real-time data helps the most educated decisions to be taken by physicians, analysts, insurers, case managers, and other partners, while simultaneously allowing consumers more influence of their own care. This difficult coordination, however, takes substantial time and can tax even the most flexible organization's capital [1, 3].

In their lifetime, the average citizen is expected to produce over 1 million gigabytes of health-related material, equal to 1.3 billion books, health information from personal fitness trackers, connected medical devices, implants, and other sensors that gather real-time data. The amount of health information currently doubles every 3 years and is expected to double every 73 days by 2020 [1].

It is reluctant to manage these growing databases of knowledge relating to healthcare, namely electronic health records, clinical studies, autopsy reports, laboratory findings, radiology photographs, voice recordings, and exogenous evidence, since they are scattered [64]. Furthermore, these sources of knowledge do not willingly incorporate important evidence about the non-clinical circumstances of a person, which can have a strong health effect. As a result, patients and their healthcare providers must make choices based on a limited data set [1, 2].

That's one factor why health professionals are among the early adopters of cognitive computing technologies that, when communicating with individuals, can comprehend, reason, and learn. Cognitive channels, from numbers and text to audio, video, pictures, sensory and other content, are meant to absorb large volumes of organized and unstructured information. The proverbial needle in a haystack will help doctors and experts locate similarities and associations, finding emerging trends and observations to accelerate findings, procedures, and insight. Simply put, cognitive structures, particularly though the magnitude and speed of data continued to explode, help scale, and enhance human intelligence [1, 2].

"The aim of cognitive computing is to build automatic IT processes that are capable of understanding without the need for human assistance" [3].

In this chapter, we first include the framework of cognitive science and the difference between classical cognitive science theory. Then, to include the popularity of knowledge that reflects the developmental phase of cognitive computation. The next move includes architecture and enabling computational computing technology. Then, to explain how the Intelligent system makes cognitive computation in healthcare and finally to include a case study on cognitive computing and healthcare research.

1.2 Cognitive Science

Cognitive Science is an interdisciplinary and empirical study of the mind as well as its mechanisms. It addresses the nature of thought, its functions, and goals (in a broad sense). Cognitive sciences study intelligence and behavior, concentrating on how central nervous system interpret, store and apply knowledge [4].

In "cognitive" the word "cognitive science" is used for "any kind of mental operation or structure that can be studied in precise terms" (Lakoff and Johnson, 1999). In certain traditions of theoretical theory, this conceptualization is rather broad and cannot be confused with how "cognitive" is used, where only formal rules and conditional semantics of truth have to do with "cognitive".

Cognitive science is a multidisciplinary field based on linguistics, psychology, anthropology, computer science, and philosophy that understands human behavior, including decision-making, reasoning, and problem solving. Cognitive science concepts have been extended to research the functionality of medicinal equipment and boundaries [6]; to identify advice, guidance and guidance [7]; to streamline and improve workflows and medical processes [8]; and to consider the complexities of clinical evaluation, logic and decision-making [9].

The nature and assessment of HIT has been influenced by analytical and methodological methods from cognitive psychology, as well as by recognizing and enhancing the efficacy of healthcare providers. Initial CI research has drawn extensively from subjects of cognitive science connected to learning, decision-making, and problem solving. Cognitive science emerged from the conceptualizations of person "thinking" and "mental processes" by Newell and Simon [10], and "human problem solving." Initial problem-solving experiments have presented protocol-analytical tactics [11], human data dispensation ideas that have therefore placed the foundations for the humanoid–computer collaboration communication discipline (HCI). Strategies such as cognitive thinking have been commonly used in CI research and have also been instrumental in improving our perception of the resolution of medical problems and judgment and thinking [5]. Similarly, Kintsch's [12] text comprehension thesis was instrumental in influencing Cognitive Informatics experiments relevant to inference and therapeutic judgment.

1.3   Gap Between Classical Theory of Cognition

There is a gap among (a) traditional cognitive philosophy that questions understanding basic concepts of human action by models of the general purpose of the brain's visual cortex, and (b) facets of human behavior that imitate real-life patterns, circumstances, and complexities that are on the context-specific, ground, and applied. For organizational innovations and workflow strategies that usually emerge from almost simple concepts of context-independent cognition, individual-centered, this difference has major implications [15].

This inconsistency is contained within the cognitive scientist Andy Clark's conventional mind-body dualistic that permeates evolutionary computation, contributing to the disappointment to react in an ordered world to situated behavior [16]. As per Clark, the initial step (the glory days of traditional cognitivism) described the attention, in lieu of a dominant logic structure, conceptual repositories, and many bordering 'sensory' units. The reductionist approach of traditional cognitivism centered on the 'primary processing system' of expert systems, viewed as a symbol-based architecture that determines the cognitive characteristics of a human agent [3]. Although computer vision has recently undergone an extreme reassessment of the existence of the internal cognitive machine, moving away from the reliance on rational, rule-following protocols for defining engine processes, the conventional disenfranchisement of the body and environment has already been tacitly adopted throughout this "revolution" [16].

In classical mind theory, this marginalization of the surrounding environment ignores a profound aspect of human nature: our ability to use intelligence, resources, technology, mutual knowledge, and associates to undertake achievements that no particular agent can achieve alone [17]. This ability is widely accessible to our community, which anthropologists sometimes refer to as "culture," and is fundamental to understanding human behaviors ranging from rural agricultural tasks to dynamic contemporary workplace, manufacturing, and healthcare jobs. Because of the essential need to manipulate objects, devices, and other individuals in cognitive practice, the complexities of complex operations requiring the organization of disparate tools for executing tasks must be discussed by examples of human presentation (and the technology and procedures employed to improve that concert). Such practices tend to be regulated by broader information management processes, systems in which persons are embedded actors, and thus need a separate research unit and separate cognition study techniques.

The evolution of the classical theory of cognition [18] has played a crucial role in medical informatics [13, 14, 18]. The differential diagnostic function of the clinician, often taken as an archetype of critical thinking, has been describing the subject matter for decades of investigations of rational thought, language comprehension, problem-solving, and experience [19, 20]. In the picture of the diagnosis and treatment clinician, a few of the better remembered "expert programs" in the field of artificial intelligence were conceived as isolated logical agents [21, 22]. More significantly, these devices have been repurposed as instruments to facilitate decision-making by clinicians [23]. Nevertheless, the basic theory underlying their creation as a mechanism for evidence representation and expert thought continues in methodology and studies on decision-making, problem solving, experience, and human achievement in healthcare [18].

Guided by the individual-centered model of cognition, the shortcomings of healthcare technologies and procedures are now attractive apparent. The state-of-the-art knowledge healthcare industry has also been hesitant to take root, has generated many unhappy customers, and has frequently triggered significant workflow problems and detrimental safety and health consequences that come with any of these technologies [23–25].

For contemporary cognitive science, Clark emphasizes the concept that needs clear diagnosis of cognitive processes that transcend the boundary of body-environment and mind-body. To achieve this requires focus rather than only "in the laboratory" to cognition "in the wild," and requires a conceptual representation vocabulary capable of treating the relationship between agents, through various body systems, as well as between their instruments and agents in organized atmospheres [26, 29]. The influences of Clark, Hutchins, and others [27, 28] were the principal one to accomplish that quality improvement studies in composite work happenings include cognitive science where: (1) entails a test unit entitled the "activity system" which allows work environment study experience involving various media; (2) the organizational characteristics of such experiments which may emerge from human behavior; (3) it depends on the idea of meaningful implementation in public situations. The cognitive science of human behavior, which relies on technologies and process improvement factors to enhance human performance in diverse working conditions, will have a significant effect on future advances in the area of medical computer science. We first study the developments in functional cognitive science intricate in this change in interpretation, and then refer to the insinuations for healthcare practices of the conversation.

1.4   Cognitive Computing's Evolution

The era of computation started in 1900 and is still in continuous improvement (Figure 1.1.) The age of computing is mainly divided into three areas, that is: (i) era of tabulating, (ii) era of programmable, and (iii) cognitive computing's era [30]. The first period of computation was an era of tabulation. Computing was done largely by tabulating machines, calculators, and vacuum systems throughout the period. The age grew from 1900 to 1950 [31]. The second era, which ranged from a vacuum tube to a microprocessor and was entirely programmatically operated, appeared in 1950. User interface architecture, such as mainframe, smart computing machines, and personal computers, was absolutely thorough in the programmable

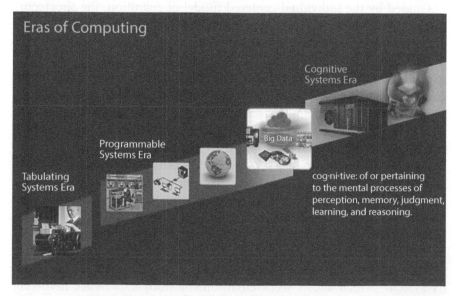

Figure 1.1 Eras of computing (2013 International Business Machine Corporation) [1].

era. This was an archetypal transition from mechanical systems to electronic systems in which storage and output benchmarks were dramatically enhanced [31]. The evolution and life of the cognitive computing age from 2011 to date. Cognitive computing's key goal is to build robotic information management structures that are capable of solving challenges without the necessity for human support. A modern methodology is cognitive computing which features the estimation and generation of theories, dynamic learning, and analysis of natural language. The quick exponential upsurge in the flow of unstructured data was the key target and catalyst of this cognitive era. Learning and collaborating in natural language rather than machine code with people [31].

A subset of analytics taught or learned is given by cognitive computing, based on machine learning. It is distinct from programmed or rules-based analytics and computation. Cognitive processing systems continually gain knowledge from the information fed into them by mining these dynamic data for particular information sources. In order to be able to predict new problems and model potential solutions, those systems themselves optimize the way they look for patterns and the way they process knowledge.

1.5   The Coming Era of Cognitive Computing

The long-standing open domain study Query Answer (QA) was approached by IBM through the TV game show Jeopardy! with a massively parallel, probabilistic architecture based on proof, known as Watson [3]. The Watson project has created a real-world sensation and influenced a big challenge in computer science to show how NLP and convergence, deep learning, information processing, knowledge representation and concurrent computing that drive open domain content are increasing and advancing in natural language content [3]. On the basis of its Jeopardy! success, IBM Watson was customized and delivered by scientists and engineers as the first computational computing capability usable commercially, a capability that marks a coming age of computing. Delivered across the cloud, the device analyzes high data volumes, understands complicated questions posed in natural language, and offers answers based on facts [3].

The ability of Watson to assist in healthcare is only one of the opportunities opening up for innovations of the next decade. Scientists from IBM Watson and elsewhere are stretching the limits of the fields of science and technology ranging from nanotechnology to artificial intelligence in order to build computers that do much more than measure and coordinate and identify trends in data – they hear, understand, reason and communicate in a powerful way with humans naturally. The exploits of Watson on TV are one of the first steps towards a new period of information technology development, the coming age of cognitive computing [3, 31].

Humans and computers would become more intertwined during this period. For civilization, the emerging age of computers is not only an opportunity; it is also a need. We would be able to cope effectively with the exploding complexities of today's environment with the help of a smart computer and effectively solve intertwined challenges such as obesity and hunger and burden on natural systems.

In the coming era of cognitive computing, the following characteristics [32] play a vital role in cognitive information.

Dynamic: Inherent value signifies the inherent natural property at the beginning of output knowledge. Extending value signifies an increasingly established social characteristic under the influence of external powers during the knowledge transmission process. To be exact, the data are viewed with an intrinsic meaning after development, which is constantly transmitted to different users on the basis of their own expectations. During this data transmission, the information is reported on and a yield of additional of the knowledge is consequently generated. As far as information is concerned, each customer, where its value is extensively excavated, assessed, and then used, measures its capacity differently. It is noted that each individual would have different associations and meanings of the same content at different times. Cognitive content, thus, changes dynamically across the communication path.

Polarity: In standard cognitive science, the measurement of knowledge is non-negative, but has positively and negatively polarities in the increasing value of cognitive deficits. The related awareness can be generated during the contact process and engagement with audiences by cognitive technologies to represent the increasing importance of information. It should be remembered that this information may have a beneficial influence on many individuals, but if it is wasted, it may have a negative impact on the dissemination of information. Discovering, for instance, that empirical experience and understanding knowledge will play a noteworthy role in its development and advancement will demonstrate the positive information polarization of a primary school student. Alternatively, if an elementary school student reflects on illogical and irrelevant information, it can have a negative effect on his/her intellect, suggesting the polarity of negative information. The understanding of data polarity is therefore of critical importance.

Evolution: During the transmission process, it will be continuously recognized until the information is produced. Knowledge can be converted into various aspects as the cognitive capacity exceeds a certain level. In order to generate new insights and viewpoints, it can be applied to the data level in other aspects after transformation. The cognitive machine imitates human thought during the training phase, constantly develops awareness through incremental learning, and eventually exceeds the cognitive ability of humans. During the knowledge delivery process, usable information is extended and compressed, based on the simple concepts of cognitive approach, to enable information to best represent the individual needs of users in a multi-dimensional world. As a consequence, the ancestral role of knowledge persists.

Convergence: Value density tends to be constant to a degree from the value of the data as the data is recalled, suggesting that the knowledge has a convergence consistency. For instance, the particulars of the definition of an object's motion can be described as the three laws of Newton's motion. According to the Shannon Intelligence Theorem, the quantity of knowledge conveyed by a standard transmitting device in a time unit is restricted to the efficiency of the channel, to be precise. However, the need for high-volume continuous data is always at odds with the capability of the communication medium. It is therefore necessary to continuously grow the capability of the communication system and to increase the amount of data transmission. In addition, it is possible to obtain the maximum value density by constantly identifying information, which decreases the quantity of information for transmission. Therefore, in order to efficiently reduce the pressure on the communication mechanism, it is important to delete redundant data on the basis of its usefulness as information. In other words, the elimination of unnecessary information and the succinct use of useful information are not limitless and agree with the theory of convergence on the basis of conformity with the minimum reduction law.

Multi-view: From the viewpoint of the consumer, as it converges, cognitive knowledge will achieve the highest density of meaning. Due to the various cognitive ability and demands of users, the importance of the same information will affect each user differently after receiving the information.

1.6   Cognitive Computing Architecture

Cognitive design refers both to the concept of the function of the human consciousness and to the technological implementation of this principle in the areas of artificial intelligence (AI) and computer cognitive science.

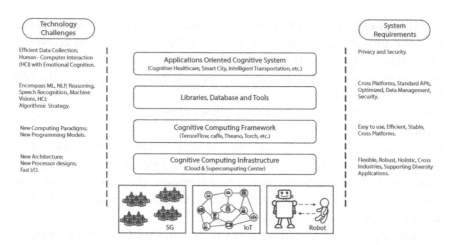

Figure 1.2 Cognitive computing system architecture [48].

One of the main goals of cognitive architecture is to summarize the various implications of cognitive science in a comprehensive computer model. The Institute for Creative Technologies defines cognitive architecture as: "A cognitive architecture is a theory of fixed constructs that include a consciousness, whether in natural or artificial settings, and how they work together to create intelligent actions in a number of diverse environments in combination with information and skills embedded within the architecture."

Figure 1.2 demonstrates cognitive computing's machine architecture. With the assistance of fundamental innovations such as the robotics, 5G-Network, and computer vision, along with Internet-of-Things (IoT) infrastructure and services, activities requiring communication between users and computers, machine vision and voice recognition can be implemented on a large scale. Each layer is accompanied in the cognitive computing environments by related technological problems and system requirements. The value of cognitive processing is researched and examined and each surface is explored.

1.6.1   The Internet-of-Things and Cognitive Computing

It is strong from the explanation above that a particular cognitive phenomenon is grounded on intelligence. The communication area highlights the transmission of knowledge, although the computational field enhances the ingestion of evidence. In definite cognitive processing systems, the data is mainly signified by data from different organized and unstructured information. In the ability to affect the data environment with the physical world, the IoT [34] collects a variety of valuable real-time statistics about substances in the objective world, forms a massive network infrastructure, and understands the interconnectedness between large measuring instruments [35]. Some innovative distributed processing fusion approaches, such as [36], can potentially also be used to boost the precision of perceived, massive data networks:

1. Using awareness technologies such as wireless sensors and RFID, satellite tracking and aligning via WiFi, and authentication, the IoT gathers data on tracked objects.
2. It extends similar network information using multiple productive means of networking, aggregation and conducts sharing.
3. Knowledge of intelligent control of physical fusion and decision-making in the information world uses intelligent computational techniques such as deep learning, cloud computing, and data mining to store and extract knowledge.

1.6.2 Big Data and Cognitive Computing

In the Big Data age, the rapid development of information and the exponential growth of machine processing capacity are irretrievably visible [37]. The growth in vast volumes of data, such as information from social networks and digital connectivity, is growing increasingly in relation to the rise in regular structured data. Cognitive Big Data contains unorganized and organized data with a feature that can be defined as 5V, i.e., veracity, velocity, value, variety, and volume. Meanwhile, during the analysis and collection of results, these requirements have created unique challenges. We discuss the relationship between, and the distinction between, extensive data mining and cognitive computing. By semantic computation, human senses are mimicked. One link between the study of cognitive computing and big data is humans' reasoning about big data. Information continually accumulates in the lives of human beings. Once the amount of knowledge from various experiences is enormous, humans' significant data reasoning can be possessed and is hierarchical as deep learning.

The problem of improving material life and the atmosphere is the first step. At the second level, moral culture is practiced, and at the third level, the meaning of life is involved. The number of employees at the highest level is the lowest. With a view to living expectations and typical psychological environments, the thinking reproduced by machine learning focuses primarily on the first and additional stages. Linked uses include medical examinations, smart healthcare, smart house, intelligent community, and emotional treatment [38, 39]. The third stage is more profoundly concerned with life's nature and gives customized advice for the user's life growth path to make the user understand a better but more fulfilling life. It cannot be achieved by robots, which is an excellent obstacle for future artificial intelligence. Under the condition that the data collection satisfies significant data characteristics, the direct approach to interpret and process the information is to follow the new machine learning technique [40].

Data size is one distinction between the study of big data and cognitive computation. The study of large facts in relation to such data sets is not inherently cognitive computation. Big data thinking stresses the mining of value and the development of knowledge from vast quantities of data. The precision and efficiency of prediction cannot be assured without a large volume of data as a basis. The aims of cognitive computing to discourse the contests of fuzziness and misperception in the genetic environment are grounded on judgment and cognition like the human intellect. Thus, multiple levels of mechanisms such as vision, memory, comprehension, logic, and problem-solving are realized. As long as ordinary citizens and domain experts are concerned, the data is supposed to be indistinguishable, but the context of the information collected by mutual individuals may fluctuate from that received by subject matter specialists. As the intensity of perception is new, there might also be a different perspective for evaluating the findings. Using semantic processing, more hidden meanings can be extracted from limited data [41].

Cognitive computing is informed by the method of human learning. Living creatures only necessitate a very short time to recognize a picture, and they can effortlessly discern cat from dog, and so on. This basic human function can be accomplished by conventional Big Data after a significant amount of preparation, for instance, while "Google Photos" by studying a lot of pictures will differentiate cat from dog [42]. The multiple cat breeds, however, may not be recognized. In addition, with multiple data sizes, there is a significant consistency and these data would consume huge storage space. Cognitive computation supports using a pathway that is lighter and more accessible than processing big data. It violates data universality and meaning, and after gaining cognitive knowledge, it not only uses "brute computing force" for big data processing. Cognitive computation was not sufficiently researched until the age of big data. The emergence of AI and the sustenance of ample cloud computing tools currently deliver compensations for the advancement of cognitive computing [43] and enable the computer to view and mine the consequences of information from the perspective of knowing the user's interior needs.

1.6.3   Cognitive Computing and Cloud Computing

Computing, band width, and storage are virtualized by cloud computing. It thus lowers the expense of implementation of information systems and offers funding for industrialization and the promotion of cognitive computing applications [33, 44]. In accumulation, cloud computing's powerful storage and computing ability offers cognitive computing with scalable, versatile, simulated, pooled, and well-organized computing infrastructure amenities [45, 46]. After the analysis of big data for a huge amount of facts information produced in real life on the technologies such as deep learning are applied to behavior data mining and the consequences are implemented in dissimilar fields. The numerous classes of knowledge concern multiple computational technologies. For instance, literal information and pictorial awareness correlate with computer vision and natural language processing, respectively.

1.7   Enabling Technologies in Cognitive Computing

The purpose of cognitive computing is straightforward: in a computerized environment, to replicate human thought processes. We may create classifications that simulate the human brain which performs through a range of existing technologies, such as mining of data, recognition and analysis of pattern, and natural language processing. To understand, learn, and respond automatically from experience without being specifically programmed, these systems rely on learning in terms of machine and deep learning algorithms. Data is the insight we offer to cognitive processing systems. Study presents the supporting technologies in this section, which comprise deep learning and reinforcement knowledge. Reinforcement learning can draw and learn from the behavior of the environment. High levels of characteristics may be learned by deep learning.

1.7.1   Reinforcement Learning and Cognitive Computing

Standard approaches to machine learning can be differentiated from unmonitored learning and supervised learning. In these techniques, systems train data models, some of which are in predefined sequence, and machines perform accomplish projects such as regression, identification, and aggregation. The knowledge that the machines will obtain, however, is limited. In non-linear instances, it is impossible for computers to learn information since they can only perform predictions depending on the information obtained. In addition, the label for much the same information may be different with different cases, which implies that perhaps the functionality of the information gathered by the machines is different for each individual. Closed teaching with data feedback is the foundation of conventional supervised learning and unsupervised learning. These standard models of learning are inadequate to fulfill the demands of sustainable improvement of machine intelligence.

In the arena of computer erudition, reinforcement learning has since become a trendy branch of research. The human learning process is very similar to reinforcement learning. Let us take the situation where the infant studies to talk as an instance. Usually, when a youngster learns a language, a grownup reads the word frequently, refers to something identified by that expression, or performs an action supported by that word with expressions. If the youngster's considerate is wrong due to missing judgment, the parent will make a correction. The adult will offer prizes if the kid has it right. During the human learning process, the environmental environment is often a very significant influence.

Reinforcement learning uses this stage as an example, and it will absorb from the atmosphere and respond to actions. A collection of incentive instruments is created, i.e., when convinced conduct is good for detached and some sentence is exercised on the conflicting, some reward is offered. Here are several decisions during the process towards the target. The choice is also not actually the optimum at any time, but it must be successful for the system to obtain further compensation. Let's take the example of AlphaGo [47]. By improving learning, chess plays with one another after fascinating millions of chess games for deep learning. Each move is not always optimal during the self-learning process, but thanks to global preparation, the action is more likely to trigger a complete win. The machine is not only based on previous information in this level, but may also pursue new paths to increase the target reward. Inarticulate play will be introduced, much like drawing learning, until the fundamental skills are learned. Data is created in the process of computer attempts, not regression, classification, or accumulation, but optimum reward is the ultimate aim. With this goal, the computer is important for both good and failed attempts.

If a machine interacts only with itself, however, so its cognition is not adequate. This is almost like learning to communicate without connecting with others would be hard for an infant. Therefore, if, regardless of external conditions, a learning system implements its theory, it is not a strong cognitive system. Therefore, contact specifically with humans should be carried out by a neural device. However, it will take a lot of manpower and time if a human were specially appointed to connect with a computer.

1.7.2   Cognitive Computing with Deep Learning

1.7.2.1   Relational Technique and Perceptual Technique

Cerebral cortex of the human has distinct functions which are divided into two sides of the brain. As for certain entities, vocabulary, thoughts, reasoning, etc. are the responsibility of the left brain. Although visual thinking and emotions are essential for the right hemisphere, typically, individuals with a mature left brain have better reasoning and are more logical. Although entities with a qualified right brain frequently have good creativity, comprehension is exceptional in space and material types. Then logical reasoning and visual thinking are divided into the human mode of thought. According to different abstractions in the material of thought, human beings' methodology to perceive the natural world is separated into the rational approach and visual procedure.

The conceptual approach is grounded on strict conception and relevance, though the perceptual process is a special relationship of mapping generated between various components. It is also uncertain whether the human brain knows 100 billion nerve cells' data coding, encoding, and storage. However, in the nervous method, the human mind's thinking function may be modeled through data investigation. The framework of manual feature production is purely established. This technique can be seen as a sort of logical system, i.e., it pretends the human capacity for analytical thought. The approach of function learning is to find the relationship of mapping between different components. It is a sort of system of vision, i.e., it replicates the potential of human visual thought [48].

As indicated in Figure 1.3, to assess that a quadrangle is a square, logical and perceptual methods have been adopted independently. To identify the characteristics of a cube, evaluate whether there were any four right angles, and determine whether or not the measurements of four sides are equivalent, the logical, analytical approach is used, as seen in Figure1.3 (a). The understanding of tilt, right angle, hand, and side span concepts requires this technique. If an illustration of a square is presented to a youngster and he or she is expressed that it is a square, that child can correctly define a court after several learning cycles, as exposed in Figure 1.3 (b). The infant does not understand the definition of side or slope, but he or she can also understand a square. The technique where the infant knows a court is a visual technique or perception. After many scenarios, the youngster discovers the relationship amid the square symbol and the unbiased definition of mapping. It is essential to look for image features to identify a square with a logical approach, and manual feature strategy can be seen as

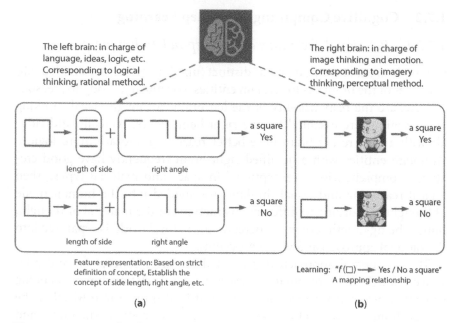

Figure 1.3 Perceptual and rational method to recognize a square. (a) Rational method. (b) Perceptual method [69].

an imitation of this process. When a youngster absorbs to identify a rectangle, the perceptual methodology is used to create the mapping relationship amid figure and definition. It is possible to see learning characteristics using a deep learning model as a simulation of this technique.

1.7.2.2   Cognitive Computing and Image Understanding

If the program is attempting to achieve glitches in the physical world, the simplest way is to mimic the human brain's thought mode. In the cognitive paradigm, the characteristics can be derived from existing classification tasks data model using the manually function development strategy to simulate the human brain's critical reasoning ability or can be taught through computer vision to replicate the human primary reward thinking ability. When computing applications grow increasingly complex, researchers realize that it is difficult to explain certain actual problems that are simple to identify by human beings using a logical approach, rendering the rational analytical method unreliable or completely impractical for machines. In other words, with the manual feature creation process, the successful data characteristics cannot be planned and it is very difficult for computers to understand the expression of the feature [48].

1.8   Intelligent Systems in Healthcare

Technologically sophisticated devices that interpret and respond to the environment in them are intelligent systems. From automatic vacuums such as Roomba to facial recognition applications to Amazon's customized shopping tips, intelligent systems can take several types.

In the late 1990s, first differentiated so-called smart information systems were from the entire collection of information systems. In this context, the word 'intelligent' is interpreted explicitly as referring to these systems' capacity to show their desire, in conditions of ambiguity, where the correct action cannot be decided algorithmically, to address the formulated query in a not utterly determined environment [49]. At the same time, these programs are the most likely to achieve success. In this way, intelligence is developed at several (intelligence) stages, determined by the system's computation and storage power, automated data search, and automatic collection of routines for the gathering of information as the process is used to find solutions to issues that are not well understood at the time of system creation, as well as the quality and quantity of information gathered in the system.

The Intelligent Device is a computer that can capture and process data and interconnect with other devices that can study from involvement and respond to existing data, etc. Intelligent systems are technologically sophisticated devices that interpret and react to the environment. Intelligent System, "The ability to perform activities generally associated with intelligent creatures by an automated machine or computer-controlled robot," having thus the competences of "Developing structures that have the features of human intellectual functions, such as the capacity to think, explore meaning, generalize, or benefit from previous experience" [50].

Each (natural or artificial) intelligence system is focused on mechanisms that help to produce beneficial behaviors. Still, each of these mechanisms derives from the human capacities and practical capabilities that make up this system. The utilization of essential tools, including instructional and creation functions and the 'instinct', is of immense significance for an intelligent system's proper functioning. Such processes (Figure 1.4 and Figure 1.5) take the same type as human intelligence functions [51].

Let's also point out that Intelligent Systems may be seen in numerous ways, along with the concept of Intelligent System's presented: from Artificial Intelligent models analyzing massive datasets to Artificial Intelligent systems commanding robots. The area of the Intelligent System describes an interdisciplinary field of study that draws together concepts

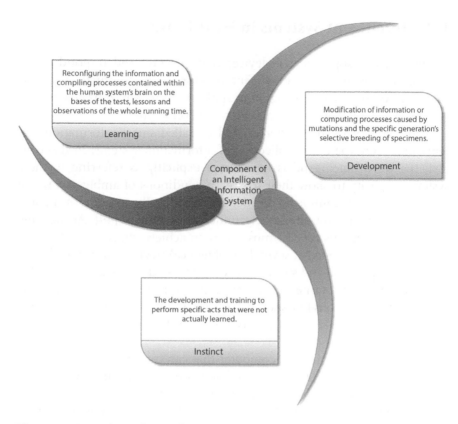

Figure 1.4 Component of an intelligent system [51].

Figure 1.5 Intelligent system [49].

from Artificial Intelligent, Machine Learning (ML) and a variety of arenas linked by multiple interdisciplinary partnerships, such as linguistics, brain sciences, and psychology.

A wide number of Intelligent Systems have been produced nowadays, such as (Figure 1.6):

- Memetic algorithms
- Hybrid models (neuro-fuzzy, neuro-genetic, fuzzy-genetic, etc.)
- Expert systems
- Particle swarm optimization
- Support vector machines

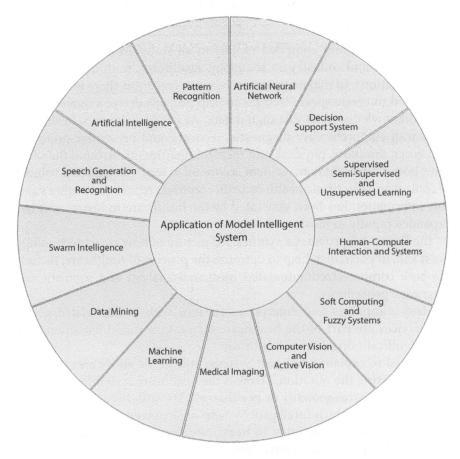

Figure 1.6 Application of model intelligent system [49].

- Artificial neural networks
- Ant colony systems
- Clustering
- Deep learning
- Bayesian model
- Fuzzy systems
- Evolutionary computation (genetic programming, evolutionary strategies, evolutionary/genetic algorithms)
- Ant colony optimization

The generic potential applications of present ISs cover the following themes:

1.8.1   Intelligent Cognitive System in Healthcare (Why and How)

Data is gathered and compiled rapidly in all study areas, from physics, meteorology, and industry to sociology, healthcare, multimedia, etc. In these conditions, to make correct decisions in real-time, there is an immediate need to create specialized ISs to help humans derive valuable information/knowledge from vast digital data. As is widely known, healthcare deals with comprehensive diagnostic, recovery, and preventive protocols for cancer, disability, physical, and mental impairments. Around the same time, hospital/patient management is covered as well. A significant volume of content and electronic health records, corporate reports, and other valuable information has been generated by the healthcare industry, as it has expanded rapidly in most nations.

The Figure 1.7 provides a synthesized picture of how smart technology assist and, in particular, help to optimize the process of healthcare, including both computerized/automated medicinal analysis and sophisticated diagnostic procedures.

Many companies and enterprises engaged with health-related goods and services are part of the healthcare sector. One might list among the most significant divisions of healthcare:

We tried to explain Intelligent Systems' role in the above area of medicine, addressing the question, "How is the healthcare system?" and "Why are Intelligent arrangements in healthcare?" We will discuss some of the essential areas in which Intelligent Systems are involved in this field. As we hear of how ISs are interested in healthcare decisions, two methods that operate in tandem come to attention.

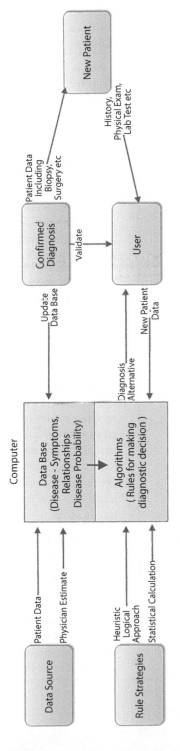

Figure 1.7 Computer-aided medical diagnosis flow.

Table 1.1 Domain of healthcare.

S. no	Healthcare domain	Details
1	Industry of Pharmaceutical	It is part of the pharmacy industry that deals with medications. It encompasses a broad variety of areas related to the discovery, manufacture, and distribution of prescription drugs.
2	Industry of Biotechnology	The biotechnology industry that produces, manufactures and markets new, proprietary drugs, essentially using gene engineering technologies, for example, sales from medical biotechnology surpass $150 billion a year. (Diehl, P., Biotech Industry, June 26, 2017).
3	Industry of Healthcare Equipment	The biomedical equipment industry, composed of manufacturers of medical equipment and surgical materials, produces a broad variety of products, such as surgical equipment, regenerative medicine, orthopedic appliances, cardiovascular, diagnostic apparatus, etc.
4	Industry of Healthcare Distribution	The healthcare delivery business, which is an integral part of the healthcare business, consists of both healthcare commodity manufacturers and wholesalers. A quick look at pharmaceutical distribution to get an understanding of the size of the healthcare distribution industry reveals that in 2015.
5	Managed healthcare	Controlled healthcare consists of a range of activities aimed at reducing the cost of delivering patient insurance and enhancing the quality of healthcare services. A form of health assurance dealing with arrangements with hospital services and treatment centers to deliver coverage to members at discounted rates is controlled healthcare policies.

Next, Natural Language Processing Systems are concerned through retrieving evidence from unorganized data to develop machine-readable structured health records. Secondly, to help human decision-making effectively, state-of-the-art DM/ML algorithms aim to retrieve useful knowledge/information using structured data in medical databases and unstructured NLP-interpreted data.

- **Natural language processing (NLP) Technology:** The umbrella concept used to define the method of using complex algorithms is natural language processing to classify essential elements in common parlance and derive meaning from unfocused spoken or written input. NLP is a computer science concept that combines expertise in artificial intelligence, cognitive science, and other fields of machine learning (Figure 1.8).

  Through constructing algorithmically based entities that can imitate human-like answers to questions or conversations, some NLP efforts are focused on beating the Turing test. Using voice recognition systems, some are seeking to interpret human speech, such as the digital customer support software used by many major corporations.
  NLP helps human beings to use natural languages to interface with the computer. In nature, The NLP can be seen to be of an interdisciplinary nature. It is a computer engineering department that derives its research connections from the field of artificial intelligence, particularly in human-computer interaction (HCI). Linguistics, social science, psychology, philosophy and mathematics logic are also related to the NLP [52].

  As the name suggests, it is possible to think of NLU as a mechanism in which the machine understands a piece of text in a natural language. Furthermore, NLU works with understanding of computer reading whose purpose is to translate text information in an unambiguous linguistic form. As a result, NLU handles texts and translates the text to a form that can be understood/understood by the computer [53, 54].

Watson Oncology is a semantic processing tool built to support doctors in the area of oncology in evaluating the treatment choices of their patients. Specifically, it interprets the health knowledge of cancer patients and describes personalized, evidence-based care choices. Let us also

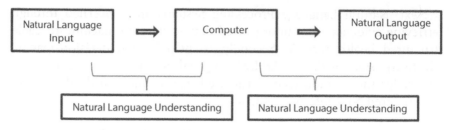

Figure 1.8 Task involved in NLP [53].

note, in this sense, the Google-Google Cloud Natural Language (https:// cloud.google.com/natural-language/) application-programming interface (API). Among the most common NLP applications, only the following are mentioned:

o Medicine, helping doctors extract and analyze information about the effects, dosage of the medication, and details on the reaction. Consequently, by identifying or flagging important items in results, one may detect potential side effects of any drug.
o Machine translation, based on maintaining intact the meaning of words along with tenses and grammar.
o Text classification, used to allocate dissimilar credentials to predetermined sections or benchmarks.
o To decide which of the incoming messages are spam and which are not, utilizing a set of protocols. Filters out e-mail spam.
o Extraction of details related to the detection of individuals, along with names, addresses, events, dates, times and costs, thereby improving the consistency and effectiveness of the search.

• **Classical and Modern DM/ML Algorithms:** Learning of Machine is a form of artificial intelligence (AI) that incorporates procedure and techniques that allow computers without specialized computer programming to solve problems. In literature and shared culture, the word AI is used quite loosely to define a wide range of critical techniques, such as self-driving cars, consumer product customization, and automated personal assistants. In this analysis, machine learning would be referred to as the primary type of applications used for statistics mining and how they put on to healthcare. While the use of Artificial Intelligent in the domain of healthcare and additional areas is encouraging, the potential of self-learning, constantly evolving machine learning procedures must be offset by the difficulties of integrating such instruments in regular medical training. Defining the purpose and reach of implementing such resources is crucial before deployment to properly frame these challenges. The key challenges and drawbacks affecting the machine learning method in healthcare conveyance will be addressed in this study.

There are many ways that Artificial Intelligence & Machine Learning can be used in healthcare:

1. AI & ML will learn features from a vast amount of health data and then use the information gained to support clinical practice in the planning of care or risk assessment.
2. The AI & ML approach can extract helpful data from a large patient population to help assess the health risk alert and the health outcomes prediction in real time;
3. AI & ML may perform repeated activities, such as research analysis, CT scans, X-rays, or data entry;
4. In human clinical practice, AI & ML programs may help to minimize medical and therapeutic mistakes that are inevitable.
5. By providing up-to-date medical information from journals, textbooks and clinical practices to provide guidance on successful patient treatment, AI & ML can support physicians;
6. AI & ML can treat patient reports and evaluate both a particular institution's success and the whole health system;
7. AI & ML will help to build accurate medication and experimental therapies on the basis of quicker mutation processing and disease links;
8. To the point of being "digital nurses" or "health bots," AI & ML will provide digital appointments and health tracking services.

The critical barriers to the development of healthcare AI systems are central to machine learning science, application management issues, and the identification that barriers to adoption and the necessary changes in essential things are to be made or pathways. As part of randomized controlled trials, rigorous peer-reviewed clinical evaluation can be used as the gold standard for evidence generation. Still, it might not always be sufficient or practical to perform them in practice. The goal of performance metrics should be to document actual therapeutic applicability and be understandable to expected consumers. To ensure that patients are not vulnerable to adverse treatment

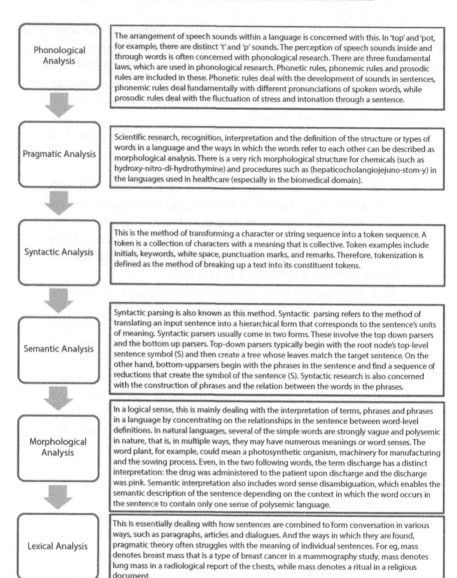

Figure 1.9 Level of NLP in healthcare [69].

or are refused access to beneficial technology, it is essential to provide a strategy balancing the pace of change with the risk for damage, along with careful post-market control. Figure 1.9 and Figure 1.10 provides the mechanisms to make direct comparisons of AI systems, including stand-alone, local, and representative test sets, need to be created. AI algorithm developers ought

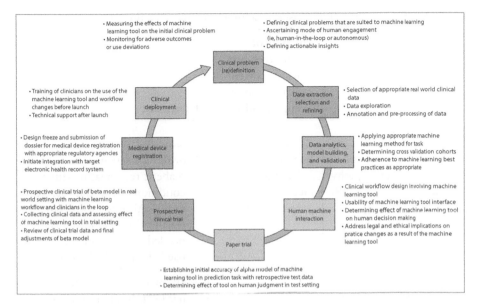

Figure 1.10 Training, clinical trial evaluation, and clinical implementation of machine learning algorithms for healthcare applications [70].

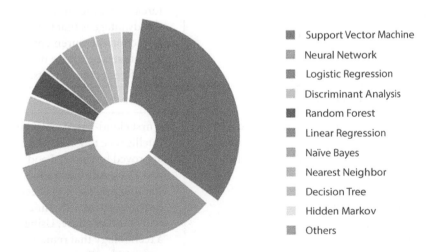

Figure 1.11 Machine learning algorithms used in clinical studies are the most common [70].

to be vigilant about possible threats, like sample movement, accidental confounding factors, unintended discriminatory bias, the challenges of generalizing new populations, and the unexpected detrimental effect on health results of new algorithms (Figure 1.11).

Table 1.2 For various clinical uses, machine learning algorithms [70].

	The type of data that was used, as well as the clinical applicability	Comment
Eye Disease		
Deep neural network to detect retinopathy of diabetes (IDx-DR, IDx Technologies, IA, Coralville) [55]	Imaging data (retinal images) Electronic health record data	Provides for much more diabetic retinopathy with a conditional read-out (i.e., yes or no). Although clinician clarification of findings is not needed, it is intended to be used along with clinicians.
Algorithm for predicting of myopia using Random Forest [56]		Adult myopia progression has been studied in school children up to 8 years before beginning, with an accuracy of 85 percent to 99 percent (area under the curve). One disadvantage is that the refraction measurements were taken by a large number of different optometrists.
Cardiac abnormalities		
Cloud-based deep neural network algorithm to detect cardiac abnormalities (Cardio DL, San Francisco, CA, Arterys) [57]	Imaging data (MRI of heart ventricles)	The first cloud-based artificial intelligence tool has been approved by the US Food and Drug Administration. Radiologists use it to check heart ventricular rhythm and blood pressure. Using a technology that removes patient identify from

(*Continued*)

Table 1.2 For various clinical uses, machine learning algorithms [70]. (*Continued*)

	The type of data that was used, as well as the clinical applicability	Comment
		images during the data collecting stage (often in hospitals), allowing only de-identified data to be analyzed. The dearth of peer-reviewed research makes it difficult to fully test the algorithm.
Fractures		
OsteoDetect (Imagen, Cambridge, UK) for detecting distal radius fractures in the wrist [58]	Imaging data (X-ray)	Especially in comparison with practitioners without any of the model, clinicians using the algorithm demonstrated greater sensitivity, accuracy, and coefficient of determination values for wrist fracture diagnosis. One drawback is that both of the supporting findings were retrospective.

(*Continued*)

Table 1.2 For various clinical uses, machine learning algorithms [70]. (*Continued*)

	The type of data that was used, as well as the clinical applicability	Comment
Pulmonary diseases		
Deep neural network algorithm (CheXNeXt) for the identification of 14 diseases, including pneumonia, pulmonary mass and pleural effusion [59]	Imaging data (chest radiographs)	Validated using subsets of the National Institutes of Health Chest X-ray dataset, which includes over 100,000 chest radiographs. The algorithm also worked on 10 diseases, better on 1 and worse on 3, in a much shorter period (1·5 min vs. 240 min for pathologists), as retrospectively compared with the results of 9 radiologists. The study, however, was retrospective, did not simulate a hospital scenario in the real world, and included only one site.
Neurological disorders		
To identify neurological problems as critical or non-critical for triage, the three-dimensional coevolutionary neural network algorithm [60]	Imaging data (CT brain scan)	Prospective, randomized controlled trials demonstrated clinician-like sensitivity but much lower accuracy. The research concerned only one hospital location, however, and lacks external confirmation
Oncology		
A significant consideration in the diagnosis of breast cancer is the PowerLook Density Assessment 3.4 (iCAD, Nashua, NH) for automatic breast density assessment [61]	Imaging data (mammogram images)	The algorithm provided evaluations comparable to those of radiologists, but with better reproducibility. The drawbacks are that the tomosynthesis algorithm has not been tested (three-dimensional mammography) and only white and Asian women have been studied.

(*Continued*)

Table 1.2 For various clinical uses, machine learning algorithms [70]. (*Continued*)

	The type of data that was used, as well as the clinical applicability	Comment
For the identification and segmentation of lung and liver tumors, cloud-based deep neural network algorithms (Oncology Lung AI and Oncology Liver AI, Arterys, San Francisco, CA) [62]	Imaging data (CT)	The efficiency of detection and segmentation has been shown to be similar to that of expert radiologists; instruments have been developed to be used before approving them in a workflow that requires clinical evaluation and potential alteration of findings. The lack of peer-reviewed research makes it impossible to test the algorithm fully.
Deep algorithm of the neural network for the identification of malignant lung nodules [63]	Imaging data (radiographs)	It outperformed any of the 18 radiologists in a retrospective analysis, and when used in conjunction with them, it boosted radiologists' efficiency. The paucity of benign lesions in the training sample means that the algorithm does not differentiate between malignant and benign lesions as well as it might.

1.9   The Cognitive Challenge

Decision-Centered Architectural emerged out of the ignorance of the cognitive mechanisms that are fundamental to the successful implementation of dynamic mental work by disciplines of information technology engineering. Here, by referring to two investigate papers that have discussed the feasibility of technical advances in healthcare, we illustrate the issues resulting from the introduction of cognitive assistance programs based on the understanding of clinical knowledge of information technology.

1.9.1   Case Study: Patient Evacuation

The US military established an electronic scheduling method to release healthcare professionals of the role of scheduling patients from first-point treatment centers for evacuation [65]. With less work, the current approach has created improved schedules for large-scale issues. However, the scheduling issue was complicated. The person could face a random order for evacuation, such as the urgent transport of a severely sick patient seeking emergency medical attention at a given facility [66]. To meet this immediate need, with the relocation of an aircraft and crew, removal schedules for other patients may be distorted such that the timetable would have to be modified.

While expected, scheduling change has always been a challenge in response to rapidly changing needs. However, workers had implicitly understood possible resource choices and contradictions in the manual scheduling process, which they could use to change a timetable following new demands. Through an unconscious sense-making mechanism, they have established a valuable degree of situation knowledge relevant to available tools and future conflicts in macro-cognitive terms. However, the restrictions enforced by the modern electronic scheduling system work from creating that understanding of possible choices and disputes.

In new hospitals, resource scheduling is a pervasive problem. For example, it will also be challenging in a big infirmary to accommodate the need for concentrated care beds [67]. This is an issue that appears perfect for computerized help. Still, there is also a pace with the immediate concern that so many of the implicit neural functions crucial to a successful result will be overlooked by those that create such a device.

1.9.2   Case Study: Anesthesiology

In a cardiothoracic surgery center, a new, fully automated, based on microprocessor, biomedical one-to-one care system for cardiac anesthesia was installed to substitute the functionality of four single-sensor systems [68]. Designers presented anesthesiologists with incentives to restructure windows on the device and show various interpretations of the same information by centralizing automated processing and patient tracking roles in a daily computer-based setting. The most important interface change from the initial relations of individual parts was a more than one layer display structure allowed by a touch screen.

Patients undergoing heart surgery are subjected to quick and reflected hemodynamic fluctuations, which can be frightening. The most current evasive numerical displays, on the other hand, have hampered an anesthesiologist's capability to quantify the severity of unanticipated blood pressure rise. The doctor relies on the anesthesiologist to document the correct cardiac rhythm in this situation. This can be easily derived from the standard waveform definition of the current scheme. Although the automated principles to compensate were learned by anesthesiologists by drawing conclusions, new residents often failed to do so, resulting in surgeon complaints. After much thinking and research that showed both blood pressures, anesthesiologists created a fixed-scale analogue window. If the anesthesiologist does other tasks, this new blood pressure window will be covered by an automatic window control system.

Before this approach is developed, the essential window monitoring should be performed during the low-work step of system startup. When the anesthesiologist tried to compute cardiac output, however, window control was a problem. Although cardiac output may be estimated in 10 to 30 seconds, the computation can be imprecise, thus anesthesiologists sometimes check it two or three times in fast succession to ensure accuracy. Cardiac output was seen by triggering a screen mark on another window added to the new operating system screen. Even when this window is activated, it has the side effect of removing the blood pressure window, degrading the doctor's capacity to track unexpected increases in blood pressure. In the old procedure, this did not really happen, since the discrete machines displayed the data in parallel. Problems were correlated to the moment of most extreme risk with the abrupt increase in blood pressure at the most routine measurement of cardiac performance.

One impact of having several functions on a single computer is that it becomes more difficult to control these processes. For begin, with the former system, a blood pressure network was reset by pushing a button on the forward-facing of a screen. The network reset includes a list of system initiations for the new device. The most recurrently utilized menu purpose of the computer system was calculating cardiac output, which required at least three menu instigations. A single press of a power-driven button activated the identical operation on the old, discrete device. In comparison, errors were common. Unintentional menu activation, for example, may cause the machine to go to a seldom utilized menu space area.

Much of an anesthesiologist's routine, for example, is intended to facilitate sense-making. In the new method, which mostly revolved around window management, workflows intended for that reason required several further steps and were more delicate than in the old framework. Sense-making was disrupted in environments that could not be grasped at a glance where any fuzzy details was seen or given. In contrast, there was a recirculation between both the anesthesiologist and the surgeon of the macro-cognitive coordination system, which was at risk because the anesthesiologist found it very difficult to convert the display readings as required by the surgeon.

1.10   Conclusion

This chapter was the first to show how cognitive calculation has progressed from four different perspectives: knowledge discovery, cognitive science, big data, and cognitive computing; then there's the cognitive computing device architecture, which is made up of three parts: IoT, big data, and cloud computing. We're also introducing technology that supports semantic computation, such as enhanced learning and deep learning. Finally, three instances of typical cognitive computing applications are presented: robot technology, emotional communication machine, and cognitive medical system. Usually most clinical evidence comes as narrative texts which are highly unstructured and not readily interpreted by the machine. It is thus an issue to have convenient and timely access to health information. However, in the field of healthcare, NLP initiatives were being used to derive useful information from the source and unstructured clinical texts, to evaluate the syntactical nature and the significance of the Clinic terms and then to convert these words into a vocabulary that clinical decision-making machines can easily interpret.

NLP thus enables the quick access and retrieval of useful and meaningful knowledge on healthcare. Healthcare function is perceptual, to a large degree. In case studies, the challenges that arise in the absence of any severe and thorough effort to consider the neural mechanisms involved in healthcare are highlighted. The creation of supporting technologies must take into account the work's cognitive criteria as well as the implicit cognitive processes used by people involved in the diagnostic process. Most importantly, we don't need procedures or field technologies that obstruct or force folks who operate well to change or abandon the cognitive processes that rely on their expertise. The last two case studies show how Decision-centered Design's verified testing and design methodologies may be applied to improve cognitive assistance.

References

1. Healthcare, I. B. M. and Point, L. S., *The future of health is cognitive. IBM Institute for Business Value*, pp. 1–12, 2016, IBM Healthcare and Life Sciences, papers3://publication/uuid/2A64FB62-8C1A-4EEB-BED6-0F507CA6FFD9.
2. Series, T.L., Emerging in Cognitive Computing and Machine AND Machine-Learning, in: *Career: Data and Analytics*, 2017.
3. Pagel, P., Portmann, E., Vey, K., Cognitive Computing, in: *Informatik-Spektrum*, vol. 41, pp. 4–9, 2018.
4. CSN, K., Choubey, S.B., Choubey, A., Approaches from cognitive neuroscience and comparative cognition, in: *Cognitive Informatics, Computer Modelling, and Cognitive Science*, vol. 2, 2020.
5. Patel, V.L. and Kannampallil, T.G., Cognitive informatics in biomedicine and healthcare. *J. Biomed. Inform.*, 53, 3–14, 2015, https://doi.org/10.1016/j.jbi.2014.12.007.
6. Zhang, J., Johnson, T.R., Patel, V.L., Paige, D.L., Kubose, T., Using usability heuristics to evaluate patient safety of medical devices. *J. Biomed. Inform.*, 36, 1 2, 23–30, 2003.
7. Patel, V.L., Yoskowitz, N.A., Arocha, J.F., Shortliffe, E.H., Cognitive and learning sciences in biomedical and health instructional design: A review with lessons for biomedical informatics education. *J. Biomed. Inform.*, 42, 1, 176–197, 2009, https://doi.org/10.1016/j.jbi.2008.12.002.
8. Malhotra, S., Jordan, D., Shortliffe, E., Patel, V.L., Workflow modeling in critical care: Piecing together your own puzzle. *J. Biomed. Inform.*, 40, 2, 81–92, 2007, https://doi.org/10.1016/j.jbi.2006.06.002.
9. Patel, V.L., Kaufman, D.R., Kannampallil, T.G., Diagnostic Reasoning and Decision Making in the Context of Health Information Technology. *Rev. Hum. Factors Ergon.*, 8, 1, 149–190, 2013, https://doi.org/10.1177/1557234X13492978.
10. Newell, A. and Simon, H.A., *Human problem solving*, Prentice-Hall, Englewood Cliffs, N.J, 1972.
11. Ericsson, K.A. and Simon, H.A., *Protocol analysis*, MIT Press, Cambridge, MA, 1984.
12. Kintsch, W., *Comprehension: a paradigm for cognition*, NY: Cambridge University Press, New York, 1998.

13. Patel, V.L. and Kaufman, D.R., Medical informatics and the science of cognition. *J. Am. Med. Inform. Assoc.*, 5, 6, 493–502, 1998, https://doi.org/10.1136/jamia.1998.0050493.
14. Thoughts, R., The Practice of. *J. Am. Med. Inform. Assoc.*, 5, 5, 421–431, 1998.
15. Hazlehurst, B., Gorman, P.N., McMullen, C.K., Distributed cognition: An alternative model of cognition for medical informatics. *Int. J. Med. Inf.*, 77, 4, 226–234, 2008, https://doi.org/10.1016/j.ijmedinf.2007.04.008.
16. Clark, A., *Being There*, MIT Press, Cambridge, MA, 1997.
17. Geertz, C., The growth of culture and the evolution of mind, in: *The Interpretation of Cultures*, C. Geertz (Ed.), Basic Books, Inc., New York, 1973.
18. Patel, V.L., Arocha, J.F., Kaufman, D.R., A primer on aspects of cognition for medical informatics. *J. Am. Med. Inform. Assoc.*, 8, 4, 324–343, 2001, https://doi.org/10.1136/jamia.2001.0080324.
19. Ledley, R.S. and Lusted, L.B., Reasoning foundations of medical diagnosis; symbolic logic, probability, and value theory aid our understanding of how physicians reason. *Science*, 130, 3366, 9–21, 1959.
20. Elstein, A.S., Shulman, L.S., Sprafka, S.A., *Medical Problem Solving: An Analysis of Clinical Reasoning*, Harvard University Press, Cambridge, MA, 1978.
21. Miller, R.A., Pople Jr., H.E., Myers, J.D., Internist-1, an experimental computer-based diagnostic consultant for general internal medicine. *N. Engl. J. Med.*, 307, 8, 468–476, 1982.
22. Reviews, B., Buchanan, B.G., Shortliffe, E.H., Rule-Based Expert Systems, in: *The MYON Experiments of the Stanford Heuristic Programming Project (Addison-Wesley, USC / Information Sciences Institute*, pp. 364–366, Addison-Wesley, 1984.
23. Ash, J.S., Berg, M., Coiera, E., Some Unintended Consequences of Information Technology in Healthcare: The Nature of Patient Care Information System-related Errors. *J. Am. Med. Inform. Assoc.*, 11, 2, 104–112, 2004, https://doi.org/10.1197/jamia.M1471.
24. Koppel, R., Cohen, A., Abaluck, B., Localio, A.R., Kimmel, S.E., Strom, B.L., Role of Computerized. *J. Am. Med. Inform. Assoc.*, 293, 10, 1197–1203, 2013.
25. McDonald, C.J., Erratum: Computerization can create safety hazards: A bar-coding near miss (Annals of Internal Medicine (2006) 144, (510-516)). *Ann. Intern. Med.*, 145, 3, 235, 2006, https://doi.org/10.7326/0003-4819-145-3-200608010-00022.
26. Hutchins, E., *Cognition in the Wild*, MIT Press, Cambridge, MA, 1996.
27. Cole, M., *Cultural Psychology*, Harvard University Press, Cambridge, MA, 1996.
28. Suchman, L.A., *Plans and Situated Actions: The Problem of Human-Machine Communication*, Cambridge University Press, 5, 1987.
29. Hazlehurst, B. and McMullen, C., Orienting frames and private routines: The role of cultural process in critical care safety. *Int. J. Med. Inform.*, 76, SUPPL. 1, S129–S135, 2007, https://doi.org/10.1016/j.ijmedinf.2006.06.005.

30. IBM Research Stakes Its Future on Cognitive Computing, 2013. retrieved from https://www.zdnet.com/article/ibm-research-stakes-its-future-on-cognitivecomputing/.

31. From Tabulating, Programming to Cognitive Computing Era, 2018. retrieved from https://www 07.ibm.com/events/th/ibmthailand65/p/tabulating_programming_cognitive_era/.

32. Chen, M., Hao, Y., Gharavi, H., Leung, V.C.M., Cognitive Information Measurements: {A} New Perspective, arxiv, 2019. CoRR, abs/1907.01719. http://arxiv.org/abs/1907.01719.

33. Chen, M., Hao, Y., Hu, L., Huang, K., Lau, V.K.N., Green and mobility-aware caching in 5G networks. *IEEE Trans. Wirel. Commun.*, 16, 12, 8347–8361, 2017, https://doi.org/10.1109/TWC.2017.2760830.

34. Chen, M., Miao, Y., Hao, Y., Hwang, K., Narrow Band Internet of Things. *IEEE Access*, 5, c, 20557–20577, 2017, https://doi.org/10.1109/ACCESS.2017.2751586.

35. Sheth, A., Internet of Things to Smart IoT Through Semantic, Cognitive, and Perceptual Computing. *IEEE Intell. Syst.*, 31, 2, 108–112, 2016, https://doi.org/10.1109/MIS.2016.34.

36. Tian, D., Zhou, J., Sheng, Z., An adaptive fusion strategy for distributed information estimation over cooperative multi-agent networks. *IEEE Trans. Inform. Theory*, 63, 5, 3076–3091, 2017, https://doi.org/10.1109/TIT.2017.2674678.

37. Fernández, A., del Río, S., López, V., Bawakid, A., del Jesus, M.J., Benítez, J.M., Herrera, F., Big Data with Cloud Computing: An insight on the computing environment, MapReduce, and programming frameworks. *Wiley Interdiscip. Rev. Data Min. Knowl. Discovery*, 4, 5, 380–409, 2014, https://doi.org/10.1002/widm.1134.

38. Chen, M., Zhou, P., Fortino, G., Emotion Communication System. *IEEE Access*, 5, c, 326–337, 2017, https://doi.org/10.1109/ACCESS.2016.2641480.

39. Chen, M., Hao, Y., Hwang, K., Wang, L., Wang, L., Disease Prediction by Machine Learning over Big Data from Healthcare Communities. *IEEE Access*, 5, c, 8869–8879, 2017, https://doi.org/10.1109/ACCESS.2017.2694446.

40. Chaturvedi, I., Cambria, E., Welsch, R.E., Herrera, F., Distinguishing between facts and opinions for sentiment analysis: Survey and challenges. *Inform. Fusion*, 44, 65–77, 2018, https://doi.org/10.1016/j.inffus.2017.12.006.

41. Hurwitz, J. and Bowles, A., *Cognitive Computing and Big Data Analytics*, Wiley, Hoboken, NJ, USA, 2015.

42. Lake, B.M., Salakhutdinov, R., Tenenbaum, J.B., Human-level concept learning through probabilistic program induction. *Science*, 350, 6266, 1332–1338, 2015, doi: 10.1126/science.aab3050.

43. Le, Q.V., Monga, R., Devin, M., Corrado, G., Chen, K., Ranzato, M., Dean, J., Ng, A.Y., Building high-level features using large scale unsupervised learning, arxiv, 2011. CoRR, abs/1112.6209. http://arxiv.org/abs/1112.6209.

44. Chen, M., Qian, Y., Hao, Y., Li, Y., Song, J., Data-driven computing and caching in 5G networks: Architecture and delay analysis. *IEEE Wirel. Commun.*, 25, 1, 70–75, 2018.

45. Zhou, L., On Data-Driven Delay Estimation for Media Cloud. *IEEE Trans. Multimed.*, 18, 5, 905–915, 2016, https://doi.org/10.1109/TMM.2016.2537782.

46. Armbrust, A. Fox and Griffith, M., R., *Above the clouds: A Berkeley view of cloud computing*, pp. 07–013, University of California, Berkeley, Tech. Rep. UCB, 2009, https://doi.org/10.1145/1721654.1721672.

47. Silver, D., Huang, A., Maddison, C.J., Guez, A., Sifre, L., Van Den Driessche, G., Schrittwieser, J., Antonoglou, I., Panneershelvam, V., Lanctot, M., Dieleman, S., Grewe, D., Nham, J., Kalchbrenner, N., Sutskever, I., Lillicrap, T., Leach, M., Kavukcuoglu, K., Graepel, T., Hassabis, D., Mastering the game of Go with deep neural networks and tree search. *Nature*, 529, 7587, 484–489, 2016, https://doi.org/10.1038/nature16961.

48. Chen, M., Herrera, F., Hwang, K., Cognitive Computing: Architecture, Technologies and Intelligent Applications. *IEEE Access*, 6, 19774–19783, 2018, https://doi.org/10.1109/ACCESS.2018.2791469.

49. Belciug, S. and Gorunescu, F., Era of Intelligent Systems in Healthcare, in: *Intelligent Systems Reference Library*, vol. 157, 2020.

50. Meystel, A.M. and Albus, J.S., *Intelligent Systems – Architecture, Design, and Control*, A Wiley-Interscience Publication John Wiley & Sons, Inc., Canada, 2002.

51. Ogiela, L., Computational intelligence in cognitive healthcare information systems. *Stud. Comput. Intell.*, 309, 347–369, 2010, https://doi.org/10.1007/978-3-642-14464-6-16.

52. Copestake, A., *Natural Language Processing: Part 1 of Lecture Notes*, Cambridge: Ann Copestake Lecture Note Series, 2003.

53. Regina, B. and Michael, C., *Natural Language Processing: Background and Overview*, Cambridge: Barzilay and Collins Lecture Note Series, 2005.

54. Saetre, R., GeneTUC: Automatic information extraction from biomedical texts. *Proceedings of Computer Science Graduate Students Conference*, Norwegian University of Science and Technology (NTNU, Trondheim, Norway, April 29 2004.

55. Abràmoff, M.D., Lavin, P.T., Birch, M., Shah, N., Folk, J.C., Pivotal trial of an autonomous AI-based diagnostic system for detection of diabetic retinopathy in primary care offices. *NPJ Digit. Med.*, 1, 1, 1–8, 2018.

56. Lin, H., Long, E., Ding, X., Diao, H., Chen, Z., Liu, R., Huang, J., Cai, J., Xu, S., Zhang, X., Prediction of myopia development among Chinese school-aged children using refraction data from electronic medical records: A retrospective, multicentre machine learning study. *PloS Med.*, 15, 11, e1002674, 2018.

57. Marr, B., *First FDA approval for clinical cloud-based deep learning in healthcare*, Forbes, Jan 20, 2017, https://www.forbes.com/sites/bernardmarr/2017/01/20/

first-fda-approval-for-clinical-cloud-baseddeep-learning-in-healthcare/#2e-0b1a44161c.

58. Voelker, R., Diagnosing fractures with AI. . *JAMA*, 320, 23, 2018.

59. Rajpurkar, P., Irvin, J., Ball, R.L., Zhu, K., Yang, B., Mehta, H., Duan, T., Ding, D., Bagul, A., Langlotz, C.P., Deep learning for chest radiograph diagnosis: A retrospective comparison of the CheXNeXt algorithm to practicing radiologists. *PloS Med.*, 15, 11, e1002686, 2018.

60. Titano, J.J., Badgeley, M., Schefflein, J., Pain, M., Su, A., Cai, M., Swinburne, N., Zech, J., Kim, J., Bederson, J., Automated deep-neural-network surveillance of cranial images for acute neurologic events. *Nat. Med.*, 24, 9, 1337–1341, 2018.

61. Henry, K.E., Hager, D.N., Pronovost, P.J., Saria, S., A targeted real-time early warning score (TREWScore) for septic shock. *Sci. Transl. Med.*, 7, 299, 299ra122–299ra122, 2015.

62. Henry, K., Wongvibulsin, S., Zhan, A., Saria, S., Hager, D., Can septic shock be identified early? Evaluating performance of a targeted real-time early warning score (TREWScore) for septic shock in a community hospital: global and subpopulation performance. In *D15. Critical Care Do We Have a Crystal Ball? Predicting Clinical Deterioration and Outcome in Critically Ill Patients*, pp. A7016--A7016, American Thoracic Society, 2017.

63. Kerlikowske, K., Scott, C.G., Mahmoudzadeh, A.P., Ma, L., Winham, S., Jensen, M.R., Wu, F.F., Malkov, S., Pankratz, V.S., Cummings, S.R., Automated and clinical breast imaging reporting and data system density measures predict risk for screen-detected and interval cancers: A case–control study. *Annal. Intern. Med.*, 168, 11, 757–765, 2018.

64. Winters, B., Custer, J., Galvagno Jr., S.M., Colantuoni, E., Kapoor, S.G., Lee, H., Goode, V., Robinson, K., Nakhasi, A., Pronovost, P., Newman-Toker, D., Diagnostic errors in the intensive care unit: A systematic review of autopsy studies. *BMJ Qual. Saf.*, 21, 11, 894–902, 2012, http://dx.doi.org/10.1136/bmjqs-2012-000803.

65. Cook, R.I., Woods, D.D., Walters, M. *et al.*, The cognitive systems engineering of automated medical evacuation scheduling, in: *Proceedings of human interaction with complex systems*, IEEE Computer Society Press, Los Alamitos, pp. 202–7, 1996.

66. Walters, M.E., The Cognitive Complexity of Event-Driven Replanning: Managing Cascading Secondary Disruptions, in: *Aeromedical Evacuation Planning*, Ph.D. Dissertation. Columbus: OH, The Ohio State University, 1997.

67. Cook, R.I., *Being BumpableJoint cognitive systems: patterns in cognitive systems engineering, chapter 3*, D.D. Woods and E. Hollnagel (Eds.), CRC Press, Boca Rotan, 2006.

68. Cook, R.I. and Woods, D.D., Adapting to new Technology in the Operating Room. *Hum. Factors.*, 38, 4, 593–613, 1996.

69. Iroju, O.G. and Olaleke, J.O., A Systematic Review of Natural Language Processing in Healthcare. *Int. J. Inform. Technol. Comput. Sci.*, 7, 8, 44–50, 2015, https://doi.org/10.5815/ijitcs.2015.08.07.
70. Ngiam, K.Y. and Khor, I.W., Big data and machine learning algorithms for healthcare delivery. *Lancet Oncol.*, 20, 5, e262–e273, 2019, doi: 10.1016/s1470-2045(19)30149-4.

2

Proposal of a Metaheuristic Algorithm of Cognitive Computing for Classification of Erythrocytes and Leukocytes in Healthcare Informatics

Ana Carolina Borges Monteiro[1]*, Reinaldo Padilha França, Rangel Arthur[2]† and Yuzo Iano[1]

[1]*Communications Department (DECOM), School of Electrical and Computer Engineering (FEEC), University of Campinas (UNICAMP), Campinas – SP, Brazil*
[2]*Telecommunications Department, Faculty of Technology (FT), University of Campinas (UNICAMP), Limeira – SP, Brazil*

Abstract

Through the use of AI in diagnostic medicine provides accurate and safe diagnoses in the evaluation of exams. Image recognition is not an easy task, as this can be achieved with the ability to organize images in an automated way provided by machine learning, classifying this based on identified patterns, particular objects, and grouping them thematically. In this panorama, pattern recognition distinguishes issues effectively, through a voluminous database containing data related to the pathology, enabling machine "learns" to do an accurate diagnosis of the patient's condition. In this context, through blood count through manual and/or automated procedure, blood is investigated, motivated by innovations in the field of medicine, implementing a Deep Learning framework for the recognition and identification of white blood cell subtypes in digital images, it is possible to employ employing a set of convolution layers, allowing to distinguish details not revealed to the human naked eye, extracting resources (from edges) from WBC digital images molding the convolution operation, also relating feed-forward layers combined for WBC augmented digital image for cell classification and qualification.

Corresponding author: decom.fee.unicamp.br; (http://orcid.org/0000-0002-8631-6617)
†*Corresponding author*: rangel@ft.unicamp.br; (http://orcid.org/0000-0002-4138-4720)
(http://orcid.org/0000-0002-7901-6691)
(http://orcid.org/0000-0002-9843-976)

D. Sumathi, T. Poongodi, B. Balamurugan and Lakshmana Kumar Ramasamy (eds.)
Cognitive Intelligence and Big Data in Healthcare, (41–66) © 2022 Scrivener Publishing LLC

With this focus, using Python language and Jupyter notebook software, the dataset encompassing 12.500 digital images of human blood smear was manipulated, integrating fields of non-pathological leukocytes. Resulting from that, with an accuracy of 86.16% testifying the elevated reliability of the developed framework. Thus, the proposed framework is evaluated as an accurate, low-cost, and effective digital method that can be used as a third practicable procedure for blood count in the underprivileged populace of underdeveloped and developing countries.

Keywords: Healthcare, biomedical signals, cognitive computing, Artificial Intelligence, deep learning, healthcare informatics, cognitive models, cognitive healthcare

2.1   Introduction

Before the advent of cognitive computing, computers were not very efficient at interacting with humans, since people needed to strive to learn languages to exploit the potential of technology. Still evaluating that even in basic tasks, such as using an algorithm to identify an image, whether it was a banana or an orange, they were too complicated to be taught to a machine. Cognitive Computing is a science related to operating and simulates thinking in a computer model, enabling the use of self-learning algorithms for recognizing patterns of data processing more efficiently [1].

Programming languages were developed by the need to program, that is, to guide a machine to perform a specific action. And in this sense, the emergence of cognitive computing was driven by its creation of the fact that natural interactions, considering speech, touch, and vision, would be a more intuitive form of interaction with the machines that surround us. In fact, cognitive computing has given systems the ability to reason close to that of a human being. This is essential for them to be able to perform complex tasks, such as medical diagnosis [2].

Improving diagnostics has been one of the most important challenges facing health systems in recent years, which can be further benefited by cognitive computing, through Neural Networks that in addition to its structure of neurons and virtual synapses, there is the focus of innovation related to optimizing the performance of human beings in their activities. With this focus in line with innovation and scientific research, related to image classification techniques, medical information management systems are brought by health technology [3].

The concept of cognitive computing with the cognitive technologies that can be used in the medical work environment goes beyond results optimization and cost reduction, reaching a level of development never seen before, thus enabling a breakthrough in the areas of prevention, early disease detection, and disease control relating that cognitive intelligence functions as a human extension capable of absorbing, learning and using all assimilated information [4].

Systems based on Artificial Neural Networks are considered neuron-based metaheuristics, evaluating that since a given neuron can have several inputs, then it can perceive different signals, and thus connect several similar neurons in a network. This type of technique depends heavily on the topology of these networks (size, structure, connections), as well as their parameters (learning rate, among others) [5, 6].

There is a known difficulty when designing efficient Neural Networks; in which some empirical knowledge is involved, which can be applied in specific cases. In this sense, blood is investigated through blood count, i.e., Complete Blood Count (CBC), which in general is subject to manual and/or automated procedures. Since the heuristic for this study is derived from the layers in operation with the articular network of hidden neurons detecting forms of simple components. Consisting of an intelligent learning algorithm finding the desired objects in the digital image, i.e., the classification and recognition of white cell subtypes in digital images that reach the criteria for reliability and efficiency of blood cell detection, making the heuristic methodology saves time in the same sense which is more accessible to diverse populations [7].

Cognitive computing applications, in turn, aim to develop data interpretation, just like the human brain. In this context, it was developed in Python programming language, using the Jupyter notebook development environment, through the use of a dataset containing 12,500 digital images of human blood smear fields comprising non-pathological leukocytes an accuracy of the cognitive metaheuristic approach of 86.16% demonstrating the high reliability of the methodology.

In the same sense, it is worth noting the great importance to create tools that facilitate the obtaining of medical reports with low cost and high reliability, since laboratory medical exams in general present costs that are inaccessible to populations of underdeveloped and developing countries. Therefore, the algorithm is considered an accurate, reliable, and inexpensive method that can be employed as a third most practicable procedure for CBC in often underprivileged people of developing and underdeveloped countries [8].

2.2   Literature Concept

2.2.1   Cognitive Computing Concept

The advent of cognitive computing has surpassed the traditional premise related to the age of computers managing data, even though capturing it was unable to process it, in the same sense that the human brain does, and even without any possibility of interacting with humans, even basic tasks like identifying whether an image was of a banana or an orange. These tasks through languages that exploited the potential of technology until then were too complicated to be taught to a machine. From this cognitive advent, technology brings the task of capacities similar to interpersonal to the way machines deal with information [9].

Still relating from the historical point of view that before man had to learn the language of the machine, nowadays, cognitive computing goes beyond simple programming, allowing the machine to speak, learn and interact using human language, being able to interpret human senses. From this, cognitive computing is considered as the third era of computing, surpassing those primitive mechanisms, which did programmable tasks and primary calculations. Given those previously computers needed to be controlled, they can now use a cognitive self-learning algorithm, natural language processing, data mining, among other characteristics, imitating the human brain in its activities and even decision making [10].

Cognitive computing is built by mixing cognition science (the study of the human brain and how it works) and computer science creating technologies that can simulate the human thought process. Empowering the ability to recognize and respond to data streams allowing to automate a variety of functions, enabling automated customer service agents, recommendation management systems, diagnosis and treatment systems, and fraud and investigation analysis systems [11, 12].

The importance of cognitive computing derives from programming languages developed by the need to program and guide a machine to perform a predetermined action, still reflecting that this created natural interactions, i.e., that take into account speech, talk, and vision. In this context, cognitive computing is a more intuitive way to interact with the machines that surround people, serving a lot of things besides making our devices more accessible [13, 14].

Cognitive computing allows systems, making machines gain the ability to interact with humans and communicate with them in natural language, bringing an enhanced era of digital transformation by allowing computers to learn, develop reasoning and make decisions, reflecting on this reasoning capacity very close to that of a human being, which is essential for machines to be able to perform complex tasks, such as medical diagnosis, for example [15, 16].

Through cognitive computing it is possible to analyze large volumes of data and then generate feasible alternatives within a set of possibilities, being able to act in large hospitals and the banking system, for example, generating answers and insights, learning every day to serve better human needs. Also listing the benefits of cognitive computing as it provides the ability to deal with elaborate systems and get the answers, they need from them, that is, where there is no longer a demand for high technical knowledge to interact with computing. This can be explained by the virtual assistants who, although still limited, bring adequate answers, just asking a question in an appropriate way for Artificial Intelligence to work on top of that [17, 18].

Also relating that the type of analysis that cognitive computing makes it possible to quickly identify bottlenecks and problems, and determining how to act in face of these scenarios, having a proactive and more responsive posture. Finally, this technology has the property of improving human performance, since it can automatically analyze structured and unstructured data and provide answers quickly, considering that otherwise, it would take years to achieve [19].

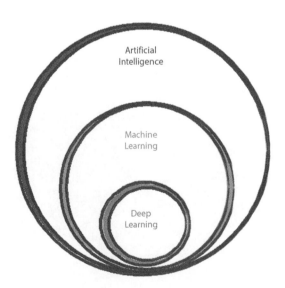

Figure 2.1 Artificial learning technologies.

Technology that reigns in cognitive computing is Artificial Intelligence (AI) (Figure 2.1), which reproduces human cognitive capacities in machines, from then on, ranging from sub-area technologies, computer vision to machine learning, enabling machines to recognize patterns, images, speech, and refine your own algorithm over time, for example. Machine Learning is allowing computational models to be trained on data sets improving automatically and gradually with the number of experiments in which it is placed to train. Having properties and characteristics to learn according to the expected responses through associations of different data, can be numbers, images, voice, and other data types that this technology can identify. Deep Learning is a digital learning capacity by using deep neural networks enhancing learning machines, using neural networks with many layers of processing, granting processing high-level resources from raw data, and even ability to learn on their own, or still to learn complex patterns and read large amounts of raw data [20–22].

Cognitive computing allows you to go beyond your structure of artificial neurons, focusing on optimizing the performance of human beings in their activities, since unlike the human brain, which makes a selection between what will be stored in memory and what would be temporary knowledge, cognitive digital intelligence functions as a human extension capable of absorbing, learning and using all the information assimilated [4, 23].

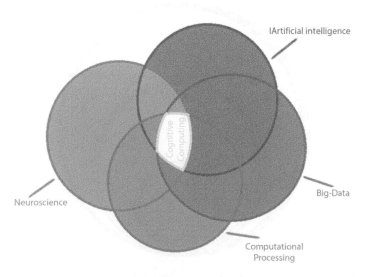

Figure 2.2 Cognitive computing illustration.

The advantages of cognitive computing (Figure 2.2), derived from neuroscience studies, come from the fact that systems that aggregate AI and cognitive intelligence have the properties of processing and analyzing data from different formats and sources, mainly concerning the speed of their computational processing, going beyond the volume of data (Big Data) to be interconnected, considering structured and unstructured data, so that in its execution, no data or knowledge is neglected. Providing decision-making is an ideal complement to the efficiency and assertiveness of human choices [4, 24].

2.2.2   Neural Networks Concepts

With neural networks, it is possible to make computers smarter by creating accurate weather forecasts, solving a partial differential equation, or even scouring the internet looking for a single web page, or even allowing a computer to differentiate between porn and Renaissance art [25].

Neural networks can have tens of millions of artificial neurons, similar to human neurons, which are arranged in layers, using AI technology to perform processing and understand information. These layers are composed of several nodes, each containing various information, which connects in different branches, creating a logical and established relationship between these nodes, emerging new connections that connect them, and so on. Thus, real-world data and information arrive at the first layer (input layer), passing to one or more layers connected to each other, still pondering that each of these layers transforms this received information into something that the final unit (output unit), allows understanding and use (Figure 2.3) [26, 27].

Computers simply cannot reason, interpret the context of real-world situations, or make differentiated decisions, in the same way as human

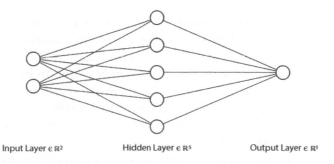

Input Layer ∈ R²   Hidden Layer ∈ R⁵   Output Layer ∈ R¹

Figure 2.3 Neural networks.

beings. In this context, through neural networks inspired by the human brain, using different layers of mathematical processing to understand more and more the information that is fed, from human speech to digital image, essentially learning and changing over time, software systems can train themselves to make sense of the human world [27].

Neural networks provide the property to classify and group a huge volume of data very quickly, facilitating the use of that data in production in any sector for which the technology is employed, qualifying the creation of insights and solutions. By learning by standards, it is possible to predict results and facilitate many processes, avoiding errors and waste, while still being able to align a planned demand with a high degree of reliability, assisting in the organization of stocks, for example [28].

Neural networks also allow recognizing commands by speech and even authoring a voice in an agile way by voice recognition, or even recognizing letters, figures, and even people, among other elements. This property configures numerous functionalities, such as parts recognition, quality control, detection, and even failure prevention. They also have characteristics that allow them to analyze, understand, and predict patterns of consumer behavior, or even predict with good chances of success the liking of customers based on their previous choices, or even assemble a streaming list of songs based on that have been heard, i.e., this can adapt and improve products according to the needs and wants of customers captured by neural networks [29, 30].

This feature deals with machine learning in an autonomous way made possible through exposure to an environment with data, being able to collect it, understand patterns, and learn from it. Starting from the premise that the more data a machine tends to learn on its own, and the more complex the tasks that it is able to perform become, managing to examine and understand different data structures without knowing them beforehand [30].

In this context, deep learning (Figure 2.4) is learning of very complex patterns that neural networks allow; it is autonomous learning that approaches the pattern of human brain processes. With this, it is possible to detect small tool failures based on any deviation from the standard behavior learned by the machine, perform part localization, classification, and recognition of product characteristics, among other applications and analysis considering several other functions that optimize any type of product. desired process [31].

Also, with parallelism, neural networks are able to process information in applications that need real-time responses. However, one of the biggest

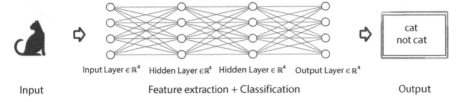

Input Layer ∈ R⁴   Hidden Layer ∈ R⁴   Hidden Layer ∈ R⁴   Output Layer ∈ R⁴

Input   Feature extraction + Classification   Output

Figure 2.4 Deep learning.

challenges is the amount of time it takes to train these neural networks, which can require a considerable amount of computational energy for more complex tasks. However, in modern days computers acquire the ability to understand the world around them in a more "human" way, due to all this artificial computational power, enhancing productivity, profitability, and competitiveness in sectors of society that employ this technology [28, 31].

2.2.3   Convolutional Neural Network

Image recognition is a challenging field of study, which evaluates the context of machine vision; it is the ability of software to identify people, places, and objects, among other elements and characteristics. To recognize digital images, computers must use machine vision technologies and AI software. Given that for a computer, identifying anything (be it a watch, a chair, humans, animals, among others) represents a much more difficult problem than the ease with which the human and animal brain recognizes objects [32, 33].

In this respect, image recognition (Figure 2.5) is a machine learning method designed to resemble the way the human brain works, allowing computers to recognize visual elements within an image. Training these machines in large databases and observing patterns results in the possibility of analyzing images and formulating relevant tags and categories that make sense [33, 34].

Through AI it has been increasingly able to bridge the gap between the capabilities of humans and machines in various areas, such as computer vision. In this sense, a Convolutional Neural Network (CNN) is a type of deep learning algorithm that captures an input image, assigning importance (weights and biases) to various aspects, and allowing objects in the image to be differentiated from each other. The architecture of a CNN was inspired by the organization of the visual cortex and is even analogous to that of the pattern of neuron connectivity in the human brain [35].

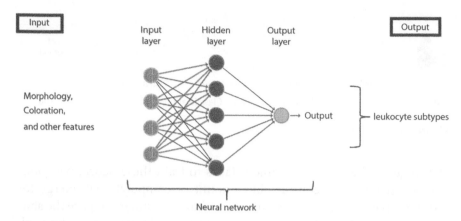

Figure 2.5 Deep learning.

Deep in Convolutional Neural Networks (CNN), they consist of an Artificial Neuron, containing Characteristic Vector, Weights, Bias, and Activation Function, which is given an input, defining a state for the neuron. This comes from the premise of how to determine the probability of each class in the output layer of the neural network, and even define the probability of a class within a multiclass problem. It is worth noting that this type of training requires high computational cost and a large number of databases; however, the pre-processing is much less in comparison to other classification algorithms, given that while in the primitive methods the filters are made by hand, in CNN it reaches the ability to learn these filters or characteristics on their own. It is also important to note that they generally consist of two major stages, extraction of Characteristics by the Convolutional Layers and then Classification [36].

A Convolutional Layer for the case of a digital image introduced as an input, which can be colored, multichannel, among others, requires a Convolution with a filter (neuron), even considering that each filter can represent a specific image attribute (straight, curved, color, among others), and a Support for that filter relative to a receptive field. As a result of this operation, an activation map (attribute map), which is generally slightly smaller than the original image because the borders are discarded. Still considering that successive convolutions detect attributes of a higher level, such as semi-circles (straight + curve), squares (four straight), among other characteristics. And even at higher levels, you can still detect handwritten text or an object of a specific color, and even receptive fields become broader with more global information) [37, 38].

Still characterizing the details concerning the Convolutional Layer there is Stride (displacement, i.e., the spacing between the masks) and Padding (filling), i.e., it is the filling (with zeros for example) to leave the convoluted image with the same size as the original. Among the convolutional layers, there is the ReLU (non-linearity) [38].

Pooling is a synthesis of information, i.e., given that the attribute is in the convoluted image (high response to the respective filter), it does not matter so much the exact location, but it reduces the number of weights (computational cost), compressing the data and controlling the overlap. training (overfitting), which results in loss of generalization. Still considering downsampling properties, max-pooling is generally more common, i.e., a filter and stride of the same size detecting the largest element in the region [39].

Dropout layer is used only in the training phase, not in the test, this eliminates a random set of activations in the layer set to zero, i.c., forces the network to be "redundant", that is, correctly classifying even if some activations are zeroed, this mitigates overfitting. The applications of a CNN in Images range from classification by assigning categories of objects to an image, or even location framing around the target object, still on detection by locating multiple objects (multiple bounding boxes and labels), or segmentation concerning the contour and label of the object of interest [40].

Deep Learning works directly with CNN and data representation at different levels of abstraction, extracting data characteristics, with a high number of parameters (Adjustment by BackProgation). However, it needs a large number of examples (data/dataset) for efficient learning, since this type of learning is geared towards understanding by the machine, that is, the data are difficult to understand/visualize humanly [41].

Finally, on a CNN (Figure 2.6), convolution is the simple application of a filter to an entry that results in activation, that repeated application of the same filter to an entry results in a resource map, indicating the locations and strength of a resource detected in an input (digital image). Innovation

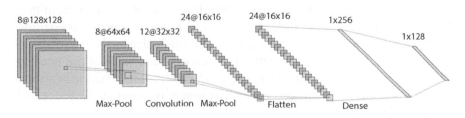

Figure 2.6 Convolutional neural networks.

is the ability to automatically learn a large number of filters in specific parallel to a set of training data under the constraints of a specific predictive modeling problem (image classification), resulting in highly specific features that can be detected in any place in the input images [42].

As it is also possible to notice in Figure 2.6, the set of convolutional layer (filters), in each step (CNN structure) to learn multiple features in parallel for a given input. This characteristic derives from different ways of extracting features from an input, this diversity allows specialization, or many different ways of both "learning" and after training related to input data, e.g., not just lines, but the specific lines digitally seen in specific training date.

2.2.4   Deep Learning

This area is a subfield of AI and computer science that has been evolving a lot in recent years, dealing with technologies that use visual data processing, such as unstructured data, such as images and videos. Deep Learning is an excellent technology to perform data recognition and classification tasks; however, it needs computational processing power and even digital memory to be executed in real-time [43].

Deep Learning is derived from Machine Learning capable of training computers to perform activities as if they were human beings, this concept concerns deep learning opportunities with the use of neural networks, improving the capacity of the machines. Deep Learning allows them to perform data analysis faster and more efficiently, recognize speech, detect objects, and describe the content, creating smarter systems and computers [44].

In Deep Learning, neural networks are more sophisticated, much larger in digital size, and with a superior ability to extract and represent information. With Deep Learning, the definition of the relevant characteristics and the extraction of them is done by the machine itself, through a large number of images necessary to capture these characteristics, that is, the machine is able to discover and define the frequent characteristics in the examples [45].

Machine Learning consists of teaching how to evolve as it is submitted to new data, it is a simpler type of AI for a computer to improve its learning capacity. Considering the main elements are predictive analysis and statistical analysis, used to detect patterns based on data, without the need to indicate where to look. Deep Learning is intuitive, while Machine Learning requires manual interventions in the selection of resources to be processed (Figure 2.7) [46].

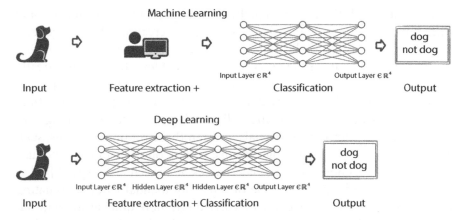

Figure 2.7 Machine learning x deep learning.

With respect to Figure 2.7, Deep Learning (DL) is related to the premise of referring to a part of ML that uses complex algorithms to "mimic the neural network of the human brain" and learn an area of knowledge with little or no supervision; it needs large amounts of data to be trained to recognize significant patterns of human behavior. From an accessible and well-organized database, in addition to a computational superpower of information processing, this is what makes it possible for machines to behave as similarly as possible to humans, i.e., the system can learn how to defend itself from digital attacks, alone. Since an algorithm that uses DL to improve the ranking of links, unlike "ML", is aimed at in-depth analysis of data in a much larger volume than usual, using algorithms that help to identify data, allowing systems and machines to be able to observe patterns and correlations in a large amount of information. Deep Learning is a technique that, through artificial neural networks, has significantly improved the ability of computers to recognize, classify, detect, and describe information. In this way, Deep Learning does the "training" of a computational model so that it can decipher the natural language, relating terms and words to infer meaning from the huge flow of data generated and processed [47].

Nowadays, Deep Learning through neural networks is used to solve specific tasks, avoiding a strictly biological approach, as the volume of structured and unstructured data increases, with many layers, they have replaced decision trees in several applications. Still pondering the aspect that it is possible to reuse the initial phases of the machine for the recognition of other types of images, through Deep Learning. Before, for each application, a different machine was needed [48].

Currently, with Deep Learning, the reuse of part of the machine in some different applications is possible, allowing the creation of more general machines for various applications. With these properties, Deep Learning has not only taken machine precision to the next level but has also greatly expanded the possibility of applications. Deep Learning has many applications and several advantages such as tasks that used to require a lot of time can be performed using machines, eliminating the costs of training staff and hiring specialized professionals, or even those routine activities, such as creating reports, monitoring systems, among others, can run automatically, running 24 hours a day, 7 days a week at a much faster speed [49].

Increased productivity capable of replacing manual labor, automating certain tasks, as these processes are carried out more quickly and without risk of failure. Better decision-making given the data flows generated by society are increasingly greater, due to the current hyperconnectivity, technology is capable of handling this volume of information, making forecasts more assertive and more accurate, and intelligent scenarios [50].

Exemplifying the use of this technology, it is seen its use in cars with the possibility of driving autonomously or almost autonomously, requiring the system to understand the environment around it. In addition to the various cameras installed around the vehicle collecting information that is analyzed by deep neural networks, analyzing several images of the car's activities compared to others, from other users, allowing and managing to avoid collisions and navigate smoothly on the roads [51].

Or even exemplifying the processing of medical images through computer vision algorithms using deep learning, making it possible to analyze several images and compare them to obtain a faster and more effective result for a person's health diagnosis, analyzing tests or symptoms. Or even used for the creation of medicines, through the realization of several combinations of substances and their possible reactions when they are combined and put in contact with the human body [52].

Or even interacting with the real world, through the augmented reality (AR) technology used by several applications, ranging from eyewear stores, making it possible to try different models, or even a clothing store, also making it possible to try different models, even mobile games. Both examples, performed through the environment, body, and people's faces, using Deep Learning technology to detect and track objects in the place and insert virtual shapes [53].

Finally, instead of organizing information to be executed using predefined equations, Deep Learning adjusts basic parameters about the data and trains the system to learn on its own. This occurs with the recognition of patterns in several layers of processing.

Thus, employing Deep Learning in a dataset of microscopic normal peripheral blood cell digital images, related to the objective of microscopy, it is possible to employ CNN to characterize five morphological cell subtypes WBC, i.e., Monocytes, Neutrophils, Eosinophils, Lymphocytes, and even Basophil, employing a set of convolution layers, allowing to distinguish details not revealed to the human naked eye, from that it is possible to extract resources (from edges) from WBC digital images molding the convolution operation, also relating feed-forward layers combined for WBC augmented digital image for cell classification and qualification.

2.3 Materials and Methods (Metaheuristic Algorithm Proposal)

A dataset was employed comprising of 12,500 blood cell digital images for the development of the proposed algorithm, categorizing into four cell morphology types Monocytes, Neutrophils, Eosinophils, Lymphocytes,

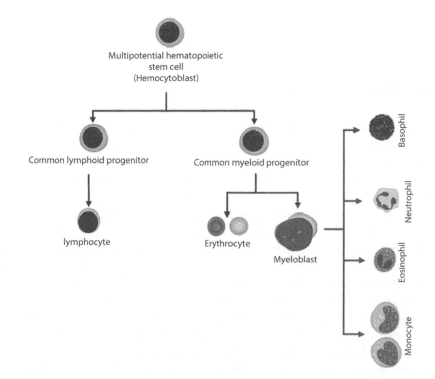

Figure 2.8 Blood cell types.

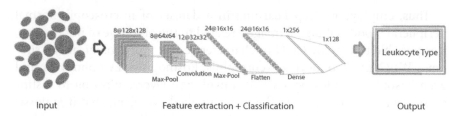

Input   Feature extraction + Classification   Output

Figure 2.9 Proposal modeling logic.

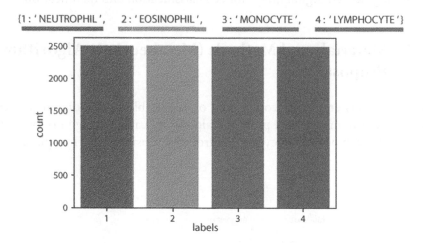

Figure 2.10 Leukocyte cell classes.

still considering implementation of a denial logic for Basophil cell type classification, as illustrated in Figure 2.8. It was still implemented in a class containing 2400 digital images for fulfillment training of CNN, as displayed in Figures 2.9 and 2.10, still assessing the employment of four more classes using 600 digital images for a test of the developed structure.

The algorithm structure was implemented on the Jupyter notebook software in version 0.35.4, utilizing Kera's environment for training models neural network written in Python 3.7 language. Still considering that this implementation was done on a hardware platform comprising of an Intel Core i3 machine with 4 GB RAM. Also, the size of the digital image was reduced to 60 × 80 × 3 favoring the training by a neural network, and then loading as numerical arrays in it, in this sense, also employed Kera's libraries for preprocessing digital images, using it through dataset processing as methods and objects. Thus, a CNN was built, summarizing a set of convolution layers and even a feed-forward associated with it, developed for digital image classification and assortment.

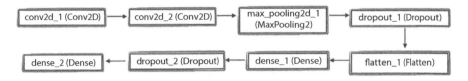

Figure 2.11 CNN architecture.

Reflecting on the dataset used, it consists of color digital images derived from blood cells introduced by a 3D matrix, provisioning a disposition of RGB colors (red, green, and blue), i.e., an additive color system summarized by these tones. Thus, CNN act in the extraction of resources (edges) from cell digital images, molding convolution operations. Since a simple neural network is unable to learn and even classify these existing resources in each cell type present dataset, i.e., it is laborious. So, CNN-developed architecture is illustrated concerning a logical flowchart in Figure 2.11.

2.4 Case Study and Discussion

As previously provided in Section 2.3, CNN has executed on a physical machine over 44 epochs, reaching an accuracy of 86.16%, as can be noted in Figure 2.12, consisting of an expressive result due to the complexity of the implemented structure of the neural network.

Testifying the accuracy and validity of the implemented CNN structure, the digital image seen in Figure 2.13 was verified regarding the trained CNN, proving the neural network's accuracy and also digital learning concerning cell classification in the digital image as a leukocyte category, particularly a monocyte type, according to that in Figure 2.14.

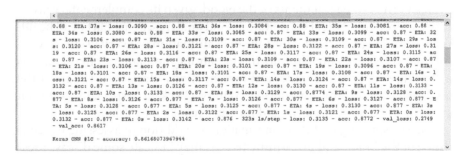

Figure 2.12 CNN accuracy.

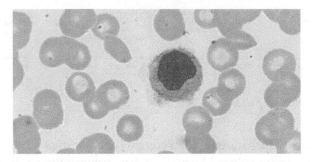

Figure 2.13 Monocyte test image.

```
In [42]:  preds = model.predict_classes(xi)
          print(preds)
          [3]
```

Figure 2.14 CNN monocyte classification.

The importance of digital classification of human blood cell biology derives from the study of the structure and functioning of cells, as well as the interaction between them, allowing a greater understanding of the functioning of the human organism. Given that this works in an integrated way with other branches of knowledge, such as biochemistry, molecular biology, genetics, and even immunology, contributing to an advance in the most diverse areas of activity related to medicine [54, 55].

Still highlighting that from these digital electron microscopy images, it is possible to use technology to contribute to the detection of structures not yet revealed by the optical microscope, or even not paying attention to the eyes of human specialists. Given that technology like the one presented in this research, it has been improved, reflecting in the constant advance of cell biology [56, 57].

In this regard, the CBC is the test that quantitatively and qualitatively evaluates the cellular elements of the blood, given its complementary property required in medical consultations and analyzes, being part of all health reviews and routine tests. This type of examination is a very useful screening that provides valuable information about the patient, often taken as a starting point for most medical investigations. Because it is part of the analysis necessary for any routine exam or check-up, especially as it is an exam that is easy to perform and measure results [58, 59].

Still considering that this examination, in addition to assessing the condition of the blood and its forming tissues, may indicate some disease present in other organs. Given that the abnormal results tend to indicate the presence of a variety of conditions that interfere in the individual's health including infections, anemias, and even leukemia, among others, still implying that many times before the individual even presents the symptoms of a certain disease [60, 61].

In this regard, this examination is intended to assess the general health of a patient, acting as part of a routine medical examination to monitor health or identifying diseases among the most serious anemias and types of leukemia, among others. In cases of weakness, fever, inflammation, bleeding, this test allows diagnosing a medical condition helping to diagnose the cause of these symptoms, helping to confirm medical suspicion of an infection, allowing for early diagnosis. Reflecting that blood plays a fundamental role in protecting and maintaining the body's balance [62, 63].

Or even, allowing monitoring medical treatment to accompany health in a situation in which there is the administration of medications that can affect the CBC. Given the properties of this test that through information obtained it is possible to measure the quantity and types of white blood cells, considering that a high number of white cells present in the blood can mean inflammation or even an infection. Or even measure the number of red blood cells, since a low number of these cells can signal anemia, still considering that in cases of anemia there may be a greater variation in the size of red cells [64, 65].

Thus, the classification and analysis of these components through Deep Learning techniques, such as CNN, allows the assessment of the patient's clinical condition, that is, to assess health and identify diseases, following the progression of any adverse medical condition and even assessing whether the treatment is having the desired effect. Since through digital imaging exams combined with Deep Learning, result in a lower cost of health costs, safe, fast, and inexpensive way, combined with the characteristics of the respective technology to increased accuracy allowing the early diagnosis of several major diseases, while improving certainty of diagnosis than previously without technology. Reflecting this context, Deep Learning is fully directed to the technological progress of the modern world implicating proportionately for medical practice, observing the diversity of technology-assisted examinations has enabled medical specialists through these precise techniques [66–70].

The use of artificial intelligence techniques brings more safety to patients for the best treatment of the numerous pathologies, achieving better accuracy in diagnosis, and consequently increasing the chances of a promising treatment. Still reflecting that it automates operational activities, improving the medical assistance experience in real-time, standardizing, and facilitating diagnoses of major, serious, and frequent diseases that can be analyzed by imaging, helping in the decision making of the clinical staff.

Reflecting the presented context and linking the results achieved in this research, it demonstrates how this is promising for medical areas, considering the application of this type of technology to a large portion of the world population that lives in situations of extreme poverty, with incompatible income or even with little or no government assistance. This population is not indifferent to developing blood disorders, which can be cured when discovered in the early stages.

From this panorama, this proposed framework can be considered as a technique that solves issues of confirmation or accuracy faced in diagnoses for blood tests, providing greater productivity and focus on the patient. Still evaluating that through blood cell rating by Deep Learning technology can be performed via a computational device produces advantages related to higher quality, lower cost, and reduction in the time of the exam result, comparing the current reality that is dependent on high-cost hematological equipment, specific reagents that restrict the use of purchasing from resellers to users.

2.5   Conclusions with Future Research Scopes

It is worth reflecting that in several locations around the globe, the cell and even whole preparation of blood collected for analysis is the sole responsibility of professional humans, mainly relating to underdeveloped and developing countries. Even so, this professional is subject to errors when it is associated with extensive working hours, fatigue, burnout, psychological exhaustion, physical exhaustion, and sometimes inadequate remuneration, resulting in aspects of motivation, i.e., a dissatisfaction that interferes in the performance of this professional consisting of crucial vectors against the reliability of tests performed manually.

In light of this, the proposed methodology, relating its impacts of digital transformation presents lower costs when compared with the automated methodologies, i.e., specific hematological equipment. Consisting of synonymous with low cost and reliability brought with the advent of Artificial Intelligence techniques in the medical routine, which can be geared towards developed countries and also for those less favored populations. Or even it is also useful for those populations with the best economic situation, can be used as a confirmatory tool to validate the results of exams that are outside the reference values, given the accuracy of this proposal which decreases the possibility of false-negative and false-positive tests in medical routines.

In this sense, it is worth noting that the proposed CNNN architecture for classification of white blood cells achieved 86,16% accuracy, consisting of a satisfactory performance due to the complexity of the studied problem, assessing that AI solutions in medicine are not methods based entirely on statistics and probabilities.

From this scenario, it can be concluded that the structure modeling parameters allowed a satisfactory distinctiveness in the classification between different blood subtypes, it is also possible to observe the positive exploration of CNN's advantage, enabling computational processing easier, with digital respect images interpreting it as values stored in an array, or even regarding maintaining the spatial characteristics of a digital image, such as height, width, and even colors. Still reflecting on the proposal reduces the possibilities of human failure, grants greater reliability diagnosed making this process smoother with much guarantee for health professionals.

Pondering the vast applicability of this research aligned with the constant requirement for advances in the medical field optimizing cell detection and classification for more accurate diagnostics. This research has its continuity according to the development of this proposal concerning identification, classification, and recognition of white blood cells in digital smear blood, refining the level of related detail differentiation of T-lymphocyte and B- lymphocyte.

Or even detecting, identifying, and classifying pathological blood cells, while recognizing each of the leukocyte subtypes based on techniques as Generative Adverse Networks (GANs), introducing a new training paradigm for neural networks although mathematically complex, creating new instances of data that resemble the training data. This technique is based on game theory, a field of applied mathematics that models situations of strategic interactions, it has the properties of achieving realism learning to differentiate the generator output from true data, distinguishing between real and counterfeit data.

References

1. Hwang, K. and Chen, M., Big-Data Analytics for Cloud, in: *IoT and cognitive computing*, John Wiley & Sons, Hoboken, New Jersey, USA, 2017.
2. Ahmed, M.N. *et al.*, Cognitive computing and the future of Healthcarre cognitive computing and the future of healthcare: The cognitive power of IBM

Watson has the potential to transform global personalized medicine. *IEEE Pulse*, 8, 3, 4–9, 2017.

3. Monteiro, A.C.B. *et al.*, Development of a laboratory medical algorithm for simultaneous detection and counting of erythrocytes and leukocytes in digital images of a blood smear, in: *Deep learning techniques for biomedical and health Informatics*, pp. 165–186, Academic Press, Cambridge, Massachusetts, EUA, 2020.

4. Chen, M., Herrera, F., Hwang, K., Cognitive computing: Architecture, technologies and intelligent applications. *IEEE Access*, 6, 19774–19783, 2018.

5. França, R.P. *et al.*, Potential proposal to improve data transmission in healthcare systems, in: *Deep Learning Techniques for Biomedical and Health Informatics*, pp. 267–283, Academic Press, Cambridge, Massachusetts, EUA, 2020.

6. Padmanaban, B. and Sathiyamoorthy, S., A metaheuristic optimization model for spectral allocation in cognitive networks based on ant colony algorithm (M-ACO). *Soft Comput.*, 24, 20, 15551–15560, 2020.

7. Monteiro, A.C.B., *Proposta de uma metodologia de segmentação de imagens para detecção e contagem de hemácias e leucócitos através do algoritmo WT-MO*, 2019. 1 recurso online (128 p.) Dissertação (mestrado) - Universidade Estadual de Campinas, Faculdade de Engenharia Elétrica e de Computação, Campinas, SP. Disponível em: https://hdl.handle.net/20.500.12733/1637257. Acesso em: 11 jun. 2022.

8. Monteiro, A.C.B., Iano, Y., França, R.P., Arthur, R., Medical-laboratory algorithm WTH-MO for degmentation of figital images of blood cells: A new methodology for making hemograms. *Int. J. Simul. Syst. Sci. Technol.*, 20, Suppl. 1, 19–1, 2019.

9. Cielen, D., Meysman, A., Ali, M., *Introducing data science: Big data, machine learning, and more, using python tools*, Manning Publications Co, Shelter Island, New York, USA, 2016.

10. Demirkan, H., Earley, S., Harmon, R.R., Cognitive computing. *IT Prof.*, 19, 4, 16–20, 2017.

11. Gudivada, V.N. *et al.*, Cognitive computing systems: Their potential and the future. *Computer*, 52, 5, 13–18, 2019.

12. Walczak, S., Artificial neural networks, in: *Advanced methodologies and technologies in artificial intelligence, computer simulation, and human-computer interaction*, pp. 40–53, IGI Global, Pennsylvania, USA, 2019.

13. Alpaydin, E., *Introduction to machine learning*, MIT Press, Cambridge, Massachusetts, EUA, 2020.

14. Bini, S.A., Artificial intelligence, machine learning, deep learning, and cognitive computing: What do these terms mean and how will they impact Healthcarre? *J. Arthroplasty*, 33, 8, 2358–2361, 2018.

15. Neapolitan, R.E. and Jiang, X., *Artificial intelligence: With an introduction to machine learning*, CRC Press, Boca Raton, Florida, USA, 2018.

16. Kashyap, P., *Machine learning for decision makers: Cognitive computing fundamentals for better becision making*, APress, New York, New York, USA, 2018.
17. França, R. P., Iano, Y., Monteiro, A.C.B., Arthur, R., Big data and cloud computing: A technological and literary background. in: *Advanced deep learning applications in big data analytics*, pp. 29-50, IGI Global, Pennsylvania, USA, 2021.
18. Gupta, S. *et al.*, Big data with cognitive computing: A review for the future. *Int. J. Inf. Manage.*, 42, 78–89, 2018.
19. Mohri, M., Rostamizadeh, A., Talwalkar, A., *Foundations of machine learning*, MIT Press, Cambridge, Massachusetts, EUA, 2018.
20. Chakraverty, S. and Mall, S., *Artificial neural networks for engineers and scientists: Solving ordinary differential equations*, CRC Press, Boca Raton, Florida, USA, 2017.
21. Raghavan, V.V. *et al.*, *Cognitive computing: Theory and applications*, Elsevier, Amsterdam, Netherlands, 2016.
22. Bini, S.A., Artificial intelligence, machine learning, deep learning, and cognitive computing: What do these terms mean and how will they impact Healthcarre? *J. Arthroplasty*, 33, 8, 2358–2361, 2018.
23. Demirkan, H., Earley, S., Harmon, R.R., Cognitive computing. *IT Prof.*, 19, 4, 16–20, 2017.
24. França, R.P. *et al.*, A proposal based on discrete events for improvement of the transmission channels in cloud environments and big data, in: *Big data, IoT, and machine learning: Tools and applications*, p. 185, 2020.
25. Stengel, R., *Introduction to neural networks*, 2017.
26. Suk, H.-I., An introduction to neural networks and deep learning, in: *Deep learning for medical image analysis*, pp. 3–24, Academic Press, Cambridge, Massachusetts, EUA, 2017.
27. Suk, H.-I., An introduction to neural networks and deep learning, in: *Deep learning for medical image analysis*, pp. 3–24, Academic Press, Cambridge, Massachusetts, EUA, 2017.
28. Levine, D.S., *Introduction to neural and cognitive modeling*, Routledge, Abingdon, England, United Kingdom, 2018.
29. Markatopoulou, F., Mezaris, V., Patras, I., Implicit and explicit concept relations in deep neural networks for multi-label video/image annotation. *IEEE Trans. Circuits Syst. Video Technol.*, 29, 6, 1631–1644, 2018.
30. Van Gerven, M. and Bohte, S., Artificial neural networks as models of neural information processing. *Front. Comput. Neurosci.*, 11, 114, 2017.
31. Aggarwal, C.C., *Neural networks and deep learning*, Springer, Berlin, Germany, 2018.
32. Wu, J., Introduction to convolutional neural networks, in: *National key lab for novel software technology*, vol. 5, p. 23, Nanjing University, China, 2017.
33. Yao, G., Lei, T., Zhong, J., A review of Convolutional-Neural-Network-based action recognition. *Pattern Recognit. Lett.*, 118, 14–22, 2019.

34. Neagoe, V.-E., Ciotec, A.-D., Cucu, G.-S., Deep convolutional neural networks versus multilayer perceptron for financial prediction. *2018 International Conference on Communications (COMM)*, IEEE, 2018.

35. Frady, E.P., Kleyko, D., Sommer, F.T., A theory of sequence indexing and working memory in recurrent neural networks. *Neural Comput.*, 30, 6, 1449–1513, 2018.

36. Wilamowski, B.M., Neural Networks Learning, in: *Intelligent systems*, pp. 11–1, CRC Press, Boca Raton, Florida, USA, 2018.

37. Kubat, M., *An introduction to machine learning*, Springer International Publishing AG, Berlin, Germany, 2017.

38. Hutter, F., Kotthoff, L., Vanschoren, J., *Automated machine learning: methods, systems, challenges*, Springer Nature, Berlin, Germany, 2019.

39. Steger, C., Ulrich, M., Wiedemann, C., *Machine vision algorithms and applications*, John Wiley & Sons, Hoboken, New Jersey, USA, 2018.

40. Dhillon, A. and Verma, G.K., Convolutional neural network: A review of models, methodologies and applications to object detection. *Prog. Artif. Intell.*, 9, 2, 85–112, 2020.

41. Kim, K.G., Book review: Deep learning, in: *Healthcare informatics research*, vol. 22, pp. 351–354, 2016.

42. Kelleher, J.D., *Deep learning*, MIT Press, Cambridge, Massachusetts, EUA, 2019.

43. Flasiński, M., *Introduction to artificial intelligence*, Springer, Berlin, Germany, 2016.

44. Jackson, P.C., *Introduction to artificial intelligence*, Courier Dover Publications, Mineola, New York, USA, 2019.

45. Gambus, P. and Shafer, S.L., Artificial intelligence for everyone. *Anesthesiology*, 128, 3, 431–433, 2018.

46. Varian, H., Artificial intelligence, economics, and industrial organization, in: *National bureau of economic research*, vol. No. w24839, 2018.

47. Hwang, K. and Chen, M., *Big-data analytics for cloud, IoT and cognitive computing*, John Wiley & Sons, Hoboken, New Jersey, USA, 2017.

48. Zhang, R., Li, W., Mo, T., Review of deep learning. arXiv preprint arXiv:1804.01653, 2018.

49. Hwang, K., *Cloud computing for machine learning and cognitive applications*, MIT Press, Cambridge, Massachusetts, EUA, 2017.

50. Flasiński, M., *Introduction to artificial intelligence*, Springer, Berlin, Germany, 2016.

51. Jackson, P.C., *Introduction to artificial intelligence*, Courier Dover Publications, Mineola, New York, USA, 2019.

52. Levine, D.S., Routledge, Abingdon, England, United Kingdom, 2018.

53. Stengel, R., *Introduction to neural networks*, 2017.

54. Wu, J., Introduction to convolutional neural networks, in: *National key lab for novel software technology*, vol. 5, p. 23, Nanjing University, China, 2017.

55. Monteiro, A.C.B., Iano, Y., França, R.P., Arthur, R., Methodology of High Accuracy, Sensitivity and Specificity in the Counts of Erythrocytes and Leukocytes in Blood Smear Images, in: *Brazilian Technology Symposium*, Springer, Cham, pp. 79–90, 2018, October.
56. Schmaier, A.H., Introduction to hematology, in: *Concise guide to hematology*, pp. 1–3, Springer, Cham, 2019.
57. Monteiro, A.C.B., Iano, Y., França, R.P., Arthur, R., Estrela, V.V., A Comparative Study Between Methodologies Based on the Hough Transform and Watershed Transform on the Blood Cell Count, in: *Brazilian Technology Symposium*, Springer, Cham, pp. 65–78, 2018, October.
58. Lazarus, H.M. and Schmaier, A.H., *Concise guide to hematology*, Springer, Berlin, Germany, 2018.
59. Wynn, R., Bhat, R., Monagle, P., *Pediatric hematology: A practical guide*, Cambridge University Press, Cambridge, UK, 2017.
60. Monteiro, A.C.B., Iano, Y., França, R.P., An improved and fast methodology for automatic detecting and counting of red and white blood cells using watershed transform. *VIII Simpósio de Instrumentação e Imagens Médicas (SIIM)/VII Simpósio de Processamento de Sinais da UNICAMP*, 2017.
61. Harbert, K.A., *Introduction to hematology*. WVU Syllabi, 7638, 2018.
62. Monteiro, A.C.B., Iano, Y., França, R.P., Arthur, R., Estrela, V.V., Rodriguez, A.D., Assumpção, S.L.D.L., Development of digital image processing methodology WT-MO: An algorithm of high accuracy in detection and counting of erythrocytes, leucocytes, blasts. In *International Symposium on Immunobiological, 4, 2019; Seminário Anual Científico e Tecnológico de Bio-Manguinhos, 7., 2019, Rio de Janeiro. Anais... Rio de Janeiro: Bio-Manguinhos*, p. 160, 2019. https://www.arca.fiocruz.br/handle/icict/32728
63. Monteiro, A.C.B., Iano, Y., França, R.P., Detecting and counting of blood cells using watershed transform: An improved methodology, in: *Brazilian Technology Symposium*, Springer, Cham, pp. 301–310, 2017, December.
64. Monteiro, A.C.B., Iano, Y., França, R.P., Razmjooy, N., WT-MO Algorithm: Automated Hematological Software Based on the Watershed Transform for Blood Cell Count, in: *Applications of Image Processing and Soft Computing Systems in Agriculture*, IGI Global, pp. 39–79, 2019.
65. Monteiro, A.C.B., Iano, Y., França, R.P., Arthur, R., Applied medical informatics in the detection and counting of erythrocytes and leukocytes through an image segmentation algorithm. *Set Int. J. Broadcast Eng.*, 5, 7, 2020.
66. Ravì, D. *et al.*, Deep learning for health informatics. *IEEE J. Biomed. Health Inform.*, 21, 1, 4–21, 2016.
67. Beam, A.L. and Isaac, S.K., Big data and machine learning in Healthcarre. *JAMA*, 319, 13, 1317–1318, 2018.
68. Srivastava, S. *et al.*, Deep learning for health informatics: Recent trends and future directions. *2017 International Conference on Advances in Computing, Communications, and Informatics (ICACCI)*, IEEE, 2017.

69. Stead, W.W., Clinical implications and challenges of artificial intelligence and deep learning. *JAMA*, 320, 11, 1107–1108, 2018.
70. Panch, T., Szolovits, P., Atun, R., Artificial intelligence, machine learning and health systems. *J. Global Health*, 8, 2, 020303, 2018, https://doi.org/10.7189/jogh.08.020303, https://www.ncbi.nlm.nih.gov/pmc/articles/PMC6199467/.

3

Convergence of Big Data and Cognitive Computing in Healthcare

R. Sathiyaraj[1]*, U. Rahamathunnisa[2], M.V. Jagannatha Reddy[3]
and T. Parameswaran[1]

*[1]Department of Computer Science & Engineering, School of Engineering and
Technology (SoET), CMR University, Bangalore, India
[2]School of Information Technology and Engineering, Vellore Institute of Technology,
Vellore, India
[3]Aditya College of Engineering, Madanapalle, Chittoor District,
Andhra Pradesh, India*

Abstract

With the development of advanced technologies, healthcare services are improved with improved treatment for diseases and improved patient outcomes. In assisting medical practitioners, cognitive computing systems process a massive amount of data instantaneously to answer specific queries and provide customized intelligent recommendation systems for decision making and diagnosis. Healthcare industries make use of data analytics to identify and diagnose several diseases. This technology supports a user-oriented approach in discovering the patterns which are hidden in the data. Big Data is utilized to facilitate analytics support from the enormous amount of data gathered for processing. Big Data and Cognitive Computing jointly make it possible to achieve accuracy and effectiveness in Healthcare. Healthcare services have been under great anxiety during recent years, particularly when the economic and financial crisis put a significant emphasis on sustainability. Hence, Cognitive Computing and Big Data analytics are more vital in the healthcare sector to meet the technical issues and to provide a solution for any complex problems. This chapter addresses the necessity of converging cognitive computing and big data in providing a proficient and valuable solution for Healthcare applications. In this chapter, we put forward two approaches which are based on cognitive computing and big data analytics. Firstly, a smart healthcare framework is proposed to detect and classify EEG Pathology. This approach uses

Corresponding author: rsr026@gmail.com

D. Sumathi, T. Poongodi, B. Balamurugan and Lakshmana Kumar Ramasamy (eds.)
Cognitive Intelligence and Big Data in Healthcare, (67–96) © 2022 Scrivener Publishing LLC

very deep convolutional networks (VDCN) and ImageNet Classification convolutional network models and it also integrates deep learning. The experimental results reveal the importance of the proposed EEG (Electroencephalography) Pathology classification system in the Healthcare domain. Secondly, a heart disease prediction system, this assists in predicting the heart related diseases. This methodology applies classifiers with neural networks and supports in prediction of the disease. The importance of the proposed frameworks is shown with suitable demonstrations in the chapter. Our proposed methodology will be a good decision making support system for doctors in medical information system.

Keywords: Big data, healthcare systems, cognitive computing, classifiers, neural networks, sensors, EEG classification, prediction

3.1 Introduction

Technology is growing at an enormous rate in today's digital market, serving its finest in many real-time applications. Today's population of the earth places at higher than 7.4 billion people [47]. Among those, nearly 3.1 billion people are digitally connected to Internet devices [12]. Smartphones had become a more important device for individual humans in their lifestyle. The number of people connected towards Smartphones and the device usage are increasing at an enormous rate every day. In few years, there is a possibility which leads to data explosion [45, 48]. The vast amount of data that is created with these devices is termed as Big Data [26]. Big Data has taken the attention of most of the researchers and the organizations in competing with the other companies in their domain. Big Data enables organizations to stay ahead of their competing companies with the integration of advanced machine learning techniques, cognitive computing, and IoT [7, 14, 28]. Big Data assists in analyzing the huge set of data thereby saving the tedious work of humans and also it improves the accuracy. Since it is a vast time-consuming activity when it is performed by humans [22]. This tedious work can be made efficient by integrating with classy cognitive systems. Cognitive computing aims to imitate the human thoughts in a computerized model process. Cognitive computing supports humans in decision making process. This is an AI-based method, where it can interact in humans and also supports in efficient analyzing. The services offered by Cognitive Computing are shown in Figure 3.1.

The convergence of Big Data along with Cognitive computing aims toward providing a strong and efficient human-based interactive system. Big Data concerns in analyzing and extracting the information from an enormous data, cognitive computing empowers the information by introducing human thoughts as an algorithmic computerized model.

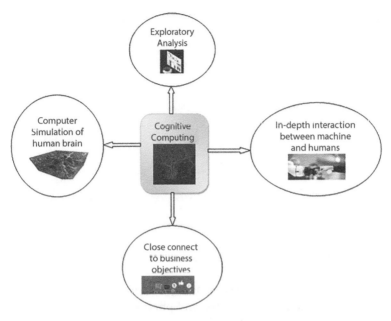

Figure 3.1 Significant services offered by cognitive computing.

This integrated model plays a crucial job in smart healthcare applications. The functions of big data in healthcare services are illustrated in Figure 3.2. A Converged big data with cognitive computing system results in an effective self-learning model that can greatly achieve the benefit in analyzing the huge set of data for better decision making process [13]. This explains the better requirement of associating cognitive computing and big data.

Big Data has proved its stability in solving data analytic problems. It has shown its unremarkable existence in smart healthcare, smart city, intelligent transportation systems, etc. With the convergence of big data with cognitive computing, the inaccessibility and erroneous information on effective decision making is achieved. This convergence holds a high impact in healthcare applications and moreover it achieves the impossible insights in clinical research. This shall be a supporting system for healthcare professionals, and also provides a platform for the top-notch doctors to arrive at the individual in a distant region furthermore saves more patients to be affected with clinical-trails, supports effectively when emergency case arises. A model has been shown in Figure 3.3 to understand the relation between cognitive computing and big data. This era of big data and cognitive computing converged healthcare system will bring together medical research and individual and public data from various healthcare sources to restructure a patient's lane towards a better and safe health. Unimagined things shall be made true with this convergence of advanced technologies.

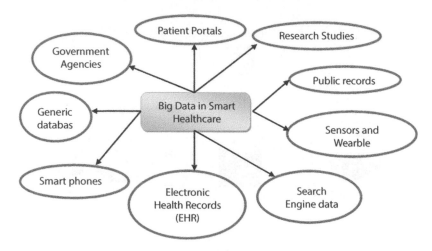

Figure 3.2 Functions of big data in smart healthcare.

This convergence facilitates researchers to discover the new insights in association with diseases, genes proteins, and phenotypes. This also supports in identifying the primary critical attributes of a patients dataset and can afford ease-to-use précised information for both healthcare experts and patients.

In this chapter, we propose to introduce a converged model of big data and cognitive computing. The objective of the proposed work is to offer an automated system capable of solving problems without human assistance. We illustrate the proposed work with a case study in healthcare.

3.2   Literature Review

In the era of growing technology and sciences there occurs enormous amount of inventions every day. Healthcare is the field in which a large number of data is being shared from personal fitness trackers to genomic records for research. Cognitive computing helps the medical data of the individuals in their reach and most importantly where the Healthcare professionals connects the top-notch doctors to get to remote areas and save more number of patients. In general cognitive computing performs difficult tasks such as classification, natural language processing, data mining, and image recognition.

3.2.1   Role of Cognitive Computing in Healthcare Applications

Cognitive computing that helps in better understanding, reasoning and learning helps people to enlarge their knowledge, improves efficiency, and deepens their expertise. This brings together the data source, individuals, and clinical research from various healthcare centers for the better health of patients. With cognitive computing we are committed to an environment where we can envisage the semi-autonomous systems to provide improved quality of life.

The future of healthcare is focused on providing personalized, transparent, integrated and high-quality care. Most important demand nowadays is to know about the complete factors that affects the individuals health. Cognitive computing is regarded as the revenge to AI. They should be regarded as "more human" artificial intelligence because their sole property is to mimic human reasoning methodologies and solving the computationally heavy processes. Cognitive computing systems uses a type of AI which aims giving back data relevant to the users in connection with the healthcare centers and social data which was formerly inaccessible [43]. More number of healthcare data is being shared nowadays than any other time in the history clearly resulting in an exponential growth in data. This AI system will enhance the responsibility of doctors, reduces cost, and moreover eventually leads to better outcomes making the world healthier and safe.

Cognitive computing creates personalized treatment plans which becomes convenient for both the physicians and patient by additionally enhancing their experience. Cognitive computing helps researchers discover relationship among phenotypes, genotypes, proteins, diseases, microbes. The features of Cognitive system are shown in Figures 3.3 and 3.4. Cognitive computing also identifies the significant attributes in a

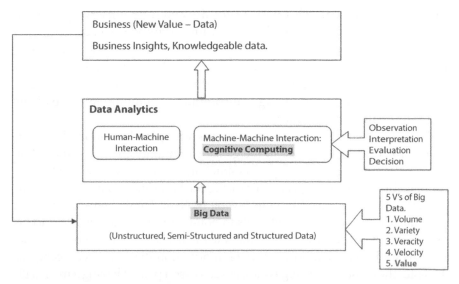

Figure 3.3 Model to understand the relation between cognitive computing and big data.

Cognitive System Features

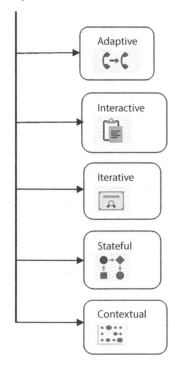

Figure 3.4 Features of cognitive system.

patient's case and makes it simple to acquire and time conserving for both patients and healthcare providers. Most importantly it is used in clinical trial matching which makes patient recruitment and selection easy. NLP and automated image tool analysis are some of the tools of cognitive computing which helps solving unstructured data for advanced research, treatment, diagnosis and improving the communication among the patients and their healthcare providers.

Cognitive computing paved way towards strong health and medical education providing better access to the global community and this can evaluate numerous amount of research papers simultaneously without wasting time by running through page by page. This makes the knowledge available at the finger tips so that students can focus less on biological and chemical processes and enhance knowledge in soft skills to bond with their patients. The access to the ample knowledge in turn makes the medical researchers more empowered. As we know the more sources of information the computers recognize the faster they assist in solving issues, in such case a patient having a mental illness he can brief about the declining cognitive functions in his body. Research has already proved that the description of the symptoms according to their demographics is used in diagnosing the cardiovascular diseases.

The necessity of computational intelligence in understanding the emotions and behavior of humans are discussed [39]. Paper [46] proposed a model using convolutional layers to handle unconstrained conditions. The model integrating behavior selection and transformation was proposed to understand the human expressions [44]. The strong power of cognitive computing in the arena of several applications with a good benchmark has motivated us to propose a convergence of cognitive with big data in offering an enhanced solutions in healthcare.

3.2.2 Research Problem Study by IBM

IBM conducted this long-standing research problem through a television show called JEOPARDY with a highly evidence-based architecture, probabilistic project called WATSON. This Watson project has hugely challenged the growing computer science and technology, aims in growing the wide range of accessibility to big data and natural language and integration, open domain, parallel QA technology. Based on this show, the scientists and engineers of IBM have declared Watson as the first commercially available cognitive computing capability in the new era. Its primary job is to analyze the high volumes of data from the cloud and answer complex natural language questions with more evidence-based answers. Watson can do this because it constantly rivals the finest human performance, by continuously gaining knowledge from each interaction.

The IBM Watson Health and The Watson Health Cloud was launched in April 2015 whose primary goal is to optimize the service of researchers, doctors and innovators from the immense amount of personal health information created and shared each day. This cloud helps to analyze, compare, identify, aggregate among the vast data that is available. In addition to this IBM Watson has tied up with many educational and research institutions, private organizations to use the cognitive computing in solving the major threatening heath issues. It has also partnered with New York's Memorial Sloan Kettering Cancer Center and the MD Anderson Cancer Center at the University of Texas to work for the data challenges of cancer treatment. This cognitive computing helps to translate the DNA sequences into personalized treatment. The role of cognitive computing here is to match the relevant clinical trials by combining with 16 cancer care institutes all over the world. Watson helps diagnosis of both acute and chronic disorders. Identifying the potential risks and evidence-based recommendations are the important tools for healthcare. In that means Watson is trained to predict the risk factors of the most cosmopolitan condition called "diabetes". By tying up with the international private companies such as apple and Johnson and Johnson, IBM uses cognitive computing in creating better platform by analyzing patient data which includes data from fitness devices, medical records, and personal records.

3.2.3   Purpose of Big Data in Healthcare

Data mining helps us to extract the data which provides meaningful information. Data mining supports to combine the statistical analysis of machine leaning with technologies related to database to pull out the hidden patterns and their relations. In building the predictive models, data mining can be used to detect unknown patterns and trends [23]. Currently Big Data Analytics has taken its path in analyzing vast amount of data. Healthcare applications are in need of Big Data analytics to process enormous dataset at a high speed. Big Data also supports in classifying and predicting the diseases and also in monitoring the health condition of the patients. It uses two types of strategy: Supervised learning and unsupervised learning. Data analytics is able to carry an evaluation of the courses in action confirm efficient through comparing and evaluation causes, symptoms and various treatments measures. The applications of big data analytics support data miners to extract from different set of problems in real-life healthcare industry whenever required. One of the best real life applications is effective working on a database which holds the medical records of heart disease. Several factors can be taken into account for the detection of a disease with its symptom. When a detection gets failed this leads to a false result which provides a path to erratic effects and failure of the system.

3.2.4   Convergence of Big Data with Cognitive Computing

In this section, we shall study the approaches related to pathology detection using cognitive computing and the importance of converging with big data.

3.2.4.1   Smart Healthcare

Smart healthcare systems have gained its attention on advanced technologies that are required to support the present healthcare systems. Nowadays, we use an automated health prediction, diagnosis and control system. Most of the hospitals are equipped with high modern technologies, which can provide treatment in an efficient manner. Most of the researchers have focused on proposing an integrated framework [4, 10, 15, 20]. A modern approach using smart device was proposed [29] that can support patients to find routes to reach hospitals during an emergency. The importance of processing and maintaining e-health records were addressed in several studies [17]. A smart framework using cognitive computing is proposed to monitor the actions of diabetic patients [33]. Robots are used as drivers for cognitive ambulance and they were also used to treat patients who require emergency assistance [19].

Finding and filtering the accurate health website for the treatment of the diseases has become hectic due to the availability of numerous websites. In America more than 1.6 billion are diagnosed with the killer disease cancer, so finding the right healthcare website becomes a significant hurdle. This is where cognitive computing comes into play; it helps find the exact information for each patient to deal with his or her disease which is called as the virtual advisor. This virtual advisor is made by the combined effort of American Cancer Society (ACS) and IBM which has detailed information of 14,000 pages about 70 different types of cancer. The patient's virtual advisor renders help on maintaining a better lifestyle. Like such there are many applications that require the efficient solutions from cognitive computing and big data. This chapter discusses in brief about the importance of cognitive computing and big data analytics in offering solutions to many complex problems in healthcare.

3.2.4.2   Big Data and Cognitive Computing-Based Smart Healthcare

Cognitive computing with smart healthcare have reshaped the healthcare facilities, particularly intended for smart hospitals in smart city applications. Processing these healthcare data's are a challenging task, even though there are many solutions are processed. Still, an advanced technique is required in processing these huge data and also it is more important to make the data secure. The convergence of cognitive computing with big data will resolve the issues addressed. Moreover to these technologies, IoT plays an essential role in communicating the devices with the sensors. The integration of IoT with Medical bioengineering is referred to as IoMT (Internet of Medical Things) [6]. Few of those healthcare applications are: intelligent disease prediction and detection, remote tracking and observing the activities of patients, smart m-healthcare, smart e-health records, remote medical assistance, etc. A few investigators have employed 5G technology to improve the communication system in a smart cognitive healthcare system [9]. They comprise cognitive systems with the other expertise like AI, IoT, ML, and Big Data to achieve the complete functionality of the system. One of the essential necessities in cognitive smart healthcare system is the support of big data technologies along with machine learning in learning the background and to process and extract the knowledge data from huge set of data. An intelligent data analytics system is required to process this unstructured form of data. With the convergence of cognitive computing and big data, an advanced framework shall be made. This can function with a minimal human intervention and has the capability to act intelligently in arriving at decisions. Paper [17] proposed a multilayer cognitive framework, which illustrates high intelligence through human behavior cognition. One more framework was proposed to process relative knowledge, which assists in human knowledge modeling [19]. A system based on NLP cognitive frameworks which have the capability of question answering was proposed [15]. Most of the recent researchers have used cognitive computing behavior in analyzing huge data [33], thus addressing the importance of converging big data with cognitive computing in achieving the better results in smart healthcare applications especially. The intelligence of cognitive computing has gained its major focus in healthcare applications like physiological [31] and psychological [9] applications. In paper [17], detection of facial expressions with an emotion-based cognitive system was proposed. A smart framework that can detect emotions using voice with facial expressions was proposed [30, 31]. In this chapter, we propose to study and resolve the problems and challenges associated to pathology detection system by applying the cognitive computing with big data. The summary of this book chapter is given in Figure 3.5.

3.3   Using Cognitive Computing and Big Data, a Smart Healthcare Framework for EEG Pathology Detection and Classification

3.3.1   EEG Pathology Diagnoses

With the recent development in deep learning, machine learning, cognitive computing, big data and IoT, there are a number of advanced

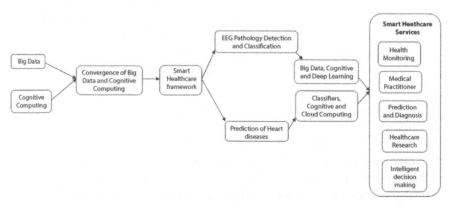

Figure 3.5 Summary of convergence of big data and cognitive in healthcare.

techniques are proposed those can be applied in modernized smart healthcare applications [5]. These also have gained its focus on automated EEG (Electroencephalogram) diagnosis. This test assists in recording the activities of the brain, which can detect electrical activity in the brain. Diagnosis shall be useful to a range of brain related diseases and disorders, such as stroke [21], epilepsy [16], brain injuries [3], Alzheimer's [34], and depression [2]. These proposed EEG diagnostic tools are based on a variety of machine learning approaches, with a few researchers moving to deep learning to improve EEG accuracy rate. The detection of EEG pathology may help practitioners in delivering appropriate care as well as determining the underlying cause or diseases that could be further examined.

Today's modernized hospitals are generating a huge size of data; few hospitals are producing more than 3000 abnormal clinical EEG recordings. Managing and predicting the possibilities of diseases from this huge data set is a complex challenge in smart healthcare applications. Moreover, the smart intelligence of cognitive computing is required to improve the accuracy of healthcare applications. Few Researchers have deployed a pathology detection mechanism, 78.8% of accuracy had been achieved by CNN-based deep network with multiple connected layers. In another research study [37], deep and shallow CNNs are applied to detect the pattern of pathology, resulted with 86% of accuracy. Several automated machine learning mechanisms are proposed to handle EEG signal, but still working with EEG signal is highly complex. The recording patterns of EGG signal are different for various patients and also vary with respect to diseases. Moreover to this, dealing with the huge complex data set with high accuracy is still challenging. There are several security challenges in processing this sort of big data, an automated EEG diagnosis tool and prediction of diseases is very challenging till today. Separating natural and abnormal EEG patterns that overlap is extremely difficult. A CNN along with a dropout method was proposed to identify seizures. A framework using multichannel EEG and CNN was proposed to detect seizures [43]. In another research work [1], CNN was used along with autoencoders for classifying EEG. In this work, we propose to detect and classify EEG pathology using a CNN model with a big data-based approach.

3.3.2 Cognitive–Big Data-Based Smart Healthcare

The framework proposed for smart healthcare applications improves the quality life of smart city. This system supports doctors, residents and especially children's and old-aged peoples to monitor their health through smart sensor connected devices. The framework also assists in accessing and monitoring health records remotely in a secure and safe way. Cognitive computing had made its remarkable feature by taking intelligent decisions independently. The data's that are collected from sensors and multiple devices, all those are processed and managed by advanced big data techniques. The proposed framework Cognitive–Big Data examines the health report and processes the real time information and thereby assisting patients to utilize the greatest medical healthcare service accessible. If required, the hospitals can upload the data to the cloud and practitioners can access those data remotely and they can also follow the diagnosis procedure accordingly. The converged Cognitive-Big Data system aims at achieving the accurate diagnosis. Smart service at reduced cost, avoids hospital visits and reduces the burden of patients and doctors, safe and easy access, less infrastructure, and improved quality of life. Our proposed system finds it position by achieving these objectives. A smart healthcare framework is proposed based on Cognitive-Big Data technologies. Further this has made us to achieve the things with fewer infrastructures, thereby promoting smart city concept to the next level and makes the public to access all these services at a low cost.

The smart framework functions as a secure channel between the healthcare sector and people and also has the ability to use the cognitive functionality of the system remotely, thereby accessing patient health records and tracking their health records are made easy to access and monitor. The patient's health condition is observed constantly to support them if there is an emergency. The patient's psychological and physiological signs are recorded in real time to keep track of his or her health. The patients' various movements, such as facial expressions, speech, and gestures, are recorded. Patients with brain disorders were required to wear a sophisticated EEG skull cap. The EEG signal will be sent, which will be managed by the deep learning system, and cognitive technology is used to access the patient's health condition. Binary classification results were provided by the deep learning module and it also assists in detecting the EEG pathology. Based on the results received, the converged Big Data and Cognitive system plans the future activities.

These health records data will be shared with practitioners for meticulous study. In an emergency, the cognitive module will issue an alert and warning alarm, and a smart ambulance will arrive at the patient in the shortest time possible. An intelligent and smart traffic control system assists in providing emergency facilities as well as ensures that passengers reach the destination in the fastest time possible by taking the shortest and most direct route possible [35, 41]. Smart traffic management is facilitated with the involvement of IoT in an effective way [32]. In this way, the converged cognitive and big data-based smart healthcare framework tenuously provides significant healthcare services to all humans.

3.3.3   System Architecture

The proposed converged cognitive and big data smart healthcare system architecture is shown in Figure 3.6. Smart sensors are used to collect and sense the data through which multimodal signal acquisition is conceded. Communication devices are deployed to transmit the obtained signals from the sensors and devices to the next level called the hosting layer. This level utilizes different categories of smart devices namely laptops, smart phones, and laptops to accumulate and pass signals. Data analytics will assist in processing the data in secure and fast manner. It also ensures the data were authenticated before being sent to the cognitive module for processing.

Sensors of both wearable and fixed types shall be used to measure medical signals such as pulse, body temperature, speech, blood pressure, facial expressions, EEG, and body movement. Few of those sensors shall also be embedded in the patient's ambiance. The hosting layer consists of smart phones, multimedia devices, where the devices can accumulate data locally and can be used for easy computation on the signals received. These devices will assist the user to acquire the general health feedback. Cloud can be used to avoid the higher expenses in establishing infrastructure and databases. The cognitive system will process the data and find out the state of the patient. The cognitive engine could make intelligent decisions and transfers EEG signals to a designated deep learning server for fast detection of EEG pathology. Deep learning unit detects and sends the results to the cognitive module; the cognitive system in turn reaches the final decision concerning the patient's state. Medical practitioners can examine the

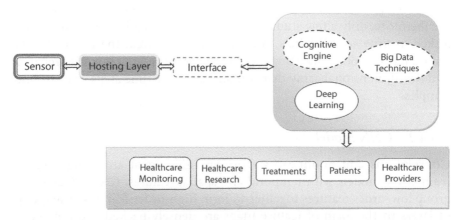

Figure 3.6 Smart healthcare framework based on cognitive computing and big data.

health records and consequences, and then track the health condition of the patients.

3.3.4   Detection and Classification of Pathology

A study EEG dataset with 1000 normal and pathology recordings was used. The average EEG recording file size was over 3500. When data volumes are large, real-time processing becomes complicated without the use of big data techniques. Furthermore, the massive dataset is more beneficial in training deep networks. The sample data were analyzed using manual marking. There are only a few methods for detecting EEG pathology that are used in the research. CNN-based deep networks were used in both of these experiments.

Paper [37] has used CNN with smaller amount of connected layers and with 86% of accuracy. For pathology detection, we use prominent CNN models such as VDCN [40] and ImageNet Classification [27]. Natural EEG recordings were used to train these CNN models. After the features from the EEG recordings have been extracted, transfer learning and fine tuning are performed, and the final classification layers are removed. SVM is used for the final classification.

3.3.4.1   EEG Preprocessing and Illustration

To feed the input to the deep learning system, several EEG illustration methods were used [18]. The CNN technique uses two-dimensional inputs; several studies have converted EEG signals to images, but only a few have converted EEG to topographical maps [42]. Just a few studies have used electrode voltage to create time series topographical images [42]. Furthermore, only a few studies have established that EEG recordings are linked to time series signals [8]. As a result, we treat the input as EEG recordings without converting them to images. The EEG input is prepared as a two-dimensional array that contains all of the time steps or recording samples.

3.3.4.2   CNN Model

Convolutions and nonlinearity from an EEG signal are being used to train CNN models with temporal and spatial features. CNN models will group low-order features together to form high-order features. The group of layers in the form of feature maps are densely packed and only contain the most important details. The intermediate features are described in this way. CNN models have shown outstanding results in an end-to-end feature learning system that uses raw signals as feedback and first extracts spatial features. The model can then mine temporal features in the deep layers as the learning improves.

VDCN [40], one of the most common CNN architectures, is used in this study. On the sample EEG dataset, this approach has been pre-trained. There are five convolution blocks in the VDCN system. Two convolutional layers make up the first two convolutional blocks. The max pooling layer comes next. In the third and fifth blocks, there are three convolutional layers and a maximum pooling layer. After each convolution layer, the rectified linear unit is used as an activation task. After all of the convolution blocks, there will be three fully connected layers. Finally, a softmax classifier is used. Certain hidden units exist in the first two completely connected blocks, and a rectified linear unit is used as an activation function. Dropout will be implemented with a certain probability after the first two completely connected layers. After all of these layers, a final fully linked layer with two units and an activation feature will be formed. Perform transfer learning and fine-tuning once the model has been developed. During transfer learning, the learning speed is slowed, and the binary Support Vector Machines swap the last fully connected layer.

This framework also uses the ImageNet Classification [27]; this is used to pretrain the EEG recording dataset. This model is comprised of five convolution layers with three completely linked layers. The other model VDCN applies transfer learning. Finally, binary SVM is placed and fully connected layer was removed. A radial basis function is deployed; this has shown its effectiveness by performing with fine results in many different applications. EEG signals at a frequency rate of 250 Hz were used in each sample of the input CNN model. For optimization, the stochastic gradient descent algorithm was used, and the Adam [24] algorithm was used to optimize the CNN parameters.

3.3.5 Case Study

The proposed structure was tested using a model dataset. The data was divided into two categories: abnormal and regular. The database was divided into two sections: assessment and training. The normal group had 110 findings in the evaluation package, while the abnormal group had 85. The average group has 745 findings in the training sample, while the abnormal group has 488. The total number of findings in the dataset is 1428. Figure 3.7 depicts the gender distribution of files in the two classes.

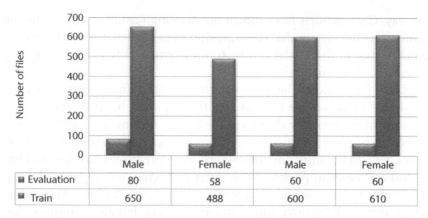

Figure 3.7 Distribution of files in gender-wise among two classes.

The two groups under consideration have no overlap. In the training sample, only a few of those observations were found more than once. Several EEG signals with the same findings were reported at different intervals in the dataset. As a result, the number of records in these training sets exceeds the number of discoveries in the dataset. The gender distribution of the records in the two classes of the collection is depicted in the graph below. A minimum of 15 standard electrodes were used to create the EEG recordings. The labeling in the training set was performed manually. Each record contains approximately 15 min of EEG data. The noise has been removed from all the recordings by removing the first minute of those recording files. The experiments were performed on two sets. VDCN and ImageNet Classification are the two models involved in the work. In both the scenarios, the RBF kernel was applied as a classifier. The below Tables 3.1 and 3.2 represents the confusion matrices of the work using the two models.

The results in the matrices show that the systems attain 82.14% and 80.35% sensitivity and also 94.48% and 96.00 specificity was achieved using the models described.

Table 3.1 System confusion matrix using the VDCN approach.

Predicted/actual	Abnormal	Normal	Sensitivity	Specificity
Abnormal	92	7	82.14%	94.48%
Normal	20	120		

Table 3.2 Confusion matrix of the system using ImageNet classification approach.

Predicted/actual	Abnormal	Normal	Sensitivity	Specificity
Abnormal	90	5	80.35%	96.06%
Normal	22	122		

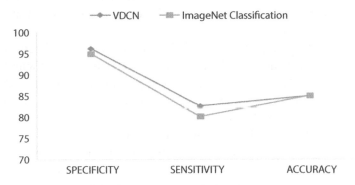

Figure 3.8 Comparison of both the approaches.

The Sensitivity, Accuracy, and Specificity of the system are compared and shown in the Figure 3.8. The system achieves 85.5% accuracy with the ImageNet Classification and 84.35% accuracy using the VDCN.

3.4   An Approach to Predict Heart Disease Using Integrated Big Data and Cognitive Computing in Cloud

Healthcare industries make use of data analytics to identify and diagnose several diseases. This technology supports a user oriented approach in discovering the patterns which are hidden in the data. Numerous amounts of data are being generated day to day. Data mining is most essential in extracting and decision making process and to provide the best support for doctors and patients. Most of the hospitals require large databases to store and process the data. With the extensive increase of population, the information gathered in a medical database are getting larger day by day and also it is hard and difficult to process these data in an efficient way. Cloud is the cost effective method that supports in data collection and storage. This will help healthcare organizations to reduce cost and time in terms of looking for a database system. Big Data analytics provides several techniques which can be applied in clinical diagnosis. In this chapter, we provide a framework to predict heart attack diseases using Rule set classifier and Neuro-fuzzy classifier. Our proposed methodology will be a good decision making support system for doctors in medical information system. It also incorporates cognitive module for intelligent decision based on the circumstances.

Cloud computing plays a major role in supporting data collections and maintenance in Healthcare industries. The two factors for efficient data analytics in huge patient's population are high volume storage and high throughput. Applying data analytics in cloud-based health services results in secure and privacy data processing. Healthcare organizations should maintain medical records in the cloud infrastructure. This can reduce the huge number of storage devices and maintenance in cost. To meet with the current advancements in IT and to utilize cloud-based services, hospitals should be committed to move from traditional paper-based approach to electronic format. With this, the accuracy can be achieved. Policies should be enforced to manage the handling of healthcare data.

Data analytics helps us to process and extract the data which provides meaningful information. Big Data analytics supports to combine the statistical analysis of machine leaning with technologies related to database to pull out the hidden patterns and their relations. In building the predictive models, data mining can be used to detect unknown patterns and trends [23]. This uses two types of strategy: Supervised learning and unsupervised learning. Big Data analytics is able to carry an evaluation of the courses in action confirm efficient through comparing and evaluation causes, symptoms and various treatments measures. The applications of big data support data miners to extract from different set of problems in real-life healthcare industry whenever required. One of the best real life applications is effective working on a database which holds the medical records of heart disease. Several factors can be taken into account for the detection of a disease with its symptom. When a detection gets failed this leads to a false result which provides a path to erratic effects and failure of the system.

In healthcare industries the techniques of big data analytics have been used to diagnose several human diseases such as Cancer, Diabetes, Heart diseases, etc., Healthcare organizations generate a large quantity of data and mining of this data is most essential. This makes the industries to deploy and maintain a large data repository. Cloud computing is an effective technology to maintain and process a large set of data so that industries may not rely on the huge data repository to be owned. Analytics prediction will be a big issue in future medical dataset. Challenges in maintaining these data repository systems can be solved by Cloud which also supports unlimited data storage and the patient data can also be shared between various healthcare Organizations [11, 25]. The features of cloud and big data analytics in healthcare industry are given in the Figure 3.9.

Health Information Technology for Economic and Clinical Health (HITECH) Act motivated all the US healthcare organizations to move from the conventional paper-based to cloud-based systems. Many of the nations like UK are also made a proposal to move from the conventional approach to an effective systematic approach to improve the patients' health-related queries and diagnosis. By this cloud-based Healthcare systems, we use a lesser amount of number of resources can be spent to hold multiple visits of patients; this can be made simple with just a computer interaction [36].

Numerous works related to diagnose heart diseases in data analytics and mining motivated to work. A prediction model [38] IHDPS was proposed with the support of mining and analytics techniques such as neural networks, Naive Bayes and Decision trees. IHDPS be competent of answering queries that the conventional DSS were incapable to do. Niti Guru *et al.*, [49] proposed an approach to forecast the heart disease, sugar and pressure with the support of neural networks. This was trained and tested with 13 variables as input such as pressure, age, blood level, etc. Carls Ordonez [50] identified the difficulty with constrained association rules for heart diseases. The medical reports of people with the attributes of high risk factors have been assessed to

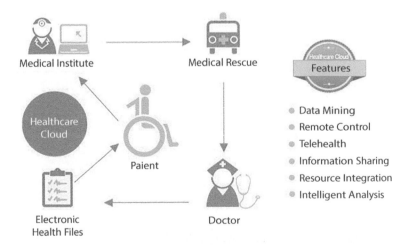

Figure 3.9 Cloud computing and big data analytics in healthcare.

predict the disease. Artery narrowing as a factor and moreover heart perfusion measurement was taken. Franck Le Duff *et al.* [51] proposed a decision tree with the data collected from the physician. Information acquisition and the need to collect enough data to create an accurate model were two major limitations of the process. By evaluating HRV from EGC, Kiyong Noh *et al.* [52] proposed a method for extracting multi parametric features.

3.4.1   Cloud Computing with Big Data in Healthcare

Cloud Computing technologies were increased rapidly in the Healthcare industries. The demand was increasing day by day. In delivering the most valuable medical services at low cost, cloud technologies are in demand in the Healthcare environment. This is in a competition between various Healthcare providers. Research clinics, doctors, and several public Healthcare organizations are looking for an alternative to offer the services with less cost. The problems that are faced by Healthcare industries can be fulfilled by the advancements in cloud computing technologies. This would benefit healthcare organizations, doctor and patients all around the world. The various advantages of using cloud computing in healthcare are shown in Figure 3.10.

Data analytics can be integrated with cloud to provide efficient prediction techniques in medical fields. Predicting diseases from huge data set is a challenging problem. Big Data Analytics provides a solution for data prediction and also processing huge data sets within a small period of time.

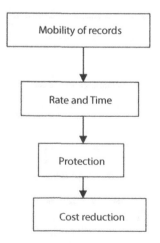

Figure 3.10 Advantages of cloud computing in healthcare.

We intend to explain the role of big data and cloud using a problem in healthcare sector. The big data algorithms for an application in healthcare is elucidated based on cloud model.

3.4.2   Heart Diseases

Heart disease is enclosed with several types of diseases that have an effect on heart. Every 34 seconds one person dies with heart disease. Categories of heart disease are: Coronary heart disease, Cardiomyopathy disease, and Cardiovascular disease.

A. Coronary Heart Diseases

It causes the coronary arteries to narrow, resulting in a reduction in blood flow and oxygen to the heart's cardinal infarctions. The CHD includes heart attacks as well as angina pectoris, or chest pain. When the heart receives insufficient blood due to a blood clot, a coronary artery is suddenly blocked, resulting in a heart attack and chest pains.

B. Cardiomyopathy

This is the disease related to heart muscle. During this disease, the enlargement of heart muscles can be seen. In some cases, rarely scar tissue will replace the muscle tissue in the heart. Various types of cardiomyopathy are given in Figure 3.11.

C. Cardiovascular Disease

Severe illness and disability are the results of this disease. In some cases, it leads to death. This disease affects blood vessels and the heart. High blood

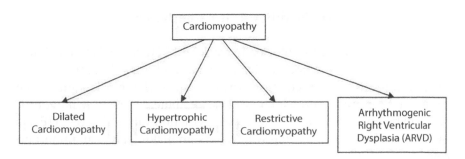

Figure 3.11 Types of cardiomyopathy.

pressure, Coronary artery disease, valvular heart disease, rheumatic fever, and stroke are the different forms of this disease.

3.4.3   Healthcare Big Data Techniques

The techniques and algorithms of data mining can be used widely in healthcare industries for disease predication and diagnosis can be suggested, which can reduce the efforts of doctor in predicting the disease. With the benefits resulting from cloud-based healthcare systems, there are always issues related with secure authentication. Cloud service providers and healthcare organizations must have certain measures to handle and process the patient's medical data in a safe manner. Governments' rules and regulations are supposed to be in position to make sure that cloud service providers should act in accordance with the legislation and concern all necessary means to care for patients' data security and privacy. The benefits of storing by electronic means the report of patients have enlarged the productivity of patient care and easy accessibility and usage. The modern technological innovation in the Healthcare is the discovery of cloud-based technology.

3.4.3.1   Rule Set Classifiers

Decision trees at complex level are difficult to understand and extract the information. A tree structure can be followed to classify the rule and also in confirming the symptom. A tree consists of a set of rules of the type, "IF P1 and P2 and P3 and ... then class X", the rules of each class will be combined in a group. We use a case to classify the findings, if the condition of the first rule is satisfied then that part will be treated else if rule is not satisfied them the default class is assigned.

IF Condition THEN Conclusion

This rule comprises of two blocks: IF block and THEN block. IF block will be the initial condition block which contains conditions about the value of the attributes used for prediction where as the THEN block contains the value used for prediction which is a goal attribute. Decision making process will be improved with this accurate prediction value. This IF-THEN is widely popular in data mining where decision making plays an important role.

(Indication) (Past ... History) → (Determinant ... of ... disease)

3.4.3.2   Neuro Fuzzy Classifiers

To construct fuzzy-based neural network Stochastic back propagation algorithm was used. The steps involved in the construction process are:

1. Random values are taken to initialize weight.
2. Compute input and output value and also error rate for each unit.
3. Calculate the degree of certainty for each node. A decision can be taken based on the computed value.

The following conditions can be applied to compute the level of certainty.

IF CE <=0.1, THEN the certainty is very less.
IF 0.1 <= CE <= 0.4, THEN the certainty is less.
IF 0.4 <= C <= 0.6, THEN the certainty is average.
IF 0.6 <= C <= 0.8, THEN the certainty is High.
IF 0.8 <= C <= 1, THEN the certainty is very high.

The network is comprised of three levels of patterns.

1. Input
2. Hidden pattern
3. Output

Input is provided with six nodes as shown in Table 3.3. Hidden layer is provided with three hidden pattern nodes. There will be only one output

Table 3.3 Input nodes.

Input node	Expansion
WBC	White blood cell
PLT	Platelet
UA	Unstable angina
HGB	Hemoglobin
GLB	Glibenclamide
RNP	Rib nucleoprotein

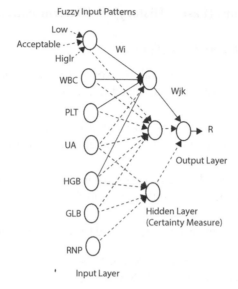

Figure 3.12 Fuzzy input patterns.

Diagnosis (Value 0 < 50% diameter narrowing (no heart disease); value 1 > 50% diameter narrowing

Key Attribute
1. Patient ID – Patient's identification number.

Input Attributes
1. Sex (Value 1: Male; value 0; Female)
2. Chest pain type   (Value 1: Typical type 1 angia
                                 Value 2: Typical type 1 angia
                                 Value 3: Non-angia pain
                                 Value 4: Asymptomatic)
3. Fasting Blood sugar (Value 1: > 120 mg/dl; value 0: < 120 mg/dl)
4. Restecg – Resting Electro graphic results (Value 0: Normal, Value 1: 1 having ST-T wave abnormally, Value 2: Showing probable or definite left ventricular hypertophy)
5. kExang – Exercise induced angina (Value 1: Yes Value 0: No)
6. Slope – The slope of the peak exercise ST segment
(Value 1: Unsloping; Value 2: flat; value 3: Downsloping)
7. CA – number of major vessels coloured by Flaursopy (Value 0–3)
8. Thal (Value 3: Normal value 6: fixed detect, Value 7: reversible defect)
9. Trest Blood pressure (mm Hg on admission to the Hospital)
10. Serum Cholestrol (mg/dl)
11. Thalach – Maximum heart rate achieved.
12. Old Peak – ST depression induced by exercise relative to rest.
13. Age in year.

Figure 3.13 List of attributes.

node in the output. According to medical recommendations, if a thrombus or blood clot occupies more than 75% of the lumen region of an artery, the outcome may be heart disease or a prediction of call death. The Fuzzy input pattern is represented in Figure 3.12.

3.4.3.3   Experimental Results

The prediction method evaluates whether respondents were ever diagnosed using attributes of dichotomous self-reported behavior. Figure 3.13 shows the complete list of attributes.

Parameters	Weightage	Value
Male and Female	Age < 30	0.1
	Age > 30 to < 50	0.3
	Age > 50 and Age < 70	0.7
	Age > 70	0.8
Smoking	Never	0.1
	Past	0.3
	Current	0.6
	Yes	0.8
Overweight	No	0.1
Alcohol Intake	Never	0.1
	Past	0.3
	Current	0.6
High salt diet	Yes	0.9
	No	0.1
High saturated fat diet	Yes	0.9
	No	0.1
	Never	0.6
	Regular	0.1
Exercise	High If age <30	0.1
	High If age >50	0.6
	Yes	0.7
Sedentary Life style/inactivity	No	0.1
Hereditary	Yes	0.7
	No	0.1
	Very High >200	0.9
Bad cholesterol	High 160 to 200	0.8
	Normal <160	0.1
	Normal: 130/89	0.1
Blood Pressure	Low: <119/79	0.8
	High: >200/160	0.9
	High: >120&<400	0.5
Blood sugar	Normal >90&<120	0.1
	Low (<90)	0.4
	Low (<60bpm)	0.9
Heart Rate	Normal (60 to 100)	0.1
	High (>100bpm)	0.9

Figure 3.14 Base model.

The above Figure 3.14 provides the various parameters related with heart attack along with the corresponding values and weightages. This supports in clinical diagnosis-based applications. Case-based reasoning systems shall be applied along with these types of systems. The proposed frameworks can be widely used in healthcare applications in providing effective treatment and also to access the electronic health records in an easy manner remotely.

3.5   Conclusion

In this chapter, we have detailed the two important applications to elucidate the necessity of integrating big data and cognitive to offer solutions for complex problems in smart healthcare. The first methodology had briefly discussed and shown its importance in pathology detection and classification. This method employed CNN models with a pretrained dataset. The framework proved its effectiveness in terms of accuracy in classification and intelligent decisions. The deployed cognitive module decides the medical support required for the patients and acts efficiently when there is an emergency. Secondly, we have shown our discussion on the role of cognitive computing and big data in heart disease prediction. This section is elaborated with the other technology named Cloud Computing. Cloud computing is shifting our life in numerous ways at a very fast velocity. Cloud solutions help the physicians to keep on contact with their patients and check their health condition at a low expenditure. Big Data and Cloud Computing are most important for medical organizations in making their system to be automated and effective. This chapter demonstrated an effective heart attack prediction method based on data mining techniques. This work used two models (1) Rule set classifiers. (2) Neuro-fuzzy. These models can be used to predict in heart attack diseases, the proposed approach can also be enhanced to different heart related diseases and more than 15 attributes can be considered as listed in the medical literature. Moreover, we plan to include few more attributes those effects human life, such as pollution, stress, financial status, depression and past medical records. Several techniques, such as Clustering and Association Rules, can be used to analyze the behavior of data and predict outcomes. Time series modeling can be used to predict the false alarm rate. It may also be used to investigate the patient's morale in order to improve clinical treatment. To improve precision, categorical data can also be avoided by using continuous data.

In the future, we wish to investigate the advanced techniques in Cognitive, AI, and Big Data and emerge with an automated system for disease identification and diagnosis. We are interested in developing an intelligent system, which can act and support humans in case of emergencies, which can also monitor and track the health condition of humans without the support of medical practitioners. We also wish to integrate smart traffic system in assisting emergency vehicles to reach the destination without any traffic delay and thereby promoting smart city to the next level.

References

1. Acharya, U.R., Oh, S.L., Hagiwara, Y., Tan, J.H., Adeli, H., Deep convolutional neural network for the automated detection and diagnosis of seizure using EEG signals. *Comput. Biol. Med.*, *100*, 270–278, 2018.

2. Acharya, U.R., Oh, S.L., Hagiwara, Y., Tan, J.H., Adeli, H., Subha, D.P., Automated EEG-based screening of depression using deep convolutional neural network. *Comput. Methods Programs Biomed.*, *161*, 103–113, 2018.

3. Albert, B., Zhang, J., Noyvirt, A., Setchi, R., Sjaaheim, H., Velikova, S., Strisland, F., Automatic EEG processing for the early diagnosis of traumatic brain injury, in: *2016 World Automation Congress (WAC)*, IEEE, pp. 1–6, 2016, July.

4. Ali, Z., Hossain, M.S., Muhammad, G., Sangaiah, A.K., An intelligent healthcare system for detection and classification to discriminate vocal fold disorders. *Future Gener. Comput. Syst.*, *85*, 19–28, 2018.

5. Amin, S.U., Hossain, M.S., Muhammad, G., Alhussein, M., Rahman, M.A., Cognitive smart healthcare for pathology detection and monitoring. *IEEE Access*, *7*, 10745–10753, 2019.

6. Bharathi, A., Balamurugan, B., Chokkanathan, K., Sathiyaraj, R., Singh, A., Internet of Things Technologies, in: *Internet of Things in Biomedical Engineering*, pp. 291–322, Academic Press, 125 London Wall, London EC2Y 5AS, United Kingdom, 2019.

7. Bumblauskas, D., Nold, H., Bumblauskas, P., Igou, A., Big data analytics: Transforming data to action. *Bus. Process Manage. J.*, 23, 3, 1–33, 2017, http://dx.doi.org/10.1108/BPMJ-03-2016-0056.

8. Canolty, R.T., Edwards, E., Dalal, S.S., Soltani, M., Nagarajan, S.S., Kirsch, H.E., Knight, R.T., High gamma power is phase-locked to theta oscillations in human neocortex. *Science*, *313*, 5793, 1626–1628, 2006.

9. Chen, M., Yang, J., Hao, Y., Mao, S., Hwang, K., A 5G cognitive system for healthcare. *Big Data Cogn. Comput.*, *1*, 12, 1–15, 2017.

10. Chen, M., Yang, J., Hu, L., Hossain, M.S., Muhammad, G., Urban healthcare big data system based on crowd sourced and cloud-based air quality indicators. *IEEE Commun. Mag.*, *56*, 11, 14–20, 2018.

11. Doukas, C., Pliakas, T., Maglogiannis, I., Mobile healthcare information management utilizing Cloud Computing and Android OS, in: *2010 Annual International Conference of the IEEE Engineering in Medicine and Biology*, IEEE, pp. 1037–1040, 2010, August.

12. eMarketer Report, in: *Worldwide internet and Mobile users: eMarketer's updated estimates for 2015*, eMarketer, New York, United States, 2015.

13. Gudivada, V.N., Raghavan, V.V., Govindaraju, V., Rao, C.R., *Cognitive computing: Theory and applications (1st edition)*, North Holland Publisher, Amsterdam, Oxford; American Elsevier, New York, 2016.

14. Habib ur Rehman, M., Chang, V., Batool, A., Wah, T.Y., Big data reduction framework for value creation in sustainable enterprises. *Int. J. Inform. Manag., Part A*, 36, 6, 917–928, 2016.

15. Hao, Y., Yang, J., Chen, M., Hossain, M.S., Alhamid, M.F., Emotion-aware video QoE assessment via transfer learning. *IEEE MultiMedia*, 26, 1, 31–40, 2018.

16. Hossain, M.S., Amin, S.U., Alsulaiman, M., Muhammad, G., Applying deep learning for epilepsy seizure detection and brain mapping visualization. *ACM Trans. Multimed. Comput. Commun. Appl. (TOMM)*, 15, 1s, 1–17, 2019.

17. Hossain, M.S. and Muhammad, G., Emotion-aware connected healthcare big data towards 5G. *IEEE Internet Things J.*, 2017, 2399–2406, 2017.

18. Hossain, M.S. and Muhammad, G., Environment classification for urban big data using deep learning. *IEEE Commun. Mag.*, 56, 11, 44–50, 2018.

19. Hossain, M.S., Muhammad, G., Alamri, A., Smart healthcare monitoring: A voice pathology detection paradigm for smart cities. *Multimed. Syst.*, 25, 5, 565–575, 2019.

20. Hu, Y., Duan, K., Zhang, Y., Hossain, M.S., Rahman, S.M.M., Alelaiwi, A., Simultaneously aided diagnosis model for outpatient departments via healthcare big data analytics. *Multimed. Tools Appl.*, 77, 3, 3729–3743, 2018.

21. Kamnitsas, K., Ledig, C., Newcombe, V.F., Simpson, J.P., Kane, A.D., Menon, D.K., Glocker, B., Efficient multi-scale 3D CNN with fully connected CRF for accurate brain lesion segmentation. *Med. Image Anal.*, 36, 61–78, 2017.

22. Kim, H.W., Chan, H.C., Gupta, S., Examining information systems infusion from a user commitment perspective. *Inform. Technol. People*, 29, 1, 173–199, 2016.

23. Kincade, K., Data mining: digging for healthcare gold. *Insurance & Technology*, 23, 2, 2–7, 1998.

24. Kingma, D.P. and Ba, J., Adam: A method for stochastic optimization, pp. 1–15, ICLR 2015, San Diego, CA, USA, 2014. arXiv preprint arXiv:1412.6980.

25. Koh, H.C. and Tan, G., Data mining applications in healthcare. *J. Healthc. Inform. Manage.*, 19, 2, 65, 2011.

26. Kreps, D. and Kimppa, K., Theorising web 3.0: ICTs in a changing society. *Inform. Technol. People*, 28, 4, 726–741, 2015.

27. Krizhevsky, A., Sutskever, I., Hinton, G.E., Imagenet classification with deep convolutional neural networks. *Commun. ACM*, *60*, 6, 84–90, 2017.

28. Li, J., Tao, F., Cheng, Y., Zhao, L., Big data in product lifecycle management. *Int. J. Adv. Manuf. Technol.*, 81, 1-4, 667–684, 2015.

29. Muhammad, G., Rahman, S.M.M., Alelaiwi, A., Alamri, A., Smart health solution integrating IoT and cloud: A case study of voice pathology monitoring. *IEEE Commun. Mag.*, *55*, 1, 69–73, 2017.

30. Muhammad, G., Alsulaiman, M., Ali, Z., Mesallam, T.A., Farahat, M., Malki, K.H., Bencherif, M.A., Voice pathology detection using interlaced derivative pattern on glottal source excitation. *Biomed. Signal Process. Control*, *31*, 156–164, 2017.

31. Muhammad, G., Alsulaiman, M., Amin, S.U., Ghoneim, A., Alhamid, M.F., A facial-expression monitoring system for improved healthcare in smart cities. *IEEE Access*, *5*, 10871–10881, 2017.

32. Muthuramalingam, S., Bharathi, A., Gayathri, N., Sathiyaraj, R., Balamurugan, B., IoT based intelligent transportation system (IoT-ITS) for global perspective: A case study, in: *Internet of Things and Big Data Analytics for Smart Generation*, pp. 279–300, Springer, Cham, 2019.

33. Samani, H. and Zhu, R., Robotic automated external defibrillator ambulance for emergency medical service in smart cities. *IEEE Access*, *4*, 268–283, 2016.

34. Sarraf, S. and Tofighi, G., Classification of Alzheimer's disease using FMRI data and deep learning convolutional neural networks, 1–5, 2016. arXiv preprint arXiv:1603.08631.

35. Sathiyaraj, R. and Bharathi, A., An efficient intelligent traffic light control and deviation system for traffic congestion avoidance using multi-agent system. *Transport*, *35*, 3, 327–335, 2020.

36. Schatz, M.C., CloudBurst: highly sensitive read mapping with MapReduce. *Bioinformatics*, *25*, 11, 1363–1369, 2009.

37. Schirrmeister, R.T., Gemein, L., Eggensperger, K., Hutter, F., Ball, T., Deep learning with convolutional neural networks for decoding and visualization of EEG pathology, in: *IEEE SPMB 2017*, pp. 1–7, The IEEE Signal Processing in Medicine and Biology Symposium (SPMB17), Science Education and Research Center, Temple University, Philadelphia, Pennsylvania, USA, 2017. arXiv preprint arXiv:1708.08012.

38. Palaniappan, S. and Awang, R., Intelligent heart disease prediction system using data mining techniques. *IJCSNS Int. J. Compu. Sci. Netw. Secur.*, *8*, 8, 343–350, 2008, August.

39. Simão, A.M.V., Ferreira, P.C., Pereira, N., Oliveira, S., Paulino, P., Rosa, H., Trancoso, I., Prosociality in cyberspace: Developing emotion and behavioral regulation to decrease aggressive communication. *Cogn. Comput.*, 13, 3, 1–15, 2021.

40. Simonyan, K. and Zisserman, A., Very deep convolutional networks for large-scale image recognition. pp. 1–14, ICLR 2015, San Diego, CA, USA, 2014. arXiv preprint arXiv:1409.1556.

41. Rajendran, S. and Ayyasamy, B., Short-term traffic prediction model for urban transportation using structure pattern and regression: An Indian context. *SN Appl. Sci.*, 2, 7, 1–11, 2020.
42. Thodoroff, P., Pineau, J., Lim, A., Learning robust features using deep learning for automatic seizure detection, in: *Machine learning for healthcare conference*, pp. 178–190, 2016, December.
43. Turner, J.T., Page, A., Mohsenin, T., Oates, T., Deep belief networks used on high resolution multichannel electroencephalography data for seizure detection. pp. 1–8, AAAI Spring Symposium Series 2014, 2017. arXiv preprint arXiv:1708.08430.
44. Tuyen, N.T.V., Elibol, A., Chong, N.Y., Learning bodily expression of emotion for social robots through human interaction. *IEEE Transac. Cogn. Dev. Syst.*, 13, 1, 16–30, 2020.
45. Veningston, K., Kadry, S., Kalash, H.S., Balamurugan, B., Sathiyaraj, R., Intelligent social network based data modeling for improving Healthcare. *Health Technol.*, 10, 1, 321–332, 2020.
46. Wang, H., Cheng, R., Zhou, J., Tao, L., Kwan, H.K., Multistage model for robust face alignment using deep neural networks. *Cogn. Comput.*, 1–17, 2021.
47. Worldometers, in: *Current World Population*, 2016, http://www.worldometers.info/world-population/.
48. Yaqoob, I., Hashem, I.A.T., Gani, A., Mokhtar, S., Ahmed, E., Anuar, N.B. *et al.*, Big data: From beginning to future. *Int. J. Inform. Manage.*, 36, 6, 1231–1247, 2016.
49. Guru, N., Dahiya, D., Rajpal, N., Decision support system for heart disease diagnosis using neural network. Delhi Bus. Rev., 8, 1, January - June 2007.
50. Ordonez, C., Improving heart disease prediction using constrained association rules. Seminar Presentation at University of Tokyo, 2004.
51. Le Duff, F., Munteanu, C., Cuggiaa, M., Mabob, P., Predicting survival causes after out of hospital cardiac arrest using data mining method. Stud. Health Technol. Infor., 107, Pt 2, 1256–1259, 2004.
52. Noh, K., Lee, H.G., Shon, H.-S. Lee, B.J., Ryu, K.H., Associative classification approach for diagnosing cardiovascular disease. Springer, 345, 721–727, 2006.

4

IoT for Health, Safety, Well-Being, Inclusion, and Active Aging

R. Indrakumari[1]*, Nilanjana Pradhan[2], Shrddha Sagar[1], and Kiran Singh[1]

[1]*School of Computing Science and Engineering, Galgotias University, Greater Noida, Delhi-NCR, India*
[2]*Pune Institute of Business Management, Pune, Maharashtra, India*

Abstract

Lately, older individuals have seen upgrades in human services IoT frameworks. Intelligent systems are utilized for extensive remote healthcare by checking nourishment quality, diet, day by day work out, physiological status, and so forth of older individuals. Seniors who are frail in general will have higher risk and gradually depend on portability helps in their everyday commute. It is exceptionally fundamental that seniors can age up where they can keep on living in their very own home and network independently securely and easily without compromising. Conventional cloud computing can barely meet the prerequisite since sensor data takes an excessive amount of time before landing at storage and processing nodes. To take care of the issue, we present different thoughts which adequately get the sensor information and give processing results to eHealth customers, e.g., neighborhood emergency clinics and social insurance suppliers, which decreases the inertness fundamentally. For example, when sensors are deployed into items that are regularly used, the system scale will extend essentially, which is probably going to bring about gigantic measure of information. We plan to execute another structure for eHealth customers utilizing IoT based framework to satisfy their necessities on information social affair and information handling. In order to accomplish this objective, we have

---

Corresponding author: indramurugesh25@gmail.com; ORCID: https://orcid.org/0000-0001-8440-2223
Nilanjana Pradhan: ORCID: https://orcid.org/0000-0002-8082-5867
Shrddha Sagar: ORCID: https://orcid.org/0000-0003-3647-1384
Kiran Singh: ORCID: https://orcid.org/0000-0003-1711-7371

D. Sumathi, T. Poongodi, B. Balamurugan and Lakshmana Kumar Ramasamy (eds.)
Cognitive Intelligence and Big Data in Healthcare, (97–120) © 2022 Scrivener Publishing LLC

to initially guarantee dependable interchanges between compact insightful sensors and haze gadgets. Because of increasing life expectancy more senior citizens become fragile whereby they experience weariness unintended weight reduction and decreased physical strength. Hence, we present in this chapter an IoT based framework which will assist older people for legitimate remote sensing of wellbeing which must incorporate wellbeing by checking nourishment observing security observing and the separate advancements which will support these applications.

Keywords: Internet of Things (IoT), healthcare, fog computing, remote monitoring, wearable device, cloud computing, sensor data, smart IoT gateway

4.1   Introduction

One of the emerging technology nowadays is IoT in which all the devices are connected to number of domains by through Internet. Rapid advancement in the internet and communication technology, actuators and affordable cost of sensing devices pave the way to the deployment of IoT devices. IoT makes intelligent and smart devices which are acknowledged as the current technological revolution. The application of IoT can be classified into technical ideas where sensors can detect physical activity automatically and human perspective and where people desire to have a sense of control over their lives, good health, social connection, and well-being. Improvement in life expectancy achieved due to advancement in technology has increased the proportion of elderly people. Weakness due to aging, vulnerability to diseases and loneliness are the major issues of elderly people. Seniors who are frail in general will have higher risk and gradually depend on portability helps in their everyday commute. Researchers are intended to develop elderly care utilities using advanced technologies especially with IoT which connects physical and virtual things for enhanced services. In this chapter, present in this chapter an IoT based framework which will assist older people for legitimate remote sensing of wellbeing which must incorporate wellbeing by checking nourishment observing security observing and the separate advancements which will support these applications.

Population aging is becoming a universal phenomenon due to declining birth rate and life longevity [1]. Surveys are declaring that the count of aged people will grow up to 1.5 billion in 2050, especially in developing countries [2]. "The Department of Economic and Social Affairs of the United Nations Secretariat" [3] stated that the population of aged persons more than 60 years holds 24.5% of entire Europe population. Ageing people are accompanied with physical and mental impairments due to age-related diseases like autism spectrum disorders, hyperactivity disorder, cognitive decline and motor handicap.

It is observed that 70% of people cannot survive independently and are in need of assistants to take care of them [4]. Hence it is forced to find robust, safe and useful but low-cost solutions to improvise the living condition of the aged population. The count of people aged above 65 is estimated to be 1.5 billion in 2050, especially in developing countries [6]. Internet of Things have an important role to overcome certain challenges and is getting lot of attention from various communities and governments by providing support to aged people who are living independently. IoT-based Ambient Assisted Living (AAL) applications [5] are evolving now to assist the elderly people to do their personal and social work.

This chapter aimed to find relevant solutions that supports the daily activities of older people in our society as full rights citizens.

4.2 The Role of Technology in an Aging Society

Technology is considered as the solution for many challenges but with a compromise in cost. The smart technologies like e-health, smart homes, remote monitoring, and e-care offer the human community to share their healthcare information to the physicians or the care takers. It is all possible with smart sensors that support people who need support or care at home. For example, elderly people or people with chronic healthcare problems can be at home and their health details are monitored by their care conveniences taker or by any physician.

Internet of Things-based devices not only provide to elderly people but also take care of the safety of the elders. For instance, the day-to-day activities of the elderly people can be monitored by the motion detection sensors. The environment of the house can be monitor by IoT sensors to monitor the humidity, air quality, and temperature. Some sensors can automatically adjust the temperature or humidity and some devices like smart locks, smart cameras, and sensors can ensure home security. With the help of these devices the caretakers of the elderly people can monitor them remotely while ensuring the safety and security. The main benefit of using IoT for the elderly is to observe and supervise the health condition remotely. Research depicts that more than 80% of the elders are suffering from at least one chronic disease and 68% of the elders are suffering from at least two of the diseases. Wearable devices based on IoT can track blood pressure, blood glucose level, heart rate, etc., Elder people who are struggling to move from one place to another in the home can get the assistance from IoT based devices like smart thermostat, smart lighting, and smart home lock.

4.3   Literature Survey

Internet of Things-based remote monitoring system solutions such as e-health; e-care makes de-territorialization in the life of elderly people [7]. Villarrubia *et al.* proposed an IoT-based application that combines Wi-Fi networks installed in the rural area to trace the elderly people in their residence [8]. This application does not require any complex hardware hence it requires minimum budget. Liouane *et al.* narrated the role of IoT in providing localization service for the elderly people when they are in need [9] using a Wireless Body Area Network that collects the physiological parameters. Chuang & Fan proposed architecture to locate elderly people [10]. Mulero *et al.* proposed an IoT architecture that can be able to provide unobtrusive variety of ICT services and applications which collect huge volume of data from the older people when they are at home or in public. Representational State Transfer (REST) API is used here that handle huge volume of data with the help "Linked Open Data (LOD) that correlate the data with the Ontology Web Language (OWL)" [11]. Proof of concept platform is proposed by Lopez-de-Ipina *et al.* to observe the city activities to endorse the development of ecosystem to assist people with disabilities. With the help of ICT, an intelligent AAL garden for elderly people was proposed as the older people like to do gardening [12]. Context-aware recommender application is introduced to instruct personalized exercise to people based on their medical condition [13]. This application gathers such as wind speed, air quality, precipitation, ultra violet radiation and temperature using neighborhood search.

Japanese followed three main concepts in implementing smart city of Kashiwanoha [14].

- Monitoring devices – scales, pedometers, wearable sensors, etc., to monitor the everyday life data.
- Provisions like diet, walking, and socializing are concentrated.
- Based on collected everyday life data, behavioral changes are considered.

The objective of the AAL application is to assist elderly people and disabled to face the life challenges of their living environment such as home and public places. "AAL environment accommodates complex networks of various information and smart devices that assist the population with special care" [14].

Smart home describes the living atmosphere with digital components like smart appliances, sensors and networks which supports people with cognitive impairment and residing alone. Service robots are engaged to help elderly people such as carrying objects, fetching, cleaning and emergency support. Many smart assistive home projects are evolving around the world. TRON, an intelligent project for living environment established in Japan [15]. Taiwan has proposed U-house and PAPI project [16]. The Sensing room and the Robotic room implemented by the university of Tokyo was meant for smart home system [9]. "Spain based Development and Innovation (RDI) group, TECNALIA, involves people with physical or cognitive disabilities, their caretakers, relatives, clinical experts as potential beneficiary in the project" [17]. Microsoft Research proposed architecture for intelligent environment called the Easy Living project with facilities of dynamic device configuration, Smart user interface and activities tracking [18]. The Architectural department of MIT proposed a multi-disciplinary project aimed to explore a novel strategies, materials and ideas to ease the life without any complexities. Health plays an important role in the older people's life as they suffering from diseases like, blood pressure, dementia, diabetic, cognitive and physical impairments. "Easing the diagnosis and treatment of these diseases not only simplify their routine life, but also enhance the safety of the older people by giving automatic alarms in case of a deteriorating health status" [19]. Residing alone is the cause of fear of unexpected things happening including accidents, falls, general safety. So, it is necessary to equip the elderly with a smart tool that assist them and their care takers.

4.4 Health Monitoring

In recent years due to increasing popularity of wearable sensors various devices are available in commercial market for personal healthcare, safety physical fitness, and activity consciousness. Researchers are actively considering applications which can be implemented in medical applications to access physiological information of patient [20].

Recent technological viewpoints help one to imagine a time in the future when the physical health examination will be preceded by a constant physiological monitoring for shorter period of time utilizing wearable sensors of reasonable price [20]. During this time, the sensors will continuously record signals relating to critical physiological markers and transmit the data to a database linked to medical records. Hence after this processing, doctor will have much detailed and accurate data in his hand along with the conventional data like lab test, blood pressure, and other static measurements [20].

A large amount of observed data for each individual can be input into decision support systems, which will provide reports that will assist a doctor in making a better health diagnosis and recommending treatment and lifestyle changes that will successfully help in improving health quality. This type of revolutionary technology not only has an impact on global healthcare systems, but it also dramatically lowers healthcare costs, resulting in enhanced physical diagnosis speed and accuracy. The vision outlined in the preceding paragraph will be implemented in the coming years [20]. As a result, wearable sensors have limited impact on current clinical practice. As shown in Figure 4.1 in remote health management systems, three-level frameworks are used. A wireless body area network is made up of wearable sensors that serve as data collection devices, connectivity, and service layers (WBAN). Sensors communicate accumulated data over Bluetooth to a gateway server. The gateway server transforms the data into an observation and measurement file, which is then stored on a remote server that doctors can access through the internet. Medical personnel may access specialized cloud-based medical data storage for tracking health systems online through a content service application.

A medical application in particular The WANDA system is designed for end-to-end remote health monitoring and analytics for the supervision of patients with high-risk heart failure. Integrating IoT devices into electronic health monitoring systems can further improve intelligence tractability and interoperability, putting traditional healthcare procedures to the test.

IoT-enabled systems are uniformly addressed and can be identified via the internet at any time and from any location. IoT-based devices are employed in remote health monitoring systems, and they are capable of not just typical sensing activities, but also of exchanging information with one another and of automatically connecting to medical institutes over the internet. The setup and management responsibilities are greatly simplified as a result of this. Systems capable of sending an automatic alert to the nearest medical facility in the event of a critical accident involving an individual.

The real-time physiological and environmental conditions can be monitored by a hybrid IoT arrange framework which stops laborers get

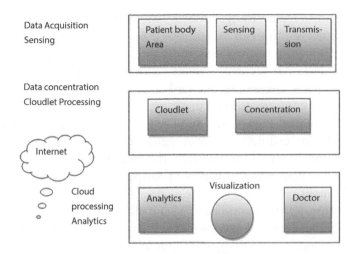

Figure 4.1 Components of remote patient monitoring system i.e. based on IoT cloud architecture.

presented to hazardous circumstances as it empowers the clients to respond in crisis or mishaps in time which impressively decreases the dangers. In this section, a hybrid wearable sensor organize framework is introduced to improve the construction industry's protected workplaces and reduce health concerns [21].

The proposed Internet of Things foundation combines two systems: a WBAN for Bluetooth low energy (BLE) data collection and an LPWAN for LoRaWAN Internet connectivity (Low Range). Temperature, humidity, UV, and CO_2 are evident conditions, and the worn sensors in the WBAN determine the subject's essential indicators (heart rate and internal body heat level).

Individual sensor data is moved via BLE within the WBAN, then aggregated and communicated via LoRa within the LPWAN to a portal. The portal will serve as a neighborhood server for edge figuring, planning sensor signals in advance, displaying data, and issuing warnings in the event of a crisis [22].

Functionalities like web monitoring and mobile applications utilize a IoT based cloud server for storing and accessing data. Protection and information security ought to be deliberately thought of while managing healthcare monitoring.

Gadgets, applications, and systems can be integrated with security systems by developers. A client server model can be used by developers for data sharing in which the server imparts a particular sort of data to customers while keeping other data protected by appropriate certifications [22].

Individual LoRa (Long Range) transmissions do not need encryption at this time; however, this can be addressed by applying data encryption to LoRa(Long Range) transmissions. Bit is a lightweight block cypher developed by the National Security Agency (NSA) that has been improved for programming use and is used in Safe Node to encrypt remote data transfers and improve information security.

For each matter, Figure 4.2 depicts two wearable sensor hubs: the Health Node for estimating physiological characteristics and the Safe Node for environmental monitoring. The Health Node has a BLE module for WBAN delivery, a PPG sensor for pulse testing, and an internal heat level sensor.

Temperature, relative humidity, CO_2, and ultraviolet light are all measured by the Safe Node's four ecological sensors. The Safe Node includes two remote modules: Bluetooth Low Energy (BLE) for WBAN (wearable body area network) communication and LoRa for low-power wide-area network (LPWAN) transmission (low-power wide-area network) [22]. The Safe Node's BLE is in charge of receiving sensor data from the WBAN's Health Node, which is then sent over the LoRa network to a remote entrance. BLE can transmit data at a high data rate with little force, but it is limited by the transmission distance. LoRa can send data over long distances while lowering data rates and rising power consumption. As a result, the current half-and-half framework plan

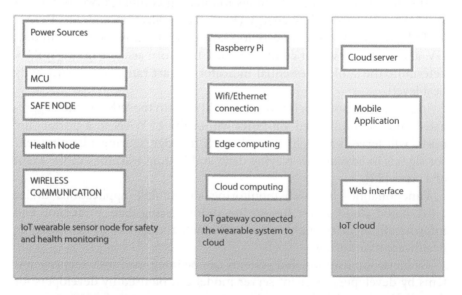

Figure 4.2 System architecture of the wearable sensor network for environmental and health monitoring.

uses LoRa for long-range data transmission and BLE for data transmission within the WBAN. The BLE will send remote data to a mobile phone for interpretation in addition to receiving data from the Health Node. An internet cell phone application is developed for this purpose [22].

4.5   Nutrition Monitoring

Combining NLP with IoT can be used to create a dietary intake monitoring system. There has been an increase in the development and use of several programs aimed to monitor and approve healthy eating habits in recent years [23]. Users' data is stored and processed via cloud-based telemonitoring technologies. Telemonitoring systems assist users in analyzing their eating habits, identifying unhealthy behaviors, and providing suggestions and activities to improve their well being. A well-balanced diet that includes all important elements in adequate amounts aids in illness prevention [23]. Various studies and applications have methods that facilitate users to adjust their dietary habits based on self-reports of food consumption. From a predefined list the users generally select their meals or type of dish recipes with the help of these methods, and the system computes the nutritional information is calculated by the system of each record. "However, these interfaces may be cumbersome to work with for some users and may lead to low adherence" [23]. Users will be able to speak about the list of meals ingested and engage more intuitively using a voice or text interface. The user interacts with the smart device and uses natural language to describe the food that has been consumed. This description is deconstructed and processed to find the necessary credentials for calculating the nutritional record.

Figure 4.3 presents a general diagram of the various advancements and components engaged with nutrition monitoring frameworks. It was discovered that smart settings for food intake checking using natural language interfaces would help a variety of resources, including demand management, data translation, and dietary data computation, all of which are usually contained in a downstream pipeline arrangement, just as explicit data models and structures are. Although natural language processing (NLP) is a notoriously unpredictably unpredictable programming challenge, extracting nutritious nutritional data necessitates many processing phases, and employs a variety of approaches of varying adequacy, those focused on keywords, statistical analysis, and formal examination are the most well-known.

However, the majority of the existing proposals present a robust, unyielding framework, forcing the designer to consume all of the administrations

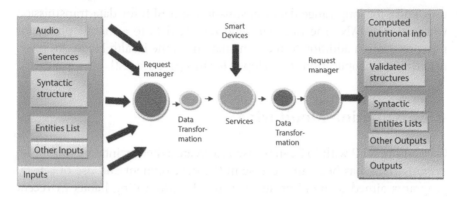

Figure 4.3 Interfaces and smart device supporting nutrition monitoring systems.

or none at all. That is, engineers cannot profit from a single piece of natural language processing from a single supplier and must seek out different administrations that can better meet their needs. Furthermore, there is no unambiguous statement that may serve as a guide and point of reference for implementing these types of service platforms and frameworks.

The suggested framework allows for continuous patient monitoring, continuous transmission of clinical information, database storage, and future control information. The suggested framework provides continuous patient monitoring, continuous transmission of clinical information, database storage, and control information for a later date.

The framework utilizes a web page that expects verification to access information of the patient. The proposed framework comprises of three level design. The level one comprises of wired sensor arrange that have less consumption of power to gather different samples of patient. Level two comprises of processing unit that incorporates processing model, probabilistic model and decision model. The framework creates live graphical presentation of different examples of information that are gathered through GPIO. Level three comprises of website page for remote access for the condition of patient and equipment model that gives component to control internal temperature of body and heartbeat of patient if there should arise an occurrence of crisis.

4.6   Stress-Log: An IoT-Based Smart Monitoring System

Overeating due to stress is a common problem among people and is the reason for obesity. The hormone released due to stress is cortisol because of which the appetite of a person increases. Appetite initially decreases during the onset of stress but eventually chronic stress results in addiction and craving for "comfort food" which are generally junk and high in calories. Uncontrolled food consumption results in obesity and associated many other health issues. Researchers have looked into this area and created a technique that can help distinguish between normal eating and stress eating. Under this scheme, users can choose from a number of wearable and non-wearable ways to monitor their food intake. In 97% of instances, the device keeps track of the amount of food eaten by the user, measures the calorie count, and then informs the user about their eating habits [4].

Sensors and devices for medical are the foundations of IoMT. The Internet of Things for medical (IoMT) is the backbone of a e-healthcare system, as well as a critical component of smart city architecture that contributes to urban intelligence [24]. As a result, a person's eating patterns may be tracked using a sensor-based system, making it easier to discern over the stress eating and normal eating.

Figure 4.4 presents the "Stress Log" system. We previously demonstrated an IoT-enabled device that tracked current food intake and predicted potential food intake to help people keep a healthy diet [24].

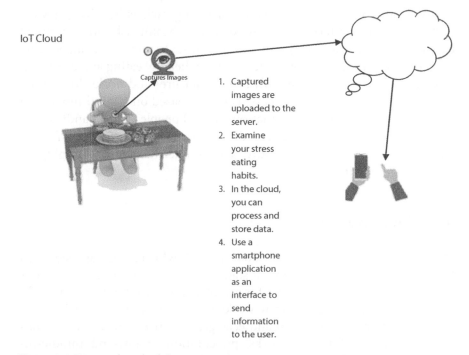

IoT Cloud

Captures Images

1. Captured images are uploaded to the server.
2. Examine your stress eating habits.
3. In the cloud, you can process and store data.
4. Use a smartphone application as an interface to send information to the user.

Figure 4.4 Proposed methodology.

"A wearable device like camera will capture the food intake of a person and sends it to a cloud server with the help of internet where the information is processed to identify the items having calories which can be calculated from a database. The processed information is then sent to the mobile application to inform or alert the user" [24].

The issues related to way of living results in increase in the number of obese people due to elevation of stress levels of people. Such people who are prone to being influenced by an increase in stress levels must be regularly monitored by a non-wearable IoT-based solution that will alert them to their food intake and recognize their stress levels.

This study helps us to enhance the quality of life at a very reasonable expense and in very less time as this is a software-based solution.

4.7   Active Aging

In modern societies various sensing and communicative devices are available which helps in the usage of multiple data sources. This in turn supports logical decision taking ability associated with health conditions. It not only ensures safety of health condition but also prevents risk and hence it is aimed to support active aging while enhancing various healthy behaviors required. Various internal and environmental health risks are monitored by the IoT system and helps in risk assessment from the available data sources. Apart from promoting active living, healthy eating and exercise it also helps old people in their daily routines leisure's and works. IoT framework deploys the decision process reasoning based on clinical inputs and situation. For example, risky situation for aged people can be handled with cognitive abilities and can act accordingly. Hence it promotes the safety for elder citizen and comfort the entire family for active and healthy aging for a specific population.

4.8   Localization

"Localization is important. IEC 60601-1: 2005, which is the basic standard for all electro- medical equipment states in clause 7.9.2.1 that instructions for use shall be in a language that is acceptable to the intended operator."

Presently a day's health frameworks have outer difficulties which are happened by monetary, social and ecological changes which require consideration on health frameworks' presentation in low-and middle-income countries (LMICs). Localization is the key component for reaction to the previously mentioned difficulties. It doles out at the local level for the production of goods and services which are diminishing reliance on non-renewable energy sources and other outside data sources. For successful execution of localization numerous progressions should be fused in administration design in the LMICs for engaging nearby networks for support in their own health.

As the change of the medicinal gadgets is extremely poor or off base this makes the client operation not the normal way. It is common model in which medical attendant of numerous emergency clinics include stickers gadgets like scans and x-ray machines to know the essential usefulness and staying away from the risky ones. Subsequently localization has gotten significant for planning gear for home consideration where fundamental concern is that individual is expected client of the gadgets.

"As required by the general standard and its USABILITY collateral standard, IEC 60601-1-6:2010 and IEC 60601-1-6:2010/AMD1:2013, accompanying documents for use in the home healthcare environment should focus on the characteristics of the intended lay operator to make the accompanying documents most effective for them."

The LoCATE localization method has a number of possible advantages [25]

- Client devices that have a telemetry interface have a lot of versatility due to their built-in computing capacity.
- Integration of cloud infrastructure and web services for scalability.
- From historical data collecting, improvements in health center processes and asset management have been made.

Human mistake, abuse, as well as misuse are only a couple of the issues that are characteristic in conventional strategies for healthcare centers. To address this problem, some healthcare facilities have begun to concentrate on implementing Real-Time Locating Systems (RTLS) in order to gain a competitive edge in asset management [26, 27]. RTLS can give clients both authentic and ongoing information. This information can be used to find tools as well as an audit tool for process improvement. Unfortunately, there are a few imperatives (specialized, financial, social/legal) that are particularly impeding the adoption of new developments in the human services industry [26]. As a result, the aim of the Localization of Health Center Assets Through an IoT Environment (LoCATE) system operation is to develop a simple, low-risk solution to these problems.

There are various developments that aid restriction, such as radio-frequency identification (RFID), which is commonly used for manufacturing platforms (433 MHz) [28], 802.11 WiFi (2.4 GHz, 5 GHz) [29] and Bluetooth (IEEE 802.15) [30]. Manufacturing, logistics, retail, and security are among the industries that are currently using these advancements for RTLS. While these innovations can possibly give an unmistakable answer for resource the management in a medical clinic condition; we pick 802.11 as the innovation of decision. Wi-Fi, or the 802.11 remote convention, is a systems management standard designed to aid wireless local area networks (WLAN). Because of the widespread use of WLANs in human resources offices and the signal loss of mobile networks within some territories of these offices due to electromagnetic obstruction, LoCATE provides a feasible RTLS solution using 802.11 [31]. This assists with lightening the underlying expenses of a RTLS by taking out interest in pointless equipment establishment, for example, RFID readers or scanners.

"The advancement of micro electromechanical innovations permits the joining of various sensors, together with wireless network is usually utilized. Wireless sensor networks (WSNs) include various little and tiny sensor hubs are implemented more than a few applications to screen the physical condition (e.g., temperature, dampness, vibration, pressure, and so on), patients' imperative signs (e.g., pulse, body temperature, blood pressure, diabetes, movement, fall identification, and so forth.)" [32], fog-supported smart city [34], fog-supported distributed WSN [33, 35], and so forth. WSN have assumed a noteworthy job in medical applications for checking old patients' major syndromes. "Physiological credentials can be checked in the older to assess their fundamental signs, for example, blood pressure and sugar, heart capacities, postures, fall, and the area of a fall episode. Among these parameters, fall location and limitation are considered right now" [35].

"A few falls recognition and limitation frameworks have been grown as of late. Fall identification can be sorted into three frameworks, to be specific, (I) vision-based, (ii) surrounding sensor-based, and (iii) wearable sensor-based" [36]. "Vision-based frameworks utilize a PC to catch pictures and recordings of fall occasions. This technique can be subdivided into three kinds: single RGB camera, 3D-based strategies using profundity cameras, and 3D-based techniques utilizing a few cameras [37]". This framework screens the shape and position of the subjects, which relies upon picture handling preprocessing and example acknowledgment strategies. "Despite the fact that this framework is helpful and non-prominent for seniors, it is more far reaching than the other two sorts since it needs numerous cameras. What's more, the RGB camera should be adjusted to permit a 3D recreation of the body, bringing about a tedious and computationally serious system" [38].

A FDS wearable device is used to monitor the fall and area of the subjects. The FDS is folded over the subject's midriff and contains a computerized tilt sensor, accelerometer sensor, shock sensor, microcontroller, Zigbee wireless protocol, and power device. The midsection is chosen as the area since it permits high segregation between activities with the accelerometer framework [39]. The subject's fall episode is detected using computerized tilt, stun, and accelerometer sensors. The RSSI of three Zigbee beacons for line-of-sight (LOS) and non-line-of-sight (NLOS) indoor situations is used to determine the size of the episode. Since no additional equipment is needed, the RSSI of the three Zigbee signals is used [40]. In light of an artificial neural network (ANN) technique, the reference points are used to determine the subject's region (i.e., the location of the fall episode). Since it can reduce the power consumption of WSN hubs, location precision is a critical factor for WSN applications [41]. When the exact location or separation between WSN hubs is known, the transmitted strength of the sensor hub's transceiver radio module can be changed to reduce power consumption while maintaining network connectivity, thereby extending battery life [42]. This approach, however, is not taken into account in the current study. The fall alert and raw RSSI data are sent to the coordinator node (CN) for estimation of older areas and prompt salvage. As a result, the risk of old people who have fallen surviving can be increased, resulting in a population effect of increased future.

4.9   Navigation Care

In stormy oceans there is the requirement of great route, with reason and heading. Likewise, the vast majority eventually in the span of their life may profit by navigating through experiences with various clinical services, offices and experts" [42]. It is not only a problem w.r.t. administration clients, there is expansive accord from human services experts that such frameworks can be intricate and quite hard to explore. Compelling route is a key component of conveying composed, individual focused consideration and backing. The people who are giving care by navigation can assume a vital job in helping individuals to get the correct help, at the perfect timing to provide benefit and deal with a wide scope of necessities. This might incorporate help with conditions that are long term, benefitting the accounts and hence segment administrations on their own will.

Navigator jobs, work titles and everyday undertakings change contingent upon neighborhood setting, including association work, people groups' current aptitudes and nearby populace need. Elderly population care givers might work in hospitals during emergency, concentrating on releasing individuals securely from medical hospitals to house, or as a genuine component for practice in a comprehensive group. While adaptability and variety to address neighborhood, issue is suitable and expected in work jobs, this structure tries to express some basic conventional ideas to enhance a steady way to deal with preparing and instruction.

There is far reaching acknowledgment that wellbeing and social consideration needs are evolving. "This incorporates an ageing population, with rising pervasiveness of individuals living life with complex issues and requirements. There is a critical requirement to move NHS administration arrangement and expert progressing in the direction of a worldview of increasingly supportable, proactive and coordinated wellbeing and social care". Hence elderly population with critical health issues regularly need to get to various health administrations, with various appraisals from numerous various experts. "This can be confounding and people and their families can experience issues. Moving between various considerations settings can be a particularly powerless time with the danger of 'sneaking past the holes" [43]. Frequently family or casual parental figures give the main 'ongoing idea' to access and organize care from an extensive rundown of health and social consideration suppliers.

Care navigation is a rising idea in the United Kingdom, together with the care coordination – which speaks to the possibility that just having administrations and prepared individuals set up are insufficient. "What at that point matters is the manner by which individuals (people, groups, administrations and frameworks) at that point cooperate – in a 'joined up' way – with the goal that individuals know when and how they can get to the correct assistance, at the appropriate time, in the ideal spot. In reality these subjects of composed, individual focused consideration reverberation points of view from patients and national and worldwide approach makers. In the midst of developing monetary weight inside mind boggling, divided health and social consideration frameworks, it is essential to utilize our assets shrewdly; these incorporate our workforce just as the patients, families, professions and non-conventional administrations for instance network and intentional segments.

"There is no all-inclusive meaning of care navigation or a 'care navigator'; navigation at its heart is a coordination procedure and key fixing to accomplish incorporated consideration arrangement to improve health and prosperity. An individual giving in care route is normally situated in a multidisciplinary group, recognizes and sign individuals to accessible administrations, going about as connection workers" [43]. The individual who gives care navigation is in this manner a significant (however alone not adequate) lynch-pin or empowering influence to accomplishing coordinated consideration provision [44]. "Macredie and associates (2014) offer one meaning of care route to be: The help offered to patients and careers in exploring through the mind-boggling wellbeing and social consideration frameworks to conquer hindrances in getting to quality consideration and treatment" [45].

From an individual viewpoint, individuals who give care navigation fabricate connections, issue unravel and help find resources, filling in as a connection between network, health and social administrations. They advocate the requirements of individuals, they are empowering and centered around recuperation, to reinforce crafted by the multidisciplinary group. A key design is to guarantee patients experience consistent, signed up care and backing. The weights and remaining burden confronting clinical staff are impractical; we have to change tack and work together toward reasonable arrangements. This needs to incorporate venturing outside of conventional 'health' and 'social' administration storehouses to build up the multi proficient workforce, with individuals outfitted with attitude and abilities to work with patients and across customary segment limits. Supporting patients to explore health and social frameworks is a territory where the remaining burden in clinical practice is expanding, including auxiliary consideration and general practice. "New jobs and broadened existing non-clinical jobs (for example experienced GP receptionists) can offer better approaches for reasonably sharing work and duty, assisting with diminishing bleeding edge clinician pressures and improve by and large nature of care for patients" [46, 47].

4.10   Fall Monitoring

The architecture of the healthcare monitoring system for elderly people is detailed in this section. Generally, it takes in four stages, namely, acquiring data, ETL process, back-end analysis and visualization of the result. This system is designed to assist the elderly people in their emergency situation by sending text message to their relatives or paramedics so as to provide immediate care.

Figure 4.5 Fall detection system.

4.10.1   Fall Detection System Architecture

Falls are the main problem for the older people who are living independently as the injuries caused by falls are the major cause of chronic disability. Hence a fall detection system as shown in Figure 4.5 is required for the caretakers to monitor the older people remotely. The fall detection system architecture consists of four major components, wearable device, smart IoT gateway, wireless communication and Cloud services.

4.10.2   Wearable Device

NUCLEOL152RE is one of the component of wearable devices and it is connected with an ARM 32-bit Cortex-M3 processor which provides maximum performance with less voltage and power. Multiple low power miniature sensors are accommodated in the sensor part. If the aged person is falling, the motion data is captured using the MEMS (LSM6DS0) sensor as it is a 3D-axis accelerometer. 6LowPAN and CoAP and IPv6 Routing Protocol for Low-power and Lossy Networks are the protocols used here.

4.10.3   Wireless Communication Network

IEEE 802.15.4 standard is used to establish a wireless communication among the device and the smart gateway. IEEE 802.15.4 standard supports connectivity, compatibility, and interoperability of heterogeneous wireless sensor with minimal technology. The best thing about the 802.15.4

standard is that it has bigger address space, minimal maintenance, and easy deployment.

4.10.4   Smart IoT Gateway

Smart IoT Gateway is a bridge which makes a connection between sensor and traditional network. It acts as a key component for fall detection. The process considered here are:

1. Interoperability
2. Transformation of Data
3. Analyzer for Big Data
4. Operator of Emergency Warnings

4.10.5   Interoperability

IoT gateways serve as a smart link between cloud providers and the 6LowPAN network, allowing for faultless communication between device components. Protocol conversion and message translation are carried out here.

4.10.6   Transformation of Data

The x,y,z axes values are collected and filtered using a first order IIR low-pass filter before being saved in a comma-separated value (CSV) file format. The values are stored locally to feed as input for the big data analysis.

4.10.7   Analyzer for Big Data

It is responsible for analyzing the collected values in all three axes to find that these values represent a fall or not.

4.11   Conclusion

This chapter examines the nature of the Internet of Things (IoT) as a support for ageing people. The literature part shows that there is a great demand for the healthcare solutions to monitor older people in their resident and in real time. Ambient Assistive Living acts as the focal point for industry and researchers alike. Assistive technology helps the elderly people to live healthy and longer irrespective of their age. Older people are experiencing many obstacles physically and mentally that isolates them from participating in social and community activities. These IoT-based assistive devices enhance the life style of elder people. In the health monitoring system, wearable device plays a vital role in the life of elderly people. For instance, the devices like blood pressure monitoring, glucose monitoring, heart rate monitoring plays an active role in the older people life. The caretakers can remotely monitor them with the help of these devices. IoT-based nutrition monitoring and stress monitoring are discussed elaborately. Elderly people probably have low memory, they forget often and this becomes worse when they go out alone. For this IoT based navigation is used and it navigates the older people to reach the location correctly. IoT-based fall detection method is discussed, as it triggers an alarm when there is some distress situation.

References

1. WHO, Global health and aging, Technical Report, National Institute on Aging, in: *National Institutes of Health*, 2012.
2. Department of Economic and Social Affairs Population Division, United Nations, in: *World Population Ageing*, pp. 1950–2050, https://www.un.org/en/development/desa/population/publications/pdf/ageing/WPA2015_Report.pdf.
3. Population Reference Bureau, The Communication from the Commission to the European Parliament, the Council, the European Economic and Social Committee and the Committee of the Regions: Towards an EU Criminal Policy: Ensuring the effective implementation of EU policies through criminal law. *Eur. Crim. Law Rev.*, 1, 3, 311–318, 2011. Available: 10.5235/219174411799494765.
4. Population Reference Bureau, America's Aging Population, 2011. URL ⟨http://www.prb.org/pdf11/aging-in-america.pdf⟩.
5. Dobre, C. *et al.*, Introduction to the AAL and ELE systems, in: *Ambient assisted living and enhanced living environments*, pp. 1–16, Butterworth-Heinemann, Elsevier Inc., 2016.
6. WHO, Global health and aging, Technical Report, National Institute on Aging, in: *National institutes of health*, 2011.
7. Milligan, C., Roberts, C., Mort, M., Telecare and older people: Who cares where? *Soc. Sci. Med.*, 72, 3, 347–54, 2011.
8. Villarrubia, G. *et al.*, Wireless sensor networks to monitoring elderly people in rural Areas, in: *5th International Symposium on Ambient Intelligence*, Springer, Cham, 2014.

9. Liouane, Z. *et al.*, A genetic-based localization algorithm for elderly people in smart cities, in: *Proceedings of the 14th ACM International Symposium/ Mobility Management and Wireless Access (MobiWac '16)*, ACM, 2016.

10. Chuang, F., Construction and value study of IT-based smart senior citizens' communities, in: *Sixth International Conference on Measuring Technology and Mechatronics Automation (ICMTMA)*, 2014.

11. Mulero, R. *et al.*, An AAL system based on IoT technologies and linked open data for elderly monitoring in smart cities, in: *2017 2nd International Multidisciplinary Conference on Computer and Energy Science (SpliTech)*, IEEE, 2017.

12. López-de-Ipiña, D. *et al.*, Towards ambient assisted cities and citizens. *2013 27th International Conference on Advanced Information Networking andApplications Workshops*, IEEE, 2013.

13. Casino, F. *et al.*, Healthy routes in the smart city: A context-aware mobile recommender. *IEEE Software*, 34, 6, 42–47, 2017.

14. Sakamura, K., Smart living environment: Ubiquitous computing approach based on TRON architecture, in: *Handbook of ambient assisted living*, p. 469, IOS Press, Amsterdam, 2012.

15. Tron Project, 2014. URL ⟨http://www.t-engine.org/tron-project⟩.

16. Adaptation, B., Sato, T., Harada, T., Mori, T., Environment-type robot system "RoboticRoom" featured by behavior media, behavior contents, and behavior adaptation. *IEEE/ASME Trans. Mechatron.*, 9, 3, 529–534, 2004.

17. Obach, M., Barralon, P., León, E., R&D projects related to Allin Tecnalia's Health Technologies Unit, in: *Handbook of ambient assisted living*, pp. 693–723, IOSPress, Amsterdam, 2012.

18. Brumitt, B., Meyers, B., Krumm, J., EasyLiving: Technologies for intelligent environments, in: *Handheld and Ubiquitous Computing, Lecture Notes in Computer Science*, vol. 1927, Springer, Berlin, Heidelberg, 2000.

19. Trencher, G. and Karvonen, A., Stretching "smart": Advancing health and well-being through the smart city agenda. *Local Environ.*, 24, 7, 610–627, 2017.

20. Hassanalieragh, M., Page, A., Soyata, T., Sharma, G., Health monitoring and management using Internet-of-Things (IoT) sensing with cloud-based processing: Opportunities and challenges, in *IEEE International Conference on Services Computing*, New York, NY, 2015.

21. Health monitoring and management using Internet-of-Things (IoT) sensing with cloud-based processing: Opportunities and challenges, in: *2015 IEEE International Conference on Services Computing*, IEEE, pp. 285–292.

22. Wu, F., Wu, T., Yuce, M.R., An internet-of-things (IoT) network system for connected safety and health monitoring applications. *Sensors*, 19, 1, 21, 2019.

23. Benítez-Guijarro, A., Callejas, Z., Noguera, M., Benghazi, K., Architecting dietary intake monitoring as a service combining NLP and IoT. *J. Ambient Intell. Humaniz. Comput.*, 1–13, 2019. Available: 10.1007/ s12652-019-01553-2.

24. Rachakonda, L., Kothari, A., Mohanty, S.P., Kougianos, E., Ganapathiraju, M., Stress-Log: An IoT-based smart system to monitor stress-eating, in: *2019 IEEE International Conference on Consumer Electronics (ICCE)*, IEEE, pp. 1–6, 2019, January.

25. Dylan McAllister, T., El-Tawab, S., Hossain Heydari James, M., *Localization of Health Center Assets Through an IoT Environment (LoCATE)*, Madison University, mcallitd@dukes.jmu.edu, eltawass, heydarmh@jmu.edu, IEEE, 2017.

26. Cao, Q., Jones, D.R., Sheng, H., Contained nomadic information environments: technology, organization, and environment influences on adoption of hospital RFID patient tracking. *Inform. Manage.*, 51, 2, 225–239, 2014.

27. Boulos, M.N.K. and Berry, G., Real-time locating systems (RTLS) in healthcare: a condensed primer. *Int. J. Health Geogr.*, 11, 1, 25, 2012.

28. Dai, Q., Zhong, R., Zhou, K., Jiang, Z., A RFID-enabled real-time manufacturing hardware platform for discrete industry, in: *proceedings of the 6th CIRP-Sponsored International Conference on 136 Digital Enterprise Technology*, Springer Berlin/Heidelberg, pp. 1743–1750, 2010.

29. Farshad, A., Li, J., Marina, M.K., Garcia, F.J., A microscopic look at WiFi fingerprinting for indoor mobile phone localization in diverse environments, in: *Indoor Positioning and Indoor Navigation (IPIN), 2013 International Conference on*, IEEE, pp. 1–10, 2013.

30. Lee, J.-S., Su, Y.-W., Shen, C.-C., A comparative study of wireless protocols: Bluetooth, UWB, ZigBee, and Wi-Fi. *Industrial Electronics Society, 2007. IECON 2007. 33rd Annual Conference of the IEEE*, IEEE, pp. 46–51, 2007.

31. Paksuniemi, M., Sorvoja, H., Alasaarela, E., Myllyla, R., Wireless sensor and data transmission needs and technologies for patient monitoring in the operating room and intensive care unit, in: *Engineering in Medicine and Biology Society, 2005. IEEE-EMBS 2005. 27th Annual International Conference of the*, IEEE, pp. 5182–5185, 2006.

32. Naranjo, P.G.V., Shojafar, M., Mostafaei, H., Pooranian, Z., Baccarelli, E., P-sep: A prolong stable election routing algorithm for energy-limited heterogeneous fog- supported wireless sensor networks. *J. Supercomput.*, 73, 733–755, 2017.

33. Saleh, N., Kassem, A., Haidar, A.M., Energy-efficient architecture for wireless sensor networks in healthcare applications. *IEEE Access*, 6, 6478–6486, 2018.

34. Naranjo, P., Pooranian, Z., Shojafar, M., Conti, M., Buyya, R., Focan: A fog-supported smart city network architecture for management of applications in the internet of everything environments. *J. Parallel Distrib. Comput.*, 132, 274–283, 2018. Available: 10.1016/j.jpdc.2018.07.003

35. Shojafar, M., Pooranian, Z., Naranjo, P.G.V., Baccarelli, E., Flaps: Bandwidth and delay-efficient distributed data searching in fog-supported p2p content delivery networks. *J. Supercomput.*, 73, 5239–5260, 2017.

36. Yang, L., Ren, Y., Zhang, W., 3D depth image analysis for indoor fall detection of elderly people. *Digit. Commun. Netw.*, 2, 24–34, 2016.
37. Yang, L., Ren, Y., Hu, H., Tian, B., New fast fall detection method based on spatIoTemporal context tracking of head by using depth images. *Sensors*, 15, 23004, 2015.
38. Diraco, G., Leone, A., Siciliano, P., An active vision system for fall detection and posture recognition in elderly healthcare, in: *Proceedings of the Conference on Design, Automation and Test in Europe, Dresden, Germany, 8–12 March 2010; European Design and Automation Association: Leuven, Belgium*, pp. 1536–1541, 2010.
39. López, J.D., Ocampo, C., Sucerquia, A., Vargas-Bonilla, J.F., Analyzing multiple accelerometer configurations to detect falls and motion, in: *Proceedings of the VII Latin American Congress on Biomedical Engineering CLAIB 2016, Bucaramanga, Santander, Colombia*, vol. 26–28 October 2016 Springer, Singapore, pp. 169–172, 2017.
40. Pal, A., Localization algorithms in wireless sensor networks: Current approaches and future challenges. *Netw. Protoc. Algorithms*, 2, 45–73, 2010.
41. El Assaf, A., Zaidi, S., Affes, S., Kandil, N., Robust anns-based wsn localization in the presence of anisotropic signal attenuation. *IEEE Wirel. Commun. Lett.*, 5, 504–507, 2016.
42. Gharghan, S.K., Nordin, R., Ismail, M., Energy efficiency of ultra-low-power bicycle wireless sensor networks based on a combination of power reduction techniques. *J. Sens.*, 7314207, 2016.
43. Windle, K. *et al.*, The national evaluation of partnerships for older people projects, 2010. Available: www.pssru.ac.uk/archive/pdf/rs053.
44. Anderson, J.E. and Larke, S.C., The Sooke navigator project using community resources and research to improve local service for mental health and addictions. *Ment. Health Family Med.*, 6, 21–28, 2009. Available: www.ncbi.nlm.nih.gov/pmc/articles/PMC2777592/pdf/MHFM- 06-021.pdf.
45. Macredie,S.*et al.*,A report on research into patient and career perspectives on the nature,effectiveness and impact of care navigation systems in Bradford,Airedale, in: *Care Navigation Wharfedale and Craven*, 2014, Available: http://health-partnership.org.uk/hp/wp-content/uploads/2014/10/Care-Navigation-Final-report.
46. Royal College of General Practitioners, *General Practice Forward View*, Gateway publication, England, 2016, Available: www.england.nhs.uk/wpcontent/uploads/2016/04/gpfv.pdf.
47. Making time in general practice, in: *Primary Care Foundation*, 2015, Available: www.primarycarefoundation.co.uk/images/PrimaryCareFoundation/Downloading_Repor ts/PCF_Press_Releases/Making-Time- in_General_Practice_FULL_REPORT_28_10_15.pdf.

5

Influence of Cognitive Computing in Healthcare Applications

Lucia Agnes Beena T.[1]* and Vinolyn Vijaykumar[2]

[1]Department of Information Technology, St. Joseph's College, Tiruchirappalli, India
[2]Department of Computer Applications, Alpha Arts and Science College, Chennai, India

Abstract

Cognitive computing employs artificial intelligence and machine learning to bridge the gap between the way the human brain grasps an idea and how the computers process a data pool. Big Data is characterized by information load. To achieve improved patient care, massive electronic health data must be converted to meaningful and expressible information. The cognitive computing system paves the way for intuitive and interactive computing that expands knowledge of the clinical domain and making informed decisions on the effective treatment of diseases with relevant content provided by Big Data analytic tools. IBM's Watson is a technology that ingests all forms of data and continuously acquires knowledge from user interactions. The confluence of big data analytics with Cognitive computing can be effectively applied to clinical guidelines and medical research. Watson Corpus is a unique repository from IBM which amasses large data sets of different domains into a single one. The objective is to aid in building a collective mechanism inspired by the potential of a human brain to enhance in the anticipation of solutions to a heterogeneous class of problems. The main focus of this chapter is to show the impact how healthcare industry can benefit out of cognitive computing and to propose a theoretical model that exploit cognitive computing for the betterment of healthcare domain.

Keywords: Cognitive computing, big data, healthcare, IBM watson, electronic medical record, watson health cloud, analytics

*Corresponding author: jerbeena@gmail.com

D. Sumathi, T. Poongodi, B. Balamurugan and Lakshmana Kumar Ramasamy (eds.)
Cognitive Intelligence and Big Data in Healthcare, (121–144) © 2022 Scrivener Publishing LLC

5.1   Introduction

The expeditious development of technologies, made the academicians as well as industrialist to apply Cognitive computing and Big Data in their domain. Another dimension that forces the adoption of Cognitive computing and Big Data is the tremendous volume of unstructured data created by Internet of Things, Mobile technologies and Social media. In the current scenario, Healthcare is one of important domains that have to embrace the Big Data and Cognitive computing to effectively handle its challenges. In recent years, patients' records are digitized and a huge amount of data is ready for processing by the physicians and the caretakers. The Cognitive systems can become a good companion for the physicians and caretakers by performing the analysis on the exploding data and providing appropriate insights for decision making. The Cognitive systems like DeepMind, Watson assist the doctors in preventing lung cancer, breast cancer and prostate cancer and diagnosis of diseases based on the statistical analysis and image pattern recognition [1]. Applying Cognitive systems in medical field, improves the observations, reduces the diagnostic errors, and decreases the cost of hospitalization. Some of the research studies that utilized cognitive principles for improving healthcare domain in different perspectives were discussed here.

Syed *et al.* [2] applied Cognitive principles with IoT and Cloud technologies for detecting and classifying pathology in Healthcare. In the framework, a normal electroencephalogram (EEG) dataset was considered and two Convolutional Neural Network (CNN) models were trained. The patient's movements, actions and emotions including EEG signals, were collected through smart sensors and processed in Cloud to regulate the patient's complaint. The deep learning system in the framework utilized the EEG signals to sense the EEG pathology and forward the results to the Cognitive Unit. The Cognitive unit notifies the situation of the patient to physicians, caretakers and the other team members to take appropriate actions. The level of accuracy of this framework was better compared to other models.

In the idea of making many people healthier, advanced technologies are deployed for better sharing of medical resources from urban areas to rural and remote places. One such initiative was proposed by Chen *et al.* [3] using 5G technology and Cognitive systems. The existing telemedicine system can only treat the patients physiologically. The proposed system understands the patients' emotional state to treat their biological diseases. This 5G Cognitive system comprises of a data cognitive engine and a resource cognitive engine. The healthcare big data is analyzed and fed to the Data Cognitive engine to treat the patient physiologically and psychologically depending on the Patient's condition. The resource cognitive engine transmits the data between the patient and the doctor with ultra-low latency and ultra-high reliability. The authors utilized this platform for remote surgery. The doctor is able to understand the current state of the patient through display devices, tactile sensor devices and respond accordingly. The doctor's arm movements are captured by the haptic device during the surgery. The captured data is forwarded to the operation terminal rapidly at the patient's end via 5G network. The operation terminal's mechanical arm follows the motion of the doctor and operation is performed on the patient. At the patient's end, the tactile feedback, audio and video information are transmitted to the doctor for further action. This communication loop is necessary for the successful remote surgery. It was found that time delay in transmission is critical and it has to be optimized.

The high speed development in computing and medical field tries to provide better healthcare services to its stakeholders. One important aspect to be concentrate is the special service needed by the patients in their emergency situations. The research made by Min Chen et al. [4] applied Edge Cognitive Computing (ECC) [5] in the smart healthcare system that observes the physical health of the patient and allocates the necessary computing assets in the whole Edge network depending on the health risk of the patient. The data cognitive engine in ECC performs exhaustive big data analysis with the help of computer and deep learning using the external data (physical signal, user behavior) and internal data (network type, communication quality, service data flow, and environmental parameters) it received. The resource cognitive engine supports the data cognitive engine by providing computing, communication and network resources at real-time for vibrant resource sharing and optimization. The investigational effects showed that the structure gave better Quality of Experience in case of the emergency situation encountered by the patients.

The increased use of wearable devices and information technology enhance the healthcare management systems. At the same time, a bulk of patient data generated from several therapeutic devices is to be stored and processed in the cloud. In order to analyze and predict the treatment, Kumar et al. [6] proposed a Cognitive Data Transmission Method (CDTM). Simulated Annealing Technique was adopted for intellectual understanding. By analyzing the data packets, the health condition of the patient is classified as critical or normal. In case of critical scenario, the data transmitted from that patient is given higher priority for further treatment. The CDTM also has a module for stochastic forecasting of most related patients depending on their current health conditions. It was observed that the CDTM provide 98% accuracy over the other models in prediction. The medical professional can offer better treatment using various medical devices and with the greater assistance given by the cognitive computing. This chapter explains the requirement of Cognitive computing and Big Data in analyzing the medical data and providing superior medication for the patients at the earliest possible time.

5.2   Bond Between Big Data and Cognitive Computing

The emerging information systems are trying to incorporate Human reasoning in the computing process in assisting human. In order to leverage computing intelligence, huge volume of data in different format with rapid speed has to be processed in real time. As the traditional data management systems fails to process these types of data, Big Data forms the basis for the data processing. Cognitive computing provides a novel way to reveal the potential in data deriving values using massive parallel processing and having interaction with human. Cognitive computing is a self-learning model that acquires the human reasoning and corrects the faults made by the system in each iteration [7].

With the introduction of Internet of Things (IoT), the information produced is intensified and flooded with different varieties of data. Big Data analytics is capable of analyzing the unstructured data to provide visualization of the information. But Cognitive computing that handles the machine learning algorithms works on objective data. Therefore, in order to apply big data analytics in Cognitive computing the unstructured data has to be converted to objective data, to train the machine learning algorithms and to predict the unseen perception derived from the data. Training of the algorithms requires massive data that may be structured, unstructured, and semi-structured with high variety, velocity, and enormous volume. Hence Big Data analytics can help the cognitive computing to identify the hidden patterns in the data and able to predict the relationship between the variables [8].

In Cognitive computing the hypothesis is framed and tested. Based on the results the hypothesis is improvised. This is similar to the human thinking process. When new data is added to the model, it checks for new variables and adds them to the model automatically and compares the results with the prior version of the model for better performance. Thus it is more dynamic than big data analytics where the new variables are to be added manually. Cognitive Computing (CC) is capable of processing natural language which is difficult in big data analytics. The efficiency of the CS improves when it is trained with exhaustive data with its context. Each iteration makes the CS stronger. Enterprises use this capacity of CS for decision making. In order to make CS to predict good decisions like human, it is vital to know the way by which human beings are taking decision making. The process of decision making is categorized as observation, interpretation, evaluation, and decision [7].

The data generated by the IoT devices and social web, grow in a rapid way. Having enormous data is good for the Cognitive system to make its observation in a better manner. The generated data is either structured or unstructured. Handling huge volume of unstructured data needs Big Data Analytics (BDA). CC needs clean data in a particular format for its analysis in decision making. BDA tools assist CC in storing, pre-processing, and managing the massive data it retrieves form various sources [9]. In order to extract the efficiency of the CC, the CC must be supported by big data infrastructure and networking to move data or information at an exact speed. Also, the public and private cloud power the CC in data service through the characteristics such as scalability, unlimited storage, and security [8]. In some scenarios, the data is captured from real time devices like medical gadgets or wearables that need security in motion. So the security techniques that are adopted should hide the sensitive personal information before sharing the data. Most of the data received by the CC is in unstructured format, though the CC may store the data in structured format for processing. For example, in healthcare applications, the request for a drug detail might be in unstructured format. But the drug details may be stored in a Standard Query Language (SQL). Therefore, there is the need for transformation of unstructured data to the structured form, which will be easily done by the Big Data Tools.

The semantics of the semi-structured or unstructured data does not pursue a particular format. The sources that generate these unstructured data are clinical trials, medical equipment, medical record of patients, demographic details of the patients, progress notes given by the physician, mobile data, and social media. These data assist the CC in understanding the issue contextually. Hence the CC need not concentrate on the data format if it adopts big data. Big Data analytics is able to handle the data collection, storage management and transformation of the unstructured data to the appropriate format the way the CC require for analysis. Big Data analytics stores data in NoSQL databases supporting different structures such as key-value pair, document database, columnar databases, graph databases, spatial databases, PostGIS, and Polyglot persistence. Big Data analytics also leverage CC to provide advance analytics by applying algorithms like sketching and streaming, dimensionality reduction, numerical linear algebra, and compression sensing [10].

Handle the streaming data or data in motion for real-time analytics is a challenge in CC. Various streaming data platforms can be implemented with CC for efficient decision making of any application at real-time. Another important fact, the log data is not taken for analysis before the introduction of big data techniques like Hadoop and MapReduce. The patterns retrieved from the log data can give some insights. For example, the log data can reveal in advance, the time at which medical equipment may fail, so that it may not be used with the critical patients. Big Data is like a fuel to the growth of the CC. The characteristics of CC with respect to volume, velocity, variety, veracity and value allow big data analytics to aid in observation, interpretation, evaluation and decision making of CC. The CC is incomplete without the usage of big data analytics. One common characteristic exists in both big data and CC is the processing of voluminous data. Through the machine learning algorithms and other techniques applied by CC offer accurate and contextual solutions or recommendations to a specific issue.

5.3   Need for Cognitive Computing in Healthcare

The recent technologies like Cloud, Big Data, Semantic Web and machine learning algorithms, empower Cognitive Computing systems to easily handle huge data generated from diverse sources and devices. These enhanced technologies open a new possibility for CC to implement effective models that to perform complicated tasks in the healthcare industry. As any other field, Healthcare industry is also generating enormous data which may give new insights in diagnosis and in preventing serious issues in the Patients. The characteristics of CC with Big Data can assist the healthcare providers in effective service. Most remarkable results have been accomplished in cancer diagnosis by the technology providers like Google, Watson, and Deep Mind [1].

The Patients' wellbeing is supported by different participants of the Healthcare Industry [10] as shown in Figure 5.1. Data required for the CS is generated by the participant of the healthcare industry. Patients have their personal background, their medical history, and test results as physical records in paper format. The Healthcare Providers possess patient medical

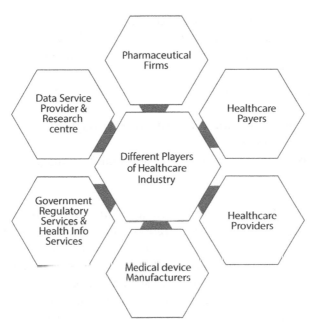

Figure 5.1 Different participants of healthcare industry.

records, reports of medical tests, reports generated from medical devices, Hospital admission history, clinical research reports, payments, and cost. The data from clinical trials and drug effectiveness from the doctor's prescriptions help the Pharmaceutical industry in preparing and designing the drugs. The Healthcare payers like insurance companies, the government and individual or the private employers assist the patient in settling their bills. All these data form a repository for the Healthcare Information Service providers, Research centers, and Medical device manufacturers. The government controls and manages the data generated by the participants of Healthcare industry for better understanding.

The data may be in structured, semi-structured or in unstructured format is organized in Cloud as Service (Data as a Service). The CC utilizes the Cloud and distributed architecture for its effective functioning. By combining the various new technologies like Machine Learning, Natural Language Processing, Big Data, Artificial Intelligence and Deep Learning, CC perform the self-learning process. As a result, the CC can predict the insights required by the healthcare authorities with full confidence. This improves the services of the Healthcare participants significantly. Hence, the CC can offer the following benefits:

- Provides better quality of experience in emergency situation
- Provides accurate reports to assist clinical decisions
- Utilize machine learning and deep learning algorithms for smart decision making
- Improves patients care by consolidating the patient's report pertaining to the problem
- Improves the patient's satisfaction through the individualized treatment.
- Helps in rectifying the anomalies found in image generated by the machines.

By using the CC, more complicated questions can be answered. Also the healthcare authorities can concentrate on their strategic initiative rather than documenting the data. Like human, the CC understands the medical history of the patients from various sources like medical images, doctor's prescriptions though they may be in structured or unstructured format. Reason out the cause for the underlying problem, by making hypothesis and arrive at the decision. Each data fed to the CC, make it accurate and perfect through self-learning. Also, interactive nature of the CC shapes it into an expert to provide intellectual awareness and probabilistic suggestions for the betterment of the patient. CC includes even the conflicting evidence and recommends that will be best. Hence CC is trying to imitate the human thinking process in assisting human.

5.4 Conceptual Model Linking Big Data and Cognitive Computing

An enormous expanse of data is at disposal from various resources and channels, though not created by any human in particular, but made to spread unknowingly. Designing and maintaining massive databases may not be the need of the hour. But there still exists the necessity to manage data so that they can be transformed into constructive information that leads to value-added production processes. This emphasizes the importance of data scientists as an emerging role in the employment sector [11].

5.4.1 Significance of Big Data

Big Data necessitates the ability to cope up with great expanse of related and unrelated data at the opposite pace and within the stipulated time to enable discerning scrutiny and analyses.

Figure 5.2 The five V's of big data.

The five fundamental attributes of Big Data, as shown in Figure 5.2, best explain the scope and dimensions of the subject concerned are: *Volume, Variety, Value, Velocity, and Veracity.*

Volume: It is the amount of information that requires to be warehoused and managed.

Variety: The data can be one of the categories: structured, unstructured, or semi-structured.

Value: The perceptions that are extracted must serve the right purpose.

Velocity: The speed with which data are transmitted, processed, and delivered matters.

Veracity: The extent of reliability of the data in consideration determines the trustworthiness of the insights [12].

5.4.2 The Need for Cognitive Computing

A system, which is grounded on Artificial Intelligence (AI), executes on the procedures and parameters which are procured as inputs. However, a system that is grounded on Cognitive Computing, executes by interpreting the commands, drawing deductions from them and suggesting probable resolutions. Cognitive Computing can be thought of as an AI-based system that empowers it to relate with human beings similar to the interaction of a fellow human, to infer the circumstantial implication, examine the user's former record, and derive inferences centered on that collaborative assembly. The Cognitive Computing system aids the individuals in decision-making. However, the AI-based systems thrive on the perception that machineries are more proficient in giving better verdicts on behalf of the human beings at large.

Cognitive Computing (CC) is deemed to be an amalgamation of Cloud Computing with the Cognitive, Data, and Neuro sciences. The purpose of CC is to construct a balanced and combined method driven by the capabilities of a human brain. The features of Cognitive computing-based systems, *viz.*, **Adaptive, Interactive, Iterative, Stateful, and Contextual** can be mapped onto the five V's of the Big Data *viz., Volume, Variety, Value, Velocity, and Veracity* [11].

5.4.3   The Association Between the Big Data and Cognitive Computing

Cognitive computing (CC) development utilizes a fusion of artificial intelligence, machine learning, neural networks, sentiment analysis, natural language processing, and contextual awareness to crack everyday difficulties just like human beings. The resolve of CC is the conception of computation of frameworks which could unravel intricate snags with no continual human involvement. The interoperability between the Big Data and Cognitive Computing leads to amalgamation of the two notions as illustrated in Figure 5.3 [13, 14].

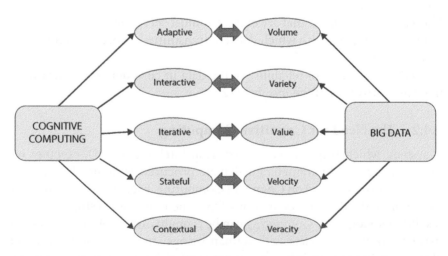

Figure 5.3 The interoperability between cognitive computing and big data.

(i) Adaptive and Volume

Adaptive is the first step towards building cognitive systems based on Machine Learning. The resolutions should impersonate the capability of human intelligence to absorb and familiarize from the surroundings. These systems cannot be automated for secluded tasks. They need to be dynamical in gathering data, understanding requirements and accomplishing the goal. This in turn leads to the necessity of access to data in large capacities. *Volume* represents the huge expanse of data that is created every second, warehoused and retrieved for data analytics. With the dawn of interconnected devices and social media, it has directed to the development of vast amount of data. These data may be structured, semi-structured of unstructured and a cognitive-based system would stabilize or regularize the data according to the format needed to gain fruitful insights. The test of data surge can be efficiently handled by using cognitive-based computing systems as it will be difficult for humans to formulate observations with huge amount of data.

(ii) Interactive and Variety

The cognitive systems need to be **Interactive** to enable users to define their needs with ease. It is essential that there is an interaction between devices, processors, and cloud services as well as human beings. Since there exist many sources from where the data gets accumulated, it leads to variety. *Variety* refers to the different types of data acquired from various avenues such as IoT devices, emails, social networking sites, Global Positioning devices, and many more. To enable Cognitive systems to cram and draw inferences, they must be provided with an assortment of data and henceforth the systems will be proficient enough to interpret the data by grasping the circumstantial sense of the issue concerned. To aid in keeping up-to-date with the advances in the arena of technology, individuals have to continually appraise their prevailing intelligence base from innumerable, probable resources of information. The Cognitive-based systems can interlink and support people in acquiring visions.

(iii) Iterative and Value

Iterative feature of the Cognitive systems pave way to solve problems which are incomplete and ambiguous. They help in defining a statement to a problem precisely by posing more queries or by discovering supplementary sources of extra information. Cognitive systems employ quantifiable predictive analyses for making decisions wherever there is an absence of exact indication. These lessen the errors made by humans when they tend to depend on presumptions. These processes can steer data repurposing which could be analyzed more for gaining added insights. As an essential attribute of Big Data, *Value* advocates that until data can be converted to knowledge the huge expanse of data is futile. The value of the data available can be realized from different contexts in which the Big Data are used, like social media, smart cities, search engines, and user-generated content.

(iv) Stateful and Velocity

Stateful, as a characteristic of Cognitive Systems, offers details to the specific application at that particular moment of need. It "remembers" the preceding interactions that were carried out in a process and "returns" information at the due time. Assessment of data to create evidence to reply a query is an inborn skill of an individual. The Cognitive Systems alter the raw facts that get collected into pictorial webs of data such that relationships within the data are created. They are capable of processing huge amount of data within a short span of time. *Velocity* is that feature of Big Data that monitors the proportion at which data gets produced and high-speed processing of the data accumulated. Though there is a massive and continuous flow of data, the cognitive systems provide data on demand and at a faster pace.

(v) Contextual and Veracity

Cognitive Systems differ from existing Computer applications in that they are **Contextual**. They recognize, categorize, and extract related components like syntax, meaning, location, time, regulations, suitable domain, process, profile of the user, goal, and task. They also can infer from numerous resources of information, whether structured or unstructured data, as well as digital or sensory inputs. Nevertheless, it is mandatory to beget effectiveness in data analyses such that the assessment is reliable and precise too. *Veracity* is a distinctive trait of the Big Data in which it pacts with anticipating the quality, ambiguity and dependability of the data. Since the data get generated from varied sources, the accuracy of the data must be checked before utilizing them for business insights. Assessing the data is crucial for a cognitive-based system and to accomplish this chore in an appropriate, accurate, and trustworthy means [13, 15].

5.4.4   The Advent of Cognition in Healthcare

Healthcare establishments nowadays have countless data bases than earlier days, but they scuffle to excerpt beneficial evidence from those figures. Hospital departments require some way to assimilate their assorted and discrete data supplies. A chief challenge in harnessing these analytics or learning algorithms is how to accrue data in a single place and single format for analysis. Predictive analytics might disclose hereditarily inherited ailments or identify associations among hospitals, doctors, and laboratories. To be precise, integration unlocks innovative potentials to explore

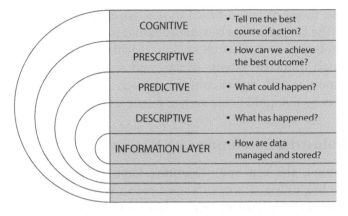

Figure 5.4 Analytics.

healthcare data and more significant, extracts meaning from the association with Cognitive Computing. Manifold database models under a single interface could be foundational to medicinal advances and could produce an innovative generation of analytic tools. The Big Data analytics help in determining the business values as to how everyone can be more right… and more often. Figure 5.4 depicts the analytics that lead to Cognitive Computing from the Information Layer [16].

5.5   IBM's Watson and Cognitive Computing

A cognitive-based computing system is not merely an unassuming mechanized processing system. It is envisioned to generate innovative levels of association between man and machine. Even though human beings have been collating evidence for an extensive period of time, there are restrictions on the perceptions and investigation that individuals can gather from those statistics employing conventional means of computing. With the invention of a cognitive-based system like IBM's Watson, the machine can discover patterns or outliers from great volumes of structured and unstructured information at enormous speed. A cognitive system becomes smarter as every successive interaction helps in advancing accurateness and analytical potential.

The association between man and machine is interdependent in a cognitive-based system. Using Machine Learning techniques, humans must do some mapping and training to get effective results from a cognitive system. By building a corpus of knowledge, people train Watson, which may be fine-tuned or broad-based to specialized areas such as finance or medicine. The corpus comprises statistics that is collated in encyclopedias, books, ontologies, and research studies. It will make Watson possible to hunt through immense extents of data and analyze those data to afford precise responses with higher confidence levels. IBM is employing Watson technologies to manifold fields such as finance, healthcare, and retail.

5.5.1   Industrial Revolution with Watson

IBM Watson is the first open Cognitive Computing platform that represents the beginning of a new-fangled era in which computers comprehend the world by means of senses, learning, and experience. With the advent of Watson, it is powering fairly some of the practical applications across an assortment of industries as shown in Figure 5.5.

With the help of the *IBM Watson IoT platform*, the manufacturers can generate easily readable control panels for their businesses, create replicas of prognostic catastrophe, and directly interact with IBM Watson to resolve the preeminent resolutions to problems, by streaming the data accumulated. Using *IBM Watson Supply Chain* and Watson Supply Chain Insights, the job of the supply chain managers is abridged. Current hiring processes become more streamlined with *IBM Watson Recruitment*. *Watson Discovery for Salesforce* is intended to transfigure customer services. The IBM Watson develops a data source based on cloud computing that is effortlessly available to customer service representatives by assembling and analyzing the data of the company from numerous sources, besides taking into consideration the account documented preceding client issues and cases. The *IBM Watson Marketing Solutions* has made it easier for industries to have a long-lasting effect on their client bases. *IBM Watson Advertising* employs numerous "dynamic and artistic" tools to deliver tailored advertisements to prospective customers. The *IBM IoT Building Insights* could be utilized in any type of infrastructures to analyze how the constructions are functioning. Healthcare professionals are always on the outlook for the utmost pioneering skill to aid them progress their exertions, and the IBM Watson Health has applications aplenty intended for that particular resolve. The IBM Watson IoT also has abundant applications in the automobile sector, inclusive of the digital assistant *IBM Watson Assistant for Automotive*, assisting the manufacturing of smarter, securer vehicles, and also informing in real time the issues faced by the vehicles. *The Watson Decision Platform for Agriculture* conjoins analytics, knowledge from industry experts, predictive insights, IBM research, and

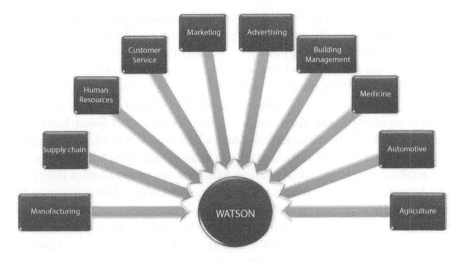

Figure 5.5 Watson's cognitive platforms.

IoT to generate an automated record of the field that is distinctive to every farmland [17].

5.5.2 The IBM's Cognitive Computing Endeavour in Healthcare

IBM engineers and scientists tailored and released Watson as the foremost commercially available Cognitive computing capability – a skill which signifies a modern age in computing. Delivered through the cloud, the computer analyses huge dimensions of data, comprehends composite queries put forward in natural dialect, and recommends solutions based on evidences. Watson incessantly absorbs and acquires valuable knowledge from every interaction with an individual over time.

The IBM Watson Health and Watson Health Cloud

The IBM Watson Health and Watson Health Cloud platform were launched in April 2015. The pursuit of this pristine section was to progress the capability of medics, insurers, and academics to modernize by evolving perceptions from the immense expanse of individual clinical data fashioned and distributed every day. The platform Watson Health Cloud permits these statistics to be recognized, distributed, and merged with a continuously developing, dynamic, and accumulated understanding of social, clinical, and research healthcare data. Hence IBM has associated with several research, private, and academic institutes to relate Watson and the Cognitive Computing in resolving the utmost puzzling and demanding complications in caring the patients. Consider the case where IBM is thriving with clinicians, researchers, and the cancer institutes to incorporate the expertise of Watson to the data confronts of treating cancer patients through collaborations with the MD Anderson Cancer Centre situated at the University of Texas, Austin and New York's Memorial Sloan-Kettering Cancer Centre. In the Minnesota's Mayo Clinic, the Watson is serving physicians map patients to associated medical tests, and also 16 foremost cancer establishments are collaborating with Watson to aid medics interpret DNA insights to treat patients with improved decisions. Watson is used to create solutions for computerized hypothesis generation by the scientists from Baylor College of Medicine in Texas. The IBM Watson Health and the American Diabetes Association have announced recently a long-standing alliance to combine the cognitive computing supremacy of Watson and the vast warehouse of research and clinical data. As part of the association, Watson will be tutored to comprehend the data about diabetes to enable it to detect probable hazards and generate "evidence-based, confidence-ranked recommendations" for an assortment of healthcare resolves. The collaboration of IBM with Johnson and Johnson, Medtronic, and Apple makes it simpler for clinical establishments to hoard and analyze data acquired from patients by means of Watson's cognitive competences, generating novel fitness-based contributions that influence data gathered from medical, personal health, and fitness appliances to offer real-time opinion, better insights, and commendations that helps in progressing the whole lot from personal fitness and health to severe and enduring care.

Usage of Cognitive Application to Augment the Electronic Medical Record

The Electronic Medical Record (EMR) is a digitized documentation of the clinical and medical data of every single patient trailed by a benefactor (independent doctor or well-built health centers collaborated with many physicians). Characteristically, the EMR is intended to hoard and retrieve data of a patient which could be utilized for analysis and therapy. It has some elementary reporting abilities like identifying a laboratory test as high or low grounded on predetermined standards. The EMR is supposed to have three foremost tasks: Think, Document, and Act. Currently, the EMR records statistics about a patient and provides support to the doctor in diagnosis and treatment. Nonetheless, the EMR does not aid with the "thinking" characteristic of defining how to deliver elite care to a patient. Through integrating cognitive capabilities, machine learning, and analytics into the Electronic Medical Record, medics could be steered to understand how the diagnoses were concluded and the concerns encompassing a treatment strategy. Overall, the healthcare establishments would wish to acquire more insights from the EMR inclusive of developing various means to control the parameters in the EMR to expand synchronization amongst diverse benefactors and giving more personalized first-class care to patients [11].

5.6   Future Directions

All the potentials that assist in the implementation of cognitive computing in healthcare have the same capabilities in other industries too. For instance, extracting patterns for diagnosing a disease and adopting therapy commendations are specific cases of the universal problem of spotting liabilities and remedies in the complex systems. This ability to detect complications has applications in businesses such as manufacturing – appliance maintenance and repair – from household machineries to oil rig apparatuses. The Figure 5.6 illustrates the steps to accelerate the Cognitive journey of an organization.

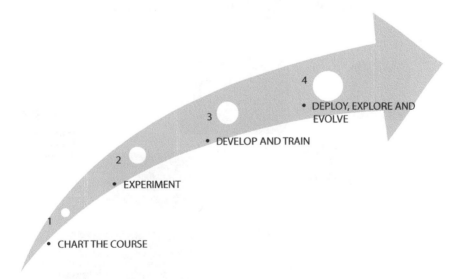

Figure 5.6 The cognitive journey of an organization.

5.6.1 Retail

Retail is a highly competitive industry, where to survive and thrive, retailers must anticipate the products to be purchased by analyzing and foretelling the recent trends beforehand. They must be able to recognize the effect of fluctuating social, economic, and demographic aspects. Retailers must also ensure that their workforces excel in both depicting the mission of the company and the goods sold. Cognitive solutions have the potentiality to assist retailers influence knowledge in innovative ways. Several retailers practice predictive analytics tools to sense motivating associations to determine perceptions based on customer loyalty-card data. For instance, big data analytics help retailers to identify changes in life situations (marriages, pregnancy, and such), changing habits, and buying preferences. It is

Figure 5.7 A coarse taxonomy of cognitive computing research areas.

probable to discriminate between an anomaly and the exact variation in buying likings [11].

5.6.2   Research

Cognitive computing can be thought of as a multidisciplinary arena of research targeting at formulating computational models and policymaking methods constructed on the bases of the neurobiological processes of the brain, psychology, and cognitive sciences to bestow computers with the faculty of knowing, faculty of thinking, and faculty of feeling. In addition, it is notable that Cognitive Computing models can be reinforced by Big Data [19, 20]. The automatic knowledge extraction mechanism of IBM Watson is the best example that incorporates both Cognitive Computing and Big Data. The contemporary research trend on cognitive computing can be categorized according to its goals as those delivering a computer system with the faculty of knowing, faculty of thinking or faculty of feeling as illustrated in the Figure 5.7 [18].

5.6.3   Travel

In the past two decades, the travel industry has seen an incredible upheaval since information about schedules and rates of transportation, lodging, and leisure activities has been made available online freely. In yesteryears, a travel agent would get to know the favorites of a particular person, find ways to satisfy the customer and look out for favorable options and innovative opportunities. But today, the traveler characteristically has to offer an outline of typical choices for each site they operate. Nevertheless, none of these websites offer interpretations that are made, created on noticeable behavior. This paves way for an application based on cognitive computing that captures information clearly by apprehending patterns of the behavior of the travelers. This leads to the potential for indirectly understanding travelers' expectations by observing social media discussions. This also helps the travelers to interrelate through a Natural Language Processing interface with the system.

5.6.4   Security and Threat Detection

For general risk management and business continuity, the commercial Network Security is a concern in virtually every industry of today. Websites, applications and networks in the cloud are becoming the most viable targets of hackers. Cybercrime is growing exponentially to exploit the vulnerabilities, which demonstrates the skill of the hacker. Hacking is made for commercial gain too and there seems to be no signs of abating. Since the attackers indulge in more and more erudite tactics to theft and hacking, even relentless vigilance with the conventional technology prove futile to keep the hackers at bay.

The following are the three significant factors need to be adopted by Cognitive Computing for threat detection:

- The swiftness at which new threats are fostered
- The rapidity with which destruction can be executed before an attack can be constrained
- The intricacy of systems that are getting beyond the skills of conventional computer systems and the network administrators to safeguard.

Earlier, as new threats were perceived, new guidelines were made available to network managers or individuals with payments to security and Antivirus Software. The delay between the detection of a threat and production of an Antivirus package could take hours, days, or weeks. Fortunately, Machine Learning solutions can supervise Network access nodes uninterruptedly and compare recent activity to past activity while observing the irregularities – without being communicated what to search for. Rather than waiting endlessly for an update, the system can spot the unanticipated anomalies in the activity and also indulge in actions such as isolating data and network sections while an administrator appraises the condition [21]. For a false-positive pattern, that is an anomaly that merely signifies an unfamiliar but harmless activity pattern, the system can absorb that the new pattern is benign and appraise its own data so that forthcoming incidences will be documented as the new normal and not record as a threat.

5.6.5   Cognitive Training Tools

It is monotonous and laborious to fabricate a corpus nowadays by training a computer system based on the knowledge previously ingested. A lot of experimental and human verdicts are tangled for each new corpus. A good deal of the training effort that is humane exhaustive currently will become computerized with the advent of the next-generation Cognitive Computing systems to scrutinize the procedure to facilitate the development of improved applications. Cognitive Computing Technology will be utilized iteratively to determine novel ways to expand the process of creating cognitive computing solutions from less-sophisticated to more complex tools. One of the most vital issues that need to be addressed is the Bias in training. With a great deal of unstructured accumulated data and with no specific protocol to analyze those data, professionals make decisions based on their personal understandings, which are prejudiced since most of them have never perceived the complete set of possible elucidations. With the advent of Cognitive-based systems and the tools that adhere to Cognitive computing, the decision-making process in complex scenarios becomes easier.

5.7   Conclusion

This chapter tries to explain the impact of cognitive computing in healthcare along with big data. The influence of big data and cloud computing is explored by cognitive computing for the better living of human beings. Medical organizations analyze complex data received from various smart devices, and wearables used by the patients. These data are in structured or unstructured format and for real-time analysis the streaming data are to be processed by the cognitive systems. The cognitive computing systems handle the huge data using big data techniques. The big data techniques convert the data received from various sources to appropriate format, so that the cognitive system can perform best in decision making. The interoperability between big data and cognitive system is deliberated in this chapter. The recent and innovative cognitive system, IBM Watson's ability is brought out in this discussion. Though cognitive computing can perform well, human intervention is must in risk management. Some industrialist's opinion is that it is costlier to train the cognitive system. Hence its adoption is slow. Also, automatic decision making is not yet included in the Cognitive systems. Finally, it can be stated that cognitive computing can assist the physicians and personals of healthcare in their activities to bring out the happiness in human beings.

References

1. Coccoli, M. and Maresca, P., Adopting cognitive computing solutions in healthcare. *J. E-Learn. Knowl. Soc.*, 14, 1, 57–69, 2018.
2. Amin, S.U., Shamim Hossain, M., Muhammad, G., Alhussein, M., Rahman, M.A., Cognitive smart healthcare for pathology detection and monitoring. *IEEE Access*, 7, 10745–10753, 2019.

3. Chen, M., Yang, J., Hao, Y., Mao, S., Hwang, K., A 5G cognitive system for healthcare. *Big Data Cogn. Comput.*, 1, 2, 2017.
4. Chen, M., Wei Li, Y.H., Qian, Y., Humar, I., Edge cognitive computing based smart healthcare system. *Future Gener. Comput. Syst.*, 86, 403–411, 2018.
5. Chen, M., Li, W., Hao, Y., Qian, Y., Humar, I., Edge cognitive computing based smart healthcare system. *Future Gener. Comput. Syst.*, 86, 403–411, 2018.
6. Kumar, M., Arun, R.V., Aravind Britto, K.R., A cognitive technology based healthcare monitoring system and medical data transmission. *Measurement*, 146, 322–332, 2019.
7. Gupta, S., Kumar Kar, A., Baabdullah, A., Al-Khowaiter, W.A.A., Big Data with cognitive computing: A review for the future. *Int. J. Inform. Manage.*, 42, 78–89, 2018.
8. Gupta, S., Kumar Kar, A., Baabdullah, A., Al-Khowaiter, W.A.A., Big Data with cognitive computing: A review for the future. *Int. J. Inform. Manage.*, 42, 78–89, 2018.
9. Abdullah, A., Hussain, A., Hussain Khan, I., Introduction: dealing with big data-lessons from cognitive computing. *Cogn. Comput.*, 7, 6, 635–636, 2015.
10. Behera, R.K., Kumar Bala, P., Dhir, A., The emerging role of cognitive computing in healthcare: A systematic literature review. *Int. J. Med. Inform.*, 129, 154–166, 2019.
11. Gupta, S., Kar, A.K., Baabdullah, A., Al-Khowaiter, W.A.A., Big Data with cognitive computing: A review for the future. *Int. J. Inform. Manage.*, 42, 78–89, 20182018.
12. Hurwitz, J., Kaufman, M., Bowles, A., Cognitive Computing and Big Data Analytics, in: *Chapter 4, The Relationship Between Big Data and Cognitive Computing*, John Wiley & Sons, Inc, Indianapolis, Indiana, 2015.
13. What is Cognitive Computing? Features, Scope & Limitations. https://marutitech.com/cognitive-computing-features-scope-limitations/.
14. Saheb, T. and Izadi, L., Paradigm of IoT big data analytics in the healthcare industry: A review of scientific literature and mapping of research trends. *Telemat. Informat.*, 41, 70–85, 2019.
15. What is Cognitive Computing? Top 10 Cognitive Companies. https://www.predictiveanalyticstoday.com/what-is-cognitive-computing.
16. Kaur, K. and Rani, R., Managing Data in Healthcare Information Systems: Many Models, One Solution, in: *Computer*, vol. 48, pp. 52–59, Mar. 2015.
17. How IBM Watson is revolutionizing 10 industries, October 2018. https://www.techrepublic.com/article/how-ibm-watson-is-revolutionizing-10-industries/.
18. Gutierrez -Garcia, J.O. and López-Neri, E., Cognitive Computing: A Brief Survey and Open Research Challenges, in: *2015 3rd International Conference on Applied Computing and Information Technology/2nd International Conference on Computational Science and Intelligence, Okayama, IEEE*, pp. 328–333, 2015.

19. Chen, M., Herrera, F., Hwang, K., Cognitive computing: architecture, technologies and intelligent applications. *IEEE Access*, 6, 19774–19783, 2018.

20. Gupta, S., Kumar Kar, A., Baabdullah, A., Al-Khowaiter, W.A.A., Big Data with cognitive computing: A review for the future. *Int. J. Inform. Manage.*, 42, 78–89, 2018.

21. Liu, B., Wu, C., Li, H., Chen, Y., Wu, Q., Barnell, M., Qiu, Q., Cloning your mind: security challenges in cognitive system designs and their solutions, in: *Proceedings of the 52nd Annual Design Automation Conference*, pp. 1–5, 2015.

6

An Overview of the Computational Cognitive from a Modern Perspective, Its Techniques and Application Potential in Healthcare Systems

Reinaldo Padilha França[1]*, Ana Carolina Borges Monteiro[1], Rangel Arthur[2] and Yuzo Iano[1]

[1]Communications Department (DECOM), School of Electrical and Computer Engineering (FEEC), University of Campinas (UNICAMP), Campinas – SP, Brazil Av. Albert Einstein, Barão Geraldo Campinas – SP, Brazil
[2]Telecommunications Department, Faculty of Technology (FT), University of Campinas (UNICAMP), Limeira – SP, Brazil Paschoal Marmo Street Jardim Nova Italia, Limeira – SP, Brazil

Abstract

Cognitive computing allows machines and systems to interpret data, collect information from them, and identify trends. It is based on models of neural networks and statistical and probabilistic models of in-depth learning, enabling systems to be able to read content and understand its domain, and also allowing these systems to be able to store all the data with which they have contact and to generate an information base, resulting in a source of knowledge; and, from there, evaluate it against certain contexts, capable of still making decisions and generating insights based on certain evidence. Cognitive computing is also based on self-learning systems that use machine learning techniques to perform specific tasks intelligently, simulating human thought processes in a computer model, through self-learning algorithms that use data mining, pattern recognition, and natural language processing. Cognitive computing has a very close relationship with AI (Artificial Intelligence), supporting productivity as support for human work, operating in

*Corresponding author: padilha@decom.fee.unicamp.com
Reinaldo Padilha França: ORCID: http://orcid.org/0000-0002-7901-6691
Ana Carolina Borges Monteiro: ORCID: http://orcid.org/0000-0002-8631-6617
Rangel Arthur: ORCID: http://orcid.org/0000-0002-4138-4720
Yuzo Iano: ORCID: http://orcid.org/0000-0002-9843-976

D. Sumathi, T. Poongodi, B. Balamurugan and Lakshmana Kumar Ramasamy (eds.)
Cognitive Intelligence and Big Data in Healthcare, (145–168) © 2022 Scrivener Publishing LLC

repetitive tasks, and helping people to solve demands. The role of cognitive computing is to interpret the data offered allowing a particular machine to understand the information that was offered, process that data, and then respond to specific and desired requests, can automate responses, and perform enrollments and schedules, in addition to handling data for strategic analysis of companies quickly and bringing results ready. Therefore, this chapter is motivated to provide an updated overview of the Computational Cognitive Techniques and application potential in Healthcare Systems, approaching its evolution and concept from a concise bibliographic background, synthesizing the potential of technology.

Keywords: Cognitive computing, healthcare, artificial intelligence, healthcare informatics, cognitive models, healthcare data, cognitive healthcare

6.1   Introduction

With the use of tools such as artificial intelligence, Cognitive Computing emerges in the field of Health, consisting of technology that impacts everyday life in Medicine. Cognitive computing arose from a mixture of cognitive science, related to the study of the human brain and how it works, along with computer science. The results have profound impacts on people's lives, especially in healthcare, business, and many other areas [1].

But AI itself, through research carried out around the world, traces its routes of transformation and development. It was among these routes, that cognitive computing emerged as an important pillar capable of offering a true revolution in Healthcare, characterized, in a very synthetic way, by the potential of self-learning of machines that, through algorithms based on data mining, using the potential of cognitive computing to analyze, for example, databases about diseases and to have the contribution of machines in the generation of insights [1, 2].

The term cognitive computing is based on the concept of artificial intelligence and machine learning (Figure 6.1) to describe a new computational era helping to reduce costs and increase the efficiency of organizations, through the crossing of data that allows more efficient management, in which systems interact with human beings through the understanding of natural language, the ability to learn, and the identification of patterns or insights that resemble human reasoning; it is also possible to work with forecasting future scenarios and prepare for them in a way more accurate, as in the case of endemic pathologies. That is, it is the intelligent machine assisting and improving the professional routine [3].

Through this technology it is possible to interpret data, language, and develop decision-making in a similar way to human reasoning; cognitive

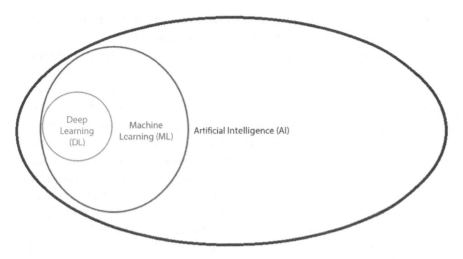

Figure 6.1 Artificial Intelligence.

computing emerges as a beacon in the scope of offering new services, treatments, and health research, and ultimately contributes to more assertive decision-making by professionals, doctors, and health managers, reflecting that doctors will see that mechanized activities will no longer be used and this change represents a benefit. Thus, it is possible to reserve more time for assistance and decision making, without worrying about the repetitive and bureaucratic part [3, 4], as well as in the organizational plans of clinics, medical centers and laboratories, and even in support of doctors and professionals in the area. These systems, when related to Health, have collaborated with oncological treatments and other specialties, with imaging exams, with the approval processes of medical requests, which start to be done more quickly, and with scientific studies [5, 6].

Making a brief analogy, traditional computing systems work from a series of instructions and algorithms, always arriving at certain answers and being unable to evolve from a certain point. In cognitive computing, systems are able to read content, understand its domain, and, from there, evaluate it in certain contexts, being able to make decisions and generate insights based on certain pieces of evidence [3, 6].

Cognitive computing came to facilitate and confront innumerable variables of information about the patient himself, with greater proficiency in diagnoses and treatments, influencing that specialists will understand this change through practical knowledge and, later, they will be able to show patients quality, speed, and the security that technology can generate. The use of cognitive computing technologies is within an Artificial Intelligence megatrend, which, according to historical records, tends to be the most innovative technological branch in the next decade [3, 7].

The goal of cognitive computing is to simulate human thought processes in a computer model, relating that with the technologies that involve cognitive computing, it is possible to cross the medical-scientific literature with the specific data of the patient at the time of the consultation. Using self-learning algorithms that use data mining, pattern recognition, and natural language processing, the computer can mimic the way the human brain works. As a result, cognitive computing systems increase the capacity of professionals beyond human limitations, so that "intelligent people and intelligent systems" can coexist in symbiosis, generating better results than the outcomes that would have been generated if they had not met [1, 8].

Inserting cognitive computing in healthcare platforms will not only be able to organize and optimize searches for patient data, having the ability to recognize and respond to data flows allows these systems to automate a variety of functions, but also assist doctors in diagnoses and decision making and even optimize research in the search for the cure of diseases, still evaluating that the performance of automated customer service agents, quality and recommendation management systems, diagnostic systems and treatments, and systems fraud analysis and investigations [8, 9].

Therefore, this chapter aims to provide an updated overview of the Computational Cognitive Techniques and application potential in Healthcare Systems, addressing and approaching its evolution, concept, with a concise bibliographic background, synthesizing the potential of technology.

6.2 Literature Concept

6.2.1 Cognitive Computing Concept

Cognitive computing is the technology that allows machines and systems to interpret data, collect information from them, and identify trends. In this relationship with information, cognitive computing also allows these systems to be able to store all the data with which they have contact, and to generate an information base, resulting in a source of knowledge [3, 4, 7, 9].

Cognitive computing (Figure 6.2) is based on self-learning systems that use machine learning techniques to perform specific tasks intelligently. The objective of cognitive computing is to simulate human thought processes

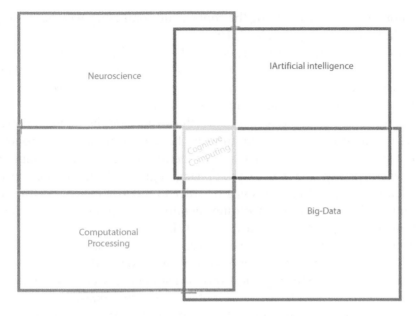

Figure 6.2 Cognitive computing.

in a computer model, through self-learning algorithms that use data mining, pattern recognition, and natural language processing [4, 10].

Over time, these systems have features that identify patterns of data and repetitions of information, enabling them to interact better with this, coupled with the premise that the more information is given, the more these systems will learn and be able to perform tasks, respond to questions, and generate insights, among other properties [10].

Cognitive Computing is a technology that has advanced to the point of making machines think and act like human beings, based on the premise of bringing them closer to a person's reasoning. Since today, any activity done in a digital environment generates data that records each action performed, and that is where the concept of cognitive computing comes in [11].

Cognitive computing uses technology and algorithms to automatically extract concepts and relationships from data, understand their meaning, and generate learning, regardless of data patterns and past experiences, expanding what people or machines could do on their own. Cognitive computing overlaps AI involving many of the same underlying technologies to power cognitive applications, including expert systems, neural networks, robotics, and virtual reality, synthesizing data from various sources of information while weighing the context and conflicting evidence to suggest the best answers possible [3, 10, 11].

Nowadays machines are increasingly able to perform functions of people, since this technology enables systems to understand data and, then, support varied demands derived from process automation, resulting in technological development derived from innovative solutions that give support to this type of activity. It is worth considering that there are three ways in which cognitive computing can be applied today, being robotic and cognitive automation to automate repetitive tasks in order to improve efficiency, quality, and accuracy; applying cognitive insights to discover hidden patterns and relationships in order to identify new opportunities for innovation; and even concerning cognitive engagement to boost client actions, offering customization at scale [12].

Cognitive computing has a very close relationship with AI (Artificial Intelligence) that enables chatbots, consisting of robots that perform simple tasks, such as answering questions in customer service chats, enabling these systems to interact with the public, answering questions as a person. The role of cognitive computing is to interpret the data offered, that is, it allows a particular machine to understand the information that was offered, process that data, and then respond to specific and desired requests [9, 12].

The relationship between cognitive computing and Machine Learning is very similar to the relationship with AI, however, it acts more on the database, enabling a system to learn from all the data it receives and understands. Thus, Machine Learning is responsible for the continuity of the work begun in the understanding that cognitive computing makes it possible, derived by making systems start to learn more and more as they come into contact with information [13].

The benefits that cognitive computing provides are combined with its adoption in processes bringing support to productivity as support for human work, operating in repetitive tasks, helping people to solve demands. Its ability to be applied in several systems helps anyone to have fewer tasks to perform, cognitive computing can automate responses, perform enrollments and schedules, in addition to handling data for strategic analysis of companies quickly and bringing results ready [14].

Automation of processes derived from automatic processes that are part of the modern work reality of any company and in most market segments such as the marketing sector with the automation of email shots, scheduling of posts on social networks, among other possibilities. Otherwise, employees would have twice as many tasks to be performed, with much greater margins of error, or even concerning financial security since it is no longer necessary for a person to conduct the entire process, no longer needing to cross-check financial data or analyze suspicious transactions, the machine solves this more simply [15].

Reduction of task complexity given that manual analysis of the result of all sales of a company, evaluating that this task, requiring time and effort, can be done by one person, without the help of software, which through complex processes and laborious can be smoothed by cognitive technology, given the volume of data. Cognitive computing performs jobs automatically, operating proactively, searching for the desired information for the best strategy as a result, ensuring that human employees have less work, redirecting that time to more technical issues [16].

It is also worth highlighting the use of cognitive systems to solve types of problems for which humans are normally asked to require large amounts of data, whether structured or unstructured, powered by machine learning algorithms. Over time, these systems are able to refine the way they identify patterns and process data to be able to anticipate new problems and model possible solutions [3, 10, 16].

6.2.1.1   Application Potential

Cognitive computing in any segment and for any level of complexity is able to offer intelligent and efficient solutions, automate tasks, and support employees. As in the case of customer service, it is one of the most common examples of the use of cognitive computing. Through chatbots they answer questions and carry out other requests from people who visit websites. Since this technological practice is more and more common, it helps real attendants to have better control over their demands, as well as to improve productivity [10, 16].

Cognitive software automates the analysis of this data, helping managers with comprehensive information to understand how departments and the company as a whole have behaved, indicating trends, repetitions and helping to evaluate the information, providing a real sense of how the company is, and then that can be done from there, giving basis to decision making. Or even concerning cognitive software, they also enable GPS technology with resources that are very inherent in the drivers' routine, through the reading of a database about traffic, street information, and dynamic events. Thus, the GPS is able to understand all of this information and then plot the best routes doing this in real-time [4, 16].

Cognitive computing also operates in investment applications by automating many of its functions, helping to reduce losses, and making notes, through the entry and exit of positions in stocks that become automated, based on the reading of the data that the financial market offers. Banks through cognitive systems come to understand behaviors acting proactively to prevent their customers from suffering any type of scam, such as improper card purchases, issuing communications to block any suspicious blocked activity. Besides, cognitive systems can still be applied to facial reading by storing details about the user's features, creating a pattern that is accessed every time a mobile device is unlocked, as a security method [17].

The use of cognitive computing provides efficiency in processes and interaction with the customer, helping companies to identify and act based on emerging patterns, given a faster and more effective response, identifies opportunities, and uncovers problems in real-time. Providing surprisingly relevant, contextual, and accurate information on broad customer-related issues [17, 18].

In financial services, a cognitive sales agent uses machine intelligence to initiate contact with promising sales and then qualify, monitor, and sustain the leadership. Analyzing through natural language to understand customers' conversation questions, dealing with hundreds, and even thousands of conversations simultaneously and in dozens of languages [18].

Cognitive technologies remove the complexity of work processes and can be used to approve a loan or financing in the financial market with the help of software, capable of processing as much data as necessary to make the best decision. Being able to read and evaluate the customer's history, their credit score, and even make predictions that consider their investment plan, still tending to make justifiable offers that align with the customer's finances and needs. Or even, this same cognitive approach can be applied to insurance companies, making it possible to predict the prices of their products with greater precision if they know the history of a driver with the aid of cognitive computing [19].

The most common uses of cognitive computing are for performing advanced classification, such as routing people and needs for the best employees to meet requirements, and for predictive analysis, how to know the best way to promote a product to a buyer [20].

Pondering on a cognitive predictive analysis (Figure 6.3), this is a technique consisting of an approach to data forwarding and interpretation that begins and ends with what is contained in the information. This unique way of approaching the totality of information (of all types and at any scale) reveals connections, patterns, and placements that enable an unprecedented and even unexpected insight. Predictive analytics can also enable meaningful business information using structured, sensor-based data, as well as unstructured data, such as unlabeled text and video, for mining customer sentiment, for example [21].

Figure 6.3 Predictive analysis.

6.2.2 Cognitive Computing in Healthcare

Generally, cognitive technology excels in cases where there is too much data for humans to classify, considering automated and fast decision making in a mass of data fundamental to modern business and where the rules of the game are well defined. Given these characteristics, cognitive computing is seen in some application examples including support for doctors in the treatment of diseases [22, 23].

Cognitive computing systems can collect information, reports, and data from different sources, such as medical journals, personal patient history, diagnostic tools, and documentation of similar treatment lines adopted in the past from different hospitals and healthcare centers, improving analysis data in the health sector. This provides the physician with evidence-based data and recommendations that can improve the level of care provided to the patient. Therefore, cognitive computing will not replace the doctor, but will simply take on the tedious job of sifting through various data sources and processing them logically [24].

Evaluating that a single patient can generate millions of gigabytes of health information in his whole life, adding the electronic medical record, medical prescription, family history, and exams provided, unfortunately, the current system present in most of the health sector, only allows us to take advantage part of this information, considering that cognitive computing allows a more informed treatment based on the patient's life data as a whole [24, 25].

Cognitive computing revolutionizes the way Health strategies are built and impacts all departments of organizations in the sector, specifically in the clinical area related to more assertive diagnoses and treatments, occurring because these solutions process data from the most varied sources extremely quickly, such as the PEP (Electronic Patient Record), data warehousing, medical knowledge portals (structured information); and even through social media and other digital sources (unstructured information) [26].

Cognitive computing can show the likelihood that a person will develop a disease based on their family history, the demographic group to which they belong, and their personal habits. Besides, it can suggest the treatment of diseases based on clinical protocols and best practices that have recently proven to be effective [10, 26].

Wearable devices act as a source of personal and individualized information about the patient; through biosensors they monitor people's vital signs and send the information, in real-time, to the hospital, clinic, or healthcare operator, due to IoT technology, objects such as watches, clothing and other accessories make it smart and essential in monitoring people in the pre, during and post-treatment period. Providing data for cognitive computing to process and analyze, even facilitating remote monitoring of patients with chronic diseases, for example. Through these preventive and predictive medicine devices, the patient understands his condition and becomes active and co-responsible for the treatment, thus avoiding that he seeks care only in emergencies, when he is ill and taking more risks, therefore needing high-cost procedures [24, 27].

Cognitive computing in Health can also help to reduce costs and increase the efficiency of organizations, by crossing data that allow more efficient management. It is also possible to work with forecasting future scenarios and prepare for them more accurately, as in the case of endemic pathologies. This method enables recommendations for therapies against cancer from the crossing of scientific literature with clinical and genetic data of the patient, bringing all possible cancer treatments and their scientific evidence, including the degree of risk and side effects. Cognitive computing also speeds up your investigation process, creating visualizations for the various possibilities, and helping to validate hypotheses, providing new perspectives for researchers to explore anticancer studies, revealing patterns [28].

Still relating that oncology is a challenging area in medicine in which cognitive intelligence has been working correlating studies, however, concerning chronic diseases, it is possible to track the entire history of a patient, acting preventively regarding diseases such as diabetes and heart disease which are treated reactively and ineffective in current medicine. Still pondering those rarer diseases, since they are those with little academic background and cognitive intelligence is able to interpret the most remote cases, bringing them together and combining real-world experience with theoretical knowledge [29].

Cognitive systems (Cognitive Computing) generally use a variety of machine learning techniques, but this technology is not a method of machine learning specifically. Instead, Cognitive Systems are more like the architecture of AI subsystems, i.e., machine learning and derivatives, that work together with associated data [28–30].

Machine Learning (Figure 6.4) emerges as a preponderant element in the area of health, dealing with an aspect of artificial intelligence, which uses a method that unites data analysis and the construction of analytical models. However, this does not happen in any way, depending on an interactive process between man and machine, concerning learning conducted by data analysts who, from the results obtained, create or improve new algorithms in order to improve your performance [30].

In Machine Learning solutions, it is possible to capture, gather, and convert a volume of data into relevant information to support decision making, considering that professionals have access to automatic responses such as the number of beds occupied, scheduled surgeries, comparison of billing per the agreement, monthly billing health institution, among others. These tools use the available databases to find and identify possible potentially pathological changes.

Machine learning techniques consist of making decisions and executing tasks based on learning by determining a set of rules, generated through the analysis of a database, or even by previously established models. The generated model recognizes patterns [31, 32].

This technology for a more practical scenario is consistent with a health plan operator using technology to mine the data records that the hospital, offices, or even each professional issued about their patients. From this selected information, it is possible to find inconsistencies or create preventive actions aimed at a specific group of users. This method can be applied in health technologies and is still a tool with the possibility of early detection of breast cancer in men and women, through an algorithm and the analysis

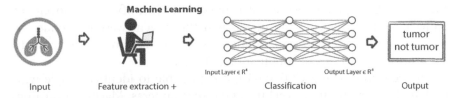

Figure 6.4 Machine learning.

of biopsies. Or even through visual analysis of individuals with diabetes to predict the possibility of developing diabetic retinopathy, a condition that can lead to blindness and significantly compromise the quality of life. Or even other fields of medicine investigating radiology with great potential to identify flaws in the interpretation of the images obtained [31, 32].

Machine Learning can have a considerable integration within the UHS (Unique Health System) mainly in developing countries like Brazil, given that the tool opens up a series of possibilities related that UHS faces many difficulties for its functioning, either due to the precarious conditions, which part of the population is submitted, due to poor management or even due to budget deviations. From the care perspective, Machine Learning can help the doctor to be more efficient, with mining and interpretation of information improving the patient's journey, and also concerning the analysis of clinical data in the country, better directing the available resources, generating even a cost reduction [33, 34].

Or even Machine Learning models of time series and prediction (techniques used to predict future results based on previously observed data) can be applied to learn the clinical states of Parkinson's disease and their corresponding progression so that doctors and patients can have a quantitative measure of an individual's illness. Disease states for chronic conditions can be considered similarly to cancer stages, with the important caveat that, in the case of chronic conditions, the connection of disease states with biological mechanisms is often not understood. However, the underlying biology of Parkinson's disease is not yet fully characterized, which makes learning and classifying stages very difficult [34].

Through Machine Learning techniques, neural networks, it is possible to assess a person's genetic sequencing in minutes, rank the most frequent and relevant mutations, cross with the most up-to-date scientific literature, and generate different treatment plans with more chances of cure, which on the contrary when analyzing traditionally, would take about hundreds of hours [35].

Or even employ Machine Learning in imaging equipment for Parkinson's patients, given that patients with this disease have a certain difficulty in performing imaging tests due to tremors, which impairs the formation of the image. Using an algorithm, it is possible to identify these movement patterns and reconstruct the image as if the patient were immobile. As well as being an alternative to sedation, that is, we have improved access to these tests for this specific population [34, 36].

Or even concerning COVID-19, it is possible to identify people with high body temperature (fever) using thermal cameras, Machine Learning, and video analysis to proactively alert employees who work in this pandemic, keep them safe, and the facilities free of the coronavirus [37].

6.2.3 Deep Learning in Healthcare

Deep Learning corresponds (Figure 6.5) essentially in deep neural networks recognizing hidden patterns and making correlations in raw data, continuously learning and improving, allowing the capture and exploration of unstructured data, such as images, videos, sounds, among others. Deep Learning architectures take simple neural networks to another level, through larger numbers of hidden layers, forming deep neural networks that enable training for machines to perform human tasks accurately, learning autonomously, without the need for human interference [28, 38].

Many diseases produce changes so small with the naked eye that they make the identification process extremely difficult since with a pattern recognition algorithm it is possible to make comparisons and distinguish problems much more effectively, issuing an accurate diagnosis of the patient's condition. For this, a large database with the most diverse types of information on cases of the same disease is used, allowing the machine to "learn" what it needs to know to make a diagnosis [38].

In addition to its great applicability with diagnoses made in advance and treatments applied as quickly as possible, it avoids complications and injuries. It is also possible that a single deep learning model associated with digital image processing can be used in various forms of diagnosis in the medical field, such as in the identification of medical complications such as diabetic retinopathy, cardiovascular risks, breast lesions, melanoma lesions, retinal diseases (from eye images), spine problems, anemia, leukocytosis, among countless other examples, even acting in the prediction of diseases [33, 38].

Or an example is in the detection of skin cancer since in diagnosis it is noticed melanomas (responsible for the highest mortality rate from skin

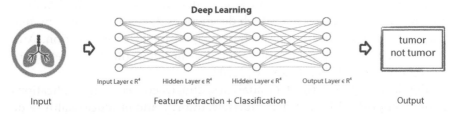

Figure 6.5 Deep learning.

cancer) and non-melanomas. Therefore, a segmentation of the images by algorithms, defining squamous cell carcinoma, basal cell carcinoma, which are the most common forms of skin cancer, or even those malignant melanomas, more lethal of skin cancer. This segmentation is done through changes in pigmentation as the characteristics most considered in detection, even though many times due to the way the image is registered, several factors must be taken into account so as not to confuse the detection algorithm, causing bad image segmentation, as is the case with lighting, environment, and instrument used in the record [39].

Deep Learning allows healthcare professionals to calculate the probability that the health status of the infected will worsen in five, ten, and thirty days, using ten variables such as age, comorbidities, and others, showing what percentage of patients infected with coronavirus that may have an aggravated state of health, which in the percentage of cases can lead to death. Or even using Deep Learning techniques to make predictions about the spread of COVID-19 with great appreciation [40].

Through the Deep Learning algorithm, it is possible to detail the operating conditions of the X-ray, Mammography, Tomography, Ultrasound, and Resonance devices, assisting in service management, performing predictive analysis from the data collected in these quality controls, which are used to predict part failures and breaks. Still calculating the exact period that the equipment will remain with acceptable levels of efficiency and credibility in the results of the exams and safety for patients and health professionals. Given the importance, if the examination involves, for example, a patient with a chronic pathology that demands numerous tests involving ionizing radiation, given that the cause of the excessively high dose to the patient can generally be attributed to the lack of procedural and technical routine of the equipment's radiographic protocols [41].

Deep Learning is transforming cancer care and medicine as a whole, given its characteristics of precision in the recognition of elements in digital imaging, it can transform radiology by distinguishing between malignant nodules and detecting patterns in medical data that can alert breast cancer. Still assessing that this pathology has a logical weakness related to time, I see that it does not grow from today to tomorrow (like COVID-19). It is a very long process, which degenerates the tissues, evaluating that the speed of its detection is the best weapon for its extermination. And pondering which Deep Learning tools are chosen as the main method of prevention against breast cancer [42, 43].

Big data (Figure 6.6), data analytics, and Deep Learning applications provide opportunities to track, illustrate, inform, and produce health value with Health Analytics. Through descriptive, predictive, and prescriptive

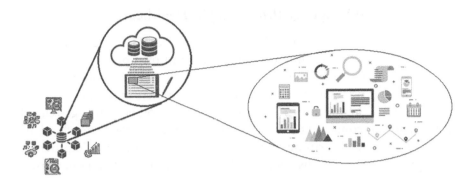

Figure 6.6 Big data.

analyses, Health Analytics models have increasingly incorporated machine learning and AI platforms, which among other features satisfy good use of analytically usable clinical data. Identifying unstructured data blocks, immersed in millions of clinical records, texts and images, without any hermeneutic rule, recognizing and providing the corresponding correspondence with the standards in Data Analytics to support health organizations in 'searching' and mining medical records doctors, separating and extracting what is relevant while coding the result obtained with standardized and interoperable terminologies [44].

It is worth mentioning the importance of anonymizing personal data from diagnostic imaging tests and biomedical signs, as they are considered personal data, all the information by which it is possible to identify the patient, such as name, age, date of birth, among others. These data are inserted in the exams of images and biomedical signs in the watermark format and are essential to ensure patient safety since this information cannot be shared with third parties without the patient's prior consent [33, 44].

Given this and based on AI and using Deep Learning methods, it is possible to generate anonymization of these personal data in medical image and biomedical signs exams, by ensuring that there is no identification of the information with the patient to which they refer, opening the way for processing large volumes of exam data in scientific research for new diagnostics and treatments [45].

Using Deep Learning it is possible to improve the way coronary heart disease is tested and treated, using a 3D human heart model, applying the technology it is possible to predict the impacts of blockages (coronary clogging) on blood flows and prescribe a treatment plan more effective and without the need for invasive surgery [46].

6.2.4   Natural Language Processing in Healthcare

Natural language processing (NLP) is an aspect of AI that enables computers to understand (Figure 6.7), interpret, and manipulate human language, seeking to bridge the gap between human communication and the understanding of computers. Also helping computers communicate with human beings in their own language and scale other language-related tasks, enabling computers to read texts, hear and interpret speech, identify feelings, and determine which passages are important. Considering the gigantic amount of unstructured data that is generated every day, from medical records to social media, automation will be essential for a complete and efficient text and speech analysis [47].

NLP applications can interpret patient questionnaires, converting text to voice, or even turning audio into writing, understanding the variations and intentions of the questions, bringing the most appropriate answer. It provides patients with the possibility of working with a kind of virtual assistant, which allows the quick search for strategic information about the Health institution in a natural, and interactive way with the receipt of responses by text or voice. The technology applied in healthcare is possible by collecting voice recordings from hundreds of patients and feeding Deep Learning software that compares the voices of potential patients with those of healthy people, in order to establish clear enough standards to recognize indicators of diseases through voices [48–50].

Based on collecting voice samples from war veterans and analyzing vocal cues such as tone, articulation, rhythm, and volume to identify invisible

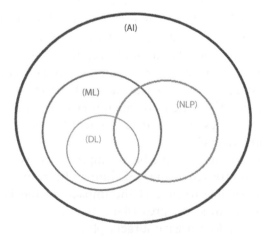

Figure 6.7 Natural language processing.

disorders such as PTSD (Posttraumatic Stress Disorder), Traumatic Brain Injury, and even Depression, using NLP techniques Through Deep Learning to explore the characteristics of the voice, the algorithms select vocal patterns in people with these conditions and compare them with voice samples from healthy people, in order to decrease the suicide rate among members of the military [50].

Software with NLP technology has the potential to transmute much of all blocked medical data in an unstructured format to a structured format, revealing information hidden in unstructured clinical data. Accelerating the analytics of the unstructured data by quickly identifying through predictive research, they are generating extraordinary silos of pandemic data that can serve in clinical pharmaceutical or epidemiological research regarding COVID-19. It is possible to apply NLP by unlocking hidden information concerning critical patient information lost in medical notes that can be extracted and mapped by NLP technology, generating better-informed care by crossing barriers between isolated data in health systems [49, 51].

Through electronic medical records, it is possible to collect data for clinical analysis, related to specific symptoms, diagnoses derived from echocardiogram reports, benchmarking classifications, which are not easily accessible and analyzed. Given the potential of NLP, the technology extracts data from clinical notes for cardiac patients. It evaluates equipment failure performance through data extracted from electronic medical records, consisting of deeper information on how to improve implants. Or those important metrics in cardiology like measuring the ejection fraction; symptoms such as shortness of breath, fatigue, and palpitations, allowing for a better analysis of structured data, thus achieving better decision-making for treatment [52].

Or even considering that through these tools powered by data it is possible to train dialogue systems, enabling high-level natural language processing. Enabling its best application in the current critical demands of clinics and health institutions, improving customer service, training virtual assistants, monitoring social networks, among other possibilities. The NLP technology can be used in health to design classification models based on medical record texts, separating the sentence by each word, space, and punctuation, thus forming a list of tokens referring to the past sequence, such as disease classification or screening for some medical specialty based on the evolution of the medical record [48, 49, 53].

Automated recognition is an essential resource for NLP in medicine since it is possible to be used to process scientific texts, in the translation of medical terms, related to the processing of clinical language by extracting information from documents by relevance [54].

6.3 Discussion

Today, Cognitive Computing is the most advanced technology for the analysis and understanding of unstructured data, making it possible to transform obscure data into valuable information and competitive advantage, which represent most of the information available in the digital environment. Only with this type of technology. This can be applied from understanding data in its most different formats such as images, films, and even in the lines.

Technological advances increasingly cover the health area, allowing the use of tools such as AI to benefit medical work, which is increasing every day and, therefore, traditional methods of care, involving paper and pen, are considered outdated by some professionals.

The technology has reached several medical procedures, providing more safety to the patient, they have also collaborated with oncological treatments and other specialties, with imaging exams, with the approval processes of medical requests, which can be done more quickly, and with studies scientific. All these factors and technological changes have potentially affected the relationship between the doctor and the patient, who now receives better and personalized service.

Cognitive technology for the future of healthcare creates an environment in which expectations are more than positive and should benefit the routine of doctors, combining data mining (functionality that aggregates and organizes data, finding patterns, associations, changes, and anomalies in them) relevant), improves the conduct of operational processes and promotes the development of personalized and more effective clinical treatments.

Still reflecting that some specialties can be highlighted by the precision effect generated by cognitive computing such as Oncology, Radiology, Dermatology, Ophthalmology, Pediatrics, Pneumology, Thoracic Surgery, Cardiology, Angiology, Neurosurgery, Nuclear Medicine and many others. Since cognitive computing came to facilitate and confront numerous variables of information about the patient himself, with greater proficiency in diagnoses and treatments.

Or even, cognitive computing is able to develop a digital health assistant to fully monitor the patient's treatment, able to remind him of the right time to take his medications, and also providing health content according to the user's illnesses.

In underdeveloped and developing countries, the existence of related problems, such as medical errors, which generate hundreds of deaths per year, or serious disorders for patients, can still be eradicated. Since the applicability of this technology has efficiency extended to other medical specialties, in this way, the patient's journey, within any health institution, is finally safe and reliable.

Through technology, medical specialists will understand this benefit through practical knowledge, which results in more time for care and decision making, without concern for the repetitive part of the profession and the medical field. Still showing patients the quality, speed, and security that technology can generate, and the trust on both sides.

Also mentioning that for a medical professional to keep up to date, it is necessary to study, specialist training, and yet hours of study per day. Likewise, cognitive systems powered by artificial intelligence increase the capacity of professionals beyond human limitations, making it possible to coexist in symbiosis, generating better results than the outcomes that would have been generated if they had not met.

Cognitive systems can also use not only data from their repository but also real-time information captured through the Internet of Things (IoT) sensors to monitor everyday actions. Assessing that the information can even come from implants, which can make doctors or emergency take preventive actions to prevent unwanted events.

Even if making an analogy, the human brain is no longer sufficient hardware to process all this information generated, derived from the enormous volume of medical knowledge and health data that exist in the world today, only tending to increase. Exemplifying the potential of cognitive technology capable of ranking personalized treatment plans according to patient's clinical data at the time of consultation, still focusing on Precision Medicine and Genomics, making it possible to identify patterns that allow, by algorithm, to predict a hypoglycemic episode three hours before in patients.

6.4 Trends

Among the next developments, computers will go beyond assisted learning, a growing trend is for machines that learn by interacting with competing algorithms or networks (GAN). This is a very advanced topic in machine learning, as it is a cutting-edge technology although mathematically complex, it is extremely simple to understand and to implement. Two neural networks are created, a generator and a discriminator, giving the objective of distinguishing between real and falsified data (discriminator), and the generator is given the objective of deceiving the discriminator, generating data that resemble reality [55].

The future is likely to be characterized by cognitive machines interacting with algorithms defined as general-purpose AI; i.e. that can be used in areas of expertise beyond the area (domain) they were originally created. That is, they are transferable and, in turn, can generate a computation code autonomously improving their own performance. Transfer Learning is related to the reuse of a pre-trained model in a new problem, that is, using a neural network trained in another set of data, usually larger, to solve a new problem. The need and reason for using Transfer Learning is the difficulty of obtaining a large enough data set about a given problem, still relating that very deep CNN (Convolutional Neural network) stems from a lot of computational processing power to be trained [56].

The fact is that Cognitive Computing is extremely powerful and there is a way to learn and understand how to get all the benefits of this technology. Given the breadth that Cognitive Systems complement and increase human capacities, they will increasingly differentiate themselves by the capacity of the 'man + machine' work [57].

6.5   Conclusions

The use of artificial intelligence and cognitive computing in health provides agility, mobility, patient safety, and assertiveness in decision-making, from the best diagnosis to competitive business strategies, engagement with patients, support for the clinical decision, and support for scientific discovery. The technology is based on the concept of computational intelligence and machine learning, describing that systems interact with human beings through the understanding of natural language, the ability to learn, and the identification of patterns or insights that resemble human reasoning

Cognitive computing can also help to reduce costs and increase the efficiency of organizations, by crossing data that allows more efficient management. From the patient's point of view, through these preventive and predictive medicine devices, the patient understands his condition and becomes active and co-responsible for the treatment, thus preventing him from seeking care only in emergencies, when he is ill and taking more risks, needing, therefore, high-cost procedures.

This is the big difference between traditional and cognitive computing, while traditional systems work from a series of instructions and algorithms, based on rigid mathematical models, always arriving at certain answers and being unable to evolve from a certain point. In cognitive computing, it is based on models of neural networks and statistical and probabilistic models of in-depth learning, enabling systems to be able to read content, understand its domain, and, from there, evaluate it against certain contexts, capable of still making decisions and generating insights based on certain evidence.

However, it is important to highlight that technology will not be a substitute for human beings, emphasizing that the physician continues to play a prominent role in the treatment and is responsible for the first contact, screening, and final diagnosis of a patient, as well as ensuring their safety throughout the process.

In this sense, with the evolution and the increased use of artificial intelligence, it was possible the advent of techniques such as cognitive computing has restructured medical work, but there is still much to transform In the same way that the telephone did not replace the human voice, but expanded its range, artificial intelligence will increase people's brain potential.

References

1. Behera, R.K., Bala, P.K., Dhir, A., The emerging role of cognitive computing in healthcare: A systematic literature review. *Int. J. Med. Inform.*, 129, 154–166, 2019.
2. Kwak, G.H. and Hui, P., DeepHealth: Review and challenges of artificial intelligence in health informatics, 2019. arXiv preprint arXiv:1909.00384.
3. Chen, M., Herrera, F., Hwang, K., Cognitive computing: Architecture, technologies and intelligent applications. *IEEE Access*, 6, 19774–19783, 2018.
4. Gupta, S. *et al.*, Big data with cognitive computing a review for the future. *Int. J. Inf. Manage.*, 42, 78–89, 2018.
5. Havaei, M. *et al.*, Deep learning trends for focal brain pathology segmentation in MRI, in: *Machine Learning for Health Informatics*, pp. 125–148, Springer, Cham, 2016.
6. Beaulieu-Jones, B. *et al.*, Trends and focus of machine learning applications for health research. *JAMA Network Open*, 2, 10, e1914051–e1914051, 2019.
7. Sangaiah, A.K., Thangavelu, A., Sundaram, V.M., Cognitive computing for Big Data systems over IoT. *Gewerbestrasse*, 11, 6330, 2018.
8. Vroegindeweij, R. and Carvalho, A., Do healthcare workers need cognitive computing technologies? A qualitative study involving IBM Watson and Dutch professionals. *J. Midwest Assoc. Inf. Syst. (JMWAIS)*, 1, 51–68, 2019.
9. Bini, S.A., Artificial intelligence, machine learning, deep learning, and cognitive computing: What do these terms mean and how will they impact healthcare? *J. Arthroplasty*, 33, 8, 2358–2361, 2018.
10. Raghavan, V.V. *et al.*, *Cognitive computing: Theory and applications*, Elsevier, Amsterdam, Netherlands, 2016.

11. Wang, Y. *et al.*, Cognitive informatics: Towards cognitive machine learning and autonomous knowledge manipulation. *Int. J. Cogn. Inf. Natural Intell. (IJCINI)*, 12, 1, 1–13, 2018.

12. Alpaydin, E., *Machine learning: The new AI*, MIT Press, Cambridge, Massachusetts, EUA, 2016.

13. Chen, W. *et al.*, Review on deep-learning-based cognitive computing. *Acta Automat. Sin.*, 43, 11, 1886–1897, 2017.

14. Tarafdar, M., Beath, C.M., Ross, J.W., Enterprise cognitive computingapplications: Opportunities and challenges. *IT Prof.*, 19, 4, 21–27, 2017.

15. Rigger, E., Munzer, C., Shea, K., Estimating the potential of state of the art design automation-tasks, methods, and benefits. *DS 84: Proceedings of the DESIGN 2016 14th International Design Conference*, 2016.

16. Tatasciore, M. *et al.*, The benefits and costs of low and high degree of automation. *Hum. Factors*, 62, 6, 874–896, 2020.

17. Kharb, L., A perspective view on commercialization of cognitive computing. *2018 8th International Conference on Cloud Computing, Data Science & Engineering (Confluence)*, IEEE, 2018.

18. Pramanik, P.K.D., Pal, S., Choudhury, P., Beyond automation: The cognitive IoT. artificial intelligence brings sense to the Internet of Things, in: *Cognitive Computing for Big Data Systems Over IoT*, pp. 1–37, Springer, Cham, 2018.

19. Zebec, A., Cognitive BPM: Business Process Automation and Innovation with Artificial Intelligence. *BPM (Ph.D./Demos)*, 2019.

20. Lytras, M., Visvizi, A., Zhang, X., Aljohani, N.R., Cognitive computing, big data analytics and data driven industrial marketing. *Ind. Mark. Manage.*, 90, 663–666, 2020.

21. Marchevsky, A.M., Walts, A.E., Wick, M.R., Evidence-based pathology in its second decade: Toward probabilistic cognitive computing. *Hum. Pathol.*, 61, 1–8, 2017.

22. Hwang, K. and Chen, M., *Big-data analytics for cloud, IoT and cognitive computing*, John Wiley & Sons, Hoboken, New Jersey, USA, 2017.

23. França, R.P. *et al.*, A Proposal Based on Discrete Events for Improvement of the Transmission Channels in Cloud Environments and Big Data, in: *Big Data, IoT, and Machine Learning: Tools and Applications*, vol. 185, 2020.

24. França, R.P., Iano, Y., Monteiro, A.C.B., Arthur, R., A methodology for improving efficiency in data transmission in healthcare. *Internet Things Healthc. Technol.*, 73, 49, 21, 2020.

25. França, R.P. *et al.*, Potential proposal to improve data transmission in healthcare systems, in: *Deep Learning Techniques for Biomedical and Health Informatics*, pp. 267–283, Academic Press, Cambridge, Massachusetts, EUA, 2020.

26. França, R.P. *et al.*, Potential model for improvement of the data transmission in healthcare systems. In: *International Symposium on Immunobiological, 4., 2019; Seminário Anual Científico e Tecnológico de Bio-Manguinhos, 7., 2019*, Rio de Janeiro. Anais... Rio de Janeiro: Bio-Manguinhos, p. 161, 2019.

27. Chen, M. *et al.*, Edge cognitive computing system. *Future Gener. Comput. Syst.*, 86, 403–411, 2018.

28. Monteiro, A.C.B. *et al.*, Development of a laboratory medical algorithm for simultaneous detection and counting of erythrocytes and leukocytes in digital images of a blood smear, in: *Deep Learning Techniques for Biomedical and Health Informatics*, pp. 165–186, Academic Press, Cambridge, Massachusetts, EUA, 2020.

29. Somashekhar, S.P. *et al.*, Early experience with IBM Watson for Oncology (WFO) cognitive computing system for lung and colorectal cancer treatment. *J. Clin. Oncol., 35, 15_suppl*, 8527–8527, 2017.

30. Chen, M. *et al.*, Disease prediction by machine learning over big data from healthcare communities. *IEEE Access*, 5, 8869–8879, 2017.

31. Holzinger, A., Machine learning for health informatics, in: *Machine Learning for Health Informatics*, pp. 1–24, Springer, Cham, 2016.

32. Dua, S., Acharya, U.R., Dua, P., *Machine learning in healthcare informatics*, vol. 56, Springer, Berlin, 2014.

33. Santos, H.G.D. *et al.*, Machine learning for predictive analyses in health: an example of an application to predict death in the elderly in São Paulo, Brazil. *Cad. Saude Publica*, 35, 7, 19, 2019.

34. Monteiro, A.C.B., Proposta de uma metodologia de segmentação de imagens para detecção e contagem de hemácias e leucócitos através do algoritmo WT-MO. 1 recurso online p. 128, Dissertação (mestrado) - Universidade Estadual de Campinas, Faculdade de Engenharia Elétrica e de Computação, Campinas, SP., 2019. Disponível em: https://hdl.handle.net/20.500.12733/1637257. Acesso em: 2 jun. 2022.

35. Salvatore, C. *et al.*, Machine learning on brain MRI data for differential diagnosis of Parkinson's disease and Progressive Supranuclear Palsy. *J. Neurosci. Methods*, 222, 230–237, 2014.

36. Sternberg, M.J.E. *et al.*, Application of machine learning to structural molecular biology. *Ser. Philos. Trans. R. Soc London B: Biol. Sci.*, 344, 1310, 365–371, 1994.

37. Kubota, K.J., Chen, J.A., Little, M.A., Machine learning for large-scale wearable sensor data in Parkinson's disease: Concepts, promises, pitfalls, and futures. *Movement Disord.*, 31, 9, 1314–1326, 2016.

38. Alimadadi, A. *et al.*, Artificial intelligence and machine learning to fight COVID-19. *Physiol. Genomics*, 52, 4, 200–202, 2020. https://doi.org/10.1152/physiolgenomics.00029.2020

39. Srivastava, S. *et al.*, Deep learning for health informatics: Recent trends and future directions. *2017 International Conference on Advances in Computing, Communications, and Informatics (ICACCI)*, IEEE, 2017.

40. Jafari, M.H. *et al.*, Skin lesion segmentation in clinical images using deep learning. *2016 23rd International conference on pattern recognition (ICPR)*, IEEE, 2016.

41. Zhao, R. *et al.*, Deep learning and its applications to machine health monitoring. *Mech. Syst. Signal Process.*, 115, 213–237, 2019.

42. Hinton, G., Deep learning—a technology with the potential to transform healthcare. *JAMA*, 320, 11, 1101–1102, 2018.

43. Brunese, L. *et al.*, Explainable deep learning for pulmonary disease and coronavirus COVID-19 detection from X-rays. *Comput. Methods Programs Biomed.*, 196, 105608, 2020.

44. Song, Y., Zheng, S., Li, L., Zhang, X., Zhang, X., Huang, Z., Chen, J., Wang, R., Zhao, H., Chong, Y., Shen, J., Deep learning enables accurate diagnosis of novel coronavirus (COVID-19) with CT images. *IEEE/ACM Trans. Comput. Biol. Bioinform.*, 18, 6, 2775–2780, 2021.

45. França, R.P. *et al.*, Big Data and Cloud Computing: A Technological and Literary Background, in: *Advanced deep learning applications in big data analytics*, pp. 29–50, 2021, IGI Global, Hershey, Pennsylvania, USA, 2021

46. França, R.P. *et al.*, Improvement of the Transmission of Information for ICT Techniques Through CBEDE Methodology, in: *Utilizing educational data mining techniques for improved learning emerging research and Opportunities*, pp. 13–34, IGI Global, Pennsylvania, USA, 2020.

47. Madani, A. *et al.*, Fast and accurate view classification of echocardiograms using deep learning. *NPJ Digit. Med.*, 1, 1, 1–8, 2018.

48. Indurkhya, N. and Damerau, F.J., *Handbook of natural language processing*, vol. 2, CRC Press, Boca Raton, Flórida, EUA, 2010.

49. Friedman, C. and Elhadad, N., Natural language processing in healthcare and biomedicine, in: *Biomedical informatics*, pp. 255–284, Springer, London, Switzerland, AG, 2014.

50. Friedman, C. and Hripcsak, G., Natural language processing and its future in medicine. *Acad. Med.*, 74, 8, 890–5, 1999.

51. Travieso, C.M. *et al.*, Detection of different voice diseases based on the nonlinear characterization of speech signals. *Expert Syst. Appl.*, 82, 184–195, 2017.

52. Neuraz, A. *et al.*, Natural language processing for rapid response to emergent diseases: Case study of calcium channel blockers and hypertension in the COVID-19 pandemic. *J. Med. Internet Res.*, 22, 8, e20773, 2020.

53. Chen, L. *et al.*, Using natural language processingto extract clinically useful information from Chinese electronic medical records. *Int. J. Med. Inform.*, 124, 6–12, 2019.

54. Wang, S., Ren, F., Lu, H., A review of the application of natural language processing in clinical medicine. *2018 13th IEEE Conference on Industrial Electronics and Applications (ICIEA)*, IEEE, 2018.

55. Khurana, D., Koli, A., Khatter, K., Singh, S., Natural language processing: State of the art, current trends and challenges, 2017. arXiv preprint arXiv:1708.05148.

56. Mirsky, Y. *et al.*, CT-GAN: Malicious tampering of 3D medical imagery using deep learning. *28th {USENIX} Security Symposium ({USENIX} Security*, vol. 19, 2019.

57. Paul, R. *et al.*, Convolutional Neural Network ensembles for accurate lung nodule malignancy prediction 2 years in the future. *Comput. Biol. Med.*, 122, 103882, 2020.

7

Protecting Patient Data with 2F- Authentication

**G. S. Pradeep Ghantasala[1]*, Anu Radha Reddy[2]
and R. Mohan Krishna Ayyappa[3]**

*[1]Department of Computer Science and Engineering, Chitkara University Institute
of Engineering and Technology, Chitkara University, Punjab, India
[2]Department of Computer Science and Engineering, Malla Reddy Institute
of Technology and Science, Telangana, India
[3]Department of Computer Science and Engineering, Mahatma Gandhi Institute
of Technology, Telangana, India*

Abstract

At present, the healthcare business is implementing new bits of knowledge hastily. Mostly, the Data Skill, which is castoff to support surgeons and patients identical individually, and to advance the conveyance of healthcare amenities. The entire vital segment of an infirmary info association currently is located in the Electronic Health Record (EHR), where patient data is stored. Moreover, an uncountable number of claims are cast off by the infirmary supervised to display the therapeutic ability's concert in rapports of fiscal effectiveness and handling triumph tariffs. In accumulation to this, regime and centralized system of government as well use IT resolutions to crisscross the eminence and protection of healthcare associations. Furthermore, patients practice several fitness intensive care applications and strategies to monitor their vitals and to interconnect with surgeons over portable and tuner devices. These days as supercomputers have turned out to be a crucial portion of our day-to-day subsistence, it is progressively significant that information safety has similarly positioned obverse and center on our tilt of significances. Primarily in the healthcare business, wherever views are frequently attentive on redeemable somebody's lifespan and accurately, therefore, but safeguarding admittance to boundaries and mainframe structures that hoard private information like therapeutic histories is

*Corresponding author: ggspradeep@gmail.com
G. S. Pradeep Ghantasala: ORCID: https://orcid.org/0000-0001-6817-0266
Anu Radha Reddy: ORCID: https://orcid.org/0000-0002-4045-1434
R. Mohan Krishna Ayyappa: ORCID: https://orcid.org/0000-0001-5672-1518

D. Sumathi, T. Poongodi, B. Balamurugan and Lakshmana Kumar Ramasamy (eds.)
Cognitive Intelligence and Big Data in Healthcare, (169–196) © 2022 Scrivener Publishing LLC

similarly a critical aspect to reflect. Information safety is a conforming deed amid monitoring admittance to data while permitting unrestricted and informal admittance to individuals who want it. One more significant motive is the feeble fortification of patient's information in health organizations. Economic organizations like tiers partake previously formed robust prearrangement of information safety. The two-factor verification has to turn out to be a widespread usual for levels. The level permits its customer admittance to the data solitary afterwards entering the One-Time Codeword. Nonetheless, on the opposite, in communal fitness connotations, such organizations have not actually instigated in a stretched period, and therefore they develop an open quarry for the replicated offenders.

Keywords: Electronic health records, information security, privacy, patient's information, authentication, big data, healthcare system

7.1   Introduction

Big data has radically altered how companies in every sector handle, evaluate, and exploit data. Fitness concern is one of the most exciting areas where you can apply appropriate big data to make a difference. Big fitness concern information has incredible potential for optimizing patient safety, predicting illness outbreaks, obtaining useful information, preventing preventable diseases, rising fitness concern deliverance costs and enhancing the overall excellence of verve. Nonetheless, it is an exigent assignment to agree on the appropriate uses of information while protecting protection and the right of a patient to privacy [1]. Big data, no matterhow important it is for advancing therapeutic research and essential to the progress of all fitness concern organizations, should only be used when resolving protection and seclusion concerns. It is important to recognize the shortcomings of current approaches and to imagine avenues for outlook exploration to ensure a stable and reliable huge information environment.

A shift for the universal fitness concern manufacturing is the new standard. In reality, for the near future, the digitization of fitness and patient records undergoes a drastic and profound change in the clinical, organizational and industry models and, commonly, in the economic world. This shift is motivated by era populations and shifts in lifestyles; the proliferation of electronic apps and mobile devices; creative treatments; increased emphasis on quality and affordability of concern; and evidence-based remedy as opposed to discretionary scientific conclusions – all of which provide significant prospects to promote clinical decision-making, enhance fitness care delivery.

Big data analytics in the fitness concern sector has various benefits, opportunities and tremendous perspective for fitness concern change, but it faces many obstacles and challenges. Nonetheless, questions about the protection and privacy of the big fitness care [2] data are growing year by year. Healthcare organizations have discovered that a hasty, technology-centric strategy from the ground up to set protection and confidentiality policies are not enough to save from harm to the business and its customers. Each of these, conversely, poses emerging problems:

(i) the cognitive sophistication of CPS-IoT may direct to volatile rising behavior;

(ii) cognitive CPS-IoT may undergo since predictable CPS-IoT susceptibility and intimidation, and novel intimidation associated with their intrinsic cognitive functionality;

(iii) 75% of the majority of widely IoT Systems Used could be hacked; 85%of such devices can radiate.

Fitness concerns and knowledge systems are further important, complex, and integrated than ever (Figure 7.1). Although enhancing clinical outcomes and changing medical delivery [3] while enhancing human life, nevertheless is increasingly concerned about the security of data and computers in healthcare. Growing interconnectivity has shown the therapeutic apparatus services and systems to novel susceptibility in cyber security. This makes the fitness concern business the most susceptible to grave refuge intimidation. The circumstances are compounded by the fitness concern classifications and infrastructures allowed by CPS-IoT, susceptible for a series of increasing cyber-attacks. CPS-IoT classifications remain known for instance decisive protection systems [4] and fortification systems, which contain complexity, interconnectivity, heterogeneity, which are cross-organizational characteristics that offer an expanded surface of attack.

Cyber security is a concept that seems old-fashioned, but as more and more people's personal information continues to be customers, health clients and patients are moving online year after year, a growing problem. In 2017, the distinctiveness Fraud Resource Center calculated that safety infringes ranked second in terms of most breaches in the area of medicinal and healthcare, representing 25.7% of the 1,600 breaches reported during the year. Credit cards among hackers were still higher, but it has become popular in the last 5 years to hold patient information hostage and some hospitals and data breaches of health system systems [5].

Cyber security attacks can potentially lead to user privacy breaches, physical injury, financial losses and human life coercion, and are vital to avoiding them. Investigation demonstrates the increase of attacks and the rise in stealing of patient information, utilizing millions of universal stolen therapeutic reports. The increase in cyber-physical assaults tells us that

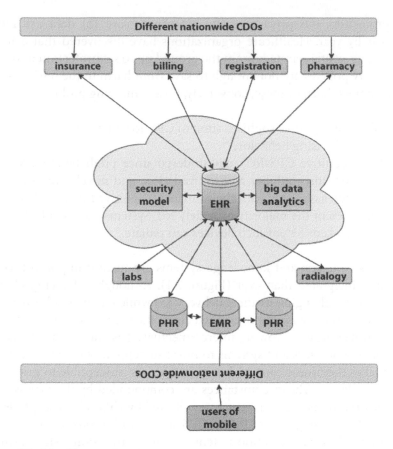

Figure 7.1 A healthcare safe system.

the existing security strategies are incapable of resolving the nature, intricacy, ambiguity andhigh connectivity of fitness services powered by CPS-IoT and decisive infrastructure. Cognitive structural design and artificial intelligence can develop programmed, elegant information security decision-making procedures utilizing expertise.

In addition, attackers can acclimatize their tactics to the security situation and contradict actions recently organized. Therefore, groundbreaking techniques for developing cognitive cyber security for healthcare environments allowed by CPS-IoT are crucially needed. This suggested and commences a methodology and theory of cognitive cyber security that facilitates the revise of the actions via understanding their intentions, anticipating and forecasting their involvement, and correlating them with the operation of To help prevent promising attacks, CPS- IoT and critical infrastructure systems.

In modern years, the e-healthcare system is gaining more popularity due to the growing influx of patients daily. For implementation as a real-time application, a multi-dimensional view is needed in the e-health-care system. Before use, we have to address the following questions: what is the computational power we need to construct the structure and what are the security steps we have taken? We need to clear up two aspects of data management [6] and the preservation of data in every sort of production of the information system. Data security [7] is one of the most relevant work fields for most of the system's information. e-Health services are one of the preeminent examples of the information system.

Medical records are the most critical personal records and useful knowledge in e-healthcare networks. Maintaining protection for this information system is very necessary to maintain discretion. Currently, many of the clinics have the best treatment with improved online facilities in e-health-care. Patients can view documents from their location, are hardcopy files, tablet information, test reports, and scan reports not to hold health records [8]. This is translated to digital data and stored at a central position call-ing as a server. The hospitals will administer the server, and a database manager will be assigned to one of the IT specialties. When a novel patient arrives for a check-up or common health Survey then the patent gathers a novel patient ID and further similar information.

The hospice will administer the server, and a documentation manager will be allocated to one of the IT specialties. When a novel patient arrives for a check-up or common fitness enquiry then the patent gathers a novel patient ID and other associated information. The hospice will keep the individual patient records and accurate every time the particulars of the check-up are altered. The digital credentials accessible from everywhere came from a distant area [9].

Each hospice goes forward and preserves an e-health appliance with appropriate sanctuary characteristics. Patients should view their informa-tion using the person's patient ID and Patient Login Password. When an endorsement is checked then access to the records is enabled. It is one of the traditional system confirmation methods and it is to assault during the susceptible strait contact by the identified/unidentified populace.

Fitness concern is a multi-dimensional program developed solely for the avoidance, analysis, and handling of individual health-related syndrome or impairments. Fitness concern practitioners, fitness concern services health centers, hospices for the precondition of medication and other investiga-tive or behavior skills and a funding action sustaining the previous two are the main components of the fitness concern method [10].

Fitness concern practitioner belongs to various fitness concern fields such as dentistry, pharmacy, midwives, nursing, counseling, physiotherapy

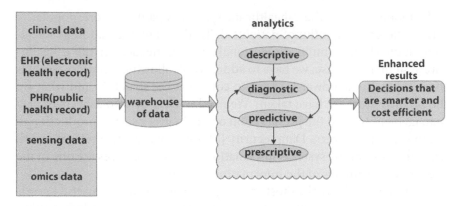

Figure 7.2 Big data analytics workflows.

and many others. Depending on the sternness of the case, fitness concern is provided on many levels. It is provided by physicians as the initial point of contact for primary care, disaster concern relating to qualified practitioners specific therapeutic investigation and treatment (Figure 7.2) and predominantly unusual analytical or surgicalmeasures.

Data warehouses hoard enormous quantities of information that are produced from a variety of resources. Such information is processed utilizing computational pipelines for smarter and other affordable fitness concern alternatives.

Comparable to EHR, the regular medical and medical information obtained from the patients are enclosed in an Electronic Medical Record (EMR) [11]. Cooperatively, Personal Health Record (PHR), EMRs, Medical Practice Management Program (MPM) [12], EHRs, and various further fitness concern expertise mechanisms can advance fitness concern eminence, service performance and expenses along with the medicinal faults. Big fitness concern information covers fitness concern person paying information such as EMRDs, pharmacy orders and medicinal proceedings as well as genomics-driven revise and further information composed from the Internet of Things smart website.

The supervising and use of this fitness concern information has become mainly reliant on IT. The creation and use of wellness tracking tools and related applications accomplished of generating cautions and substitute a patient's fitness interrelated information utilizing the particular fitness concern providers has gained traction, in particular by increasing a biomedical and security supervising association in real time. These apparatus construct a huge quantity of information that can be evaluated to endow with therapeutic [13] or medical concern in real-time.

For a long time, software users have had access to two-factor authentication, and organizations and institutions started introducing to improve digital security, optional two-factor authentication a few years ago. More colleges and sanatoriums are now switching from discretionary to obligatory verification with two factors and staff worn for two-factor authentication must adapt to using two-factor authentication in their workflow for their personal digital life.

7.2   Literature Survey

Kim *et al.* [14] suggested two ID-based secret word verification systems, utilizing smart card and fingerprint, which do not include a secret word lexicon or verification tables. Instigator assertsthat users can freely change their passwords in these schemes. This system, even without synchronization clocks, can withstand the message reaction attack. The two schemes proposed to require a scheme to validate every addict by every user's awareness, tenure and biometrics, and the dramatist asserts that this facet allows the planned schemes additional consistent.

Ming Chen *et al.* [14] suggested tripartite key substitute etiquette for authenticating passwords. Instigator claims that the proposed system is stable with a Stolen Assault on Smart Cards. Ming Chen *et al.* endow with a sanctuary evaluation to exhibit that the etiquette is immobile protected whether an intruder steals confidential data stored in a smart card.

Diffie and Hellman [15] developed a Model of the key configuration known as the Diffie–Hellman Key swap over many of revise with investigate papers [16] are written. Use of the AuthenticDiffie and Hellman [17] developed The Diffie-Hellman Key Exchange is a key setup model and a lot of study and analysis papers [18] are written. Using the Authenticated Key Exchange Protocols (AKE) definition, the rationale of the AKE protocol is to allow authenticating and creating a common session key used for encryption and definition, two communications entities.

An efficient statement and computation, authenticated three-party key agreement protocol devoid of synchronization of password, and clock and systematic sanctuary analysis using rationale from Burrows-Abadi-Needham were proposed by Xiong Li *et al.* [19].

Different AKE protocols consent to contestants holding details like that a secret, such as a hashed value [20]. Of course, the safest way to keep these secrets in mind might be, but realizing that it is simply unworkable for humans. That's why, to store this sensitive information, we need a computer. The definition of the Authenticated Key Exchange Protocols (AKE). The AKE protocol aims to enable the authentication of two communication entities and to build used for encryption and definition, a standard session key.

SK Hafiz Islam *et al.* [21] proposed An ECC-based protocol for two-factor authentication that was anonymous moreover proved effective. The random oracle model tests our protocol and has been formally guarded against The Diffie-Hellman Computational Dilemma is the assumption of hardness. The performance review showed that it outperformed by our protocol other current designs as of the viewpoint of the sanctuary, reliability along with device costs.

Xian *et al.* [22] prove that the Farah and Atari protocol [23] are unable to avoid impersonation Attacks Guessing Attacks and Offline Login. Xian *et al.* planned an enhanced 3 PAKE Chaotic maps-based protocol through the same advantages to address their security limitations. Furthermore, he applied the structured testing method Pro Verify based on pi-calculus to demonstrate that the projected 3 PAKE protocol accomplishes substantiation and protection.

Farah *et al.* [24] showed that if the smart card is compromised and the information stored on the smart the Yen *et al.* [25] the device is defenseless to off-line password presumption assault, user imposture attack, and server imposture assault. The card is exposed. Farah *et al.* implemented an enhanced method of authentication based on smart cards that not only overcome the security flaws of the related systems but also reduce the cost of computing.

Farah *et al.* [26] scheme offers confidentiality and intractability to the user and enables a user without notifying the remote server to change his/her password. Islam *et al.* [27], suggested strengthening the protocol for Xu *et al.* [28], a two-factor authentication protocol for TMIS, using elliptic curve cryptography (ECC). They also asserted that their enhancement Protocol is effectiveand that all safety criteria are met.

Chaudhry *et al.* [29] have shown that the protocol Islam *et al.* [30] is suffering from consumer attacks on impersonation and impersonation websites. In addition to this, Chaudhry *et al.* suggested an improved policy and procedure, thus providing every principle of Islam *et al.* that holds back the entire suspected attacks.

Zhang *et al.* [31] suggested that the framework of Mishra *et al.* undergoes as of man-in-the-middle attacks, replay attacks, and does not have full forward defense. Zhang *et al.* [32] introduced a three-factor authenticated key conformity system to resolve the limitations of the Mishra *et al.* scheme that would enable patients to benefit from privacy in secluded healthcare services security through TMIS.

A narrative key protocol of agreement based on chaotic maps with user anonymity was proposed by Tseng *et al.* [33]. They suggested that their proposed etiquette could include common server-user authentication.

To create a shared session key, the user may communicate anonymously with the server. In 2011, however, Niue *et al.* [34] found to [35] was unable to pay for user anonymity and absolute privacy, and then a trusted third party suggested the design of their protocols.

7.3   Two-Factor Authentication

Two-factor authentication, or 2FA, validates the uniqueness of a person throughout two (or more) identification devices, like a password and a supplementary one user-linked device confirmed process. Due to the entire seclusion and sanctuary apprehensions neighboring details and medications for patients, two-factor authentication is especially significant for healthcare systems. The Fitness Indemnity Portability and Liability protects electronic health information for patients which allows patients seeking to display patient health records to check their identity which validates their access authority to that information. Controlled Substances Prescriptions of the United States Act. In 2010 Drug Enforcement [36] Administration prepared an addendum allowing two-factor authentication since it is easy to bypass or guess memory-based authentications such as passwords or security questions alone.

Confirmation user approaches include:

> - Email authentication or authentication of text messages depending on the protection of electronic message and telephone services to demonstrate the distinctiveness of the personage;
> - Computer verification using a secondary computer to demonstrate the identity of the user to the principal software;
> - Hard-token verification involving an individual's physical key or token As secondary evidence of personality;
> - Biometric verification, as identity proof, is a technique based on fingerprints, iris scanning or voice recognition.
>
>   Electronic mail the mainly fashionable two-factor authentication techniques are text messages, for personal accounts, in particular, since it is easy for users to easily submit and log in the process. More recent two-factor authentication methods are simpler, software or hard-token authentication, for example, but need additional user steps, like purchasing and synchronizing a physical key or using another software system.

7.3.1   Novel Features of Two-Factor Authentication

Facial and biometrics identification [37] can be emergent parts of significance on behalf of distinctive endorsement techniques because individual-inherent physical features appear to have fewer hacks for email messages and codes for text messages. In 2013, Apple implemented biometrics as a tool for accessing phones with Touch ID, and with 3D facial recognition, the iPhone X brought authentication further. Social networking sites such as Twitter are now processing two-dimensional facial recognition images, Law enforcement authorities, however, still use driver's license photos in some states to link to facial recognition databases.

A few arguments to facilitate the category of 3D facial recognition [38] revealed health data will soon be on the iPhone X protection norm, predominantly because cell phones that enhance facial recognition accessing electronic health records are also being used.

Hospice uses facial identification and biometrics to validate the identity of fitness concern specialized requiring access to protected patient records and to verify patient identification to make certain that the patient in question is prescribed the right drugs and procedures. Certain hospitals now use iris recognition and palm vein biometrics for patient authentication, although some have articulated concern regarding patient compliance to partake and potential patient seclusion [39] concern.

Only facial recognition was considered for at-home drug administration. A Canadian company recently announced that in its home drug dispensers it would include facial recognition, making it easy to track drug enforcement and remain drugs from the hands of non-patients [12]. Fitness issue is concerned with facial detection as the device is non-invasive, cannot pretend to be or conciliation is precise, does not necessitate further apparatus.

In the future, it seems worth monitoring the use of biometrics and face recognition for patients or retailers As a branch of a two-factor scheme for authentication, the technology will need to become more reliable to be successful with this authentication process, seclusion laws will take expertise to keep up, and cyber security will need to be quick to deter hackers from hunting for hackers around the world vulnerabilities to abuse [40].

7.3.2   Two-Factor Authentication Sorgen

As one would assume, the protection, anonymity, and the hackable flaws of the methods are the downsides of two-factor authentication. Facial recognition and other biometrics tend to be relatively secure since the physical identification of a person is part of who they are. However, hackers confirmed that the technology was released within a week to crack Apple's Face ID 3D iPhone X facial recognition apps and gelatin can be used to quickly scythe the Contact ID.

It is more difficult to hack the hard token authentication technique as of remoteness for the reason that it relies on a physical token conceded by the user, but because they can be lost or stolen, corporal indications are dangerous, at which summit acquaintance of the secret code and tenure of the token are the bare barrier linking whichever unauthorized person and the one-off data.

Derivative apps email and text message authentication rely on secondary systems for endowing theirs possess systems fortification besides that afforded by the major data coordination. If certain secondary systems, including telecommunications companies, are a reduced amount of apprehensive with safety or uncomplicated to hack, then the second authentication method possibly will not pass to make available the additional sanctuary of two-factor authentication and might essentially be an explanation in the branch of the scythe.

A few cyber security connoisseurs are starting to advocate the utilize of three-factor authentication or multifactor authentication because two-factor authentication protection be able to be broken with exertion. Efficient attacks and two-factor authentication scheme infringements contain revealed users and web applications that two-factor authentication is not the mere solution.

In addition, authentication may as encryption fails to protect sensitive information and private data; it often goes beyond physical or digital barriers [16]. Attackers are searching for vulnerabilities to abuse. Google is allowing for using machine learning taking into account variables such as online user habits and authentication patterns and banks look at behavioral biometrics, such as how people determine the identity of the individual, use a mouse to individual.

7.3.3   Two-Factor Security Libraries

Medical libraries [41] ought to be incredibly involved in two-factor authentication, as sanatoriumsare fretful. The protection of private data and privacy is incorporated into broader private data-related identities. Libraries can, however, also recommend for their databases, dual authentication mechanisms, catalogues, as additional hospitals and universities need two-factor authentication for personnel, proxy servers along with virtual private networks are used for off-campus access to library services, libraries are likely to be caught up in those initiatives in those institutions.

Both libraries are involved in preserving customers' private information, from personal information to the practice of lending. Libraries, however, often fail to encourage people to use library services rather than services that are freely accessible on the web with suspicious copyright and authority. When libraries begin to require users could feel more irritated than comfortable in the absence of simple access to the two authentication levels, user accounts or library access services can be checked. Libraries may also assist as supporters of two-factor authentication and assistance in directing users to sheltered applications and tokens build it easier for other workers or agencies to move to mandatory two-factor authentication.

7.3.4   Challenges for Fitness Concern

At present, the majority of the developed nations are faced with major quality complications and the price of different wellness and well-being programs. Some difficulties would escalate even further as the population ages; this translates into a massive amount of chronic diseases [42] and a large demand for different healthcare facilities. As a consequence, the fitness care industry's costs may not be sustainably competitive and, thus, developing countries require to develop and sketch guiding principles and approaches to fitness care to make more productive and effective use of limited economic capital.

This need for sustainable fitness treatment programs contributes to a range of problems in science and technology [43]. Technology that, if it is resolved, may ultimately support theglobal economy and culture. In particular, it would be extremely advantageous to use information and communication technologies to employ healthcare programs that are autonomous and responsive. Healthcare powered by customers, in tandem with web-based services and EHR, has led to a range of improved options for healthcare over the past decades. We have also seen the introduction of some smartphone apps in recent years, which physiological status monitoring is becoming easily accessible [44]. Conversely, while medicines are these solutions also suffer from scalability, security problems, and privacy, which are an essential step towards personalization. In addition, these solutions can only include a snapshot of physiological conditions for several years, rather than a continuous view of optimal health.

This requires sustainable healthcare systems face a range of scientific and technical problems. Technology that, if resolved, will eventually sustain the global economy and culture of ours [45]. In fastidious, it would be extremely

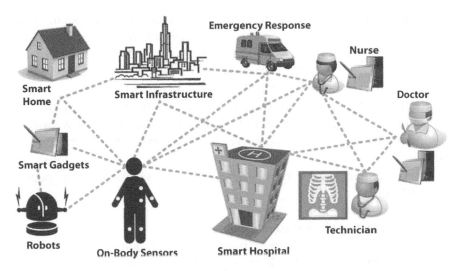

Figure 7.3 Illustration of interconnected fitness concern connected with smart sensor.

advantageous to use information and communication technology to employ self-sufficient and responsive healthcare systems. In tandem with web-based services and EHR, consumer-driven healthcare has led to a range of improved healthcare options over the last few decades (Figure 7.3).

We have also witnessed the emergence of some mobile apps in recent years which are appropriate readily available for physiological status monitoring. Nonetheless, while medicines are an essential step towards personalization, scalability also affects these solutions, security concerns, and privacy concerns. Moreover, for several years, these solutions can include only an overview of physiological conditions rather than a continuous vision of optimum health. Low-cost, innovative healthcare monitoring systems embedded in the home and livings, with recent advances in sensor network research conditions are already on the way.

7.4   Proposed Methodology

The purpose of such proposed loom remains to build an incorporated cognitive architecture for the protection of CPS-IoT-enabled healthcare environments against complex and adaptive attacks. This adds to the global security issue of cyber security. By applying cognitive computing, optimization, formal methods, cyber security [46], faith, forensics, artificial intelligence and mathematics awareness, an interdisciplinary [47] approach is needed to achieve this objective.

Figure 7.4 illustrates the general architecture of cognitive system cyber security for CPS-IoT has made ecosystems for fitness concern with four-layer building blocks: Fitness Concern Collaboration layer, Awareness also information layer, Adaptive Data compilation along with Actuation Layer as well as Infrastructure Layer for fitness concernstakeholders.

The goal of the strategy is to act as a base for a pioneering approach in favor of the averting of complex and hierarchical processes fitness concern environments have allowed adaptive attacks on evolving smart CPS-IoT [48].

The subsequent parts outline in brief the features of the key components of each layer:

1. **Privacy-Collaboration Conscious**
   In a privacy-aware way, mitigation techniques, a modern, sophisticated and risk management evidence-based frame-work perspective is needed [49]. This is supposed to illustrate the ambiguity as well as awareness, not just the likelihood, of the dynamic environments of fitness concern that is marked by profound uncertainties. It should provide opportunities to promote the collaboration of stakeholders through mutual situational knowledge, information exchange, common reporting, and visualization in a privacy-preserving manner. Fitness concerns interoperability, engagement and

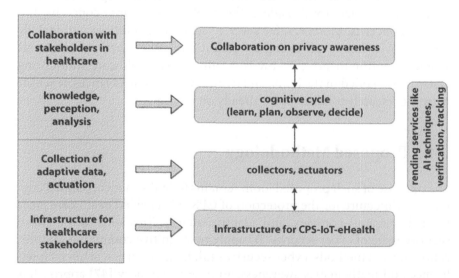

Figure 7.4 Suggested approach.

communication are mostly powered by data sharing. This brings freshness with its safety and privacy, technology, rewards, and governance issues and criteria that should be targeted.

A decentralized approach could be another successful solution. A strategy that usesblockchain technology through five mechanisms to promote this: rules of data aggregation, digital access, liquidity of information, patient identification, and data in mutability and immutability [50]. Blockchain technology can improve the sharing of user centered data and protect privacy through clear access rules that allow efficient and effective cyber security and privacy collaboration at different levels of complex fitness concern environments to encourage cognitive cyber security and seclusion by designing.

2. The Model Cognitive Loop

The ultimate approach of this model is to use trade-offs, AI, controllers, and creative methods to close the cognitive cycle model, to dynamically interpret the circumstances of CPS-IoT and activities of the human and social world, and to take action and learn from those acts. The answer is available at all stages of the loop/cycle. Increased safety tolerance for shifting priorities and adversarial situations, this will help to gain awareness of the situation. It has been disputed in the literature that a person who this loop can be processed faster than his adversary can get further from one of the decision cycles of the opponent with this win the decision cycle of the opponent 'Gain.' [51–53].

In favor of these CPS-IoT, the revealing contrivances and variation of defense are defined by detection (orient and observe), preparation, implementation (act and decide), and learning phases in a cognitive cycle security model. This general confrontation is how human cognition processes, together with those essential control, learning, adaptation, perception, Choice-making, and deed functions, are captured at the computational level. The further elementary problem is how to address the overall cognitive cyber security architecture by adapting to the limitations and competence of the various CPS-IoTs, as well as the probable complexities of these limitations and capacity. To illustrate how to best help user-centered confidentiality protection and managing, it uses cognitive representations for user contexts in a physical world.

When communicating collaborates and contending with others in these areas to preserve protection and seclusion in social, personal, public spaces also through various human stakeholders, cognitive models of the human upbringing of users are often used. We define the building blocks in the following at each point of the succession with added focus on the steps of Decide and Act and Observe and Orient.

i)   **Scrutinize and Adjust:** The Observe Process tracks and perceives compound stimulus at this stage. The Scrutinize Process uses adaptive information collectors like sensors/probes in the adaptive data assortment then automation layer to achieve this. The observation stage looks at observable variables, including configuration, user behavior, Vulnerabilities, emerging threats, fragmentary assaults, and physical environment contact. Exhausting a variety of collecting/sensing and automatic auditing tools like as configuration management traps for network management protocols, dynamic detection implements like as Nmap or trace path, log management implements, intrusion detection schemes like Snuffle, automated vulnerability scanners like Nessus detection also development of algorithms; this interaction is achieved to properly fuse along with fuse aggregation in real-time of sensed data from different sources [54–57].

Trade-offs are stuck between the on-demand pulling of collectors/sensors and for different sensors, push notifications can be used. The process of the Orient decides the importance of scrutiny by analyzing the importance of the findings actions and the effect concerning the security circumstances in the immediate upcoming. Using ontology, an explication system and Big Data Analytics approach methods are used for optimum point of reference. Because of the multitude of sensors and the vast number of sensors, Uh. Data. Wearables may also be sources of sensing, smart Telephones, social media, and so on. The methodsof AI are used to interpret these findings to classify possible variables (or root variables and causes) of conditions, to assess progress towards security output targets, to forecast potential circumstances and the possibility of achieving objectives and of agreeing on the urgency of reacting to issues.

ii) **Trained:** This stage is based on awareness, learning, Observation, choices, and conduct. In order, the dispute for this arena is how to discover user habits, relevance habits, to upgrade models and/or information for other models in other stages, and system levels to make precise predictions. To learn the environmental conditions and capabilities of opponents, it can use either explicit human input or performance data on empirical protection. Another obstacle for this move is how to learn faster than a potential intruder. In this instance, it is possible to use inverse reinforcement training. Learning agents change actions to perform better in real-time learning and adapt every minute by adapting the approach to current circumstances.

iii) **Plan:** This stage creates policy and takes into account time. Rationale by defining tasks to be accomplished. Several claims that preparation includes reasoning for causality, temporal reasoning, conditional Planning, reasoning with constraints, and supply administration. Multi-aimed trade-offs concerning preparation are determined utilizing sufficient planning. The processes in diverse environments, the approach it is important to track and updated tactics to ensure reliability plans and reaction to the changed circumstances. Multi-agent preparation, dynamic, is traditional techniques programming, partially-observable Markov processes judgment, contentment with limits, and distributed algorithms for optimization [58–60].

iv) **Decide and be active:** Centered on observations of changing conditions of protection and privacy, with the filtering and description of problems, the Decide process decides between candidate security plans. The Input and derived data for the Agreed Process are defined by the annotations from the Observe and Orient stages and their descriptions appropriate to the difficulty. At this point, decision-making, different trading-offs to speed up the decision and information ambiguity, suitable to speed up the resolution practice and swell the degree of sensory confidence, models like fuzzy logic, Bayesian networks, and subjective logic may be used [61–63].

The Act mechanism launches internal and/or external processes chosen to explicitly enact countermeasures or modify the physical CPS-IoT in CPS-IoT devices, devices in the Adaptive Data Collection via the actuators, Layer, and Automation [64–67].

3.   **Vibrant sanctuary acquaintance base:** A complex vulnerability and security information threat intelligence knowledge base can confine a variety of threats dynamically. Data starting its environments with CPS-IoT. This knowledge provides a perspective in which multifaceted networks and the mounting omnipresence of healthcare technologies are organized environments pose a major challenge.

Ontologies are the most promising method because of their expressiveness, strong and formal and the possibilities for the application of ontological reasoning methods, background modeling, and management. The dynamic capabilities can be enabledby using these capabilities within ontologies. Dynamic vulnerability [68] scanning and pen testing, the continuous testing and tracking of changes, discrepancies, new vulnerabilities and risks, unsecured protection and privacy properties, etc., are often usedas proof of the proper functioning of the complex healthcare cognitive intelligence assets environments.

7.5   Medical Treatment and the Preservation of Records

Patients hospitalized whose physiological state requires utilizing IoT-driven, non-invasive monitoring, near attention can be continuously monitored. This sort of approach uses sensors to gather detailed knowledge about physiology [69–71] and to analyze and archive the information using gateways and the cloud, and then return the examined information wirelessly for further review and assessment to caregivers. This eliminates the mechanism of making a health professional come through to track the imperative signs of the patient at regular intervals, instead of providing the corresponding doctors with a constant automated knowledge flow. In this manner, continuous attention concurrently increases the eminence of treatment and reduces the treatment costs by removing the necessitate for a caregiver to participate in data collection and analysis daily. The findings give clinicians a full, accurate image of patient status to review wherever they might be.

7.5.1   Remote Method of Control

A variety of patients are available worldwide and their well-being would undergo since they do not have equipped admission for reliable check of their well-being. However, lightweight, powerful IoT-connected wireless solutions are now available allowing the coming of these patients to be monitored as a substitute of vice versa. Those relevant are worn in a protected manner to obtain uncomplaining health information from using sophisticated algorithms to evaluate a variety of sensors. The information and then communicate it via wireless communication with health practitioners who can make relevant health decisions. Patients with chronic illnesses, as a result, complications and acute conditions could be less likely to happen. It is possible to diagnose complications [72] sooner than they ought to be.

7.5.2   Enabling Healthcare System Technology

The health monitoring framework based on the IoT relies mostly on some enabling technologies. Without these, in fields such as the control of health, the accessibility, connectivity, and capabilities needed for applications will be difficult to achieve. Smart sensors, combining a sensor and a microcontroller, allow the supremacy of the IoT to be leveraged some health status measures are accurately assessed, tracked, and analyzed for fitness care.

This may include essential signs such as heart rate and blood pressure, blood glucose or levels of saturation of oxygen. You can also add smart sensors to the pill. Bottles and the network connected to show if a scheduled dosage of medication [73] has been taken by a patient. The microcontroller components must integrate many critical capabilities for smart sensors to function efficiently.

To keep the device's footprint small and prolong the battery life, the low-power operation is essential; features helping to render IoT products as functional as possible. Precision-analog optimized capabilities allow sensors at a low cost to achieve high accuracy. By allowing display systems to provide in vivid factors and through the ease of contact the data, a lot of details, graphical user interfaces maximize usability.

Gateways are data hubs that collect, analyze, and then communicate sensor data through Wide Area Network (WAN) technologies to the cloud. For clinical or home environments, gateways may be configured; in the latter, they can be part of a wider networking utility that often handles power, distraction, and other domicile systems.

Infrastructure and healthcare facilities are more important, refined and it is more interrelated than always. While enhancing clinical upshots and changing deliverance, of treatment, however, there is a rise in human life, thereby enhancing human life. Concerns about the protection of data and equipment in fitness care. Medical equipment has been exposed to increasing interconnections of current cyber protection vulnerabilities and facilities. This makes for the most exposed healthcare sector to major security issues threat [74, 75].

The problem is compounded by the healthcare programs and facilities funded by the CPS-IoT, which are defiant to an assortment of cyber attacks that are up-and-coming. CPS-IoT schemes were characterized as critical security and security schemes with extended attack surface features and current disintegration, heterogeneity, interconnectedness, and cross-organizational existence. Cyber security potentially, attacks will contribute to user privacy being breached, physical injury, loss of money, and threats to human lives; it's important to stop and prevent them. Growth is illustrated by reports of attacks and the climb of fraud of patient identity, with millions of stolen health records around the world.

The growth of cyber-physical assaults indicates to us to complexity, dynamicity, volatility, CPS-IoT and high connectivity powered healthcare facilities and essential infrastructures cannot be solved by current security solutions. Artificial intelligence and cognitive design can improve automated decision-making processes for intelligent cyber security with expert-level capabilities.

In addition, attackers can acclimatize their tactics to the sanctuary circumstances, and countermeasures recently implemented. There is therefore a vital requirement for novel methods for CPS-IoT-enabled cognitive cyber security creation ecosystems for fitness care behavior by capturing their purpose, forecasting their determination and estimating their determination and these are associated with CPS-IoT behavior and decisive systems of infrastructure to facilitate deter evolving attacks.

7.6 Conclusion

The e-healthcare system maintains responsive users/patients common-place details and other knowledge. The devices are prone to attack. The majority of information systems fail to provide successful remote access authentication.

Although two-factor authentication is not an old idea for digital devices and applications, the growing in large organizations, such as healthcare systems and colleges, and the prevalence of multi-level authentication suggest that the technology will not quickly vanish. While the final solution for cyber security is not two-factor authentication, it is more reliable than passwords alone. A significant way to work constantly towards securing private information is to study the advantages and existing issues of two-factor or multi-factor authentication methods.

The primary objective of the proposed methodology is to stop imposers impersonate in the remote health system, legitimate users, but also make certain that justifiable users are not denied and the consistency of the scheme is strong. Here, the researchers recommended that keystroke dynamics be used for machine admittance, which does not cost and requires little external hardware other than the keyboard. Conversely, analysis of keystrokes by itself may not be capable of providing a high degree of precision due to its poor repeatability as a behavioral bio-metric feature. Two-factor authentication is proposed for this purpose, integrating hidden PIN verification with keystroke analysis to improve the degree of precision of authentication.

The investigators proved that their algorithms are in this area, it is versatile, simple to implement and more realistic than other known approaches for consumers. The results show that Compared to only using one keystroke factor, the degree of accuracy in two-factor authentication is improved. The effort of the researchers is on the analysis of different problems in this area and on the determination of potential final solutions. The suggested keystroke logic is changed by considering many basic parameters of the application and a versatile data collection. The expanded groundbreaking approach for authenticating remote health end-users will then be the proposed two-factor authentication version, which would benefit society from several points of vision.

References

1. Vickers, N. J., Animal communication: When i'm calling you, will you answer too?. *Curr. Biol.*, 27, 14, R713–R715, 2017.
2. Jang, J., Cyber Security Intelligence (CSI) team. Retrieved 2022, from https://researcher.watson.ibm.com/researcher/view_group.php?id=4354.
3. Wigmore, I., Cognitive security, 2017, August. Retrieved 2022, from https://www.techtarget.com/whatis/definition/cognitive-security.
4. Lenders, V., Tanner, A., Blarer, A., Gaining an Edge in Cyberspace with Advanced Situational Awareness. *IEEE Secur. Privacy*, 13, 2, 65–74, 2015.
5. Yelizarov, A. and Gamayunov, D., Adaptive Visualization Interface That Manages User's Cognitive Load Based on Interaction Characteristics, in: *Proc. of VINCI*, ACM, New York, USA, pp. 1–8, 2014.
6. Schaffhauser, D., UK University Staff Seeks Security with Tokenless 2-Factor Authentication, in: *Campus Technology*, August 4, 2015, https://campustechnology.com/ articles/2015/08/04/uk-university-staff-seeks-security-with-tokenless-2-factor-authentication. aspx.
7. Shacklett, M. E., ProVerif: Cryptographic protocol verifier in the formal model, 2016, October 31. Retrieved 2022, from https://bblanche.gitlabpages.inria.fr/proverif/.
8. Pham, T., Hospitals Increase Infrastructure Support for Two-Factor Authentication, in: *The Duo Security Bulletin*, December 7, 2015, https://duo.com/bloghospitals-increase-infrastructure-support-for-two-factor-authentication.
9. Harris, J., Why Two-Factor Authentication Can Help Keep Your Data Safe, in: *Hospitals and Health Networks Magazine*, May 12, 2016, https://www.hhnmag.com/ articles/7182-two- factor-authentication-for-hospitals.
10. Healthischool. Health Standards, in: *Is your face the future of patient identification?*, October 21, 2016, http://healthstandards.com/blog/2016/10/21/face-recognitionpatient- identification/.
11. Brostoff, G., 3D Facial Recognition Gives Healthcare Data A New Look, 2017, October 6. Retrieved 2022, from https://www.clinicalresearchnewsonline.com/news/2017/10/06/3d-facial-recognition-gives-healthcare-data-a-new-look.
12. Siwicki, B., Iris recognition, palm-vein, fingerprinting: Which biometric is best for healthcare?, 2016, March 30. Retrieved 2022, from https://www.healthcareitnews.com/news/iris-scanning-palm-vein-fingerprinting-which-biometric-best-healthcare.
13. Pocius, D.M., Using Facial Recognition with Prescription Drugs, in: *Dark daily*, July 9, 2018, https://www.darkdaily.com/canadian-company-prepares-to-usebiometric-Facial-recognition-for-positive-patient-identification-with-an-in-home-prescription drug- dispensing-device/.

14. Kumari, S., Li, X., Wu, F., Das, A.K., Arshad, H., Khan, M.K., A user friendly mutual authentication and key agreement scheme for wireless sensor networks using chaotic maps. *Future Gener. Comput. Syst.*, 63, 56–75, 2016.

15. Li, X., Niu, J., Karuppiah, M., Kumari, S., Wu, F., Secure and efficient two-factor user authentication 570 scheme with user anonymity for network based e-healthcare applications. *J. Med. Syst.*, 40, 12, 268, 2016.

16. Lee, C. C., Hwang, M. S., Liao, I. E., Security enhancement on a new authentication scheme with anonymity for wireless environments. *IEEE Trans. Ind. Electron.*, 53, 5, 1683–1687, 2006.

17. Wu, F., Xu, L., Kumari, S., Li, X., An improved and anonymous two-factor authentication protocol for healthcare applications with wireless medical sensor networks. *Multimed. Syst.*, 23, 2, 195–205, 2017.

18. Li, W. and Wang, P., Two-factor authentication in industrial internet-of-things: Attacks, evaluation 615 and new construction. *Future Gener. Comput. Syst.*, 101, 694–708, 2019.

19. Gupta, M. and Chaudhari, N.S., Anonymous two factor authentication protocol for roaming service in global mobility network with security beyond traditional limit. *Ad Hoc Netw.*, 84, 56–67, 2019.

20. Luo, E., Liu, Q., Wang, G., Hierarchical multi-authority and attribute based encryption friend discovery scheme in mobile social networks. *IEEE Commun. Lett.*, 20, 9, 1772–1775, 2016.

21. Weerasinghe, D., Elmufti, K., Rajarajan, M., Rakocevic, V., Securing Electronic Health Records with Novel Mobile Encryption Schemes. *Int. J. Electron. Healthcare*, 3, 4, 395–416, 2007.

22. IBM, Using two-factor authentication, 2022. Retrieved 2022, from https://www.ibm.com/docs/en/acvfc?topic=security-using-two-factor-authentication.

23. Karnan, M., Akila, M., Krishnaraj, N., Biometric personal authentication using keystroke dynamics: A review. *Elsevier J. Appl. Soft Comput.*, 11, 2, 1565– 1573, 2011.

24. Monrose, F. and Rubin, A., Authentication via keystroke dynamics. *Proceedings of Fourth ACM Conference on Computer and Communications Security (CCS)*, pp. 48–56, 1997.

25. Office for civil rights, United State Department of Health and Human Services, in: *Medical privacy- national standards of protect the privacy of personal health information*, http://www.hhs.gov/ocr/privacy/hipaa/administrative/privacyrule/inde x.html.

26. Kumar, P., Lee, Y.D., Lee, H.J., Secure health monitoring using medical wireless sensor networks. *6th International conference on networked computing and advanced information management*, vol. II, pp. 491–494, 2010.

27. Haque, M.M., Pathan, A.S.K., Hong, C.S., Securing UHealthcare sensor networks using public key based scheme. *10th International conference of advance communication technology*, pp. 1108–1111, 2008.

28. Fu, Z., Ren, K., Shu, J., Sun, X., Huang, F., Enabling personalized search over encrypted outsourced data with efficiency improvement. *IEEE Trans. Parallel Distrib. Syst.*, 27, 9, 2546– 2559, 2016.

29. Ren, Y., Shen, J., Wang, J., Han, J., Lee, S., Mutual verifiable provable data auditing in public cloud storage. *J. Internet Technol.*, 16, 2, 317–323, 2015.

30. Xu, J., Zhu, W.T., Feng, D.G., An improved smart card based password authentication scheme with provable security. *Comput. Stand. Interfaces*, 31, 4, 723–728, 2009.

31. Wang, Y.Y., Liu, J.Y., Xiao, F.X., Dan, J., A more efficient and secure dynamic ID-based remote user authentication scheme. *Comput. Commun.*, 32, 4, 583–585, 2009.

32. Song, R., Advanced smart card based password authentication protocol. *Comput. Stand. Interfaces*, 32, 5, 321–325, 2010.

33. Chen, B.L., Kuo, W.C., Wuu, L.C., Robust smart-card-based remote user password authentication scheme. *Int. J. Commun. Syst.*, 27, 2, 377–389, 2014.

34. Kumari, S. and Khan, M.K., Cryptanalysis and improvement of 'a robust smart-card-based remote user password authentication scheme. *Int. J. Commun. Syst.*, 27, 12, 3939–3955, 2014.

35. Li, X., Niu, J., Khan, M.K., Liao, J., An enhanced smart card based remote user password authentication scheme. *J. Netw. Comput. Appl.*, 36, 5, 1365–1371, 2013.

36. An, Y.H., Security improvements of dynamic id-based remote user authentication scheme with session key agreement. *15th International Conference on Advanced Communication Technology (ICACT)*, IEEE, pp. 1072–1076, 2013.

37. Amin, R., Islam, S.H., Biswas, G., Khan, M.K., Li, X., Cryptanalysis and enhancement of anonymity preserving remote user mutual authentication and session key agreement scheme for e-healthcare systems. *J. Med. Syst.*, 39, 11, 1–21, 2015.

38. Sood, S.K., Secure dynamic identity-based authentication scheme using smart cards. *Inf. Secur. J. Glob. Perspect.*, 20, 2, 67–77, 2011.

39. Nyang, D. and Lee, M. K., Improvement of Das's two-factor authentication protocol in wireless sensor networks. *Cryptology EPrint Arch.*, 2009.

40. Raja, K.N. and Beno, M.M., On securing wireless sensor network novel authentication scheme against dos attacks. *J. Med. Syst.*, 38, 10, 1–5, 2014, doi: 10.1007/s10916-014-0084-3.

41. Wang, D. and Wang, P., On the anonymity of two-factor authentication schemes for wireless sensor networks: Attacks, principle and solutions. *Comput. Netw.*, 73, 41–57, 2014.

42. Wang, D. and Wang, P., Understanding security failures of two-factor authentication schemes for real-time applications in hierarchical wireless sensor networks. *Ad. Hoc. Netw.*, 20, 1–15, 2014.

43. Wang, D., He, D., Wang, P., Chu, C. H., Anonymous two-factor authentication in distributed systems: Certain goals are beyond attainment. *IEEE Trans. Dependable Secure Comput.*, 12, 4, 428–442, 2014.

44. Wu, F. and Xu, L., Security analysis and improvement of a privacy authentication scheme for telecare medical information systems. *J. Med. Syst.*, 37, 4, 1–9, 2013.

45. He, D., Kumar, N., Chen, J., Lee, C.-C., Chilamkurti, N., Yeo, S.-S., Robust anonymous authentication protocol for healthcare applications using wireless medical sensor networks. *Multimedia Syst.*, 21, 1, 49–60, 2015. http:// dx.doi.org/10. 1007/s00530-013-0346-9.

46. Wu, F., Xu, L., Kumari, S., Li, X., An improved and anonymous two-factor authentication protocol for healthcare applications with wireless medical sensor networks. *Multimed. Syst.*, 23, 2, 195–205, 2017.

47. Srinivas, J., Mishra, D., Mukhopadhyay, S., A mutual authentication framework for wireless medical sensor networks. *J. Med. Syst.*, 41, 5, 80, 2017.

48. Vickers, N. J., Animal communication: When i'm calling you, will you answer too?. *Curr. Biol.*, 27, 14, R713–R715, 2017.

49. Amin, R., Islam, S.H., Biswas, G., Khan, M.K., Leng, L., Kumar, N., Design of anonymity preserving three-factor authenticated key exchange protocol for wireless sensor network. *Comput. Netw.*, 101, 42–62, 2016.

50. Yuan, C., Sun, X., Lv, R., Fingerprint liveness detection based on multi-scale lpq and pca. *China Commun.*, 13, 7, 60–65, 2016.

51. Xia, Z., Wang, X., Zhang, L., Qin, Z., Sun, X., Ren, K., A privacy-preserving and copy deterrence content-based image retrieval scheme in cloud computing. *IEEE Trans. Inf. Forensics Secur.*, 11, 11, 2594–2608, 2016.

52. Fu, Z., Ren, K., Shu, J., Sun, X., Huang, F., Enabling personalized search over encrypted outsourced data with efficiency improvement. *IEEE Trans. Parallel Distrib. Syst.*, 27, 9, 2546–2559, 2016.

53. Fu, Z., Sun, X., Liu, Q., Zhou, L., Shu, J., Achieving efficient cloud search services: multi- keyword ranked search over encrypted cloud data supporting parallel computing. *IEICE Trans. Commun.*, 98, 1, 190–200, 2015.

54. Li, X., Ma, J., Wang, W., Xiong, Y., Zhang, J., A novel smart card and dynamic ID based remote user authentication scheme for multi-server environments. *Math. Comput. Modelling*, 58, 1, 85–95, 2013.

55. Li, X., Niu, J., Khan, M.K., Liao, J., An enhanced smart card based remote user password authentication scheme. *J. Netw. Comput. Appl.*, 36, 5, 1365–1371, 2013.

56. Wu, F., Xu, L., Kumari, S., Li, X., A novel and provably secure biometrics-based three-factor remote authentication scheme for mobile client–server networks. *Comput. Electr. Eng.*, 45, 274–285, 2015.

57. Wu, F., Xu, L., Kumari, S., Li, X., Alelaiwi, A., A new authenticated key agreement scheme based on smart cards providing user anonymity with formal proof. *Secur. Commun. Netw.*, 8, 18, 3847–3863, 2015.

58. Amin, R. and Biswas, G., A secure light weight scheme for user authentication and key agreement in multi-gateway based wireless sensor networks. *Ad. Hoc. Netw.*, 36, 58–80, 2016.

59. Ma, T., Zhou, J., Tang, M., Tian, Y., Al-dhelaan, A., Al-rodhaan, M., Lee, S., Social network and tag sources based augmenting collaborative recommender system. *IEICE Trans. Inf. Syst.*, 98, 4, 902–910, 2015.

60. Jiang, Q., Wei, F., Fu, S., Ma, J., Li, G., Alelaiwi, A., Robust extended chaotic maps based three-factor authentication scheme preserving biometric template privacy. *Nonlinear Dynam.*, 83, 2085–2101, 2015.

61. Blanchet, B., Modeling and verifying security protocols with the applied pi calculus and ProVerif. *Found. Trends® in Priv. Secur.*, 1, 1–2, 1–135, 2016.

62. Messerges, T.S., Dabbish, E.A., Sloan, R.H., Examining smart-card security under the threat of power analysis attacks. *IEEE Trans. Comput.*, 51, 5, 541–552, 2002.

63. Wu, F. and Xu, L., An improved and provable self-certified digital signature scheme with message recovery. *Int. J. Commun. Syst.*, 28, 2, 344–357, 2015.

64. Wu, F., Xu, L., Kumari, S., Li, X., Das, A.K., Khan, M.K., Karuppiah, M., Baliyan, R., A novel and provably secure authentication and key agreement scheme with user anonymity for global mobility networks. *Secur. Commun. Netw.*, 9, 16, 3527–3542, 2016.

65. Wang, D. and Wang, P., On the anonymity of two-factor authentication schemes for wireless sensor networks: Attacks, principle and solutions. *Comput. Netw.*, 73, 41–57, 2014.

66. Wang, D., He, D., Wang, P., Chu, C.-H., Anonymous two-factor authentication in distributed systems: certain goals are beyond attainment. *IEEE Trans. Dependable Secure Comput.*, 12, 4, 428–442, 2015.

67. Kumari, S., Khan, M.K., Atiquzzaman, M., User authentication schemes for wireless sensor networks: A review. *Ad. Hoc. Netw.*, 27, 159–194, 2015.

68. Yelizarov, A. and Gamayunov, D., Adaptive Visualization Interface That Manages User's Cognitive Load Based on Interaction Characteristics, in: *Proc. of VINCI*, ACM, New York, USA, pp. 1–8, 2014.

69. Cho, J.H., Xu, S., Hurley, P.M., Mackay, M., Benjamin, T., Beaumont, M., Stram: Measuring the trustworthiness of computer-based systems. *ACM Comput. Sur. (CSUR)*, 51, 6, 1–47, 2019.

70. Ullah, F. and Babar, M. A., Architectural tactics for big data cybersecurity analytics systems: A review. *J. Syst. Softw.*, 151, 81–118, 2019.

71. Narayanan, S., Ganesan, A., Joshi, K., Oates, T., Joshi, A., Finin, T., Cognitive techniques for early detection of cybersecurity events. arXiv preprint arXiv:1808.00116, 2018.

72. Torjusen, A.B., Abie, H., Paintsil, E., Trcek, D., Skomedal, A., Towards Run-Time Verification of Adaptive Security for IoT in eHealth, in: *Proceedings of ECSAW*, vol. 14, ACM, NewYork, NY, USA, p. 8, 2014.

73. Xu, X., Zhu, P., Wen, Q., Jin, Z., Zhang, H., He, L., A secure and efficient authentication and key agreement scheme based on ECC for telecare medicine information systems. *J. Med. Syst.*, 38, 9994, 2014.

74. Xue, K.P. and Hong, P.L., Security improvement on an anonymous key agreement protocol based on chaotic maps. *Commun. Nonlinear Sci. Numer. Simul.*, 17, 7, 2969–2977, 2012.
75. Yeh, H.L., Chen, T.H., Shih, W.K., Robust smart card secured authentication scheme on sip using elliptic curve cryptography. *Comput. Standards Interfaces*, 36, 2, 397–402, 2014.

8

Data Analytics for Healthcare Monitoring and Inferencing

Gend Lal Prajapati[1], Rachana Raghuwanshi[2]* and Rambabu Raghuwanshi[3]

*[1]Computer Engineering, Devi Ahilya University, Khandwa Road Indore,
Madhya Pradesh, India*
*[2]Computer Engineering, SAGE University, Bypass Road, Kailod Indore,
Madhya Pradesh, India*
*[3]Technical Consultant, Price Water House Coopers Pvt. Ltd., Indore,
Madhya Pradesh, India*

Abstract

Big Data has changed the manner in which we manage and explore data in all types of sectors. Healthcare analytics has potential to decrease expenses of treatment and predict all types of pandemics. We can also avoid and control contagious diseases to improve the quality of life.

The average human life of expectancy is also increasing continuously, which presents new challenges to treatment conveyance strategies.

Nowadays, healthcare information are generating from various applications like patient data storage and monitoring in healthcare management systems. Healthcare data is continuously increasing and distributed in a manner for sharing among medical experts and healthcare service provider. Cloud gives most incredible strategies to explore the information arrange from medical care by analyzing continuous previous medical data.

As of now existing framework could not support both analysis and procedure for large quantity of healthcare data.

In this book chapter, we present a study on data analytics and machine learning techniques using R and Python programming for efficient inference, monitoring, and transmission of medical data in healthcare industries. We also brief about bioinformatics approaches in order to see usefulness in dealing with pandemics like COVID-19 situation.

*Corresponding author: rachana.raghuwanshi1990@gmail.com

D. Sumathi, T. Poongodi, B. Balamurugan and Lakshmana Kumar Ramasamy (eds.)
Cognitive Intelligence and Big Data in Healthcare, (197–228) © 2022 Scrivener Publishing LLC

As a reader progresses through this book chapter, he or she will be able to:

1. Define key terms in healthcare.
2. Identify the challenges and opportunities facing healthcare organizations.
3. Summarize the role of oversight and research in healthcare infrastructure.
4. Describe how value, quality, and variation in healthcare impact outcomes and expenditures.
5. Summarize current healthcare trends.
6. Understand the Bioinformatics Data Analytics for COVID-19 pandemic.

Keywords: Data analytics, healthcare, COVID-19, machine learning, bioinformatics

8.1   An Overview of Healthcare Systems

Healthcare services are a basic and fundamental need and constitutionally assured to every citizen of society; it is a fundamental human right and available to every citizen in affordable cost irrespective of social and economic status [1]. As per World Health Organization under united nation is also working for improvement in global healthcare system and also focusing some specific set of disease as per specific healthcare improvement targets in 2015, and also set of the Sustainable Development Goals and target up to 2030 [2]. Which is included a broad health goal to ensure a good and healthy lives for all irrespective of ages.

8.2   Need of Healthcare Systems

According to the annual report of world health organization (WHO) is observed remarkable progress. The most recent data are showing given below:

i.   At least 50% of the world's populations are not getting the basic necessary health services, which is 3.65 billion populations and 7.3 billion total world's population as per WHO United Nation 2020 [3].

ii.   According to WHO, an estimated 5.4 million children died before reaching age of 5, which is, one out of 14 children dies before reaching age 5 in 2017 and the global children under 5 age mortality rate is reducing, which dropped by 49% since 2000.

iii.   Around 100 million in population were pushed into extreme poverty due to lack of affordable healthcare services.

iv.   The probability and risk of a 30-year-old dying before reaching the age of 70 owing to cardiovascular, respiratory, diabetes, and cancer diseases, which were affected in low and medium income countries of 22% for men and 15% for women [5].

8.3   Basic Principle of Healthcare Systems

i.   The government system should design systematic structure and provide essential healthcare services for well-being of all people in affordable cost rather than profits. There are following principles, which are given below:

ii.   Healthcare services are a human fundamental right rather than a profitable product, which can be equal and easily accessible [4].

iii.   Essential cost effective healthcare services delivery is the accountability of the state;

iv.   The public should be participating in the healthcare development program [6].

v.   Empowerment of all citizens through information, technology, and transparency.

vi.   Provide awareness about global health standards and it should be published in public domain for all citizens.

vii.   Provide basic medical treatment knowledge training program or basic nursing program for all citizens through basic education system [8].

8.4   Design and Recommended Structure of Healthcare Systems

Primary healthcare is basic and essential in a healthcare system; it should be based on a practically, scientifically, and publically acceptable process

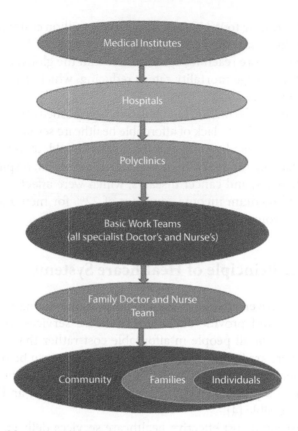

Figure 8.1 Healthcare organizational structure.

with the use of latest technology made easily reachable to individuals for closing the gap between the rich and the poor in the community through their major contribution. Systematic healthcare system should be designed and structured in proper manner to meet all basic requirements of the single citizen, and to sustain a wellness efficiency model of healthcare system [7]. Healthcare organizational structure is shown in Figure 8.1.

8.4.1   Healthcare System Designs on the Basis of these Parameters

    i.   Physical environment like type of housing, nutrition, geography, weather, clean water, and air [9].

    ii. Social environment like urban or rural, education, occupation.

iii. Personal attributes like habits, age, sex, genetic history
iv. Other parameters like accessibility, quality, primary care focus, and health promotion focus.

8.4.2 Details of Healthcare Organizational Structure

i. Mcdical institutes: Medical institutes are generating medical experts and advance research in different diseases; these medical institutes also provide treatment of highly specific disease, and especially these institutes are reserved for tertiary treatment and care like cardiology, nephrology, and endocrinology [10].

ii. Central and local government hospitals: The use of hospitals for treatment and care is restricted to severe secondary-level illnesses.

iii. Polyclinics: Polyclinics focus on four health initiatives: promotion of health, wellness, and curative measures for immediate illnesses, and rehabilitation, and include rooms for admission, observation, and autoclaves. Polyclinics help control dengue fever, a mosquito-borne illness, by providing more specialized treatments and the coordination of teaching, research, and community preventive health programs. Bone specialty, speech therapy, physical therapy, adult and children's gyms, acupuncture, massage therapy, heat therapy, and electromagnetic therapy are among the other services available [11].

iv. Basic work team (all specialists): These basic teams of all specialists who operate in policlinics, such as a gynecologist [12], a psychologist, a pediatrician, an obstetrician, and, in many cases, a social worker, are in charge of a certain number of family doctor and nurse offices.

v. There is a need for various developed specialized preventative care programs that include [13]:

- Tuberculosis
- Obesity
- Immunization
- Smoking
- Diabetes
- Hypertension
- Cancer
- Alcohol abuse

- AIDS/HIV
- Asthma
- Geriatrics
- Gynecology

- Sexually transmitted diseases
- Stress and depression
- Dental

Services such as maternity homes for women with high-risk pregnancies, disabled child-care facilities, and senior day-care facilities are also included in primary-level care [14].

vi. Family Doctor and Nurse Team: Family Doctor and Nurse Team should be available and reach to provide consultations for the community, family, and individual citizen. The purpose of the Family Doctor Program is to have a doctor and nurse team in every neighborhood. The neighborhood consultorio in Cuba and the Mohalla clinic in Delhi provide the most basic level of healthcare (India) [15].

8.5   Various Challenges in Conventional Existing Healthcare System

i.   Insufficient reform
ii.   Insufficient funding
iii.   Raising drug cost
iv.   Growing patients
v.   Consumerism
vi.   Uncertainty
vii.   Technology up gradation

8.6   Health Informatics

Health informatics is the way to collect, analyze, communicate, and share health related information by using latest technology, with the goal of improving healthcare system to reduce costs, and patients engagement; Details are shown in Figure 8.2 [16].

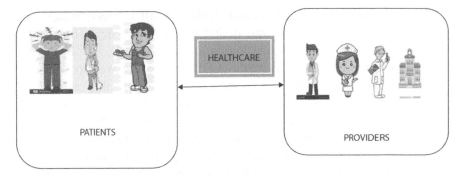

Figure 8.2 Interaction between patients and healthcare provider.

8.7 Information Technology Use in Healthcare Systems

Healthcare information technology (HIT) has been characterized as "the use of information and processing by using both hardware and software [17] that manage the storage capacity, sharing, recovery, and utilization of knowledge for communication and decision making."

List of various applications, which are given below:

a. Electronic prescribing
b. Electronic medical record systems EMRs
c. Electronic health records EHRs
d. Personal health records PHRs
e. Telehealth

8.8 Details of Various Information Technology Application Use in Healthcare Systems

a) **Electronic prescribing (E-prescribing):** It's easy to misplace or misread a paper prescription. E-prescribing allows your doctor to communicate directly with your pharmacist. This means you won't need to bring your paper prescription with you when you go to the drugstore [18].

b) **Electronic medical record (EMR): EMR** Convert paper based health record into digital record of physician office within clinics or hospitals computer system [19].

c) **Electronic health records (EHRs):** It is the way to collect patient's data and convert paper based health record into digital record in structured form of data in electronic platform, which can use data analysis and visualization to provide full electronic documentation systems and share through health information exchanges (HIEs) platform to connect patients with all clinics and doctor to exchange medical history [21].

   EHRs let doctors maintain track of your health information and may allow them to access it at any time and data can be updated and accessed real time from any location by an authorized person and organization.

d) **Personal health records (PHRs):** A PHR keeps track of personal information, such as tracking what is your intake of food, how much you keep fit by doing several exercises, and your blood pressure [20].

e) **Telehealth:** It is the way to healthcare delivery services, which may interact through telephone or video conferencing between patients and healthcare providers separately by distance [23]. Telehealth can help to achieve universal health coverage by enhancing patient access to high-quality, low-cost healthcare in rural areas, vulnerable groups, and the elderly [22].

8.9   Healthcare Information Technology Makes it Possible to Manage Patient Care and Exchange of Health Information Data, Details are Given Below

a) Accurate and understandable prescriptions: E-prescribing systems are the way to solve messy handwriting problem on a paper prescription, which automatically sends prescription to patients in understandable language to the all pharmacies or medical stores. E-prescribing can also help to eliminate the risk of pharmaceutical mistakes, accurate and complete information about a patient's health [24].

b) Reduced paperwork: Identical questions about personal information and medical history have been answered multiple times as a patient [26]. There's no need to write down and answer the same facts over and over if your healthcare providers share your electronic health information.

c) Rapid information sharing: The facility to better coordination between various healthcare providers. When any healthcare provider needs the history of patients, that information may be available, so that any authorized healthcare provider can have access information to aid in the early detection of health concerns, the reduction of medical errors, and the provision of safer care at reduced costs [25].

d) Reduced unnecessary tests expenditure and repeatedly: Every healthcare provider or doctors order tests that already have been completed [30]. Suppose, if you have completed your tests earlier and results are recorded in EHRs, then it could be easy for a healthcare provider to review the test results in common platform and suggest the required tests, which helps to save time, money.

e) Secure access to information: Having your information in an EHR should make it easier to reconstruct your records and make them available to clinicians outside of your house if you need to relocate temporarily or permanently in the case of a natural disaster or other tragedy [27].

f) Quality and outcomes improvement: It comes from the clinical decision support capabilities, as well as other clinical alerts that are able to be generated within the systems in real-time [28].

g) Health informatics allows doctors and hospitals to share clinical information and educational materials with patients via patient portals.

8.10 Barriers and Challenges to Implementation of Information Technology in Healthcare Systems

i. Lack of awareness of the benefits and advantages of utilizing healthcare information technology [29]

ii. Lack of capital resources due to high initial expenditure and infrastructure

iii. On a hospital level, there are no policies or procedures that control EMRs.
iv. On a national level, there are no laws or regulations governing EMRs.
v. Lack of healthcare information technology professionals
vi. Lack of financial resources,
vii. Lack of personnel, privacy and security concerns
viii. Difficulty in integration and interoperability
ix. Lack of technological resources

8.11   Healthcare Data Analytics

Healthcare Data Analytics is a technique of analysis of data that lets in healthcare professionals to discover possibilities for improvement in health system, patient appointment, and diagnosis in micro and macro level. Healthcare analytics can be used to analyze current and historical data to predict latest trends, management of the various diseases, and drive long-term growth [31]. Healthcare is a new generation of healthcare technology, which changes various medical models from patient to disease-centered care from clinical to regional medical information, and also changes in the idea of prevention and cure to focus on disease and preventive healthcare [33]. Smart Healthcare system involves updated digital use of various devices and various technologies like Internet of Things (IOT), Artificial Intelligence (AI), big data analytics, machine learning in healthcare system, which work through sensors and operate remotely [32].

This can store large patient data and examined by healthcare professionals like doctors, researchers to provide better diagnosis and clarifications through real time data collection and assessment with possible prompt outcome.

8.12   Healthcare as a Concept

The idea of Smart healthcare system was suggested by IBM. Smart healthcare system is used in sensors, Internet of Things (IOT), Artificial Intelligence (AI); it can also coordinate with social systems, integrate and actively manage the ecosystem [35].

8.13   Healthcare's Key Technologies

Smart healthcare involves a wide range of participants, including patients and doctors, hospitals, and research organizations, as well as multiple dimensions such as disease prevention, treatment, and diagnosis, as well as hospital management using modern technologies such as mobile Internet, cloud computing, IoT, big data, and artificial intelligence. From the patients' point of view, they can use various healthcare monitor devices, and also use remote services; from the doctors' point of view, they use various intelligent support systems to assist treatment and diagnosis.

8.14   The Present State of Smart Healthcare Application

Smart healthcare system can be divided into three basic categories [34]:

   i.   Family or individual users
   ii.   Hospitals/clinical/scientific research
   iii.   Regional health decision-making institutions

a) Assisting Diagnosis and Treatment
Disease treatment has gotten more sophisticated, thanks to the use of technologies such as surgical robots, mixed reality, and artificial intelligence. It has detected hepatitis, lung cancer, and skin cancer among other disorders [17].
b) Health Management
The prevalence of many chronic diseases has gradually increased; prolonged diseases have a protracted progress of disease that is incurable and expensive, and the traditional healthcare system is hospital and doctor-centered. Patients and various diseases are dealt with via the healthcare management system. It combines health data from a variety of portable devices to produce health decision support and to make optimal use of the data collected for disease diagnosis [35].
c) Risk Monitoring and Disease prevention
Traditional disease risk estimation depends on the health authorities' initiative to gather patient data, compare that data to authorized organization guidelines, and then provide the forecast results. This method faces the

issue in time and does not offer individuals with correct recommendations. Disease risk prediction is dynamic and tailored in smart healthcare [26]. It allows patients and doctors to take part, proactively monitor their illness risk, and implement chosen prevention strategies which depend on their own monitoring data [36].

d) Virtual Assistants

Virtual assistants converse with users using speech recognition algorithms, respond to the user's choices, and rely on large data from various sources [37]. For doctors, the virtual assistant may respond to pertinent information automatically based on the patient's fundamental information, making it easier for them to manage patients and organize medical procedures, allowing them to save time [13].

e) Smart Hospitals

Smart hospitals rely on information and communication technology-based settings, particularly those based on IoT optimization and automated operations, to improve existing patient care procedures and introduce new features [38]. Smart hospitals offer three types of services: medical staff services, patient services, and administrative services. The needs of these service consumers must be considered when hospital management decisions are made [25].

f) Assisting Drug Research

In order to uncover appropriate action locations, traditional drug target displaying manually crosses known medications with numerous possible target molecules in the human body [21]. This strategy is not only time-consuming, but it is also frequently neglected. The Internet of Things, big data, and artificial intelligence are all used in drug studies. To begin with, using artificial intelligence to evaluate and match a large number of cases can make it easier to screen for exclusion criteria and find the most suitable target subjects, saving time and improving target population targeting [28].

8.15 Data Analytics with Machine Learning Use in Healthcare Systems

Big Data tends to the data that is massive, rapid, complex, and huge volume being created by machines, people, and organizations. It is an enlarged stream of data [16]. This refers to the fact that data appears to be arriving in a steady stream and at a faster rate. Structured, unstructured, and semi-structured are the three types of it.

Data can come from a variety of places, including media-generated data from sites like Facebook, Twitter, and LinkedIn, as well as video, audio, image, text, and relational data. As a result, the data could be small or large. Big data entails a lot of speed, a lot of volume, and a lot of variation. As a result, we employ machine learning to examine large amounts of data [39].

The Block diagram starts with data sources, which in medical care and biomedicine may consist of patient records, financial records, medical record, and administration record. The second stage is feature extraction, which allows us to extract some features from the data and then analyze it to reveal hidden patterns. Then we apply machine learning methods to examine the massive data, such as linear regression, logistic regression, anomaly detection, clustering, and classification [27]. The next stage is

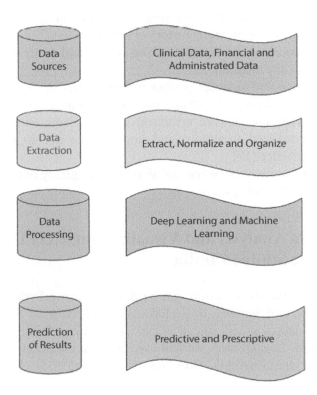

Figure 8.3 Workflow of big data analytics.

result prediction, which can be done using descriptive, predictive, or prescriptive methods. As a result, we mix machine learning with big data.

Machine learning techniques using data analytics, as illustrated in Figure 8.3. Picture, text, and relational data, may be comprehended with the help of the diagram.

8.16 Benefit of Data Analytics in Healthcare System

a) Performance improvement by delivering data-based quality in healthcare system
b) Increase efficiency of doctors and specialist to use telepathy techniques in treatments
c) Improvement of patient's data compilation for future reference
d) Reduce human error in testing and treatment by using digitalization of previous history of patient
e) Improvement of health tracking system and easily accessible in any location
f) Reduce and manage patient waiting times by measuring and scheduling of staff and patient procedures
g) Provide special care arrangement of patients with more personalized treatment and improve the overall patient experience [17]
h) Improvement of patient satisfaction and quality of services in healthcare system

8.17 Data Analysis and Visualization: COVID-19 Case Study in India

Data analysis and visualization can be done by using Python, NumPy, SciPy, Pandas, and Seaborn to perform. We will focus on the four vital steps for any data analysis project: analysis, describing, cleaning, and visualizing of data. In each step, we will use the most common and popular tools like Jupyter Notebook, Skill Network lab, and IBM cloud for data analysis [22].

Step 1: Importing datasets like pandas, Matplotlib, Seaborn, and Numpy. Pandas are libraries which are used for data manipulations. Matplotlib and seaborn are libraries which are used for visualization and Numpy library which is used to create and manipulate array.

```
import pandas as pd
from matplotlib import pyplot as plt
import seaborn as sns
import numpy as np
```

Step 2: Load the dataset covid_19_india.csv and we have a column called Date normally this is string type so we will have to convert that string type into date type and set the day first with True and successfully set the COVID 19 dataset into df.

Importing Covid 19 dataset

```
#importing main dataset
df = pd.read_csv('covid_19_india.csv', parse_dates=['Date'], dayfirst=True)
```

Step 3: The head() function is used to return the top five rows (by default).

```
df.head()
```

Output:

Time	State/UnionTerritory	ConfirmedIndianNational	ConfirmedForeignNational	Cured	Deaths	Confirmed
6:00 PM	Kerala	1	0	0	0	1
6:00 PM	Kerala	1	0	0	0	1
6:00 PM	Kerala	2	0	0	0	2
6:00 PM	Kerala	3	0	0	0	3
6:00 PM	Kerala	3	0	0	0	3

Step 4: Purely integer-location based indexing for selection by position.

```
df.iloc[:,1:]
```

Output:

	Date	Time	State/UnionTerritory	ConfirmedIndianNational	ConfirmedForeignNational	Cured	Deat
0	2020-01-30	6:00 PM	Kerala	1	0	0	
1	2020-01-31	6:00 PM	Kerala	1	0	0	
2	2020-02-01	6:00 PM	Kerala	2	0	0	
3	2020-02-02	6:00 PM	Kerala	3	0	0	
4	2020-02-03	6:00 PM	Kerala	3	0	0	
...	...	...	...	...	...	...	...
7011	2020-10-05	8:00 AM	Telengana	-	-	172388	11
7012	2020-10-05	8:00 AM	Tripura	-	-	21876	2
7013	2020-10-05	8:00 AM	Uttarakhand	-	-	41740	6
7014	2020-10-05	8:00 AM	Uttar Pradesh	-	-	362052	60
7015	2020-10-05	8:00 AM	West Bengal	-	-	237698	51

Step 5: The info() method is used to print a DataFrame's summary. This method prints data about a DataFrame, including the index and column dtypes, non-null values, and memory usage.

Inspect the Data Frame

```
df.info()
```

Output:

```
<class 'pandas.core.frame.DataFrame'>
RangeIndex: 7016 entries, 0 to 7015
Data columns (total 9 columns):
 #   Column                    Non-Null Count   Dtype
---  ------                    --------------   -----
 0   Sno                       7016 non-null    int64
 1   Date                      7016 non-null    datetime64[ns]
 2   Time                      7016 non-null    object
 3   State/UnionTerritory      7016 non-null    object
 4   ConfirmedIndianNational   7016 non-null    object
 5   ConfirmedForeignNational  7016 non-null    object
 6   Cured                     7016 non-null    int64
 7   Deaths                    7016 non-null    int64
 8   Confirmed                 7016 non-null    int64
dtypes: datetime64[ns](1), int64(4), object(4)
memory usage: 493.4+ KB
```

Step 6: Calculate the number of missing value in each column in Pandas dataframe we use isnull() method with axis=0.

Identify Null values in each colume

```
df.isnull().sum(axis=0).sort_values()
```

Output:

```
Sno                             0
Date                            0
Time                            0
State/UnionTerritory            0
ConfirmedIndianNational         0
ConfirmedForeignNational        0
Cured                           0
Deaths                          0
Confirmed                       0
dtype: int64
```

Step 7: Calculate the number of missing value in each row in Pandas dataframe we use isnull() method with axis=1.

Identify Null values in each Row

```
df.isnull().sum(axis=1).sort_values()
```

Output:

```
0          0
4683       0
4682       0
4681       0
4680       0
          ..
2333       0
2332       0
2331       0
2342       0
7015       0
Length: 7016, dtype: int64
```

Step 8: Print the dataset by using df command.

Total Covid 19 Cases Month Wise

```
df
```

Output:

	Sno	Date	Time	State/UnionTerritory	ConfirmedIndianNational	ConfirmedForeignNational	Cured	Deaths	Confirmed
0	1	2020-01-30	6:00 PM	Kerala	1	0	0	0	1
1	2	2020-01-31	6:00 PM	Kerala	1	0	0	0	1
2	3	2020-02-01	6:00 PM	Kerala	2	0	0	0	2
3	4	2020-02-02	6:00 PM	Kerala	3	0	0	0	3
4	5	2020-02-03	6:00 PM	Kerala	3	0	0	0	3
...	...	...	...	...	...	...	...	...	...
7011	7012	2020-10-05	8:00 AM	Telengana	-	-	172388	1171	200611
7012	7013	2020-10-05	8:00 AM	Tripura	-	-	21876	299	27033
7013	7014	2020-10-05	8:00 AM	Uttarakhand	-	-	41740	652	51481
7014	7015	2020-10-05	8:00 AM	Uttar Pradesh	-	-	362052	6029	414466

Step 9: Renaming column name using df.columns command and use head() method to print top five records.

```
import datetime as dt
```

```
#keeping only required columns
df = df[['Date', 'State/UnionTerritory','Cured','Deaths','Confirmed']]
#renaming column names
df.columns =['date', 'state','cured','deaths','confirmed']
```

```
df.head()
```

Output:

	date	state	cured	deaths	confirmed
0	2020-01-30	Kerala	0	0	1
1	2020-01-31	Kerala	0	0	1
2	2020-02-01	Kerala	0	0	2
3	2020-02-02	Kerala	0	0	3
4	2020-02-03	Kerala	0	0	3

Step 10: This tail() method returns last five rows (by default)

```
df.tail()
```

Output:

	date	state	cured	deaths	confirmed
7011	2020-10-05	Telengana	172388	1171	200611
7012	2020-10-05	Tripura	21876	299	27033
7013	2020-10-05	Uttarakhand	41740	652	51481
7014	2020-10-05	Uttar Pradesh	362052	6029	414466
7015	2020-10-05	West Bengal	237698	5194	270331

Step 11: We will extract all of those records where date is 05/10/2020 because we want to analyze the latest cases and store into today.

```
#current date
today = df[df.date == '2020-10-05']
```

```
today
```

Output:

	date	state	cured	deaths	confirmed
6981	2020-10-05	Andaman and Nicobar Islands	3649	53	3884
6982	2020-10-05	Andhra Pradesh	658875	5981	719256
6983	2020-10-05	Arunachal Pradesh	7577	18	10548
6984	2020-10-05	Assam	152127	749	186200
6985	2020-10-05	Bihar	175458	915	188168
6986	2020-10-05	Chandigarh	10598	174	12445
6987	2020-10-05	Chhattisgarh	93731	1045	123324
6988	2020-10-05	Dadra and Nagar Haveli and Daman and Diu	2980	2	3087
6989	2020-10-05	Delhi	260350	5510	290613
6990	2020-10-05	Goa	30033	456	35328
6991	2020-10-05	Gujarat	122233	3496	142538
6992	2020-10-05	Haryana	120341	1470	133878
6993	2020-10-05	Himachal Pradesh	12361	217	15851
6994	2020-10-05	Jammu and Kashmir	62404	1242	79106
6995	2020-10-05	Jharkhand	75531	743	87210

Step 12: Sorting the cases to be in descending order of number of confirmed cases. We are using today.sort_values() method.

#Sorting the data w.r.t number of confirmed cases

```
max_No_Confirmed_Cases=today.sort_values(by="confirmed",ascending=False)
max_No_Confirmed_Cases
```

Output:

	date	state	cured	deaths	confirmed
7000	2020-10-05	Maharashtra	1149603	38084	1443409
6982	2020-10-05	Andhra Pradesh	658875	5981	719256
6996	2020-10-05	Karnataka	515782	9286	640661
7010	2020-10-05	Tamil Nadu	564092	9784	619996
7014	2020-10-05	Uttar Pradesh	362052	6029	414466
6989	2020-10-05	Delhi	260350	5510	290613
7015	2020-10-05	West Bengal	237698	5194	270331
7005	2020-10-05	Odisha	202302	907	232713
6997	2020-10-05	Kerala	144471	836	229886
7011	2020-10-05	Telengana	172388	1171	200611
6985	2020-10-05	Bihar	175458	915	188168
6984	2020-10-05	Assam	152127	749	186200
7008	2020-10-05	Rajasthan	121331	1545	144030
6991	2020-10-05	Gujarat	122233	3496	142538

Step 13: Extract the top five states with maximum number of confirmed cases. By using sns.barplot() method we are able to make a bar plot in x and y axis. We are mapping the state column on to the x axis and confirmed column on to the y axis. We also analyze the number of confirmed cases with respect to each state.

```
#Getting states with maximum number of confirmed cases
top_states_confirmed_cases=max_No_Confirmed_Cases[0:5]
```

```
sns.set(rc={'figure.figsize':(15,10)})
sns.barplot(x="state",y="confirmed",data=top_states_confirmed_cases,hue="state")
plt.show()
```

Output:

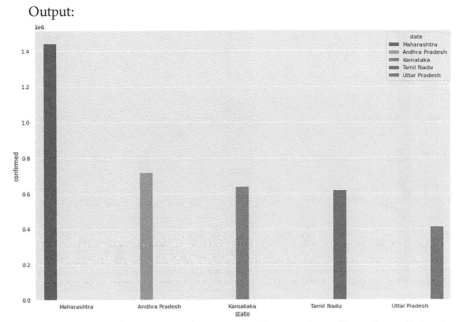

Step 14: Sorting the cases to be in ascending order of number of death cases. We are using today.sort_values() method.

```
#Sorting data w.r.t number of death cases
max_No_death_cases=today.sort_values(by="deaths",ascending=False)
max_No_death_cases
```

```
#Getting states with maximum number of death cases
top_states_death=max_No_death_cases[0:5]
```

Extract the top five states with maximum number of death cases. By using sns.barplot() method we are able to make a bar plot in x and y axis. We are mapping the state column on to the x axis and state column on to the y axis. We also analyze the number of deaths cases with respect to each state [32].

```
#Making bar-plot for states with top death cases
sns.set(rc={'figure.figsize':(15,10)})
sns.barplot(x="state",y="deaths",data=top_states_death,hue="state")
plt.show()
```

Output:

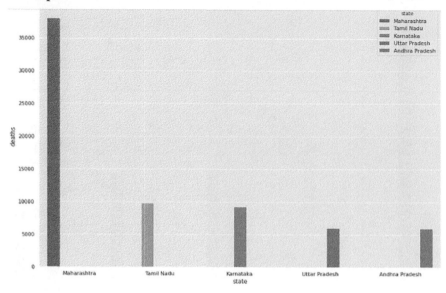

	date	state	cured	deaths	confirmed
7000	2020-10-05	Maharashtra	1149603	38084	1443409
7010	2020-10-05	Tamil Nadu	564092	9784	619996
6996	2020-10-05	Karnataka	515782	9286	640661
7014	2020-10-05	Uttar Pradesh	362052	6029	414466
6982	2020-10-05	Andhra Pradesh	658875	5981	719256
6989	2020-10-05	Delhi	260350	5510	290613
7015	2020-10-05	West Bengal	237698	5194	270331
7007	2020-10-05	Punjab	100977	3603	118157
6991	2020-10-05	Gujarat	122233	3496	142538
6999	2020-10-05	Madhya Pradesh	113832	2434	135638
7008	2020-10-05	Rajasthan	121331	1545	144030
6992	2020-10-05	Haryana	120341	1470	133878
6994	2020-10-05	Jammu and Kashmir	62404	1242	79106
7011	2020-10-05	Telengana	172388	1171	200611
6987	2020-10-05	Chhattisgarh	93731	1045	123324

Step 15: Getting the states with maximum no of cured cases.

```
#Getting states with maximum number of cured cases
top_states_cured=max_No_cured_cases[0:5]
```

Extract the top five states with maximum number of cured cases. By using sns.barplot() method we are able to make a bar plot in x and y axis. We are mapping the state column on to the x axis and cured column onto the y axis. We also analyze the number of cured cases with respect to each state.

```
#Making bar-plot for states with top death cases
sns.set(rc={'figure.figsize':(15,10)})
sns.barplot(x="state",y="cured",data=top_states_cured,hue="state")
plt.show()
```

Output:

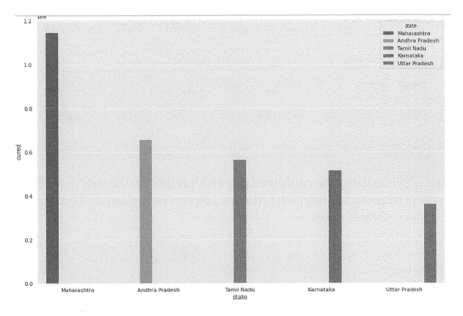

Step 16: We analyze the statistics with respect to the state of Madhya Pradesh.

```
#Madhya Pradesh
madhya_Pradesh = df[df.state == 'Madhya Pradesh']
```

```
madhya_Pradesh
```

Output:

	date	state	cured	deaths	confirmed
256	2020-03-21	Madhya Pradesh	0	0	4
279	2020-03-22	Madhya Pradesh	0	0	4
302	2020-03-23	Madhya Pradesh	0	0	6
325	2020-03-24	Madhya Pradesh	0	0	7
349	2020-03-25	Madhya Pradesh	0	0	14
...	...	...	...	...	...
6859	2020-10-01	Madhya Pradesh	104734	2316	128047
6894	2020-10-02	Madhya Pradesh	107279	2336	130088
6929	2020-10-03	Madhya Pradesh	109611	2372	132107
6964	2020-10-04	Madhya Pradesh	111712	2399	133918
6999	2020-10-05	Madhya Pradesh	113832	2434	135638

199 rows × 5 columns

Step 17: Visualizing the confirmed cases with respect to the state of Madhya Pradesh by using sns.lineplot() where x axis represents date and y axis represents confirmed cases.

```
#Visualizing confirmed cases in #Madhya Pradesh
sns.set(rc={'figure.figsize':(15,10)})
sns.lineplot(x="date",y="confirmed",data=madhya_Pradesh,color="g")
plt.show()
```

Output:

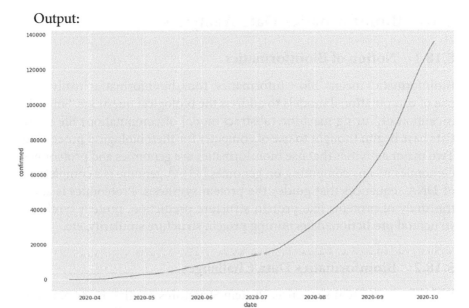

Step 18: Visualizing the death cases with respect to the state of Madhya Pradesh by using sns.lineplot() where x axis represents date and y axis represents death cases.

```
#Visualizing death cases in Madhya Pradesh
sns.set(rc={'figure.figsize':(15,10)})
sns.lineplot(x="date",y="deaths",data=madhya_Pradesh,color="r")
plt.show()
```

Output:

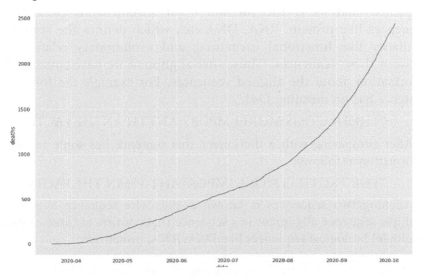

8.18   Bioinformatics Data Analytics

8.18.1   Notion of Bioinformatics

Bioinformatics means 'Bio + Informatics'. Thus, bioinformatics involves the use of computational models to address the biological questions. Since the invention of Turing machine (abstract model of computation) life scientists have begun thought to use of computer for their biological processing. Two major activities that use bioinformatics are genomics and proteomics. Genomics means computing on genomes [33]. A genome is a complete set of DNA sequences that guides the protein synthesis. Proteomics is about the study of proteins like protein structure prediction, protein synthesis, structural prediction, determining protein structure similarity, etc.

8.18.2   Bioinformatics Data Challenges

DNA, RNA, Protein sequence, Protein Structures are the major bioinformatics data. The size of bioinformatics data is not small, hence reading, storing, and analyzing these biological data remain challenging. Finding the accurate similarity between the two DNA/Protein sequences is still a computationally hard problem. Also, efficient storage of DNA, RNA, and Protein structures is still a challenging task. Moreover, making efficient phylogenetic analysis, and developing Killer App like personalized medicine are emerging research challenges.

8.18.3   Sequence Analysis

Sequence analysis is the method of arrangement (alignment) of sequences like protein, RNA, DNA etc., which defines the region of similarity like functional, structural, and evolutionary relationship between these sequences. Thus, after alignment we have some useful information about the aligned sequences. For example the following sentence has no meaning [34].

"THETR UTHIS MOREI MPORT ANTTH ANTHE FACTS"

After comparing with a dictionary, this sentence has some semantic information as follows:

"THE TRUTH IS MORE IMPORTANT THAN THE FACTS"

Aligning two sequences is known as pair-wise sequence alignment. Multiple sequence alignment is a sequence that consists of three or more (multiple) biological sequences like DNA, RNA, protein, etc.

Multiple sequence alignment is an important problem in biological computations. Accuracy of many practical problems including Phylogenetic analysis and determining motif depend on the result of the multiple sequence alignment algorithm [40]. However, doing multiple sequence alignment is computationally hard problem in bioinformatics. Hardness of doing multiple sequence alignment has given rise to many approaches including soft computing based on genetic algorithm (GA).

Multiple sequence alignment using GA and dynamic programming – The use of combined techniques of and pairwise dynamic programming for multiple sequence alignment is the approach for efficient and robust search. This approach is used for obtaining efficient solution. In particular, GA is used to find match block in the sequences and pairwise dynamic programming is used in subsequences between the match block. Combination of two techniques achieved high efficiency and quality of alignment. The combined method reduces both memory space and time while also handling both matches and mismatches. The system can efficiently deal with many, long, and complex sequence data by combining the two advanced methodologies.

The approach is built on a multiple populations GENITOR-type GA and uses local search heuristics to solve the sum of the pairs of multiple protein sequence alignments.

A natural extension of two-sequence alignment is multiple sequence alignment (MSA). The emphasis was on multiple sequence alignment in multiple sequence alignment. To solve the Multiple Sequence Alignment problem, a simple prototype was created using a combination of Genetic Algorithm and Simulated Annealing. The Genetic Algorithm phase discovered fresh regions of solution, whilst Simulated Annealing can be used to improve the alignment of any near-optimal solution found by GAs.

A new technique to solve MSA assignments was to utilize a combination of Genetic Algorithm and Simulated Annealing. Simulated Annealing was used as an alignment improver while the Genetic Algorithm was used to locate a new region of feasible solution. There were various factors to consider, including representation, evaluation functions, and operators. In comparison to Dynamic Programming, simulated annealing helps to avoid local minima problems.

8.18.4   Applications

Following applications are implemented through multiple sequence alignment: predicting protein structure, predicting protein function, polygenetic analysis, pattern identification, domain identification, DNA regulatory etc.

These applications are used in forensic investigation and many bioinformatics applications.

The abovementioned applications and many related applications can be implemented through multiple sequence alignment, but still there is no convenient approach for multiple sequence alignment.

8.18.5   COVID-19: A Bioinformatics Approach

Bioinformatics methodologies can be used to identify genes and pathways, those shared among patients with comorbidities and having severe **COVID-19**. This is the advanced bioinformatics application to identify the similar persons by doing the gene profiling to identify the disease at earliest, and also emerging active research area to prepare drug cocktails (personalized medicine) in extremely short period of time which is suitable for a particular person without any side effect.

8.19   Conclusion

Healthcare services are a basic need for every citizen of society and every government should be on top priority to provide basic healthcare facility at an affordable cost; the healthcare community has also realized the potential of Big Data and Big Data analytics in healthcare system. The exponential growth of medical data is big challenge for management, integration and implementation. Advance healthcare system is a combination of bioinformatics and health informatics. Furthermore, new healthcare strategies and technology, spanning from medical data management to drug discovery programs for complicated human diseases such as cancer and neurodegenerative disorders, should be developed. Smart Healthcare system involves updated digital use of various devices and various technologies like Internet of Things (IOT), Artificial Intelligence (AI), big data analytics, machine learning in healthcare system, which work through sensors and operate remotely. In future, different devices and applications will warn for patients and healthcare service provider to be careful, when early symptoms appear. Healthcare service providers will be more easily reachable to patients, and the patients also have medical history and it will be more accessible for healthcare providers.

References

1. Zhang, C. and Wong, A.K.C., Toward efficient multiple molecular sequence alignment: A system of genetic algorithm and dynamic programming. *IEEE Trans. Syst. Man Cybern.-Part B: Cybern.*, 27, 6, 918–932, 1997.

2. Nguyen, H.D., Yoshihara, I., Yamamori, K., Yasunaga, M., A parallel hybrid genetic algorithm for multiple protein sequence alignment. *IEEE*, 0-7803-7282-4/02, 309–314, 2002.

3. Othman, M.T.B. and Abdel-Azim, G., Multiple sequence alignment based on genetic algorithms with new chromosomes representation. *IEEE*, 978-1-4673-0784-0/12, 1030–1033, 2012.

4. Harik, G.R., Lobo, F.G., Goldberg, D.E., The compact genetic algorithm. *IEEE Trans. Evol. Comput.*, 3, 4, 287–297, 1999.

5. Suzuki, J., A further result on the Markov chain model of genetic algorithms and its application to a simulated annealing-like strategy. *IEEE Trans. Syst. Man Cybern.-Part B: Cybern.*, 28, 1, 95–102, February 1998.

6. Omar, M.F., Multiple sequence alignment using genetic algorithm and simulated annealing. *IEEE*, 3, 212–17, 2004.

7. Ying-Ding, Z., Research on optimal multiple sequence alignment. *International conference on e-business and e- government*, pp. 221–226, 2010.

8. Smith, S.F., RNA gene finding with biased mutation operators. *Proceedings of the IEEE Symposium on Computational Intelligence in Bioinformatics and Computational Biology*, pp. 268–274, 2007.

9. Connors, D.P. and Kumar, P.R., Simulated annealing and balance of recurrence order intime-inhomogeneous markov chainst. *IEEE*, 1, 225–238, 1987.

10. Naznin, F., Sarker, R., Essam, D., Progressive alignment method using genetic algorithm for multiple squence alignment. *IEEE*, 1, 378–382, 2011.

11. Chambers, B., *Spark: The definitive guide: Big data processing M made simple*, O'Reilly Media, Inc, Sebastopol, California, 2018.

12. Karau, H., Konwinski, A., Wendell, P., Zaharia, M., *Learning spark: Lightning-fast big data analysis*, O'Reilly Media, Inc, Sebastopol, California, 2015.

13. Wills, J., Ryza, S., Laserson, U., Owen, S., *Advanced analytics with spark: Patterns for learning from data at scale*, O'REILLY, Sebastopol, California, 2009.

14. Luu, H., Beginning Apache Spark 2: With Resilient distributed datasets, spark SQL, in: *Structured streaming and spark machine learning library*, A press, 2018.

15. Shalev-Shwartz, S. and Ben-David, S., *Understanding machine learning: from theory to algorithms*, Cambridge University Press, Cambridge, MA, USA, 2014.

16. Bironneau, M. and Coleman, T., *Machine learning with go quick start guide: Hands-on techniques for building supervised and unsupervised machine learning work flows*, Packt Publishing Ltd, Birmingham, UK, 2019.

17. Grange, J., *Machine learning for absolute beginners: A simple, concise & complete introduction to supervised and unsupervised learning algorithms*, Create Space Independent Publishing Platform, Scotts Valley, California, 2017.

18. Geron, A., *Hands-on machine learning with scikit- learn, keras, and tensor-Flow: Concepts, tools, and techniques to build intelligent systems*, O'Reilly Media, Inc, Sebastopol, California, 2017.

19. Marsland, S., *Machine learning: An algorithmic perspective*, CRC Press, Boca Raton, Fla, 2014.

20. Amirghodsi, S., Hall, B., Rajendran, M., Mei, S., *Apache Spark 2.x machine learning cookbook*, Packt Publishing Ltd, Birmingham, UK, 2017.

21. Mayer-Schönberger, V. and Cukier, K., *Big data: A revolution that will transform how we live, work, and think*, Houghton Mifflin Harcourt, Boston, MA., USA, 2013.

22. Ankam, V., *Big data analytics*, Packt Publishing Ltd, Birmingham, UK, 2016.

23. Walkowiak, S., *Big data analytics with R*, Packt Publishing Ltd, Birmingham, UK, 2016.

24. Wickham, H. and Grolemund, G., *R for Data Science: Import, Tidy, Transform, Visualize, and Model Data*, 1st, Shroff/O'Reilly, India, 2017.

25. Bahga, A. and Madisetti, V., *Big data analytics: A hands-on approach*, VPT, Blacksburg, VA, 2018.

26. Kuma, U.D. and Pradhan, M., *Machine learning using python*, Wiley, USA, 2019.

27. DT Editiorial Services, *Big data, black book*, DT Editorial Services Dreamtech Press, Darya Ganj, Delhi, India, 2015, ASIN:B01LZEWQH6.

28. Marr, B., *Big data in practice: How 45 successful companies used big data analytics to deliver extraordinary results*, 1st, Wiley, USA, 2016, ASIN:B01DCOYDUS.

29. Flach, P., *Machine learning: The art and science of algorithms that make sense of data*, Cambridge University Press, Cambridge, MA, USA, 2012.

30. D'Arcy, A., Kelleher, J.D., Namee, B.M., Fundamentals of Machine Learning for Predictive Data Analytics: Algorithms, in: *Worked examples, and case studies*, MIT Press, Cambridge, MA, USA, 2015.

31. Grus, J., *Data science from scratch*, O'Reilly Media, Inc., Sebastopol, California, 2015.

32. Chandarana, P. and Vijayalakshmi, M., Big data analytics frameworks, in: *International Conference on Circuits, Systems, Communication and Information Technology Applications (CSCITA)*, 2014.

33. Keim, D., Ma, K.-L., Qu, H., Big-data visualization. *IEEE Comput. Graph,. Appl.*, 3, 199–210, 2013, doi: 10.1109/MCG.2013.54.

34. Golfarelli, M., Pirini, T., Rizzi, S., Goal-based selection of visual representations for big data analytics, in: *Proceedings of the MoBid*, Springer, Valencia, Berlin, pp. 47–57, 2017.

35. Börzsönyi, S., Kossmann, D., Stocker, K., the skyline operator, in: *Proceedings of the ICDE*, IEEE, Heidelberg, New York, pp. 421–430, 2001.

36. Ardagna, C., Bellandi, V., Damiani, E., A model-driven methodology for big data analytics-as-a-service, in: *Proceedings of the IEEE international congress on big data*, 2017.

37. Bouali, F., Guettala, A.E., Venturini, G., Viz Assist an interactive user assistant for visual data mining. *Visual Comput.*, 1, 1447–1463, 2016.

38. Ibrahim, I.A., Albarrak, A.M., Li, X., Constrained recommendations for query visualizations. *Knowl. Inf. Syst.*, 1, 499–529, 2017.

39. Wongsuphasawat, K., Moritz, D., Anand, A., towards a general-purpose query language for visualization recommendation, in: *Proceedings of the HILDA*, San Francisco, CA, p. 4, 2016.

40. Oprea, A., Li, Z., Yen, T., Detection of early-stage enterprise infection by mining large-scale log data, in: *Proceedings of the DSN*, Rio De Janeiro, Brazil, pp. 45–56, 2015.

9

Features Optimistic Approach for the Detection of Parkinson's Disease

R. Shantha Selva Kumari*, L. Vaishalee and P. Malavikha

Department of Electronics and Communication Engineering, Mepco Schlenk Engineering College, Sivakasi, Tamil Nadu, India

Abstract

The dreadful neuro-degenerative disorder, Parkinson's disease (PD) is hard to detect in its early stage. Even in the early stages of the disease, Single photon emission computed tomography (SPECT) has proven to be efficient in diagnosis. In this paper, SPECT images of healthy normal, early PD, and Subjects without Deficit of Dopamine Deficit (SWEDD), are obtained from the Parkinson's Progression Markers Initiative (PPMI) database, and processed to compute distinguishable shape-based features. Along with it these features are compared with striatal binding ratio (SBR) features, which are well established and clinically used by computing feature importance score. Using Random Forest Technique, feature importance estimation is carried out and those importance features are used for classification. Classification of the patients is done with the help of support vector machine (SVM) and other classifiers like KNN and Naïve Bayes. The performance measures of the classifier: accuracy is 98.6%, Specificity obtained is 98.2%, Sensitivity is 99% and Precision is 97% which is higher than the performance obtained through the methods discussed in the previous literatures. With the help of using only important/minimal features, it is possible to achieve higher accuracy in classification of subjects. Shape analysis is found to be a promising method for extracting discriminatory features develop diagnostic models and is having the potential to help clinicians in the diagnostic process.

Keywords: Parkinson disease (PD), Parkinsonian Syndrome (PS), Single Photon Emission Computed Tomography (SPECT), Subjects Without Deficit of Dopamine Deficit (SWEDD), Dopamine Transporter (DAT) shape features, Parkinson's Progression Markers Initiative (PPMI) database, Support Vector Machine (SVM)

Corresponding author: rshantha@mepcoeng.ac.in; ORCID: https://orcid.org/0000-0003-4123-7744

D. Sumathi, T. Poongodi, B. Balamurugan and Lakshmana Kumar Ramasamy (eds.)
Cognitive Intelligence and Big Data in Healthcare, (229–256) © 2022 Scrivener Publishing LLC

9.1   Introduction

9.1.1   Parkinson's Disease

The organic chemical dopamine, belonging to the catecholamine family is highly responsible for the activities of brain. The amino compound is synthesized by the elimination of carboxyl compound levodopa. Generally dopamine concentration is found in most living organisms like plants and animals. Dopamine acts as a neuro-transmitter. The endogenous compound responsible for neurotransmission is known as neurotransmitters. From synaptic vesicles, it is released into synaptic left.

These neurotransmitters are responsible for motor activities like moving, writing and other limb activities. Parkinson's disease is characterized by the reduced presence or mere absence of this dopamine compound. Resting tremor is one of the visible symptoms [7] i.e., even in the resting position, the affected individuals suffer from tremor disorders thereby leading to reduced activity of limbs as compared to the normal subjects [6]. Some other visible symptoms may include, Bradykinesia, slow movement, even the simpler tasks may seem difficult for them and it consumes more time to get completed, e.g., they will be dragging their feet, if they are in an attempt to walk.

This explains the DaT scanning process: Initially, the injection of the imaging agent is given to PD patient. After injection, gamma camera, a special detector, is used to visualize the compound. This scan gives the dopamine transporter (DaT), and it will be helpful for a doctor to determine if patient is having tremor due to This scan will reveal the dopamine transporter (DaT), which will assist a doctor identify whether the patient's tremor is caused by Parkinson's disease or another Parkinsonism (a condition that affects dopamine systems and causes symptoms similar to Parkinson's disease). Only minor side effects are present (e.g. dizziness, headache, creepy crawly feeling under the skin and increased appetite). The "function" of the brain is examined using imaging techniques like DaT/SPECT and PET scans, rather than its anatomy (appearance). In contrast to strokes and malignancies, the brain anatomy of a Parkinson's disease patient is mostly normal. These scans give brain chemistry reveal changes, such as a decrease in dopamine, which may aid in the diagnosis of Parkinson's disease and other forms of Parkinsonism. There are a variety of compounds available that can be used in both PET and SPECT scanning; however, DaT/SPECT scans indicates the activity of the dopamine transporter, whereas PET scans typically shows the glucose (sugar) metabolism.

A frequent pattern in persons with Parkinson's disease is cell loss that begins on one side and progresses to the back of the basal ganglia. Cells in the basal ganglia, a region of the brain related with movement, will be lost.

Over time, these affected areas spread across the entire region. It is also normal due to aging process some of these cells may lose. Scanning patterns may appear. As a result, it takes a specialist/doctor to examine these scans and determine if the changes are related to disease or natural ageing. The larger the decline in uptake on the scan, the more advanced the degeneration.

An interpretation of DaT's scans is essential. The first step is to assess whether the scan is normal. The specialist will then look to see if the scan shows signs of Parkinson's disease or Parkinsonism. Finally, the severity of brain cell will be determined.

9.1.2   Spect Scan

In order to visualize physical anatomy and structure of the brain wide variety of scans are prevailing in the market. Those include MRI, CT, etc., as CT may sometimes lead to allergic reactions as it uses X-ray, whereas MRI is found safe as it uses strong magnetic fields and radio waves for scanning. Though MRI is costlier as twice as much of CT, MRI provides a detailed account of tumors, aneurysms in brain etc., MRI is considered to be less harmful than CT, MRI probes a detailed account of soft brain tissues.

As Parkinson's disease is characterized by the presence or absence of dopaminergic activity, MRI and CT may sometimes fail to provide the account on dopaminergic concentration. The brain activity depends on blood flow and SPECT scan is the only method that provides detailed account of blood flow [5].

SPECT scan has proved to be the efficient technique in neural science. The gamma emitting radioisotope, a radionuclide is injected to provide true 3D information of the target. SPECT images can be normal or abnormal, symmetric, and intense; DAT binding [23] in putamen and caudate on two hemispheres look like the shape of a comma and characterize normal scans [1]. The comma-shaped characterizes the presence of dopaminergic activity, whereas dot-shaped characterizes the deficit of dopamine.

During the investigation of PD, clinical professionals coined the term Scans without Evidence of Dopaminergic Deficit (SWEDD) or normal dopaminergic activity [20]. SWEDD subjects suffer from resting tremor, therefore they are characterized under PD [3], but actually they don't possess the disease. Their SPECT scans reveal that they too have the dopaminergic activity as that of normal subject, but they are misinterpreted that they have Parkinson's disease.

Single-photon emission computed tomography (SPECT) Imaging using I-Ioflupane has proved as the most sensitive imaging techniques as it helps in efficient and early detection [9]. Accurate detection is difficult for management of the patient effectively because the disease progress, diagnosis, and treatment differ substantially from other patients/tremor diseases. In this chapter, distinguishable shape-based features are extracted from the Parkinson's Progression Markers Initiative (PPMI) database. SPECT images of healthy people, people with early Parkinson's disease, and people with SWEDD.

SPECT doesn't involve the injection of external radiation like that of detective X-rays, in order to extract the information on inner organs. In this scenario, radiopharmaceuticals come into picture. Radiopharmaceuticals emit radiations that are used for therapeutics and diagnosis.

9.2   Literature Survey

A group of movement of disorders called Parkinson's syndrome (PS) is characterized by rigidity, resting tremor, and bradykinesia symptoms. The diagnosis of Parkinson's disease (PD) based on clinical symptoms is a favorable response to levodopa [20] and is straightforward. SPECT scan has proved to be the efficient technique in neural science. While the disease is in early stages, the symptoms are less and unusual with responses non-convincing to levodopa, therefore the diagnosis is somehow inconclusive and difficult. Imaging using I-Ioflupane has proved to be the most sensitive imaging techniques as it helps in efficient and early detection [4]. The gamma emitting radioisotope, a radionuclide is injected to provide true 3D information of the target. Accurate detection is difficult for management of the patient effectively because the prognosis, course of the disease, and treatment differ significantly from other disorders or non-degenerative tumor variations [7].

Clinically, SPECT images are valued either via visually or using Region-of-Interest (ROI) analysis. As expertise and knowledge are the key dependent factors of visual analysis and it may also lead to many pitfalls, PPMI has provided Striatal Binding Ratio (SBR) as quantified striatal values computed by PPMI Nuclear medicine experts. These help to avoid ambiguity in visual assessments. An alternate approach [16] is shape analysis and surface fitting. As it has its own advantages like, there is no need of positioning ROI as it can be automated or semi-automated. The regions in which the striatum's greater uptake portions [22] were segregated and quantified by fitting an ellipse to the region. Overall, the following is a summary of the work: The SPECT scan imaging data of healthy normal, SWEDD, PD were used. In order to extract the region of high activity, segmentation is done. This is followed by shape analysis and surface fitting. For surface fitting polynomial equation of order 3 is used. Classification based on SVM is developed to classify early PD from SWEDD. The accuracy obtained is also compared with the accuracy obtained using the SBR features along with the shape features. The result obtained through shape analysis and surface fitting [12, 17] gives accuracy better than that of clinically obtained feature, i.e., Putamen and Caudate SBR. But the surface fitting of data tend to cause run time complexity.

Table 9.1 Shape features for all the three classes of subjects and its asymmetric index value.

Features (Mean)	Normal	SWEDD	PD	P1	P2
Area	106.69	110.41	58.56	0.8	≈0
Major Axis Length*	16.44	16.40	10.39	0.89	≈0
Minor Axis Length	8.62	8.87	7.094	0.09	≈0
Aspect Ratio	1.12	1.14	0.8358	0.45	≈0
Eccentricity	0.84	0.83	0.6901	0.06	≈0
Orientation	8.15	5.10	05.1122	0.26	≈0
Area AI*	0.48	1.58	-2.2788	0.82	≈0
MajorAxisLengthAI	0.05	0.04	0.0767	0.37	≈0
MinorAxisLengthAI	-0.01	0.10	-0.2677	0.34	≈0
AspectRatioAI	-0.03	-0.03	-0.0238	0.73	≈0
Eccentricity AI	0.008	0.005	0.0302	0.25	≈0
Orientation AI*	13.51	10.95	31.5050	0.44	≈0

*Proved as important features.

In order to overcome the complexity caused by computation due to both shape and surface analysis this work proposed an optimized technique which provides better performance due to classification with the help of minimal features. First all shape features mentioned in Table 9.1 and from this the exclusive features are extracted. Through random forest technique the feature importance are computed. Instead of using all the features, then only a few features which contribute much for distinguishing the early PD and SWEDD are used. These few features are considered to be important features and used the important features for classification. The performance of SVM with the help of these important features is higher than that of the performance through shape and surface analysis and also clinically computed features.

9.3   Methods and Materials

9.3.1   Database Details

As PPMI serves as a landmark and multi centered study for categorizing PD progression biomarkers, dataset (www.ppmi-info.org/data) discussed in this chapter is from the PPMI Database [2] SPECT images of healthy people, people with SWEDD, and people with early PD were used in this work. The subjects considered were 201 healthy normal, 111 SWEDD, and 209 PD subjects. The SPECT image obtained through PPMI were DICOM images.

9.3.2   Procedure

Image is received from PPMI database [2]. The preprocessed image available in the database is considered for further process. PPMI database provides access to students, researchers, and clinicians to obtain the clinical data, database, biomarkers etc., These SPECT images are of processed or in raw format. The patient's privacy is maintained and the identity is de-identified. PPMI provides a specimen of data as biomarkers for clinical research. This database acts as a central hub for scientific community, who carry out their research on clinical data. PPMI has data in modalities like DaTSCAN SPECT, AV-133 PET (positron emission tomography), DTI (diffusion tensor imaging), and f-MRI [4].

Recently voxel-based analysis [14] plays a major role in clinical research because reduction in uptake can be clearly visualized via the voxel clusters. Selecting Region of Interest and visual assessments are the peer practices. Visual assessment cannot be accurate as it solemnly depends on the observer's decision.

In ROI technique, the target area is nigro-striatum. It is located in midbrain and it is mainly responsible for motion. This striatum region appears to be blacker than the other regions due to the presence of dopamine concentration in that area rather than its neighboring parts. Here the occipital cortex is taken as reference region. The striatal binding ratio is computed with these quantitative methods.

This is computed using the concept of background subtraction. With the help of sound knowledge of nuclear medicine experts, Striatal Binding Ratio (SBR) values are available via the database. Because of many pitfalls and human errors that occurred via human assessment, this quantitative analysis has proved to be the efficient and effective tool for classification.

The obtained images are normalized and segmented. The segmented image is used for shape and surface features extraction. All the shape features and surface features along with SBR values are used as feature inputs. The statistically important features are analyzed with the help of rank test and classifications of groups are justified. Previous works are based on giving all extracted features as input to the classifier. The proposed work classifies the subjects with the help of minimal feature input in order to eliminate the overhead. These features are considered as highly contributing features for accurate classification. The important feature is estimated and classification in made using SVM.

9.3.3   Pre-Processing Done by PPMI

The SPECT scan images present in the PPMI database are already preprocessed and hence they can be readily used for further processing steps.
Pre-processing is done to ensure that all the scan images were in the same
anatomical alignment. Anatomically aligned, in the sense they were spa-
tially normalized.

9.3.4   Image Analysis and Features Extraction

9.3.4.1   Image Slicing

Slicing of an image includes dividing the entire image into smaller segments in order to extract our region of interest.

We mainly concentrate on the presence of dopaminergic activity in the
brain and therefore the slice that clearly depicts the dopaminergic concentration has to be isolated for further process. According to the Society of
Nuclear Medicine(SNM), as there are 91 trans axial slices in SPECT image
and striatum is the region were the deterioration in DAT imaging is visualized because radio ligand binds to the striatal DAT specifically. Whenever
dopaminergic degeneration occurs, striatal uptake gets reduced with
decrease in reduction of density of DAT. This decrease in DAT characterizes the presence of PD. The Region of Interest is 42nd slice as this is the area
where highest striatal uptake is recorded. Therefore the slices meant for
consideration ranges from 35th to 48th slice. Image slicing is an enhanced
approach to optimize the complexity and to make the further processes
to concentrate much on the specific area. Therefore effective computation
can be done. Dataset is obtained from Parkinson's Progressive Markers
Initiative. SPECT images are obtained in dicom format. The sample dataset
for normal, SWEDD and PD subjects are given Figures 9.1 and 9.2.

Figure 9.2.a: the SPECT scan of normal subject indicates the abundant
presence of dopamine concentration. Figure 9.2.b depicts the SPECT scan
of SWEDD subjects, where there is sufficient amount of dopamine presence, but sill they are misinterpreted as PD. Figure 9.2.c shows the SPECT
scan of PD, as compared to other subjects, there is reduction of dopamine
concentration [5].

As there are 91 trans axial slices in SPECT image and striatum [18] is
the region were the deterioration in DAT imaging is visualized because
radio ligand binds to the striatal DAT specifically. Whenever dopaminergic degeneration occurs, density of DAT decreases and meanwhile striatal
uptake is also reduced. The region of interest is the 42nd slice as this is the

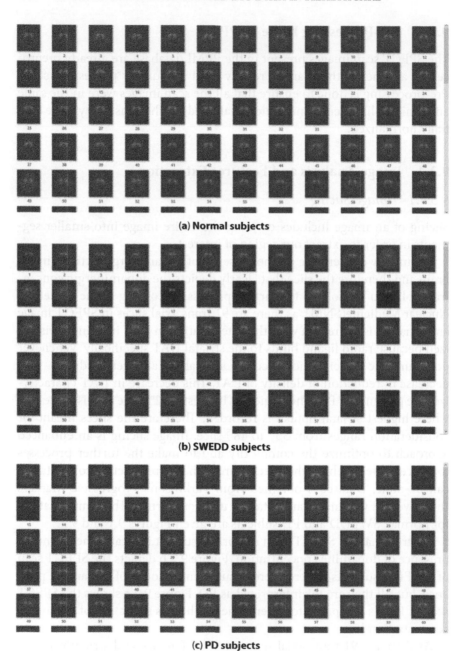

Figure 9.1 SPECT images obtained from PPMI database in dicom format.

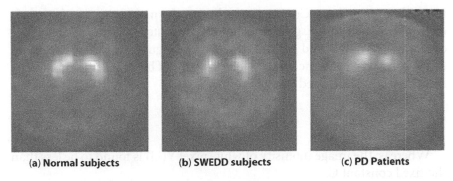

(a) **Normal subjects**   (b) **SWEDD subjects**   (c) **PD Patients**

Figure 9.2 Zoomed version SPECT images obtained from PPMI database in dicom format.

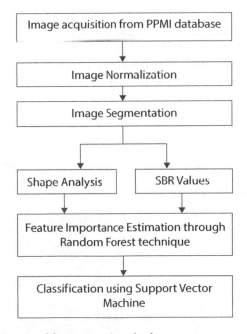

Figure 9.3 Block diagram of the proposed method.

area where highest striatal uptake is recorded. Therefore the slices meant for consideration ranges from 35th to 48th slice. Figure 9.3 gives the block diagram of the proposed method for Parkinson's disease detection.

9.3.4.2   Intensity Normalization

Generally, slices of an image have different pixel intensity values and in order to confine the pixel intensity values to range between [0,1], intensity normalization is done. Contrast stretching is the main purpose of normalization. For each image, gray threshold is computed. The normalized slice of normal, SWEDD and PD are discussed in Figure 9.4. A fixed constant (C) is considered and the image intensity Z(i,j) of black pixel is found to be less than that of the fixed constant C:

$$Z(i,j) < C \qquad (9.1)$$

Whereas, the image intensity of white pixel Y(i,j) is found to be less than the fixed constant C.

$$Y(i,j) > C \qquad (9.2)$$

Gray threshold is calculated for each image. It is plotted as histogram. Histogram reveals the pictorial representation of numerical data. It is highly accurate than other distributions and so it is preferred for clinical data analysis. Before plotting the histogram, the axis coordinates for x-axis

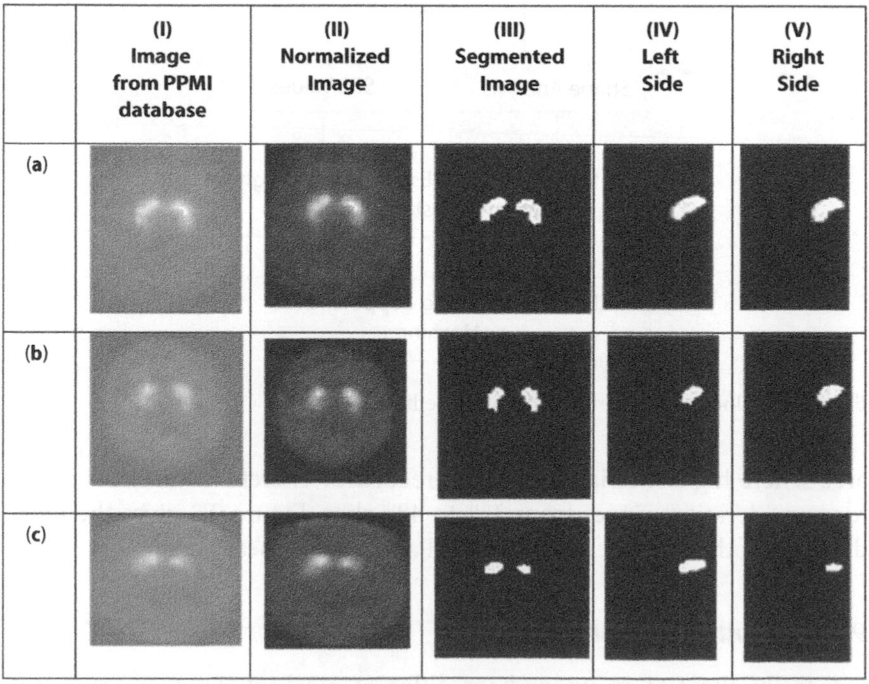

	(I) Image from PPMI database	(II) Normalized Image	(III) Segmented Image	(IV) Left Side	(V) Right Side
(a)					
(b)					
(c)					

Figure 9.4 (a) Normal (b) SWEDD patient (c) PD patient.

and y-axis have to be carefully chosen. The axis coordinates can be linearly spaced and the values in scale must be non-overlapping. Because overlapping values in scale may result in more sensitive errors. The output of the histogram is represented by rectangular boxes.

As the histogram output is in continuous scale, there should not be any space between the adjacent consecutive rectangular boxes. The term 'Histogram' has its origin from Greek ascent meaning something that is straight. Histogram differs from bar graph as the latter deals with the two constraints but histogram deals with single variable. The rectangle found at output may be of variable widths and need not be fixed. While extracting the statistical property, histograms play a crucial role in medical field due to its accurate estimation. The major difference between histogram and bar chart is histogram delivers the continuous distribution whereas bar chart delivers the discrete distribution of data. In order to find the threshold, the histogram is plotted against threshold versus frequency.

9.3.4.3   Image Segmentation

In order to have accurate analysis, image has to undergo a process known as segmentation. Segments possess a relevant characteristics like contour, pixel intensity etc., are grouped. Segmentation has its own application in medical field like tumor detection and Planning for surgery. Other significant applications include face and iris recognition, fingerprint detection, etc.

Segmentation using thresholds is mainly used to convert the processed binary slice to binary format. Otsu method of segmentation is the recently developed method for segmentation as it delivers better results than other methods when CT images of the brain are considered. This method uses obtained from the X-rays rather than normal images therefore the true 3D information leads to better accuracy in detection.

To obtain the high uptake region of dopamine, segmentation is done on images after normalization. The threshold value from the histogram of each category of subjects is calculated and the segmented image is shown in Figure 9.4. Empirical experiments and histogram results are used to fix the threshold for three classes of subjects.

As the region of interest is Nigro-striatum, segmentation is done in the striatum region. Then the mean threshold value for each group of subjects is calculated. As the dopamine concentration is found lost in putamen and then subsequently in caudate, the threshold value of PD subjects are found relatively higher than the other group of subjects.

To confine the image of different pixel intensity values between [0,1] normalization of image is done on the preprocessed image obtained from the database. In order to obtain the high uptake region of dopamine, segmentation is done on images after normalization. Empirical experiments and histogram results are used to fix the threshold for three classes of subjects. The method used for computing threshold value is found in Section 9.3. Following segmentation, shape features are computed for the subjects on the region of interest. Segmented image is divided into left and right side. Left is taken as reference image, with the right side flipped to the left side. Shape Features are separately computed for both sides and asymmetric index is calculated.

9.3.4.4   Shape Features Extraction

Shape features accounts for the dimensions, geometric profile and density, etc. Dimensions in the sense, it deals about the shortness or length of certain feature. Geometric profile deals with the shape, i.e., for example square, triangle, hexagon etc. Density constraints include whether the region is found to be less dense or denser. Scale invariance is the important aspect of shape feature, the extracted features should not be subject to change with respect to the changes in scale [16]. Extracted features should be as robust as possible as it should not be affected by disturbances like noise.

Shape features can be extracted by the help of two methods, one by using the boundary points and the other by using interior points placed inside the image. The image taken for processing has two sides right and left [8]. The shape features to be extracted were Area, Minor Axis Length, Major Axis Length, Eccentricity, Orientation, Aspect Ratio, Area Asymmetric Index, Minor Axis Length Asymmetric Index, Major Axis Length Asymmetric Index, Eccentricity Asymmetric Index, Orientation Asymmetric Index, and Aspect Ratio Asymmetric Index [21]. These shape features are computed by the formulas discussed below.

Area
A boundary is formulated and based on the points plotted along the boundary, and the distance from the adjacent boundary points with respect to the boundary is calculated.
Minor Axis Length
The shortest dimension in an elliptical image of the slice in terms of pixels is termed as major axis length.

Major Axis Length
The longest dimension in an elliptical image of the slice in terms of pixels is termed as major axis length.

Eccentricity
Eccentricity of the elliptical slice is formulated using Equation 3. If the eccentricity value tends to be 1, then it indicates that the ellipse has become a circle.

Aspect Ratio
Aspect ratio of the elliptical slice is calculated using the height and width of the elliptical slice.

Orientation
Orientation of the elliptical slice indicates how far the major axis length gets deviated from y-axis.

Dopamine concentration is first lost in putamen followed by caudate [16], 'comma' shape that represents the presence of dopamine is changed to dot shaped. For extracting shape features from the image, left side is taken as reference and the right side of the image is flipped to the left and its Asymmetric index (AI) is computed.

Shape features to be extracted are Area(1), Minor Axis Length, Major Axis Length, Aspect Ratio(2), Eccentricity(3), Orientation, and its corresponding AI[8] given in Table 9.1.

Shape features are computed using the formula given below:

$$\text{Area} = \pi ab/4 \qquad (9.3)$$

$$\text{Aspect ratio} = h/w \qquad (9.4)$$

$$\text{Eccentricity} = c/a \qquad (9.5)$$

where a,b – major axis length and minor axis length, h,w – height and width of the segmented image, and c,a – distance from the center to the focus and to a vertex of the ellipse respectively. The features obtained are efficient enough to classify SWEDD from PD [3].

9.3.4.5 SBR Features

Four SBR-based features, i.e., SBR features in striatal regions namely caudate and putamen on left and right side which are available in PPMI database is taken into consideration [13]. Caudate left, Putamen left are taken directly whereas for caudate AI and putamen AI, left is taken reference to that of right.

9.3.4.6 Feature Set Analysis

Along with 12 shape features are four SBR features that count 16 features on the whole. These features are statistically test under Wilcoxon rank sum test. Feature whose p value is less than 0.05 are statistically significant for the classification of PD from SWEDD patients. It is inferred that these features give the same result (p > 0.05) for SWEDD and Normal. They are grouped as single entity which is helpful for binary classification.

9.3.4.7 Surface Fitting

Following the segmentation, the segmented slice is take for surface fitting. Surface fitting is done using polynomial of order 3 Equation (9.6). More complicated fitting greater than the order 2 can be represented in order 3. Cubic polynomial is used where ellipsoid and parabolic fitting becomes inefficient. Surface fitting has its importance in medical field, especially in detection of ocular and cranial abnormalities. Especially in detecting abnormal disorders occurring in lens, iris etc., Curve fitting is method for 2D images. It includes interpolation and smoothing. Extrapolation comes into the picture while discussing on over-fitting.

The polynomial of order 3 is given by:

$$f(x,y) = P_{00} + P_{10}x + P_{01}y + P_{20}x^2 + P_{11}xy + P_{02}y^2 + P_{30}x^3 + P_{12}xy^2 + P_{21}x^2y + P_{03}y^3 \tag{9.6}$$

where p_{ij} – model coefficients; $i,j - \{1,2....n\}$

The coordinates $\{x_i, y_i\}$ are normalized by setting the mean value to be o and the standard deviation value to be 1, before using in the fitting process. This does not influence the fitting process. Certain performance measure like Goodness of fit is estimated. This estimate is done using sum of squares due to error, root Mean square error, R^2, and adjusted R^2.

Sum of Squares Due to Error
It can be calculated by finding average of all the data and by subtracting the original value from the mean. The resultant difference is squared.

Root Mean Square Error
It deals with how much the observed value differs from the predicted value. The root mean square value is computed from Equation (9.7).

$$\text{RMSE} = \sqrt{\frac{\left(\sum_{i=1}^{n}(P_{i\_}O_i)^2\right)}{n}} \qquad (9.7)$$

R-Squared
The R-squared value can be computed using Equation (9.8).

$$R^2 = 1 - \frac{SSE}{SST} \qquad (9.8)$$

Where   SSE – Sum of Squares due to Error
            SST – Sum of Squares Total

Adjusted R-Squared
The Adjusted R-Squared can be computed using the Equation (9.9)

$$adj = 1 - \frac{n-1}{n-p} \times \frac{SSE}{SST} \qquad (9.9)$$

Where,   n - no of observations;   p - no of regression coefficients

Striatal Binding Ratio
The striatal binding ratio values were calculated and available at the database. There are four different SBR values: Caudate SBR, Caudate SBR AI, Putamen SBR, and Putamen SBR AI [18]. Caudate left, Putamen left are taken directly whereas for caudate AI and putamen AI, left is taken reference to that of right.

The Nigro-striatum is taken as reference and the caudate and putamen is observed in order to understand the dopamine uptake found in caudate and putamen.

9.3.5 Classification Modeling

Support Vector Machine classification is used for binary classification. Here, Normal and SWEDD are grouped as a single class and PD as other class.

SVM, the supervised learning model is used for classification as well as regression [10]. With the help of sufficient number of training sets, each one is categorized other any of the two groups and thus SVM develops the learning model which assigns a new data to any of two categories. It is a non-probabilistic binary linear classifier.

SVM segregates the two classes with the help of hyper-plane [17]. The best hyper plane is chosen whose distance is a maximum from the support vectors. Also, the distances from one of the support vectors to the hyper plane must be equal that of another.

The SVM defines that a decision surface (hyper plane) should be possibly long distance from any data point. The classifier *margin* is the distance from the plane to the closer data point. These points form *support vectors*. Maximizing the *margin* will contribute better classification [15].

A decision hyper plane is determined by an intercept '*b*' and hyper plane normal vector ŵ perpendicular to the hyper plane. This vector is called as the *weight vector*. To choose best among all the hyper planes which are perpendicular to the normal vector, intercept *b* is specified. As the hyper plane is perpendicular to the normal vector, all points '*a*' on the hyper plane satisfy. Figure 9.5 shows hyper planes for SVM classifier.

$$\vec{w}^T\vec{a} = -p \qquad (9.10)$$

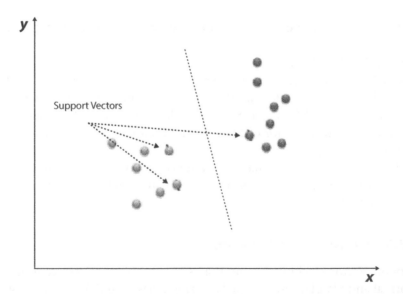

Figure 9.5 Hyper planes for SVM.

A set of training data points is given as $\mathbf{D} = \{(\mathbf{a}_i, \mathbf{b}_i)\}$, where each member is a pair of a point $\mathbf{a}_i$ and a class label $\mathbf{b}_i$. For SVMs, the two data classes are normally named +1 and −1, and the intercept term is represented as p. The linear classifier is then:

$$f(\vec{a}) = sign(\vec{w}^T \vec{a} + p)$$ (9.11)

A value of *-1* indicates one class (PD), and a value of *+1* the other class (Normal/SWEDD). The classification is good if the data point is far away from the decision boundary. The shortest distance between a point and a hyper plane should be perpendicular and parallel to the plane and $\hat{w}$ respectively. A unit vector is $\hat{w} / |\hat{w}|$. The label point on the hyper plane closest to $\vec{a}$ is considered as $\overrightarrow{a'}$.

Then

$$\vec{w}^T \left(\vec{a} - br \frac{\vec{w}}{|\vec{w}|} \right) + p = 0$$ (9.12)

The *geometric margin* is the maximum width of the plane which is drawn separating the support vectors of the two classes. It is twice the minimum value over data points for r. Any scaling constraint can be imposed on $\hat{w}$ without affecting the geometric margin. As scaling the functional margin is done, for convenience in solving large SVMs, here for all data points with functional margin at least 1 is equal to 1 for at least one data vector. That is, for all items in the data:

$$b_i \left(\vec{w}^T \vec{a} + p \right) > 1$$ (9.13)

The geometric margin is $\rho = \dfrac{2}{|\vec{w}|}$

The sum of influence of the support vector is expressed as kernel function. There are many kernel functions. Here radial basis function (RBF) is used. RBF is given by:

$$K(a, a') = \exp \left(\frac{\|a - a'\|^2}{2\sigma^2} \right)$$ (9.14)

Where $\|a-a'\|^2$ is the Euclidean distance. $\gamma=1/2\alpha^2$ which is given as 0.0625.

Usually in prediction model having binary classification is used 10-fold cross validation. The cross validation statistically estimates the potential of the learning model. It is evaluated on a limited data sample. Optimal value is chosen so as to get low bias. The procedure for k-fold cross-validation is as follows:

➤ Training dataset is shuffled randomly.
➤ Since 10-fold is chosen, dataset is decomposed into 10 groups.
➤ For each group,
    1. Some groups are taken as a training data set
    2. The remaining groups as a test data set
    3. A model obtained from the training set is used to evaluate the test set
    4. The evaluation score is retained and the model is discarded.
➤ The potential of the model is précised using the score.

Here, each group is given an opportunity to be used as test dataset for some time and also as train data during the procedure. The performance analysis of other classifiers is tabulated in Table 9.3. Thus the classification is made with the help of features obtained through shape and surface features.

9.3.6   Feature Importance Estimation

9.3.6.1   Need for Analysis of Important Features

Computation of various features using surface fitting cause greater runtime. In order to achieve higher accuracy with less computational complexity important feature estimation is done through random forest technique. Features computed through surface fitting and shape analysis is about 28. As surface fitting of data causes greater run-time, only shape features are compared with SBR values and importance is estimated. It is calculated through random forest technique. The performance of the other classifiers is tabulated in Table 9.3.

9.3.6.2 *Random Forest*

In random forest decision trees are used. Decision trees learn to split the dataset in smaller and smaller subset in the best way to achieve the target [19]. The decision is represented as *branches* and condition is represented as *node*. The splitting is done until the maximum depth is reached.

Random forest uses many decision trees for classification and regression process. The prediction of all the decision trees are taken and pooled to obtain the final result [11]. This is an ensemble technique as it uses the output of final decisions of many trees.

Apart from classification and regression, feature importance can be computed from this technique. Feature importance can be found by the decrease in the node impurity value which is weighted by probability of reaching that node.

$$Node\ Probability = \frac{\text{Number of samples that reach the node}}{Total\ no\ of\ nodes}$$

For each decision tree, node importance is carried out with the help of Gini importance. It assumes that the tree is a binary tree.

$$ni_j = w_j c_j - w_{left(j)} c_{left(j)} - w_{right(j)} c_{right(j)} \tag{9.15}$$

Where ni_j – node j importance; w_j – weighted number of samples reaching the node; c_j – impurity of the node j; $left_j$, $right_j$ – left and right child at each split.

The import feature of each node on a decision tree is computed by,

$$fi_i = \frac{\sum_{j:node\ j\ splits\ on\ feature\ i} ni_j}{\sum_{k \in all\ nodes} ni_k} \tag{9.16}$$

where fi_j – importance of feature i; ni_j – importance of node j.

$$normfi_i = \frac{fi_i}{\sum_{j \in all\ features} fi_j} \tag{9.17}$$

The feature importance $RFfi_i$ is calculated by sum of importance of feature $normfi_{ij}$ in each tree divided by total number of trees T,

Table 9.2 SBR values of caudate, putamen values.

SBR features (mean value)	Normal	SWEDD	PD
Caudate	2.98	2.78	1.989
Putamen	2.13	1.989	0.75
Caudate AI	0.0355	0.0366	0.059
Putamen AI	-0.003	-0.0026	-0.0013

$$RFfi_i = \frac{\sum_{j \in alltrees} normfi_{ij}}{T}$$

This gives the important feature among all the 28 features and those features are given for classification of subject using SVM instead of providing all the features estimated. Table 9.2 gives the SBR values of caudate, putamen values.

9.4 Results and Discussion

9.4.1 Segmentation

Threshold-based segmentation is carried out for three classes of subjects separately. Threshold for each subject is found and the histogram is plotted. The mean threshold value of Normal is 0.63 0.04, SWEDD is 0.64 0.03,

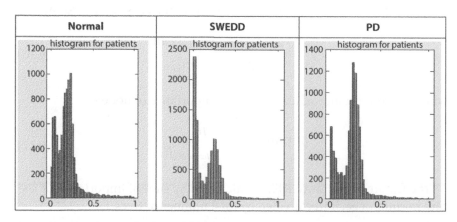

Figure 9.6 Histogram of thresholds for patients.

and for PD 0.690.05. Figure 9.6 shows histogram of threshold for all the three subjects.

9.4.2   Shape Analysis

Shape features as discussed in Section 2.3 are extracted and tabulated in Table 9.1. P1 signifies the rank test carried out between Normal and SWEDD and P2 is the rank test value for Normal/SWEDD versus PD. P1 > 0.05 for all features and P2 < 0.05 for all shape features. Left side value is used as reference and calculating the asymmetric index value.

The following inferences are observed from the table:

1. As the size of uptake regions reduces in Parkinson's Disease, Area, Major Axis Length, Minor Axis Length reduces in PD compared to that of other groups.
2. The size of uptake region looks like circle or dot in PD hence the aspect ratio and eccentricity is close to 1 and 0 respectively.
3. SWEDD scan corresponds to normal uptake in both anterior and posterior striatum whereas in PD the loss of dopamine activity leads to decrease to orientation value.

9.4.3   Classification

The shape features are given for statistical analysis using Wilcoxon Rank Sum test. It is used to determine any two dependent samples selected from populations having the same distribution. $p < 0.05$ is considered be to a statistically significant feature which can be used for distinguishing patients. No feature gives $p < 0.05$ while comparing SWEDD and Normal from Table 9.1 P1 whereas all the features give rank value $p > 0.05$ when SWEDD compared with PD [9]. Therefore we consider SWEDD and normal together as single entity for further classification.

For binary classification (SWEDD/Normal and PD) support vector machine can be used. Random forest technique [19] is performed to estimate the feature importance among all the features. Among all the shape features and SBR values only two features found to be important feature through Random forest technique. The number of trees chosen is 200 based on lower 10-fold cross validation [15]. From Figure 9.7 it is clear that the important features are Major Axis Length, Area, and Orientation AI. Area decreases for PD due to less dopamine activity than SWEDD patients.

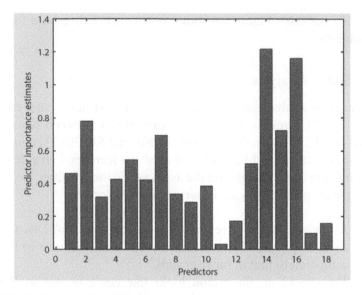

Figure 9.7 Predictors 1-18 with its importance.

Orientation also decreases for PD due to loss of posterior striatum activity, which is similar to Staff *et al.* [21] study.

Figure 9.7 shows Predictors 1–14 represents shape features 15–18 represents SBR features. Area, Orientation AI, and Major axis Length are the best among shape features. Putamen Left is the best among SBR feature. From this we consider Area, Orientation AI and Major axis length as exclusive feature among shape feature for further classification. The performance measures are obtained for SVM [10] and also for other classifiers like KNN, Naïve Bayes [12]. The accuracy found to be higher for all classifiers when important features were used than all shape features and SBR values. SVM gave accuracy of 98.6%. Radial Basis Kernel function is used for support vector machine (SVM) classifier [14]. RBF is given as:

$$K(x,x') = \exp(-\gamma \|x-x'\|^2) \tag{9.19}$$

Where x,x' are input feature vectors, $\|x-x'\|^2$ is Euclidean distance and $\gamma = 1/2\alpha^2$. The γ parameter is obtained for SVM using 10-fold CV as 0.0625, respectively.

From Table 9.3 it is proved that important features i.e., Major axis length, Area, and Orientation AI alone give more accuracy. Usage SBR feature along with shape features did not substantially provide better performance than exclusive feature that are obtained. This signifies that the

Table 9.3 Performance measures of various classifiers

Performance measures	Features	SVM	KNN	Naïve Bayes
Accuracy	a	97.4%	95.8%	97.7%
	b	98.6%	96.7%	97.9%
Sensitivity	a	97.9%	94%	99%
	b	99%	95%	98%
Specificity	a	98%	96%	96%
	b	98.2%	97%	97%
Precision	a	97	94	95
	b	97	96	96

'a' represents performance with all shape features computed in Table 9.1 and SBR values in Table 9.2.
'b' represents performance by using only the important estimated feature(Major axis length, Area, and Orientation AI).

Table 9.4 Performance comparison with related works.

Study	Proposed work	Accuracy
Proposed work	Major axis length, Area, and Orientation AI are considered as efficient features and SVM classifier is used for classification	98.6%
R. Prashanth *et al.* [13]	Shape features, Surface fitting coefficients, SBR values are considered for classification	97.29%
R. Prashanth *et al.* [9]	SVM Classification is done by considering striatal uptake values as features	96.14%
Staff *et al.* [21]	Segmentation is done on high uptake regions and fitting is done using aspect ratio	94%
Towey *et al.* [23]	Single Vector Decomposition is done followed by classification using Naïve Bayes classifier	94.8%
Illan *et al.* [4]	Voxels of brain is considered as feature and trained using SVM	96.8%

proposed optimized features give high-performance in the classification. This method has potential to be used in clinical diagnosis of Parkinson patients by distinguishing from SWEDD patients. The performance of all the classifier is improved by using only the important features (Major axis length, Area, and Orientation AI). From this work it is proved that by using the only three important features (Major axis length, Area, and Orientation AI) the classifier out-performs as given in Table 9.3 (b) than that used all the features as given in Table 9.3 (a).

Table 9.4 represents the previous works carried out in the field of detection of Parkinson's disease using different features like Striatal Binding Ratio (SBR), Aspect Ratio, Voxel-based approach, etc., whereas the proposed work focuses on using the most deviating features as efficient shape features for further classification.

Previous studies were aimed in achieving accuracy using the SBR based features and also by using surface fitting coefficients. In past works surface fitting coefficients proved to be the well-distinguishable feature and results in achieving greater accuracy but run-time complexity is high. It is inferred from this method that accounting the most deviating feature i.e., major axis length, area and orientation AI contribute much for higher accuracy with optimum features in turn faster computation, resulting in lowering the complexity. This work gives better performance than the previous works available in the literature. The Shape analysis especially with important features that are mentioned, achieve not only good performance than others but also minimize the computation process.

9.5   Conclusion

In this chapter, the images from the PPMI database are used to compute distinguishable shape-based features. Along with it these features are compared with the SBR features, which are clinically used to determine feature importance score. Random Forest algorithm is utilized to estimate the important features that are used for classification. Classification is done with the help of support vector machine (SVM). The accuracy is 98.6%, Specificity obtained is 98.2%, Sensitivity is 99%, and Precision is 97%, which is higher than the performance obtained through the methods discussed in the previous literatures. Wrong medication to even limbs may result in deadlier effects; therefore a small mistake in dosage to brain may even lead to comma or may result in death. The novel research in detection of PD in early stages helps to provide right treatment to PD subjects and avoids wrong medication to SWEDD. This will serve to save many lives from wrong medication in future.

References

1. Booth, T.C., Nathan, M., Waldman, A.D., Quigley, A.M., Schapira, A.H., Buscombe, J., The role of functional dopamine-transporter SPECT imaging in Parkinsonian syndromes Part 1. 36, 236–44, Feb. 2015.

2. Marek, K., Jennings, D., Lasch, S., Siderowf, A., Tanner, C., Simuni, T., Coffey, C., Kieburtz, K., Flagg, E., Chowdhury, S., Poewe, W., Mollenhauer, B., Klinik, P.-E., Sherer, T., Frasier, M., Meunier, C., Rudolph, A., Casaceli, C., Seibyl, J., Mendick, S., Schuff, N., Zhang, Y., Toga, A., Crawford, K., Ansbach, A., De Blasio, P., Piovella, M., Trojanowski, J., Shaw, L., Singleton, A., Hawkins, K., Eberling, J., Brooks, D., Russell, D., Leary, L., Factor, S., Sommerfeld, B., Hogarth, P., Pighetti, E., Williams, K., Standaert, D., Guthrie, S., Hauser, R., Delgado, H., Jankovic, J., Hunter, C., Stern, M., Tran, B., Leverenz, J., Baca, M., Frank, S., Thomas, C.A., Richard, I., Deeley, C., Rees, L., Sprenger, F., Lang, E., Shill, H., Obradov, S., Fernandez, H., Winters, A., Berg, D., Gauss, K., Galasko, D., Fontaine, D., Mari, Z., Gerstenhaber, M., Brooks, D., Malloy, S., Barone, P., Longo, K., Comery, T., Ravina, B., Grachev, I., Gallagher, K., Collins, M., Widnell, K.L., Ostrowizki, S., Fontoura, P., Ho, T., Luthman, J., vander Brug, M., Reith, A.D., Taylor, P., The Parkinson progression marker initiative (PPMI). *Prog. Neurobiol.*, 95, 629–635, 2011.

3. Schwingenschuh, P., Ruge, D., Edwards, M.J., Terranova, C., Katschnig, P., Carrillo, F., Silveira-Moriyama, L., Schneider, S.A., Kagi, G., Palomar, F.J., Talelli, P., Dickson, J., Lees, A.J., Quinn, N., Mir, P., Rothwell, J.C., Bhatia, K.P., Distinguishing SWEDDs patients with asymmetric resting tremor from Parkinson's disease: A clinical and electrophysiological study. *Mov. Disord.*, 25, 560–569, 2010.

4. Illan, J.M., ., Ramirez, J., Segovia, F., Jimenez-Hoyuela, J.M., Ortega Lozano, S.J., Automatic assistance to Parkinson's disease diagnosis in DaTSCAN SPECT imaging. *Med. Phys.*, 39, 5971–5980, Oct. 2012.

5. Scherfler, M.N., Dopamine transporter SPECT: How to remove subjectivity? *Mov. Disord.*, 24, S721–S724, 2009.

6. Marshall, V.L., Reininger, C.B., Marquardt, M., Patterson, J., Hadley, D.M., Oertel, W.H., Benamer, H.T., Kemp, P., Burn, D., Tolosa, E., Kulisevsky, J., Cunha, L., Costa, D., Booij, J., Tatsch, K., Chaudhuri, K.R., Ulm, G., Pogarell, O., Hoffken, H., Gerstner, A., Grosset, D.G., Parkinson's disease is overdiagnosed clinically at baseline in diagnostically uncertain cases: A 3-year European multicenter study with repeat [123I]FP-CIT SPECT. *Mov. Disord.*, 24, 500–508, 2009.

7. Schneider, S.A., Edwards, M.J., Mir, P., Cordivari, C., Hooker, J., Dickson, J., Quinn, N., Bhatia, K.P., Patients with adult-onset dystonic tremor resembling parkinsonian tremor have scans without evidence of dopaminergic deficit (SWEDDs). *Mov. Disord.*, 22, 2210–2215, 2007.

8. Prashanth, R., Dutta Roy, S., Mandal, P.K., Ghosh, S., Shape features as biomarkers in early Parkinson's disease. *Proc. 6th Int. IEEE/EMBS Conf. Neural Eng.*, 517–520, 2013.

9. Prashanth, R., Dutta Roy, S., Mandal, P.K., Ghosh, S., Automatic classification and prediction models for early Parkinson's disease diagnosis from SPECT imaging. *Expert Syst. Appl.*, 41, 3333–3342, 2014.

10. Cortes, V.V., Support-vector networks. *Mach. Learn.*, 20, 273–297, 1995.

11. Breiman, L., Random forests. *Mach. Learn.*, 45, 5–32, 2001.

12. Ng, Y. and Jordan, M., II, On discriminative vs. generative classifiers: A comparison of logistic regression and naive Bayes, in: *Advances in neural information processing systems (NIPS)*, pp. 841–848, 2001.

13. Prashanth, R., Dutta Roy, S., Mandal, P.K., Ghosh, S., High-accuracy classification of parkinson's disease through shape analysis and surface fitting in 123i-ioflupane SPECT imaging. *IEEE Biomed. Health Inform.*, 21, 3, 794–802, May 2017.

14. Oliveira, F.P. and Castelo-Branco, M., Computer-aided diagnosis of Parkinson's disease based on [123I] FP-CIT SPECT binding potential images using the voxels-as-features approach and support vector machines. *J. Neural.Eng.*, 12, 026008, 2015.

15. Krstajic, L.J.B., Leahy, D.E., Thomas, S., Cross-validation pitfalls when selecting and assessing regression and classification models. *J. Cheminform.*, 6, 1–15, 2014.

16. Kish, S.J., Shannak, K., Hornykiewicz, O., Uneven pattern of dopamine loss in the striatum of patients with idiopathic Parkinson's disease. *N. Engl. J. Med.*, 318, 876–880, 1988.

17. Chang, C.-C. and Lin, C.-J., LIBSVM: A library for support vector machines. *ACM Trans. Intell. Syst. Technol.*, 2, 1–27, 2011.

18. Piggott, M.A., Marshall, E.F., Thomas, N., Lloyd, S., Court, J.A., Jaros, E., Burn, D., Johnson, M., Perry, R.H., McKeith, I.G., Ballard, C., Perry, E.K., Striatal dopaminergic markers in dementia with Lewy bodies Alzheimer's and Parkinson's diseases: Rostrocaudal distribution. *Brain*, 122, 8, 1449–1468, Aug. 1999.

19. Breiman, L., Random forests. *Mach. Learn.*, 45, 5–32, 2001.

20. Marek, K., Jennings, D.L., Seibyl, J.P., Long-term follow-up of patients with scans without evidence of dopaminergic deficit (SWEDD) in the ELLDOPA study. *Neurology*, 64, A274, 2005.

21. Staff, R.T., Ahearn, T.S., Wilson, K., Counsell, C.E., Taylor, K., Caslake, R., Davidson, J.E., Gemmell, H.G., Murray, A.D., Shape analysis of 123I-N-ω-fluoropropyl-2-β-carbomethoxy-3β-(4-iodophenyl) nortropane single-photon emission computed tomography images in the assessment of patients

with parkinsonian syndromes. *Nucl. Med. Commun.*, 30, 3, 194–201, March 2009.

22. Meena Prakash, R. and Shantha Selva Kumari, R., Spatial fuzzy C means and expectation maximization algorithms with bias correction for segmentation of MR brain images. *J. Med. Syst.*, 41, 15, 2017, https://doi.org/10.1007/s10916-016-0662-7.

23. Towey, J., Bain, P.G., Nijran, K.S., Automatic classification of 123I-FP-CIT (DaTSCAN) SPECT images. *Nucl. Med. Commun.*, 32, 699–707, Aug. 2011.

10

Big Data Analytics in Healthcare

Akanksha Sharma, Rishabha Malviya* and Ramji Gupta

Department of Pharmacy, School of Medical and Allied Sciences, Galgotias University, Greater Noida, Gautam Buddha Nagar, Uttar Pradesh, India

Abstract

The chapter aims to describe the data analytics role in the healthcare field. It is an irresistible way to handle huge data of healthcare in less time. They can increase operating performance and support to anticipate and schedule responses to disease outbreaks. It can enhance the standard of clinical trial surveillance and maximize healthcare expenditures at each level from patients to hospitals to government systems. The chapter emphasizes the need for Big Data analytics in the health management system which helps to increase prevention and also raise the patients and physician's gratification. It can also help in better performance during the analysis of Chronic Obstructive Pulmonary Disease in an individual patient. This chapter describes the different benefits in healthcare system of Big Data analytics. It is a significant part of evidence-based care, increases the care quality, helps in early detection, and increases the communication between patients and physicians. It is also useful in health surveillance and also reduces healthcare costs. The various characteristics of data analytics related to 10V's which are used in healthcare management are also described in this chapter. The 10V's includes Veracity, Variety, Value, Virility, Variability, Visualization, Validity, Viscosity, Volume, and Velocity. It can also describe the various platforms and software related to data analytics which is used in the medical field like Hadoop Distributed File System, Hive, MapReduce, Zookeeper, Jaql, HBase, Cassandra, Lucene, Mahout, and Oozie. These platforms can enhance the quality of the healthcare field. The paper discusses the various diseases and their management with data analytics in brief. Mainly there are four diseases are discussed in this chapter that is heart disease, diabetes, chronic disease and neurological disease. Data analytics are used for

Corresponding author: rishabhamalviya19@gmail.com;
rishabha.malviya@galgotiasuniversity.edu.in

D. Sumathi, T. Poongodi, B. Balamurugan and Lakshmana Kumar Ramasamy (eds.)
Cognitive Intelligence and Big Data in Healthcare, (257–302) © 2022 Scrivener Publishing LLC

clinical purpose such as in the processing of an image, processing of the signal, genomics, bioinformatics, and clinical informatics is also discussed.

Keywords: Big data analytics, bioinformatics, image processing, signal processing, clinical informatics, patient care, health management

10.1   Introduction

Healthcare with Big Data denotes the multifaceted and large electronic data sets of health which is difficult to handle by using conventional hardware and software, nor can be handled easily by using old style or popular aid and approach of data management. Big Data in the health management was noxious not just because of magnitude also due to different variety of data or the rate on that has to be handled. A report sent in August 2012 to the United States Congress which describes Big Data as 'massive quantities of elevated speed, complicated and variable data requiring advanced technologies and methods to collect, store, transit, handle and analyze the information [1].

Healthcare is an instant of the 3 Vs of data, velocity (data processing speed), volume, and variety, which are an essential characteristic including its data that engender. The generated information was distributed amongst various medical management networks, health plan, academics, and government bureau. All these data depositories are silted and incapable to provide a global stage for the transparency of data. In addition to the three Vs, the healthcare data veracity is also essential which is used in producing translational research [2].

Big Data analysis could transform the healthcare sector. It can boost operating efficacies, help to anticipate and prepare results related to disease epidemics, enhances efficiency of clinical trials tracking, and maximize healthcare expenditure from patients to hospital systems to governments at all levels. The Big Data healthcare applicability, some of the research works were in development and a potential perspective on how Big Data analytics will increase the overall characteristic of the healthcare sector [3].

Big Data investigative can analyze a large ambit of complicated data or produce useful visions that would otherwise have been difficult to obtain. When analytics used for healthcare data, it can recognize trends and contribute to enhanced quality of healthcare, cost reduction, and timely decision-making. According to the McKinsey Global Institute study, by making efficient use of Big Data, US Healthcare can generate an annual value of more than $300 billion, of which two-thirds will be spent on healthcare by decreasing spending around 8%. Hidden information can be revealed through an automated review of results [4].

In the recent scenario, medical devices which is wearable play a critical part in several environments like individuals regular monitoring of health, control of traffic on road, forecasting of weather and in automated home. These sensors aid produce a large quantity of data continuously which is collected in cloud storage. Architecture on the Internet of Things can collect and manage scalable sensor data which is further used in healthcare. The suggested planning involves two major sub-designs such as MetaFog-Redirection, architecture grouping and choosing. While cloud computing offers scalable storage of data, powerful computing frameworks must be used to process it [5].

The quick growth of patients Electronic Health Records, incorporation of social, omics and behavioral data based on eHealth, mHealth, digital health and telehealth apps focused on development of new healthcare framework that indorse personalized medicine and patient care. Current analysis efforts have shown that complex healthcare approaches have resulted in architectural structures supporting multiple hierarchical services levels. The concept behind the creation of this system is to efficiently integrate the Big Data sources in the identification of healthcare. These platforms indorse healthcare strategies from a disease centered model to the patient centered model, in which patients were actively involved in their treatment [6].

Big Data analytics emerges from business intelligence and decision support systems that allow organizations of healthcare to determine volume, velocity, or variety of data across a vast range of network associated with health management which supports evidence-based decision making and taking of action. It also includes several analytical methods like mining/predictive analytics and descriptive analytics which are good for processing a big amount of text-based health records and unstructured clinical data. Current management systems of database like MarkLogic, Apache Cassandra, and Mongo DB allow data to be shared between conventional and modern operating systems for integration of data and their recovery. Such Big Data analytics devices with high level functionalities promote the integration of clinical information and offer fresh business perceptions which help the organizations of healthcare to meet with patients need and future trending demand, thereby improving care quality and financial performance [7].

10.2   Need for Big Data Analytics

Big Data investigation in Medicare delivery summary shows variations that occur in the modern healthcare system such as developed, additionally effective, cost-reduced, and accomplished quality of healthcare system than ever. The healthcare organization needs to develop and change constantly to provide quality services to the people. The main fact which makes the health center efficiency better and makes the people live better is measure, store, and analysis of the data which enhances the quality of treatment. The income costs are managed by decreasing excessive tests. It can enhance preventive treatment and also the satisfaction between patients and doctors [8].

Big Data analytics was used to obtain data on healthcare from various resources to achieve perceptions into the quality and understand best practices in the Big Data technologies field which is unique to healthcare. The United States is actively seeking future changes to the Quality of Service of their healthcare system. Current development in regulations of the sharing of data such as the nature of the current Affordable Healthcare Act altered the directions of the game and created a new collection of observable variables in quality of health for the United States that they could not ignore anymore. Peoples in those states without health insurance prefer to avoid attending the doctor even though they experience the signs of a disease, as well as healthy young people's with insurance, can also be treated with the same behavior. Health specialists are still indorsing closer immersion in individual well-being and more attention towards preventive healthcare [9].

Big Data Analytics aims to bring healthcare researchers and professionals together for growth in the field of computing which manages the data efficiently and to draw inferences from heterogeneous and broad health management data. Chronic obstructive pulmonary disease is an important reason for mortality and morbidity worldwide resulting in a social and financial gist that was for the both extensive or rising. This work explores Data mining method of Big Data, in this method Decision Tree procedure is applied for an individual patient which shows the improved results during the analysis of chronic obstructive pulmonary disease. The centralized clinical data depository comprises the details of the patient concerning a specific aadhaar number, which allows learning about treatments received by the individual patient in various hospitals. The experimental outcomes indicate the promising accuracy of chronic pulmonary intransigent disease patient diagnosis and reliability of the suggested program [10].

The tools of Big Data analytics for management of population include limited and tentative case-finding applications but the management of population may be a significant way to use the Big Data in health management. Inhabitants' administration is commonly characterized by effective monitoring of patients by a hospital, clinical or health management system. The case outcome shows that practice of performing regular examination for populations or patients at risk of a specific condition treated before the condition get manifest. These strategies can increase the importance of reformation in healthcare, mainly with the emergence of alternate payment structures like Accountable Care Organizations and usefulness basic models of payment such as the US Hospital Readmission Reduction Program [11].

Big Data analytics method is used to increase patient-based service, for detection of diseases earlier before spread, create unusual awareness into disease mechanisms, observe the clinical and healthcare institutions quality and also offer improved treatment methods. Data mining methods employed on Electronic Health Record, social media and web data allow to identify the hospitals optimum practical guidelines, recognizing the association rules in the Electronic Health Record and exposing disease monitoring and health based trend. Additionally, incorporation and data analysis with various natures like scientific and social can lead toward new intelligence and knowledge, exploring novel hypothesis, characterizing unseen patterns. In the recent scenario, smart phones are perfect tools for delivering personal messages to patients in order to engage them to make lifestyle improvements that will improve their health and well-being. The mobile phone messages can use as an alternate option to deliver motivational and medical advice to the patients [12].

The natural-language detersion, pattern identification, or machine learning is at front of the quickly evolving artificial intelligence techniques. Those artificial intelligence skills can be useful in many fields, specifically in life sciences and biomedicine. Google's algorithm used to monitor diseases that are called Google Trends. Google Trends and another method for monitoring diseases using geospatial maps are an intimidating challenge for Big Data, analyzing a huge amount of knowledge and making quick decisions. Google Trends will note the increase in Google's search demands for words like 'flu symptoms' and 'flu remedies' until there is a rise in people with flu going to hospital emergency rooms in particular areas. Methods for classifying word demand in the field of illnesses are only the main features in biomedical big-data investigative. That information-based approach is currently having an enormous effect on health monitoring and disease control [13].

The use of the internet and computer technologies often helps to build tools for handling of diseases. Data sources were designed to direct physicians and patients suffering from diseases like cancer and help them to find the best treatment for their type of disease, which is one of the pillars of personalized medicine. The related tool is the 'My Cancer Genome' portal produced by researchers in the USA at Vanderbilt University. The portal lists mutations in various forms of cancer, also drug therapies which may or may not help patients. The drugs listed on the website are mostly in clinical trials and US Food and Drug Administration has granted only few them. The portal is free and it can be utilized by physicians, researchers, patients, relatives and institutions, making it easier for patients to translate the results in research labs [13, 14].

Research in bioinformatics analyzes the molecular level difference in the biological system. With recent developments in personalized medicine, these large datasets are increasingly needed to be produced, stored, and analyzed within a convenient time frame. The next-generation sequencing method facilitates the attainment of genomic data in less time. In bioinformatics applications, the role of Big Data methods is to offer data sources, computing resources, and effective data processing methods for researchers to analyze and gather biological information. Big Data methods or tools are classified into four groups such as storage of data and their retrieval, detection of errors, analysis of data and implementation of platform integration. For example, utmost data input applications can embrace simple data interpretation or vice versa and these classifications are related and can overlap [15].

Big Data offers a powerful platform to collect actionable data from the sea of information. Big Data analytics from the McKinsey report was the tool to provide five principles to healthcare that is right living, the right provider, right care, right innovation, and right value. Such principles offer boundless incentives to improve healthcare delivery and on the other hand, to reduce waste and costs. Healthcare analytics can help the patient not only based on basic conventional demographic characteristics like gender, age or lifestyle not only the specific health or clinical features appertained to medical conditions, genetic character, hazard tendencies or therapeutic possibilities. Medical evidence provides capability to customize or alter course of care of every patient depend on several variables that determine medical treatment plan for these patients such as past case history, allergies, precautions, genetic conditions, variables of personal risk, work, lifestyles or management of safety [16].

Big Data has recently attracted attention because it combines social data analytics with conventional analytics, although the fact that data analytics has been important in the practice of science and healthcare. Google Flu Trends forecasting began in February 2013, has drawn interest outside the healthcare industry, and shows the emerging importance and benefit of social media and Big Data analytics. This advanced approximation of flu occurrence of Google Flu Trends has opened up and inspired new possibilities of handling long-lasting healthcare problems through the use of social data in cyberspace. Numerous stakeholders have found that Big Data analytics can offer prospects for forecasting, identifying preliminary needs and mitigating risks, also provides real-time sensing, personalized services and counter-measures more effectively [17].

Big Data will increase operational effectiveness, help to plan, and predict responses to disease outbreaks enhance the clinical trial tracking quality and maximize healthcare expenditure at all levels. The main area of Big Data is the processing of genomics which is considered to be the healthcare future [18].

Big Data analytics utilizes effective computational tools to determine secret correlations, trends, and additional intuitions from Big Data. It makes remarkable price benefits, increases efficiency of making the decision, and develops novel products to reach the customer requirements. This strategy has several usages in healthcare and bioinformatics. It can be enhanced with different methods like intelligent tools, network analysis, and machine learning. Due to all processes or the provision of large throughput devices, a large volume of data has increased in bioinformatics research at a lower price. Processing cost decrease and enhance the analytic quantity which helps this trend raises the amount of data resulting from the Big Data technologies development. In recent years, data size of bioinformatics information gets increased [19].

Rapid progress in clinical analytics methods to analyze vast volumes of data and collecting new information from the research is also a key element of Big Data. Big Data in United States provide unprecedented opportunities to decrease healthcare costs. The Big Data reduces the cost of different cases like high-cost patients, triage, readmissions, improvement in treatment and adverse effects for diseases affecting various organ systems as well as decompensation (when a patient's health deteriorates) [20].

The Internet of Things shows the great rise towards wearable devices which are linked with healthcare and technology. This contributes to personalized treatment which improves the access to healthcare and convenience which has never been shown. Such innovations must be implemented with precaution because there are still valid questions about performance, the effectiveness of cost, safety and many more. Internet of Things eHealth technology includes wearable sensors for smart healthcare,

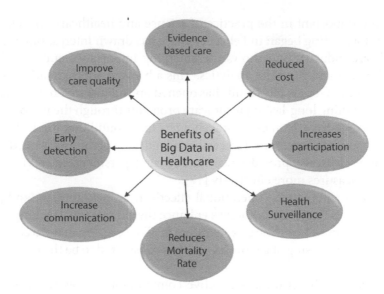

Figure 10.1 Schematic diagram showing the health management benefit of big data.

sensors for the body environment, advanced prevalent healthcare networks, and Big Data analytics to deliver healthy lifestyles by using eHealth services to individuals [21].

Figure 10.1 illustrates diagram for the advantages of Big Data in healthcare.

10.3 Characteristics of Big Data

Big Data played an important role in a broad range of environments, including business, healthcare, science, industry, and organization, the management of natural resources, public administration, and social networks. The large data are divided into 10Vs as follows.

10.3.1 Volume

Data produced by the various medical tools are larger compared to traditional data so is represents the Big Data. Sources of generation of data are increased and this generates the range of data like video, audio, images, and text with large size. The traditional systems of data processing have developed paw the broad volume of data.

10.3.2 Velocity

Amount of information stream by the medical network is much less compared to the annual data storage capacity of an entire hospital system. The velocity expresses the speed of data generation. Social media data explosion has changes the data variety.

10.3.3 Variety

Conventional format of data means less adoption and growth of a new type of sensor data types. However non-conventional data like medical devices can easily be adjusted for change. The Big Data must reflect the variety of data. Recently, data forms are also being collected rapidly. Many of the administrations use various kinds of data formats including Excel, CSV, database that can store the plain text file. The information was always not in the desired format which creates problems during the processing. To decrease this administration problem there is needs to recognize the data storage system that can analyze the data variety.

10.3.4 Veracity

Veracity is about unsure or vague data. In conventional data centers, the supposition was always that the data was safe, clean, and reliable, but it is not same in case of Big Data. This data of veracity reflects the Big Data. Veracity shows the incomprehensibility of data; it does not denote the quality of the data. Significantly, the organization should accomplish data analysis to avoid the accumulation of 'dirty data' in the systems [22, 23].

10.3.5 Value

Value of data reflects the Big Data. It is not beneficial to have a constant amount of data until it can be transformed into value. While performing Big Data analytics advantages and price of processing and gathering of Big Data are more importable.

10.3.6 Validity

Either the data are reliable and accurate for future use or not, it is important to confirm. Associations will substantially monitor the data for the right decisions in the future.

10.3.7   Variability

Variability denotes the consistency of data and their value.

10.3.8   Viscosity

The delay or lag time between the source and destination during data transmission is defined by viscosity which is an aspect of velocity.

10.3.9   Virality

The speed at which data is sent and retrieved from different sources is referred as virality.

10.3.10   Visualization

To represent Big Data, visualization is used in a complete view. It aids in regulating the concealed values. Visualization is a key element in the determination basics process which Big Data is made useful [23].

Figure 10.2 shows the Big Data analytics 10 V's.

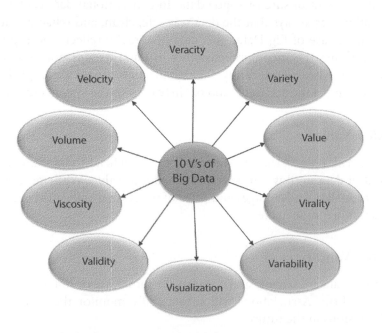

Figure 10.2 Schematic diagram of 10 V's of big data analytics.

10.4   Big Data Analysis in Disease Treatment and Management

10.4.1   For Diabetes

Modernizing the healthcare industry is moving towards the managing of enormous health records and accessing records for consideration and implementation will increase the difficulties. Diabetes mellitus is a non-communicable disease which is a main hazardous disease in developing countries. Diabetes mellitus is acute and associated with various health disorders and long term complications. For a potential solution, it is important to emphasize its structure and size into a minimal value. Health Information Exchange can excerpt clinical knowledge from different databases and merge that data into a consolidated health record of a patient that can be easily accessed by all care providers safely. The method of predictive analysis method integrates a range of services from statistics, game theory, and data mining. It utilizes the recent and previous data to regulate or predict future events by using analytical or statistical models and methods. Predicting the ubiquitous forms of diabetes, problems, and treatment uses the predictive analysis algorithm such as Hadoop, Map Reduce. This program provides an effective method of cure and treatment for patients with improved results like availability and affordability based on research [24].

The principal of the linear regression model is employed as a portentous model. Mainly, there must be 2 types with portentous models: parametric or nonparametric models. Parametric models used to create theories about the fundamental data distribution and nonparametric models also known as semi-parametric models make less or no hypotheses about underlying distribution. These models often employ a broad range of approaches, including pattern recognition or machine learning, and are largely, and not limited to tree categorization, neural networks and neighbors. A model is usually examined in a wide range of patients and validated in a different cohort data or results from another study. Normally, singular observations or perhaps a time sequence can be included in data. In many other cases a certain type of signal processing or mathematical transformation involves removing certain predictors. The basic parametric methods such as linear regression, c-statistics, and specificity or sensitivity are used to determine the execution of the predictive model [25].

Bai *et al.* had been discussing about Data mining technology like Gaussian Naove Bayes, the order point of the clustering structure (OPE) and balanced iterative hierarchical reduction and categorization (BIRCH) were discussed for diabetes prediction. Methods for the diagnosis and clustering of diabetic disease patients are effective. Classification of the Gaussian Naive Bayes is used in probability. OPTICS and BIRCH are used to assemble the same type of persons, while the points in the cluster are arranged with BIRCH. The study and evaluation of clustering algorithms is measured by different performance metrics. OPTICS was found to be extremely effective and to be suitable as diagnostic clusters with different clusters for the same number of diabetes. This research helps doctors to diagnose and deliver suitable medication early. The aim of the work is to reduce costs and improve treatment [26].

Kalyankar *et al.* have been utilized the MapReduce and Hadoop depend machine learning method use for the Pima Indian diabetes information set to identify absent significances and to determine the patterns from it. This research indicates that the algorithms executed might attribute the missing values and the data set are used in the determination of patterns [27].

Kumar *et al.* have found during the study that the diabetes data set was used to calculate the diabetes type and to test the appropriate machine learning model to give precise predictions. Machine learning algorithms including random forest, vector support machine, cocaine, or amphetamine were used to predict disease, k-nearest neighbor, or linear discriminant analysis. These algorithms were used to collect semi-random algorithm according to their learning style model and representational diversity. The comparative research was carried out by using several metrics like Precision, Kappa, Accuracy, Recall, Specificity, and Sensitivity [28].

10.4.2   For Heart Disease

Data mining can play a significant part in developing a smart model for medical systems to diagnose the disease of heart by using patient's data sets. It involves risk factors related to disease of heart. Practitioners can assist patients in detecting heart disease before it happens. By using data mining techniques vast data obtained from diagnosis was examined and the obtained useful outcomes are known as extracted knowledge. The data mining approach explores massive data sets to take out patterns that were hidden, formerly unspecified associations and information identification patterns to aid in progressing comprehension of medical information to avoid disease of heart. There are different data mining methods are available such as Naive Bayes, Neural Network, Artificial Intelligence, Genetic Algorithm, Decision Tree and Clustering algorithm like K-Network

Neighbor and Support Vector Machine. Data mining is a non-trivial outcome of tacit. Big Data and Data Mining are the two methods and similar in assembling the enormous amount of data, managing it and compiling a data report by taking out the knowledgeable information. Data Mining used to observe important data trends with detailed knowledge by using the Big Data [29].

An Apache Hadoop open source program was used to store or technique a vast number of information sets on commodity hardware. In the healthcare industry, Hadoop is used in labeling segregated data set to different servers (endpoints) to handle a very vast amount of information, each node interprets a small part of a specific problem and then sets results to achieve the final results. Hadoop analyses and arranges the data simultaneously at same time. Big Data is used for heart diseases to figure out how the Hadoop method can be used to boost the efficiency of the performance of investigating massive data-sets and extend this work to allow better use of different resources. Large databases are being developed that can put diverse data types together and allow multivariate analysis of information on every patient. Population-based methods have been especially used in comparing specific anatomy with a population or in the quantifying, detecting and tracking the progression of the disease between sub populations [30].

Big Data is used to establish a centralized surveillance network for patients. A large collection of medical records is taken as inputs in this system. This medical dataset was intended to use a map reduction technique to obtain the necessary required information from the heart patient record. Cardiovascular disease is a big concern and certain features like QT interval, RR interval, and QRS interval are evaluated for the identification of disease. The classification method identifies either patient is abnormal or normal and using the Map Reduce method to identify disease and decrease dataset in detection phase. Big Data can estimate the uncertainty of recovery from congestive cardiac failure for 30 days. Firstly, data are used from and increased by patient data collected from Multicare Health System from the national hospital dataset. Then scalable data mining models are developed using the combined data set to analyze the readmission risk. The random forest algorithm is used since it can work with predictable variables of all types [31].

Heart disease is predicted by using the Big Data approach. This method is useful for the prediction, based on certain parameters like age, chest pain, resting blood pressure, lack of cholesterol etc. This system will improve decision making as well as being fast [32].

10.4.3   For Chronic Disease

Current management and management of chronic diseases depend on the provider's willingness, including heart failure, diabetes, chronic diseases, on their potentiality, to prevent high risk or economic conditions from developing. Big Data analytics has the advantage of encouraging healthcare providers to take informed and timely decisions based on evidence to provide a more effective and personalized treatment and reduce patient healthcare costs. Big Data analytics included various methods used to analyze significant sections of text-based health records and other proeutectoid clinical information, such as written physician notes, prescriptions, and medical imaging, including analytics that describe, predict, and prescribe [33].

Big Data are accustomed to manage the improved health planning. The methodologies can be used for data analytics in the healthcare sectors, which helps to make smarter decision to raise the market value and consumer engagement and offer eHealth services to different healthcare stakeholders using messaging standards like Health level 7, Message broker, Health Insurance Accountability and Portability, Communication, and Digital Imaging in Medicine. Big Data tools are used in developing early disease diagnostic systems and to understand the link between HIV/AIDS Tuberculosis and Silicosis as well as to grow combined data analytics platforms [34].

Telehealth in the healthcare sectors allows the sensors to be used inside or on the body of a human. Wearable sensors like activity monitor and ECG are a precise form of medical sensors placed on the body of a human that allow the collection of non-invasive, unobtrusive, and 24×7 data for monitoring of health. These tools have been installed in homes covering the body of humans and delivering telehealth services for people pursuing accessible healthcare while staying in direct contact with medical practitioners. Application of telehealth is an exemplar of use of Big Data to collect a broad proportion of the information with a variety of data that requires real time and rapid processing to deliver better healthcare. Echo Wear is a modern smart watch used to deliver a home-based speech teletherapy which produces approximately 100 Mb data per day per patient. Wearable sensor data contains valuable information. It can also carry non-deterministic errors like data corruption issues, motion artifacts and unwanted signals which are also uploaded which increases the requirements of storage and power consumption. Fog computing could play a major role in increasing efficiency and decreasing the storage requirements for medical Big Data solutions [35].

10.4.4   For Neurological Disease

The computerized diagnostic systems are known as a computer-aided diagnosis that can identify neurological disorders automatically using the Big Data in the medical field. This program increases the diagnostic accuracy and increases treatment effectiveness, reduces cost and time, and saves lives. To detect the neurological disorders from Big Data, the computer-aided diagnosis systems are implemented for the specialists and neurologists. The computer-aided diagnosis system assists the practitioners to analyze the medical Big Data properly. It helps to maintain the analysis precision and continuity and also reduces the time of diagnosis [36].

Big Data produces, incorporates, and analyzes massive, heterogeneous dataset that provide in-depth visions into multifaceted process and have ability to untangle neuro inflammatory complexities. In particular, the introduction of 'omics' analysis is a suitable standard practice in biomedical science, and neuroimaging generates vast sets of complex data. In several neurological conditions, including chronic and autoimmune neurodegenerative disease like Alzheimer's disease, multiple sclerosis, neuro inflammation, is suggested. In research, it was evaluated that the neuro-inflammatory processes included in these condition are being complex and Big Data analysis reinforced this definition [37].

The use of deep learning in Big Data neuro imaging helps in the neurological diseases diagnosis. Identification of patterns using deep learning will obtain characteristics of neuro imaging signal specifically to different neurological disorders, proceeding to improved diagnosis. Aoe *et al.* develop the MNet, new deep neural network for the multiple neurological disorders classification by using magneto encephalography signals from the resting-state [38].

10.4.5   For Personalized Medicine

The security of biomedical data, effective and stable models for integration, storage, data-driven analysis, and discovery will differentiate Big Data analytics methods for personalized medicine. Personalized brain models created under the Human Brain Project, a European Commission Flagship program for the patient with intractable epilepsy. Through the FP7 and Horizon 2020 programs, the European Commission has spent more than 2.6 billion in research of personalized medicine and introduced the International Personalized Medicine Consortium, whose achievement reports contain BLUEPRINT of the project related to the study of hematopoiesis epigenetic processes. A recent scenario, a large number of imaging, medical devices, multi-omics, and Electronic Health Record data are accessible from large-scale cohort and population studies, exposing variations in the human genetics and enabling involvement in personalized medicine [39].

Exome and selective sequencing in comparison to whole genome sequencing, provides a balance between benefit and cost. Intact exome sequencing aims about 3% of the entire genome that is the origin of protein-coding genes. For a large implementation, it has the features of Big Data. Whole exome sequencing has been assimilated into The NHLBI 'Grand Opportunity' Exome Sequencing Project and the exertions by the Exome Aggregation Consortium to catalog variants of the population and to detect diseases related with rare variants. This enhances personal medicine by matching and providing the most beneficial treatment to the genetic profile of specific patients [40].

Using Big Data in the health management field offers significant prospects for analyzing patients' fitness and health status by using communication tools. Personalized treatment may also be achieved by contrasting two or more peoples in an identical health condition. The Big Data used to improve accuracy and decision making about personalized healthcare. Big Data were used for study, diagnosis, treatment, or prevention of high blood pressure. Medical experts use machine learning techniques with help of Big Data to get diagnostic information. Big Data used to treat high blood pressure, which can be personalized with social, medical, smartphone etc. for people. With the advancement of healthcare technologies, Big Data utilized for the investigation of structured data from demands associated

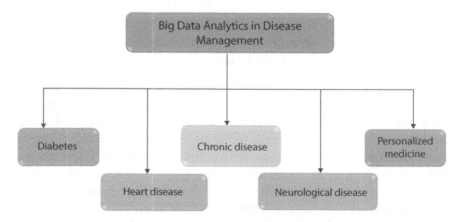

Figure 10.3 Schematic diagram to show the role of Big data analytics in disease management.

Table 10.1 Big data analytics and their use in the treatment of diseases.

S. no.	Disease	Big data analytics in treatment of disease
1.	Diabetes	Analysis and comparison of the various algorithms of mechanical learning is carried out with the closest neighbor, Random forests, vector grading machinery and regression trees, and linear discriminant analysis algorithms to find an appropriate prediction algorithm depending on multiple metrics: precision, accuracy, recall, kappa, sensitivity, speciality, and diabetes dataset [42].
		Data analytics proposed the manner of the prediction model and recognized different risk aspects in diabetes by utilizing text mining methods [43].
		The diabetes prevention program has tried to recognize peoples with reduced glucose tolerance and interfere to avoid or prolong their diabetes development. This study analyzed the alterations between women joined in diabetes prevention programs with and without gestational diabetes mellitus a reported history background [44].
		The risk of diabetes has been checked by a possible personality sleep and incident diabolic analysis in women because of the increase in sleep time [45].
		The 5G smart program for diabetes incorporates the art skills which develops the wearable device 2.0. Big Data and machine learning produce robust sensing and investigation for diabetes patient. 5G smart diabetes data exchange system and personalized data analysis model were also introduced [46].
		More than 4,000 patients from an isolated people in western Finland were recognized for non-parametric linkage analysis to augment 26 families (containing 217 peoples) for non-insulin dependent diabetes mellitus or genome wide scan method were implemented. When the families were analyzed together, no substantial indication of linkage was found, but a clear indication of linkage was listed when families were listed according to mean insulin levels (in oral glucose tolerance tests) [47].

(Continued)

Table 10.1 Big data analytics and their use in the treatment of diseases. (*Continued*)

S. no.	Disease	Big data analytics in treatment of disease
2.	Heart disease	Big Data used to predict heart attacks and impulsive medical study using the Internet of things and Hadoop techniques. This is an end-user of professionals to supports the online project. Hereby application targets to grants users to receive immediate feedback on their heart disease through an online intelligent system [48].
		The Random Forest method is used to predict heart diseases with well-set characteristics and great precision [49].
		Development of MEDLINE for large-scale blood pressure reduction trials for cardiovascular disease and prevention of death and inverse variance weighted fixed-effect meta-analysis was used to assemble estimations [50].
		Various collaborative methods like Random Forest, Bagged Tree, or AdaBoost are used in healthcare to improve and reliably analyze the manifestation of the heart disease in a specific patient, alongside the feature selection technique. Experimental results show that the Bagged Tree and Particle Swarm Optimization are more precise [51].
		Heart disease is investigated by using the Hadoop and Map Reduce tools of Big Data analytics. The improved K-Means method is used for clustering and the Decision Tree Algorithm like ID3 is used for classification. This system will enhance the clinical decision making process as well as be fast. It will improve the progress of the treatment process and use in heart disease prediction [52].

(*Continued*)

Table 10.1 Big data analytics and their use in the treatment of diseases. (*Continued*)

S. no.	Disease	Big data analytics in treatment of disease
		The availability of large datasets for healthcare and advances in machine learning methods, computers are now well fortified to diagnose health problems. This helps in the development of an Apache Spark, a cloud-based, open source Big Data processing engine that focuses on streaming machine learning models, for remote health prediction in real time. In this technology the user tweets his health reports which are received in real time by the system, separates reports, and utilizes the machine learning model to assess a user's health status, which is then sent immediately user to take appropriate action [53].
		In area of healthcare, data mining is a major part of cardiac disease determination. Rough set concept was propounded in 1982 as a method for analyzing cardiovascular data. The theory of the raw set is based on the theory of the interplay and the ability to define the difference in attribute value between objects [54].
		The feature selection methods and algorithms are used to analyze several datasets of heart disease and to demonstrate the increase in precision. The Rapid Miner, Decision Tree, Support Vector Machine, Naive Bayes, Logistic Regression, and Random Forest algorithms are utilized as feature selection methods and the results indicate progress by showing the accuracy [55].
		Pravastatin therapy was tested on an elder population of men and women having a high possibility to develop cardiovascular disease or stroke. The combination of coronary death, non-fatal or fatal stroke, or non-fatal myocardial infarction was endpoint of test [56].

(*Continued*)

Table 10.1 Big data analytics and their use in the treatment of diseases. (*Continued*)

S. no.	Disease	Big data analytics in treatment of disease
3.	Chronic disease	Extract, Transform, Load is a method used in the processing of data bases mainly in the warehousing of health data. This tool used in the fields of health as a software item responsible for collecting information from various provenance including chronic disease or data sources for health tracking, their cleansing, customization and insertion into a warehouse of data [57].
		It was calculated that depression dominance in respondents was based on ICD-10 guidelines. Prevalence levels were also calculated for four chronic physical diseases of arthritis, angina, diabetes, and asthma using algorithms resulting from Diagnostic Item Probability analysis [58].
		Groups of Facebook and Twitter related to different diseases like colorectal cancer, breast cancer, and diabetes. The words breast cancer, diabetes and colorectal cancer are used to search for such diseases on Facebook. Analyzing the number of people, aspirations, or URLs of the site was used in each large group [59].
		Governments around the world were concerned about the inconvenience of illness caused by different chronic diseases and a large portion of this comes from actually preventable hospital admissions. Such admissions can be prevented by taking preventive steps which in turn can decrease costs and health risks [60].
		The Healthcare industry has moved towards transformation, producing electronic health records that produce enormous data. One of the major contributors to mortality and morbidity is a non-communicable disease, chronic kidney failure. Prompt discovery of the disease becomes necessary and requires further attention and can be evaluated using a predictive approach by utilizing the capacity of the Hadoop and Map Reduce tool [61].

(*Continued*)

Table 10.1 Big data analytics and their use in the treatment of diseases. (*Continued*)

S. no.	Disease	Big data analytics in treatment of disease
		Chronic disease causing long-term deaths. They are only being regulated but cannot be completely cured. Chronic disease affects most people in the world; few of the chronic disease includes asthma, allergy, heart disease, cancer, diabetes, obesity, glaucoma, viral disease like HIV/AIDS and Hepatitis C. For analysis of data the Hadoop Big Data analytical structure is used. It was used for storage of large data sets. Research is carried out using an algorithm reduction map [62].
		DIETOS (DIET Organizer System) was introduced; it is a recommender system for the integrated distribution of dietary materials to both diet-related chronic disease patients and healthy subjects including chronic kidney disease, diabetes, and hypertension. DIETOS prepares consumer health profiles and offers recommendations for individuals related to their diet [63].
4.	Neurological disease	Genome-wide was done by, single nucleotide sequencing genotyping of widely existing samples from patients of Parkinson's disease and neurologically regular controls and producing widely available genotype data for patients of Parkinson's and controls to allow these data to be extracted by other researchers to identify common genetic variation resulting in a negligible and normal risk for disease [64].
		The genome-wide organization investigates for Parkinson's disease and linked two loci (*Microtubule-associated protein tau* and alpha-synuclein) to predict the risk of Parkinson's disease [65].

(Continued)

Table 10.1 Big data analytics and their use in the treatment of diseases. (*Continued*)

S. no.	Disease	Big data analytics in treatment of disease
		An electroencephalogram is an important method for evaluating certain neurological conditions and for measuring overall cerebral function. In various studies electroencephalogram are computed by applying power spectral density used in the determination of electroencephalogram sample. This work deals with power spectral density attained from normal, alcoholic, and epileptic electroencephalogram esticulation. The power range was determined to use the rapid Welch method, the Burg method, or the autoregressive Yule–Walker method [66].
		Data sets with different considerations like gender, age, rate of glucose fasting and post prandial, rates of blood pressure and cholesterol that affects the people collected from the specific record. The Map Reduce, Hive, and Pig are used as an effective technique for the execution of time and performance [67].
		Predictive analytics uses clinical data to determine chronic kidney disease. Logistics and regression, decision-tab classifiers and support vector machines, such as machine-to-neighbor learning methods. Probabilistic models were compared to the appropriate method for forecasting renal chronic conditions with chronic kidney disease data sets [68].
		Chronic disease patients face risk and various adverse health outcomes. Bayesian multitasks learning model is used to coordinate with baseline models and communicate information on training across the models. Bayesian multitasks learning model permits healthcare providers to achieve multifaceted risk profiling. It can also help to decrease the delays and failures in clinical trials [69].

with demographics, laboratory results, cost and few related information. Big Data are used to identify and locate the patients endure from diseases such as blood pressure or prescribe medication or other care interventions which are appropriate to the individual needs [41].

Figure 10.3 shows the data analytics use in the management of various diseases while Table 10.1 describes Big Data investigative and their use for treatment of diseases.

10.5   Big Data: Databases and Platforms in Healthcare

Software and their use in the healthcare are described in Table 10.2.

Table 10.2 Software and their use in the management of the healthcare.

S. no.	Software/tool	Description	Roles and uses in personalized healthcare
1.	Hadoop Distributed File Structure	Hadoop apportion File structure allows Hadoop cluster for underlying storage. It breaks the data into small part and spreads them through different servers or nodes [70].	Predicting the diabetes common forms, problems associated with it and the type of cure to be offered [71].
2.	MapReduce	MapReduce offers platform for the sub tasks delivery and for collecting results. When tasks are implemented, MapReduce monitors each server processing [70].	Used to protect the healthcare dataset [72].

(*Continued*)

Table 10.2 Software and their use in the management of the healthcare. (*Continued*)

S. no.	Software/tool	Description	Roles and uses in personalized healthcare
3.	Hive	Hive was architecture for Hadoop that controls the query language structure using the Hadoop Platform. This helps developers to change Hive Query Language statements closely to their conventional text [70].	Hive is used only for analytics, to create graphs and charts from the Hive data warehouse the data can be easily submitted to reports application. The predictive analysis is helpful for doctors and researchers to treat patients with different drugs, based on several variables such as lifestyle, family background, smoking habits and health problems like blood pressure and diabetes [73].
4.	Jaql	For Big Data sets, Jaql was a practical declared query language. Jaql turns "high quality issues" into "low level" issues, which consist of MapReduce tasks that enable parallel processing [70].	It advances and personalizes treatment, improves patient relationships with providers and decreases medical expenses [74].

(*Continued*)

Table 10.2 Software and their use in the management of the healthcare. (*Continued*)

S. no.	Software/tool	Description	Roles and uses in personalized healthcare
5.	Zookeeper	Zookeeper allows a consolidated network with different services, enabling connectivity through a servers cluster. Big Data analytics system uses these tools to organize processing in parallel across large clusters [70].	It personalizes information by using Big Data analytics to transform life-care and provide customized management and treatment plans to individuals at their doorstep [75].
6.	HBase	HBase is a column-based administration structure for a database located above the Hadoop Distributed File structure. It used as a non-SQL procedure [70].	Propose a single mapping structure for the newly created and enduring prototype, between the open electronic health record prototype or NoSQL (HBase) column family [76].

(*Continued*)

Table 10.2 Software and their use in the management of the healthcare. (*Continued*)

S. no.	Software/tool	Description	Roles and uses in personalized healthcare
7.	Cassandra	Cassandra is a distributed network of the database. This is classified as a top-level project focused on managing massive data spread across multiple utility servers. It also offers consistent service without a common failure point [70].	Key-value stores clinical data indirectly [77].
8.	Oozie	Oozie was an open source platform that harmonizes workflow and cooperation between tasks [70].	Personalized treatment planning can be done based on each particular patient's medical history, diagnosis can be made to assess the correct treatment and medications for that patient. Analysis of real time can be performed using MapReduce and Oozie based on the analytics results, the patient will have personalized treatment for them [78].

(*Continued*)

Table 10.2 Software and their use in the management of the healthcare. (*Continued*)

S. no.	Software/tool	Description	Roles and uses in personalized healthcare
9.	Lucene	This software is commonly utilized in text analysis or searching and has been integrated into different open source projects. In java application its extent contains library search and full text indexing [70].	The software works as a program for a command prompt with various user options, allowing oriented human literature evaluation by using Natural language processing for the pursuit in identified articles of biomedical publications for personalized genes and illnesses [79].
10.	Mahout	Mahout is another Apache project that develops application software of scalable or distributed machine learning algorithms to endorse Hadoop Big Data Analytics [70].	In the healthcare sector, broad numbers of data can be analyzed using Big Data to guarantee meaningful patient prognostication and to alert the health consumer to taking adequate steps before this happens [80].

The Apache Hadoop was an open source structure that was initially conducted and this system runs various Big Data specialist software projects. For the management of massive information volumes, Hadoop was optimized. The Hadoop Distributed File Systems and MapReduce Systems are two major components. MapReduce has been developed as a key Internet search engine provider for Google's Big Data processing application; billions of web pages get indexed quickly and meaningfully. A common cluster file system delineate to govern large quantities of data effectively was its Hadoop Distributed File Systems. In order to management huge data groups, MapReduce uses procedural programming by dividing them into small task blocks. Hive is a platform for open source information, queries and analysis. Supports mass studiation of massively stored data systems or compatible file systems like Amazon S3 file system on Hadoop Distributed File Systems. These questions were translated into the work of MapReduce and sent to Hadoop for execution. Mongo DB is a NoSQL database which supports non-relational text format substitution in conventional SQL. It is primarily developed for offering high efficiency and scalable data storage and employs a robust syntax query language which resembles object-oriented query languages. Spark offers memory computing with a flexible platform for data analysis, which is offered for direct use including language processing or machine learning algorithms [81].

Big Data sources can usually be used for pharmacovigilation in spontaneous systems and medical repositioning systems containing patient's medical claims or medical records. Information on adverse conditions and medicinal defects is contained in the food and drug administration or adverse reaction program. Other civic-accessible spontaneous databases such as Vigibase (nearly 15 million World Health Organization adverse drug reactions) and Eudra Vigilance (nearly 11 million depository adverse drug reactions reporting by the European Arznei Agency) are very relevant. International networks have been developed for the marketing of drug and vaccine trials in the last few years, such as SAFE-GUARD, ARITMO, SOS, ADVANCE, CNODES in Canada, Europe's EUROmediCAT, and Asia-Australia Asian Pharmaceutical Network. The Observational Health Data Sciences and Information Technology research alliance used methods and tools to build infrastructure in database networks. Data collaboration such as Innovative Medicines Initiatives PROTECT has demonstrated how numerous associations can be implemented with standard protocols, rather than centrally analyzing summary data [82].

10.6   Importance of Big Data in Healthcare

The Big Data are utilized to extract values from healthcare data. Big Data benefits from advanced methods and tools in healthcare are elaborated below.

10.6.1   Evidence-Based Care

Modern medical practice moves from decision-making to healthcare based on evidence. Evidentiary medicine was a type of method by which existing scientific evidence is based on the care of patients. Big Data helps to promote evidence-based care by adding data sets from different resources [83, 84].

10.6.2   Reduced Cost of Healthcare

A survey conducted by the Health Research Institute exposes that Big Data helps to decrease healthcare costs. The survey can also reveal that patients prefers non-traditional forms of healthcare like urinalysis tests performed at home using a low cost smart phone attached device [84, 85].

10.6.3   Increases the Participation of Patients in the Care Process

The Big Data enables patients to retrieve correct and update information. It makes patients understand their options, deciding on their treatment and change their lifestyle to prevent chronic disease [84].

10.6.4   The Implication in Health Surveillance

Healthcare data analyzed with creative methods help in identify trends of the disease, monitor outbreaks of disease and transmission. Big information investigative utilized in education, observe of health and prompt response [84, 86].

10.6.5   Reduces Mortality Rate

Big Data helps to reveal, identify and diagnose the diseases. This helps to make the great decisions in an appropriate and timely way for treating a specific disease. This decreases the morbidity and mortality rate in patients [84, 87].

10.6.6   Increase of Communication Between Patients and Healthcare Providers

The use of Big Data increases ability to communicate effectively between patients and healthcare providers. In social media, patients with a specific health problem and healthcare providers with specific specialties across the world will share information on the cure and prevention of a specific disease. This method helps to facilitate interoperability across healthcare institutions [84, 88].

10.6.7   Early Detection of Fraud and Security Threats in Health Management

Big Data may be utilized to identify trends easily and anomalies which suggest the existence of fraud and risks of safety in healthcare [84, 89].

10.6.8   Improvement in the Care Quality

Big Data enhances the patient care quality by order to ensure that choices are made on huge amounts of meaningful as well as up-to-date data. The quality of care increased by using Big Data analytics with wearable technology [84, 90].

10.7   Application of Big Data Analytics

10.7.1   Image Processing

Medical images were a foremost provenance of data frequently used to evaluate, plan and diagnose therapies. A few good examples are well-established imaging techniques: Magnetic resonance imaging, computational tomography, molecular imaging, X-ray, photoacoustic imagery, and ultrasound. The data ranges of medical pictures in less megabyte are used in a single study, for example histological images. Tomography computed. These data, if stored for long term, would require large storage capacities. This also requires quick and precise algorithms if the data is to be used to perform some decision assist automation. Also, when other forms of data collected for each patient are used throughout the phases of diagnosis, care and prognosis then it becomes difficult to provide coherent storage and design effective methods for encapsulating the wide range of data [91].

Big Data are produced by social media, digital processing, internet, computer systems, mobile devices and various types of sensors. The maximum generated Big Data are in the form of images and videos. Yan *et al.* have been created an image processing cloud project which helps to promote the work on image processing by controlling the Big Data analysis and cloud computing technologies. The project used to fill void between intricate modern architecture and evolving algorithms for image processing. The image processing cloud project aims to create a research environment for high-performance and high-productivity image processing that participated in a cloud computing network. The cloud will provide the appropriate storage and computing resources to image processing researchers and also provide an open and sharing environment for image processing [92].

The machine learning and image processing play a critical role in analyzing and diagnosing diseases. It helps physicians to make rapid decisions related to diseases which accurately and efficiently treat the disease. The advancement in computer-aided diagnosis systems is used for the different types of imaging tests in the classification and detection of disease in the digestive systems. These imaging tests were enteroscopy and endoscopy, wireless capsule endoscopy, radio-opaque dyes, sigmoidoscopy or colonoscopy, deep small bowel enteroscopy, computed tomography, intraoperative enteroscopy. Jia and Meng used a deep sophistication neural network in 10,000 wireless capsule endoscopy images to detect bleeding in gastrointestinal disease [93].

The graphics processing units is instantly parallel to several core processors which are used to speed up a broad variety of parallel data applications such as analysis and image processing, in addition to graphics processing. Hadoop framework is accelerated by a compute unified device architecture providing a manifesto for distributed, fast, computationally intensive data sets of processing. To make a high execution distributed image processing system, compute unified device architecture can be incorporated into the Hadoop platform. It can create very large, distributed computing frameworks which are cost and power effective [94].

10.7.2   Signal Processing

In contrast to medical image, medical signals often experience volume and rapid restriction, particularly when data from a variety of patients connected to monitoring systems are continuously acquired and stowed in high resolution. Besides data size problems, physiological signals often create challenges in space-time. By combining physiological and situational signals, analyzing physiological signals is more useful to develop continuous tracking systems and predictive systems to verify their effectiveness and intensity [91].

The convexity of signal clarification dates back to the beginning of the industry, and difficulty including squares are omnipresent in most subsections. Because of development of new hypothesis for organized absence or the belittlement of classifications or effical statistical training models, such as vector supporting machines, the importance of convex optimization and wording has become more serious during the last decade. This formulation is presently used for a variety of applications including medical imaging, compression detection, bioinformatics and signal-processing geophysics [95].

Independent Component Analysis is used in the biomedical signal processing field. Independent Component Analysis includes various fields such as digital imaging, financial and economic markets and psychometric testing as well as analyzes of biomedical signals which includes neurophysiological and cardiac signals and also in fMRI [96].

10.7.3   Genomics

As the high-performance sequencing method progresses, the cost of sequencing of human genome (which comprises 30,000 to 35,000 génes) has slowly fallen. In the computational biological field the analysis of data of genome scale in order to quickly produce actionable recommendations represents a major challenge. Researchers use a predictive, preventive, participation and personal health (SCH) paradigm and an integrative personal omics profile to examine 100,000 subjects in the 20–30-year period to deal with this complex matter. In the P4 initiative, a systematic approach is adopted to (a) evaluate genome scale data sets to evaluate disease status, (b) transfer into blood-based diagnostic methods for continuous subject monitoring, (c) explore new drug discovery methods, develop tools for the large data capture, process, validate, integrate, and (d) model data for each person. Data modeling the integrative profile combines physiological surveillance with different high-performance sequence methods for the delivery of comprehensive health and disease conditions [91].

As taxonomy for observing in the next generation, on the basis of profound algorithms, state-of-the-art software is the solution for sequencing. The next-generation sequence defines the many modern applications for DNA sequences which generate broader genomic data that is easier to determine. Furthermore, complex contrivance and highly efficient side-by-side detersion structure are required for interpretation and collection of information from a broad range of molecular or genomic data. In terms of information sharing or scalability of computer resources, the research community could benefit from the next generation of cloud computing services based on Deep Learning algors [97].

Hadoop technology is used in two paradigms that apply to vast medical data and genomics set. Hadoop has the immense capacity, if and when applied to life sciences, to make scientific discoveries. However, given that public clouds like Amazon Web Services now provide DaaS by offering a repository of public data sets like Ensembl, GenBank, 1000 Genomes, DNA Elements Model Organism Encyclopaedia, Influenza Virus, Unigene, this potential is becoming an impending reality. The ability of cloud computing's to analyze all variables at once is a significant enabler of the new field of system biology which is a holistic approach that helps to visualize the 'omics' as an interconnected network, allowing a paradigm change from hypothesis-driven analysis to hypothesis-generating research [98].

Talukder *et al.* have been found in the study that Next Generation Sequencing data implemented in evidence-based medicine an aspect of data-driven mechanistic science-bringing in mathematicians and computer scientists to support a physician. Genomics, which began with the Human Genome Project which explains nature of a living systems disease and the genotype–phenotype relationship. Today, genomics is used as a screening method for genetic and non-communicable diseases. Genomics uses the Big Data genomic analytics for the asymptomatic disease onset. It is used to treat and cure patient disease with heart disease or some other environmental or genetic disorders that are non-communicable [99].

10.7.4   Bioinformatics Applications

The research related to bioinformatics analyses alternatives at the molecular level to the biological system. For personalized medicine, the large data sets must be generated, processed, and analyzed in an accomplishable time frame. Next-generation sequencing method allows for the genomic data achievement in less time period. A part of Big Data methods in bioinformatics is to deliver computing infrastructure to researchers, data repositories and efficient data processing tools for the collection and analysis of biological information [15].

Bioinformatics needs a broad range of software resources for several varieties of data analysis. Software as a Service is a type of software that offers online services and accelerates remote access to bioinformatics software tools. Software as a service has significance to abolish the need for local deployment and simplify software updates and maintenances that provide update cloud-based services for web-based data exploration in bioinformatics. Over the past few years, attempts have been put together to produce cloud scale utensil, which include alignment, sequence mapping, expression analysis, analysis of succession, assembly, ChIP-seq data for peak caller, orthology detection, variants functional annotation from multiple personal genomes, recognition of different cloud-based applications for Next-Generation Sequencing data analysis, and Single-Nucleotide Polymorphisms epistatic interactions [100].

Yanjun *et al.* have developed a Database of Adverse Event Notifications to predict the proteins local properties which is based on their sequence. Many of the expected properties were determined such as surface area of available solvent, signal peptides, secondary structure, DNA-binding residues, and transmembrane topology. The amino acid succession is used as an entry to predict class labels Adverse Event Notifications database. The approach has three levels, including an amino acid extraction layer and a sequence extraction layer, and the artificial neural networks layer. The latest findings of this approach were obtained. In 2014 Lyons *et al.* used an Adverse Event Notifications database to predict the Cα angles or dihedrals depend on protein succession [101].

A most common and useful data types in bio-informatics are gene expression data that are used to represent cellular changes resulting from different chemical and physical conditions as well as genetic disturbances. The cost of profiling the whole genome is high. In order to reduce gene profiling costs, the researchers have developed an affordable method for profiling about 1000 selected landmarks and predict that the other target genes are expressed using computer-based and landmark methods for gene expression [102].

BioPig is an Apache's Hadoop framework or the Pig Latin data flow languages for bioinformatics processing. BioPig has three main advantages as opposed to conventional algorithms, such as the programmability of BioPig reduces the time required to develop parallel bioinformatics applications; BioPig was tested with sequences until 500 GB, which determines that the BioPig is automatically scale with data size. The software is called Cloudburst and is performed furthermore the Hadoop framework to examine next-generation sequence data. The Dryad, Message Passing and Hadoop MapReduce Programme's programming framework were used in three bioinformatics applications for comparative studies. In Hadoop, algorithms for BLAST or Gene Set Enrichment Analysis have been used both to stream computations on huge data sets and to compute multipasses on relatively small datasets [103].

The PEI is the first genome sequencing facility worldwide to use the Hadoop platform for cloud based investigation workflow called Gaea. Gaea is used at large scales in which parallel analysis of the genome has been carried out on hundreds of cloud-based devices. In terms of the Bina box hardware part, Bina Technologies will spin off a cloud-based genome analysis system. It's being used to prepare genome data and to analyze pre-processed data cloud-based. Bina Box decreases quantity of the genome data in order to allow successful cloud transmission. This magnitude order must more than conventional techniques be extended to the output of genome analytics [104].

The European Bioinformatics Institute has set up a cluster of Hinxton data center comprising 17,000 cores and 74 terabytes of RAM. The National Institute of Genetics, Japan, and the US National Center on Biotechnology Information are using this technology. Five different types of data are extensive and are used in bioinformatics research, including data on protein-protein interaction, gene expression, pathway information, RNA information, DNA data, protein sequence data, and gene ontology. There are other forms, like the relationship between gene and human disease, also used in numerous research areas [105].

10.7.5   Clinical Informatics Application

Clinical informatics emphasizes on use of healthcare information technology. This involves activity-based analysis, it investigation the cause of death which is determined by the collection of data from electronic health records or other sources such as electrophysiological data. Clinical informatics deals with structured in addition unstructured data and produces particular ontologies and use natural language processing significantly. Sahoo et al. or Jayapandian et al. suggested a distributed system for huge amounts of Electroencephalogram data being stored and queried. The Cloudwave frameworks store clinical data using Hadoop-based data processing modules. They developed a web-based interface for visualizing and retrieving data in real-time. The Cloudwave team analyzed a 77-GB Electroencephalogram signal dataset and compared Cloudwave to a stand-alone device. Cloudwave, processed 5 Electroencephalogram studies in 1 minute, but the stand alone device took more than 20 minutes [106].

The abundance of Big Data, the healthcare analytics has generated an increasing need for experts in clinical informatics which can help to bridge the gap between information and medical science. Clinical informatics experts influence information technology like telemedicine to increase the safety and delivery of healthcare, Electronic Health Records, and evidence-based medicine methods use technologies like clinical decision systems and data analytics to improve healthcare. The Big Data produced by patients were recognized as a potential platform in data mining and the advancement of computerized diagnostic software for personalized healthcare and medical diagnostics [107].

The importance of patient-centered informatics and clinical information systems focus to improve health results and promoting the ability to provide effective and quality care. Health and clinical data are tools that can improve healthcare. Clinical informatics is a sub-discipline of health informatics. It provides the scientific simplification to use information effectively in patient care, medical education, and clinical research. Data needs a combination of analytics, visualization, and interpretation to create the information that subsidizes health policy and decision making services [108].

The American Medical Informatics Association for clinical informatics and biomedical informatics is a research organization and professional home. It develops a code of ethics and funded workshop, policy, education and research programs [109]. The amount of data produced within Health Informatics has grown very fast and Big Data analysis contributes potentially endless possibilities for acquiring information. This information helps the patients to escalate the quality of healthcare. The foremost involvement of Health Informatics was to take medical data from all aspects of human life into the real world to further advance knowledge of medicine and medical practice. Clinical informatics research includes making predictions that can help doctors to make safer, quicker, and more reliable decisions [110].

The Big Data analysis attained by Electronic Health Record enables for a fast learning healthcare system that combines clinical research and clinical care. This involves clinical data which helps in health learning and assists large-scale observational trials and large reasonable trials for rapid evidence generation and validation using Electronic Health Record data. Big Data was renowned to be the backbone of a learning health system and tools for optimizing clinical research design. The PCORnet has been launched by Patient-Centered Outcomes Research Institute which necessitates 13 clinical data research networks and 19 patient-powered research networks. It covers most states in the United States to perform both randomized trials and observational comparative effectiveness studies using Electronic Health Record data [111].

In addition to genomics, proteomics, and other biological data, the most effective means to enhance the analysis are the clinical bioinformacy tools and services as major biological databases contain clinical data. The concept collections and methods used to explain new biological processes and to lead to translation development in individualized healthcare are included in clinical bioinformatics. The main focus of clinical bioinformatics is lung cancer and metastasis patients, such as patients, therapies, clinic signs and symptoms, history, biochemical analyses, physician exams, imaging profiles, paths, etc. The use of multi-dimensional evidence includes clinical data sets and played an important role in understanding level of lung cancer [112].

Clinical bioinformatics is designed to provide different methods and tools to assist decision-makers. It must contribute to tackling clinical genomics such as biomarker discovery, genomic medicine such as genotype and phenotype correlations, genetic epidemiology, and pharmacogenomics during the treatment. It mainly supports the purposes of researchers. Clinical bioinformatics can also support the research. In the last decades, novel genome sequencing and experimental high-throughput techniques have produced large quantities of molecular data, combined with clinical data. If appropriately utilized by researchers, it can contribute to significant biomedical discoveries. The regular growth in publicly accessible data, sources of information and the probability of simply accessing at low cost. Bioinformatics and computational technology have been predicted to be used in genomic medicine through the high amount of molecular technology. The cloud computing technology is accepted as a key technology for future of genomic research to assist the translational research on a wide scale [113].

10.8   Conclusion

This chapter discussed the data analytics role in healthcare. Big Data is mainly used to enhance the performance in response to disease in less consumption of time. It can improve the healthcare facility at different levels. The chapter describes the need of Big Data in the healthcare management. It can discuss the different software characteristics which are involved in disease management and treatment. It can also focus on the benefits and application of data analytics in medical field. It can describe the signal processing, image processing, genomics, bioinformatics and clinical informatics related to data analytics which is used in the management of the disease.

References

1. Raghupathi, W. and Raghupathi, V., Big Data analytics in healthcare: Promise and potential. *Health Inf. Sci. Syst.*, 2, 1, 1–10, 2014.
2. Priyanka, K. and Kulennavar, N., A survey on Big Data analytics in healthcare. *Int. J. Comput. Sci. Inf. Technol.*, 5, 4, 5865–5868, 2014.
3. Nambiar, R., Bhardwaj, R., Sethi, A., Vargheese, R., A look at challenges and opportunities of Big Data analytics in healthcare, in: *IEEE international conference on Big Data*, IEEE, pp. 17–22, 2013.
4. Mehta, N. and Pandit, A., Concurrence of Big Data analytics and healthcare: A systematic review. *Int. J. Med. Inform.*, 114, 57–65, 2018.
5. Manogaran, G., Lopez, D., Thota, C., Abbas, K.M., Pyne, S., Sundarasekar, R., Big Data analytics in healthcare Internet of Things, in: *Innovative healthcare systems for the 21st century*, pp. 263–284, Springer, Cham, 2017.
6. Palanisamy, V. and Thirunavukarasu, R., Implications of Big Data analytics in developing healthcare frameworks–A review. *J. King Saud Univ. Comp. & Info. Sci.*, 31, 4, 415–425, 2019.
7. Wang, Y., Kung, L., Byrd, T.A., Big Data analytics: Understanding its capabilities and potential benefits for healthcare organizations. *Technol. Forecast. Soc Change*, 126, 3–13, 2018.
8. Sharma, A., Malviya, R., Awasthi, R., Sharma, P.K., Artificial Intelligence, Blockchain, and Internet of Medical Things: New Technologies in Detecting, Preventing, and Controlling of Emergent Diseases, in: *Advances in Multidisciplinary Medical Technologies-Engineering, Modeling and Findings*, A. Khelassi and V.V. Estrela (Eds.), pp. 127–154, Springer, Cham, 2021, https://doi.org/10.1007/978-3-030-57552-6_10.
9. Batarseh, F.A. and Latif, E.A., Assessing the quality of service using Big Data analytics: with application to healthcare. *Big Data Res.*, 4, 13–24, 2016.
10. Koppad, S.H. and Kumar, A., Application of Big Data analytics in healthcare system to predict COPD, in: *2016 International Conference on Circuit, Power and Computing Technologies (ICCPCT)*, pp. 1–5, IEEE, Nagercoil, India, 2016, March.
11. Rumsfeld, J.S., Joynt, K.E., Maddox, T.M., Big Data analytics to improve cardiovascular care: promise and challenges. *Nat. Rev. Cardiol.*, 13, 6, 350–359, 2016.
12. Ristevski, B. and Chen, M., Big Data analytics in medicine and healthcare. *J. Integr. Bioinform.*, 15, 3, 1–5, 2018.
13. Costa, F.F., Big Data in biomedicine. *Drug Discovery Today*, 19, 4, 433–440, 2014.
14. Noor, A.M., Holmberg, L., Gillett, C., Grigoriadis, A., Big data: The challenge for small research groups in the era of cancer genomics. *Br. J. Cancer*, 113, 10, 1405–1412, 2015.

15. Luo, J., Wu, M., Gopukumar, D., Zhao, Y., Big Data application in biomedical research and healthcare: A literature review. *Biomed. Inform. Insights*, 8, 1–10, 2016.
16. Sakr, S. and Elgammal, A., Towards a comprehensive data analytics framework for smart healthcare services. *Big Data Res.*, 4, 44–58, 2016.
17. Ryu, S. and Song, T.M., Big Data analysis in healthcare. *Healthc. Inform. Res.*, 20, 4, 247–248, 2014.
18. Bhardwaj, R., Sethi, A., Nambiar, R., Big data in genomics: An overview, in: *2014 IEEE International Conference on Big Data (Big Data)*, IEEE, pp. 45–49, 2014.
19. Gharajeh, M.S., Biological Big Data analytics, in: *Advances in computers*, vol. 109, pp. 321–355, Elsevier, Tabriz, Iran, 2018.
20. Bates, D.W., Saria, S., Ohno-Machado, L., Shah, A., Escobar, G., Big Data in healthcare: Using analytics to identify and manage high-risk and high-cost patients. *Health Aff.*, 33, 7, 1123–1131, 2014.
21. Firouzi, F., Rahmani, A.M., Mankodiya, K., Badaroglu, M., Merrett, G.V., Wong, P., Farahani, B., Internet-of-Things and Big Data for smarter healthcare: From device to architecture, applications and analytics. *Future Gener. Comp. Sy.*, 78, 2, 583–586, 2018.
22. Augustine, D.P., Leveraging Big Data analytics and Hadoop in developing India's healthcare services. *Int. J. Comput. Appl.*, 89, 16, 44–50, 2014.
23. Alonso, S.G., de la Torre Diez, I., Rodrigues, J.J., Hamrioui, S., Lopez-Coronado, M., A systematic review of techniques and sources of Big Data in the healthcare sector. *J. Med. Syst.*, 41, 11, 1–9, 2017.
24. Eswari, T., Sampath, P., Lavanya, S., Predictive methodology for diabetic data analysis in Big Data. *Proc. Comput. Sci.*, 50, 203–208, 2015.
25. Cichosz, S.L., Johansen, M.D., Hejlesen, O., Toward Big Data analytics: Review of predictive models in management of diabetes and its complications. *J. Diabetes Sci. Technol.*, 10, 1, 27–34, 2016.
26. Bai, B.M., Nalini, B.M., Majumdar, J., Analysis and detection of diabetes using data mining techniques—a Big Data application in healthcare. *Emerg. Res. Comput. Inform. Commun. Appl.*, 882, 443–455, 2019.
27. Kalyankar, G.D., Poojara, S.R., Dharwadkar, N.V., Predictive analysis of diabetic patient data using machine learning and Hadoop, in: *2017 International Conference on I-SMAC (IoT in social, mobile, analytics and cloud)(I-SMAC)*, IEEE, pp. 619–624, 2017.
28. Kumar, P.S. and Pranavi, S., Performance analysis of machine learning algorithms on diabetes dataset using Big Data analytics, in: *2017 International Conference on Infocom Technologies and Unmanned Systems (Trends and Future Directions)(ICTUS)*, IEEE, pp. 508–513, 2017.
29. Banu, N.S. and Swamy, S., Prediction of heart disease at early stage using data mining and Big Data analytics: A survey, in: *2016 International Conference on Electrical, Electronics, Communication, Computer and Optimization Techniques (ICEECCOT)*, IEEE, pp. 256–261, 2016.

30. Thakur, S. and Ramzan, M., A systematic review on cardiovascular diseases using big-data by Hadoop, in: *2016 6th International Conference-Cloud System and Big Data Engineering (Confluence)*, IEEE, pp. 351–355, 2016.

31. Vaishali, G. and Kalaivani, V., Big Data analysis for heart disease detection system using map reduce technique, in: *2016 International Conference on Computing Technologies and Intelligent Data Engineering (ICCTIDE'16)*, IEEE, pp. 1–6, 2016.

32. Mane, T.U., Smart heart disease prediction system using Improved K-means and ID3 on Big Data, in: *2017 International Conference on Data Management, Analytics and Innovation (ICDMAI)*, IEEE, pp. 239–245, 2017.

33. Bhardwaj, N., Wodajo, B., Spano, A., Neal, S., Coustasse, A., The impact of Big Data on chronic disease management. *J. Healthc. Manage.*, 37, 1, 90–98, 2018.

34. Thara, D.K., Premasudha, B.G., Ram, V.R., Suma, R., Impact of Big Data in healthcare: A survey, in: *2016 2nd International Conference on Contemporary Computing and Informatics (IC3I)*, IEEE, pp. 729–735, 2016.

35. Dubey, H., Yang, J., Constant, N., Amiri, A.M., Yang, Q., Makodiya, K., Fog data: Enhancing telehealth Big Data through fog computing, in: *Proceedings of the ASE Big Data & social informatics 2015*, pp. 1–6, 2015.

36. Siuly, S. and Zhang, Y., Medical Big Data: neurological diseases diagnosis through medical data analysis. *Data Sci. Eng.*, 1, 2, 54–64, 2016.

37. Dendrou, C.A., McVean, G., Fugger, L., Neuroinflammation using Big Data to inform clinical practice. *Nat. Rev. Neurol.*, 12, 12, 685–698, 2016.

38. Aoe, J., Fukuma, R., Yanagisawa, T., Harada, T., Tanaka, M., Kobayashi, M., Inoue, Y., Yamamoto, S., Ohnishi, Y., Kishima, H., Automatic diagnosis of neurological diseases using MEG signals with a deep neural network. *Sci. Rep.*, 9, 1, 1–9, 2019.

39. Cirillo, D. and Valencia, A., Big Data analytics for personalized medicine. *Curr. Opin. Biotech.*, 58, 161–167, 2019.

40. Suwinski, P., Ong, C., Ling, M.H., Poh, Y.M., Khan, A.M., Ong, H.S., Advancing personalized medicine through the application of whole exome sequencing and Big Data analytics. *Front. Genet.*, 10, 1–16, 2019.

41. Clim, A., Zota, R.D., Tinica, G., Big Data in home healthcare: A new frontier in personalized medicine. Medical emergency services and prediction of hypertension risks. *Int. J. Healthc. Manage.*, 12, 3, 241–249, 2019.

42. Kumar, P.S. and Pranavi, S., Performance analysis of machine learning algorithms on diabetes dataset using Big Data analytics, in: *2017 International Conference on Infocom Technologies and Unmanned Systems (Trends and Future Directions)(ICTUS)*, IEEE, pp. 508–513, 2017.

43. Duggal, R., Shukla, S., Chandra, S., Shukla, B., Khatri, S.K., Predictive risk modelling for early hospital readmission of patients with diabetes in India. *Int. J. Diabetes Dev. C.*, 36, 4, 519–528, 2016.

44. Ratner, R.E., Christophi, C.A., Metzger, B.E., Dabelea, D., Bennett, P.H., Pi-Sunyer, X., Fowler, S., Kahn, S.E., Diabetes Prevention Program Research

Group, Prevention of diabetes in women with a history of gestational diabetes: Effects of metformin and lifestyle interventions. *J. Clin. Endocr. Metab.*, 93, 12, 4774–4779, 2008.

45. Ayas, N.T., White, D.P., Al-Delaimy, W.K., Manson, J.E., Stampfer, M.J., Speizer, F.E., Patel, S., Hu, F.B., A prospective study of self-reported sleep duration and incident diabetes in women. *Diabetes Care*, 26, 2, 380–384, 2003.

46. Chen, M., Yang, J., Zhou, J., Hao, Y., Zhang, J., Youn, C.H., 5G-smart diabetes: Toward personalized diabetes diagnosis with healthcare Big Data clouds. *IEEE Commun. Mag.*, 56, 4, 6–23, 2018.

47. Mahtani, M.M., Widen, E., Lehto, M., Thomas, J., McCarthy, M., Brayer, J., Bryant, B., Chan, G., Daly, M., Forsblom, C., Kanninen, T., Mapping of a gene for type 2 diabetes associated with an insulin secretion defect by a genome scan in Finnish families. *Nat. Genet.*, 14, 1, 90–94, 1996.

48. Das, N., Das, L., Rautaray, S.S., Pandey, M., Big Data analytics for medical applications. *Int. J. Modern Educ. Comput. Sci.*, 11, 2, 1–18, 2018.

49. Singh, Y.K., Sinha, N., Singh, S.K., Heart Disease Prediction System Using Random Forest, in: *International Conference on Advances in Computing and Data Sciences*, Springer, Singapore, pp. 613–623, 2016.

50. Ettehad, D., Emdin, C.A., Kiran, A., Anderson, S.G., Callender, T., Emberson, J., Chalmers, J., Rodgers, A., Rahimi, K., Blood pressure lowering for prevention of cardiovascular disease and death: a systematic review and meta-analysis. *Lancet*, 387, 10022, 957–967, 2016.

51. Yekkala, I., Dixit, S., Jabbar, M.A., Prediction of heart disease using ensemble learning and Particle Swarm Optimization, in: *2017 International Conference On Smart Technologies For Smart Nation (SmartTechCon)*, IEEE, pp. 691–698, 2017.

52. Mane, T.U., Smart heart disease prediction system using Improved K-means and ID3 on Big Data, in: *2017 International Conference on Data Management, Analytics and Innovation (ICDMAI)*, IEEE, pp. 239–245, 2017.

53. Nair, L.R., Shetty, S.D., Shetty, S.D., Applying spark based machine learning model on streaming Big Data for health status prediction. *Comput. Electr. Eng.*, 65, 393–399, 2018.

54. Yekkala, I. and Dixit, S., Prediction of Heart Disease Using Random Forest and Rough Set Based Feature Selection. *Int. J. Big Data Anal. Healthcare (IJBDAH)*, 3, 1, 1–12, 2018.

55. Bashir, S., Khan, Z.S., Khan, F.H., Anjum, A., Bashir, K., Improving Heart Disease Prediction Using Feature Selection Approaches, in: *2019 16th International Bhurban Conference on Applied Sciences and Technology (IBCAST)*, IEEE, pp. 619–623, 2019.

56. Shepherd, J., Blauw, G.J., Murphy, M.B., Bollen, E.L., Buckley, B.M., Cobbe, S.M., Ford, I., Gaw, A., Hyland, M., Jukema, J.W., Kamper, A.M., Pravastatin in elderly individuals at risk of vascular disease (PROSPER): A randomised controlled trial. *Lancet*, 360, 9346, 1623–1630, 2002.

57. Lin, R., Ye, Z., Wang, H., Wu, B., Chronic diseases and health monitoring Big Data: A survey. *IEEE Rev. Biomed. Eng.*, 11, 275–288, 2018.

58. Tarn, A., Dean, B., Schwarz, G., Thomas, J., Ingram, D., Bottazzo, G.F., Gale, E.M., Predicting insulin-dependent diabetes. *Lancet*, 331, 8590, 845–850, 1988.

59. De la Torre-Diez, I., Diaz-Pernas, F.J., Anton-Rodriguez, M., A content analysis of chronic diseases social groups on Facebook and Twitter. *Telemed. e-Health*, 18, 6, 404–408, 2012.

60. Khan, A., Uddin, S., Srinivasan, U., Adapting graph theory and social network measures on healthcare data: a new framework to understand chronic disease progression, in: *Proceedings of the Australasian Computer Science Week Multiconference*, pp. 1–7, 2016.

61. Batra, A., Batra, U., Singh, V., A review to predictive methodology to diagnose chronic kidney disease, in: *2016 3rd International Conference on Computing for Sustainable Global Development (INDIACom)*, IEEE, pp. 2760–2763, 2016.

62. Ramkumar, N., Prakash, S., Sangeetha, K., Data analysis for chronic disease-diabetes using map reduce technique, in: *2016 International Conference on Computer Communication and Informatics (ICCCI)*, IEEE, pp. 1–5, 2016.

63. Agapito, G., Simeoni, M., Calabrese, B., Guzzi, P.H., Fuiano, G., Cannataro, M., DIETOS: A Recommender System for Health Profiling and Diet Management in Chronic Diseases, in: *HealthRecSys@ RecSys*, pp. 32–35, 2017.

64. Ayas, N.T., White, D.P., Manson, J.E., Stampfer, M.J., Speizer, F.E., Malhotra, A., Hu, F.B., A prospective study of sleep duration and coronary heart disease in women. *Arch. Intern. Med.*, 163, 2, 205–209, 2003.

65. Singh, Y.K., Sinha, N., Singh, S.K., Heart Disease Prediction System Using Random Forest, in: *International Conference on Advances in Computing and Data Sciences*, Springer, Singapore, pp. 613–623, 2016.

66. Faust, O., Acharya, R.U., Allen, A.R., Lin, C.M., Analysis of EEG signals during epileptic and alcoholic states using AR modeling techniques. *IRBM*, 29, 1, 44–52, 2008.

67. Ramkumar, N., Prakash, S., Sangeetha, K., Data analysis for chronic disease-diabetes using map reduce technique, in: *2016 International Conference on Computer Communication and Informatics (ICCCI)*, IEEE, pp. 1–5, 2016.

68. Charleonnan, A., Fufaung, T., Niyomwong, T., Chokchueypattanakit, W., Suwannawach, S., Ninchawee, N., Predictive analytics for chronic kidney disease using machine learning techniques, in: *2016 Management and Innovation Technology International Conference (MITicon)*, IEEE, pp. 80–83, 2016.

69. Lin, Y.K., Chen, H., Brown, R.A., Li, S.H., Yang, H.J., Healthcare predictive analytics for risk profiling in chronic care: A Bayesian multitask learning approach. *Mis. Q.*, 41, 2, 473–496, 2017.

70. Raghupathi, W. and Raghupathi, V., Big Data analytics in healthcare: Promise and potential. *Health Inf. Sci. Syst.*, 2, 1, 1–10, 2014.
71. Eswari, T., Sampath, P., Lavanya, S., Predictive methodology for diabetic data analysis in Big Data. *Proc. Comput. Sci.*, 50, 203–208, 2015.
72. Madhavi, D. and Ramana, B.V., De-Identified Personal healthcare system using Hadoop. *Int. J. Electr. Comput. Eng.*, 5, 6, 1492–1499, 2015.
73. Chennamsetty, H., Chalasani, S., Riley, D., Predictive analytics on electronic health records (EHRs) using hadoop and hive, in: *2015 IEEE International Conference on Electrical, Computer and Communication Technologies (ICECCT)*, IEEE, pp. 1–5, 2015.
74. Wang, L. and Alexander, C.A., Big Data analytics in healthcare systems. *Int. J. Math. Eng. Manage. Sci.*, 4, 1, 17–26, 2019.
75. Khan, W.A., Idris, M., Ali, T., Ali, R., Hussain, S., Hussain, M., Amin, M.B., Khattak, A.M., Weiwei, Y., Afzal, M., Lee, S., Correlating health and wellness analytics for personalized decision making, in: *2015 17th International Conference on E-health Networking, Application & Services (HealthCom)*, IEEE, pp. 256–261, 2015.
76. Kalogiannis, S., Deltouzos, K., Zacharaki, E.I., Vasilakis, A., Moustakas, K., Ellul, J., Megalooikonomou, V., Integrating an openEHR-based personalized virtual model for the ageing population within HBase. *BMC Med. Inform. Decis. Mak.*, 19, 1, 1–15, 2019.
77. Chrimes, D. and Zamani, H., Using distributed data over HBase in Big Data analytics platform for clinical services. *Comput. Math. Methods Med.*, 2017, 1–17, 2017.
78. Sathiyavathi, R., A Survey: Big Data Analytics on Healthcare System. *Contemp. Eng. Sci.*, 8, 3, 121–125, 2015.
79. Kolker, E., Janko, I., Montague, E., Higdon, R., Stewart, E., Choiniere, J., Lai, A., Eckert, M., Broomall, W., Kolker, N., Finding text-supported gene-to-disease co-appearances with MOPED-Digger. *Omics J. Intgr. Biol.*, 19, 12, 754–756, 2015.
80. Shobana, V. and Kumar, N., A personalized recommendation engine for prediction of disorders using Big Data analytics, in: *2017 International Conference on Innovations in Green Energy and Healthcare Technologies (IGEHT)*, IEEE, pp. 1–4, 2017.
81. Manogaran, G., Thota, C., Lopez, D., Vijayakumar, V., Abbas, K.M., Sundarsekar, R., Big Data knowledge system in healthcare, in: *Internet of things and Big Data technologies for next generation healthcare*, Springer, Cham, pp. 133–157, 2017.
82. Trifiro, G., Sultana, J., Bate, A., From Big Data to smart data for pharmacovigilance: The role of healthcare databases and other emerging sources. *Drug Saf.*, 41, 2, 143–149, 2018.
83. Gandomi, A. and Haider, M., Beyond the hype: Big Data concepts, methods, and analytics. *Int. J. Inf. Manage.*, 35, 2, 137–144, 2015.

84. Olaronke, I. and Oluwaseun, O., December. Big Data in healthcare: Prospects, challenges and resolutions, in: *2016 Future Technologies Conference (FTC)*, IEEE, pp. 1152–1157, 2016.
85. Srinivasan, U. and Arunasalam, B., Leveraging Big Data analytics to reduce healthcare costs. *IT Prof.*, 15, 6, 21–28, 2013.
86. Eckmanns, T., Fuller, H., Roberts, S.L., Digital epidemiology and global health security; an interdisciplinary conversation. *Life Sci. Soc Policy*, 15, 1, 1–13, 2019.
87. Bosl, W.J., Tager-Flusberg, H., Nelson, C.A., EEG analytics for early detection of autism spectrum disorder: a data-driven approach. *Sci. Rep.*, 8, 1, 1–20, 2018.
88. Youssef, A.E., A framework for secure healthcare systems based on Big Data analytics in mobile cloud computing environments. *Int. J. Ambient Syst. Appl.*, 2, 2, 11, 2014.
89. Baesens, B., Van Vlasselaer, V., Verbeke, W., *Fraud analytics using descriptive, predictive, and social network techniques: a guide to data science for fraud detection*, pp. 270–312, John Wiley & Sons, 2015.
90. Wu, J., Li, H., Cheng, S., Lin, Z., The promising future of healthcare services: When Big Data analytics meets wearable technology. *Inf. Manage.*, 53, 8, 1020–1033, 2016.
91. Belle, A., Thiagarajan, R., Soroushmehr, S.M., Navidi, F., Beard, D.A., Najarian, K., Big Data analytics in healthcare. *Biomed. Res. Int.*, 2015, 1–17, 2015.
92. Yan, Y. and Huang, L., Large-scale image processing research cloud. *Cloud Comput.*, 88–93, 2014.
93. Razzak, M.I., Naz, S., Zaib, A., Deep learning for medical image processing: Overview, challenges and the future, in: *Classification in Bio Apps*, pp. 323–350, Springer, Cham, 2018.
94. Malakar, R. and Vydyanathan, N., A CUDA-enabled Hadoop cluster for fast distributed image processing, in: *2013 National Conference on Parallel Computing Technologies (PARCOMPTECH)*, IEEE, pp. 1–5, 2013.
95. Cevher, V., Becker, S., Schmidt, M., Convex optimization for Big Data: Scalable, randomized, and parallel algorithms for Big Data analytics. *IEEE Signal Process. Mag.*, 31, 5, 32–43, 2014.
96. James, C.J. and Hesse, C.W., Independent component analysis for biomedical signals. *Physiol. Meas.*, 26, 1, 15–39, 2004.
97. Malviya, R. and Sharma, A., Applications of computational methods and modelling in drug delivery, in: *Machine learning and analytics in healthcare systems*, H. Bansal, B. Balusamy, T. Poongodi, K. Firoz Khan (Eds.), pp. 1–28, CRC Press, India, 2021.
98. O'Driscoll, A., Daugelaite, J., Sleator, R.D., Big Data', Hadoop and cloud computing in genomics. *J. Biomed. Inform.*, 46, 5, 774–781, 2013.
99. Talukder, A.K., Genomics 3.0: Big-data in precision medicine, in: *International Conference on Big Data Analytics*, Springer, Cham, pp. 201–215, 2015.

100. Dai, L., Gao, X., Guo, Y., Xiao, J., Zhang, Z., Bioinformatics clouds for Big Data manipulation. *Biol. Direct*, 7, 1, 1–7, 2012.
101. Pastur-Romay, L.A., Cedron, F., Pazos, A., Porto-Pazos, A.B., Deep artificial neural networks and neuromorphic chips for Big Data analysis: Pharmaceutical and bioinformatics applications. *Int. J. Mol. Sci.*, 17, 8, 1–26, 2016.
102. Li, Y., Huang, C., Ding, L., Li, Z., Pan, Y., Gao, X., Deep learning in bioinformatics: Introduction, application, and perspective in the Big Data era. *Methods*, 166, 4–21, 2019.
103. Mohammed, E.A., Far, B.H., Naugler, C., Applications of the MapReduce programming framework to clinical Big Data analysis: Current landscape and future trends. *Bio Data Min.*, 7, 1, 1–23, 2014.
104. Kashyap, H., Ahmed, H.A., Hoque, N., Roy, S., Bhattacharyya, D.K., Big Data analytics in bioinformatics: A machine learning perspective. *J. Latex Class Files*, 13, 9, 1–20, 2014.
105. Kashyap, H., Ahmed, H.A., Hoque, N., Roy, S., Bhattacharyya, D.K., Big Data analytics in bioinformatics: Architectures, techniques, tools and issues. *Netw. Model. Anal. Health Inform. Bioinform.*, 5, 1, 1–28, 2016.
106. Wang, X. and Liotta, L., Clinical bioinformatics: A new emerging science. *J. Clin. Bioinform.*, 1, 1–3, 2011.
107. Simpao, A.F., Ahumada, L.M., Galvez, J.A., Rehman, M.A., A review of analytics and clinical informatics in healthcare. *J. Med. Syst.*, 38, 4, 1–7, 2014.
108. Smith, S.E., Drake, L.E., Harris, J.G.B., Watson, K., Pohlner, P.G., Clinical informatics: A workforce priority for 21st century healthcare. *Aust. Health Rev.*, 35, 2, 130–135, 2011.
109. Detmer, D.E. and Shortliffe, E.H., Clinical informatics: Prospects for a new medical subspecialty. *Jama*, 311, 20, 2067–2068, 2014.
110. Herland, M., Khoshgoftaar, T.M., Wald, R., A review of data mining using Big Data in health informatics. *J. Big Data*, 1, 1, 1–35, 2014.
111. Weng, C. and Kahn, M.G., Clinical research informatics for Big Data and precision medicine. *Yearb. Med. Inform.*, 25, 1, 211–218, 2016.
112. Wu, D. and Wang, X., Application of clinical bioinformatics in lung cancer-specific biomarkers. *Cancer Metastasis Rev.*, 34, 2, 209–216, 2015.
113. Bellazzi, R., Masseroli, M., Murphy, S., Shabo, A., Romano, P., Clinical Bioinformatics: Challenges and opportunities. *BMC Bioinf.*, 13, 1–8, 2012.

11

Case Studies of Cognitive Computing in Healthcare Systems: Disease Prediction, Genomics Studies, Medical Image Analysis, Patient Care, Medical Diagnostics, Drug Discovery

V. Sathananthavathi* and G. Indumathi

Mepco Schlenk Engineering College, Sivakasi, India

Abstract

Computer-assisted diagnosis of the retinal diseases are reliable and takes less time to process the vessels. Glaucoma is mostly caused by the gradual increase of pressure in the eye which is known as intraocular pressure (IOP). It is the silent thief of vision. As early as treatment it is possible to slow or stop the progression of the disease with proper medications, laser treatment, or surgery. The effective way in preventing the rise in eye pressure is by early detection. The early detection is possible through the application of cognitive algorithms on the detection of symptoms of Glaucoma.

This chapter provides a framework to help in the early detection using only frontal eye images. Firstly, the sclera and the iris are segmented using Fully Convolutional Network (FCN) on frontal eye images. Using these extracted areas, features that include mean redness level of the sclera, red area percentage, and Pupil/Iris diameter ratio are calculated. Based on the features extracted, the given frontal eye image can be classified into normal or Glaucoma image.

Keywords: Computer vision, eye segmentation, fully convolutional network, glaucoma, intraocular pressure, Pupil/Iris ratio, redness of the sclera

Corresponding author: sathananthavathi@mepcoeng.ac.in
V. Sathananthavathi: ORCID: https://orcid.org/0000-0002-8732-8652.

D. Sumathi, T. Poongodi, B. Balamurugan and Lakshmana Kumar Ramasamy (eds.)
Cognitive Intelligence and Big Data in Healthcare, (303–326) © 2022 Scrivener Publishing LLC

11.1   Introduction

Internal organs of our body and other pathological conditions are imaged and the relevant information are gathered with the help of innovative technology available nowadays. Biomedical imaging techniques use the x-rays in the computed tomography, sound in the ultrasound imaging, magnetism in magnetic resonance imaging, nuclear medicines or light to find the present situation of the organ or tissue of the patient and helps to monitor them continuously for their treatment. During scanning itself, image processing techniques help the doctor's necessity to perform operation to view the status of internal tissue or organ. If the image processing was not discovered then the doctor would have to perform surgery every time to examine the organ, which may provide pain to the patient and it also infects the patient as the disease causing microbes may enter the body if the invasive procedures are performed many times. Medical imaging produces images of the internal body structures without the invasive methods. Due to the use of fast processors and arithmetic and logical energy conversion, the medical images are produced.

Biomedical imaging helps in analyzing, enhancing and displaying the images though different imaging technologies. Due to the emerging nature of artificial intelligence in medical field, disease can be diagnosed earlier before noticeable to the person. Some of the computerized algorithms afford analysis based on spatial or temporal to identify tumors and other ailments. Image processing analysis can be used to determine the diameter, volume and tissue of organs, and blood vessels for diagnosis.

11.1.1   Glaucoma

Glaucoma is a complicated eye disease that results in damage to the optical nerve and may cause vision loss and blindness. This is due to the abnormal increase in pressure produced in the eyes. Glaucoma is a hidden disease because it causes no pain and no prior symptoms until noted vision loss takes place. It is prominent reasons for blindness among the elder persons over the age 60, but it is possible among any age. The greatest danger of this illness is that once glaucoma has caused blindness, it cannot be corrected. As a result, it's critical to have frequent eye exams and testing, which involve measuring eye pressure, so that the diagnosis may be arrived earlier and treated effectively. Vision loss can be delayed or prevented if glaucoma is detected early.

Glaucoma is a disorder that occurs when the optical nerve is damaged. Blind spots emerge in the visual field when this nerve starts to deteriorate. Nerve damage is frequently caused by increased pressure in the eyes. The main cause of the pressure is an uneven secretion of fluid (aqueous humor) in the eyes. This fluid generally drains from a tissue called the trabecular meshwork, which would be found in the ciliary body near the base of the cornea via the anterior chamber. When this fluid overflows or the fluid doesn't drain out properly through the trabecular, the fluid's inability to flow at its standard rate, ocular pressure rises.

Glaucoma(G) is of three types. They are Open-angle glaucoma (OG), Angle-closure glaucoma (AG) and Normal-tension glaucoma (NG). The much more prevalent kind of glaucoma is open-angle glaucoma (OG), which arises when the angle of draining formed by the cornea and iris. The trabecular meshwork is slightly obstructed, yet it is remains open, causing the pressure in the eyes to gradually rise. Angle-closure glaucoma (AG), commonly known as closed-angle glaucoma, is a type of glaucoma that usually occurs when the iris bulges. This blocks the drainage angle formed by the cornea and iris. Thus, the fluid can't circulate through the eye which tends to increase the pressure of the eye. The people with the narrow drainage angles are at the high risk of getting affected with this angle-closure glaucoma. Angle-closure glaucoma (AG) might befall unexpectedly which is termed as acute angle-closure glaucoma which is a medical emergency should be treated as soon as possible.

The immediate occurring involves in drastic eye pain, mid-dilated pupil, and severe redness of the eye, nausea, and blurred vision. The eye pressure value greater than 21 mmHg or 2.8 kPa is a high pressure which leads to greater risk. Normal-tension glaucoma takes place once the optic nerve is damaged. Although the pressure is now within acceptable bounds, this happens. The specific cause for this kind is unknown. The people with sensitive optic nerve or having less blood stream to the optic nerve are affected by this category of glaucoma. Atherosclerosis inside the arteries or other factors that induce poor circulation of blood could be the source of the restricted blood flow. Normally, the intraocular pressure (IOP) should be below 21 mmHg. If the IOP of a person is greater than 30 mmHg then the danger of blindness due to glaucoma is 40 times greater than the person with the IOP of 15 mmHg or lower. As early as treatment it is possible to moderate or halt the development of the disease with proper medications, laser treatment or surgery. The main motto or object of these treatments is to decrease the pressure of the eyes. There are number of different medications which are available for glaucoma. Laser treatments are effective in both open-angel and closed-angle glaucoma. The surgeries may be performed when the above treatments are not producing the sufficient or expected results.

The second most common causes of blindness in the world are the glaucoma. It was evaluated that about 4.6 million people are blind because of glaucoma. Especially in India, there are 12 million cases of glaucoma in which 1.2 million people are losing their vision due to this disease. More than 90% of glaucoma cases are being undiagnosed. So, it is good to diagnose and treat as early as possible. A tonometer is used to measure your intraocular pressure or IOP by using different types of tonometers. Some of the tonometer is noncontact tonometer, Applanation tonometry, and electronic indentation method tonometer. Some of the other testing and screening methods for glaucoma are Pachymetry, Ophthalmoscopy, Pupil dilation, Visual Field Testing, Gonioscopy, etc. The traditional way of diagnosing the glaucoma was carried out by Tonometry, in which the diagnosis may take few minutes to few hours. So, the rate of diagnosis or testing is low.

Computer-assisted diagnosis of the retinal diseases are reliable and takes less time to process the vessels. Glaucoma is produced by a progressive rise in intraocular pressure inside the eye (IOP). It is the silent thief of vision. As early as treated it is possible to slow or stop the progression of the disease with proper medications, laser treatment or surgery. Early detection is the most efficient strategy to prevent an increase in eye pressure. The early detection is possible through the application of cognitive algorithms on the detection of symptoms of glaucoma.

11.2   Literature Survey

Mohammad Aloudat *et al.* [1] used well-known methods to compute the blood vessels present in color photographs of the retina in order to determine the human eye's intraocular pressure (IOP). This is done with histogram analysis. This paper gives an overview of the familiar methods used in the calculation of the vasculature in color retinal image. In addition, a histogram analysis survey was done to address the first stages in detecting intraocular pressure (IOP). Mohammad Aloudat and Faezipour *et al.* [2] proposed to calculate the angle of open and closed glaucoma. These calculations are done as a first step to determine the viscosity of the liquid present inside the cornea. To get rid of vision loss this method very helpful.

The performance is established to be highly systematic and accurate by gaining the simulation results.

Chen *et al.* [3] performed morphological reconstruction functions like erosion, dilation, opening and terminating are used to retrieve and manipulate the shape attributes present on an image. Function and set processing (FSP) is used to perform dilation and erosion of a given gray scale image. This reconstruction method is used to remove the light reflection on the images. Chiou *et al.* [4] presented a on-lens intraocular pressure monitoring system which is based on the wireless mode. This comprises of a capacitance to digital converter and also wirelessly powered radio frequency identification (RFID) compatible communication system. This is used to control sensor and for data communication. The maximum detectable distance with 30-dBm incident RF power was 11 cm.

Dutta *et al.* [5] used an automatic image processing approach. This is to determine glaucoma. This method may also act as a diagnostic method as well. The proposed technique is based on computing the cup-to-disc ratio and segmenting the blind spot and hence the eyecup. A dual threshold approach is utilized to segment the eyecup and the blind spot. The first threshold is used to remove blood vessels and background, while the second is used to segment the high intensity pixels in the blind spot and eyecup. The Hough Transform is also used to estimate the radius of the blind spot as well as the eyecup. Inside the fundus image, the vertical cup to disc ratio is used as a measure for detecting glaucoma symptoms.

Khary Popplewell *et al.* [6] provide a multispectral iris recognition using Circular Hough Transform (CHT) and a modified Local Binary Pattern (mLBP) feature extraction technique. They also apply the Binary thresholding and edge detection techniques to find the boundaries of iris and pupil. Mansouri *et al.* [7] compared the accuracy by the measurement of frontal chamber angle by anterior segment optical coherence tomography and ultrasound bio microscopy in patients with suspected primary angle closure (PAC). The results like open or closed glaucoma are found by the angles.

Mariakakis *et al.* [8] used smart phone for the detection of intra ocular pressure. Here the system based on smartphones can be operated by the users even with minimum training to compute IOP and this system imitates fixed-force tonometry with a mechanical attachment to the smartphone of low cost. Mashhadi *et al.* [9] proposed a repetitive method using adaptive thresholding for the purpose of reconstructing voice from non uniform level crossing. It will take the estimated range of the voice or image level. This refers to the range higher than threshold value. This technique is applied in image to split the foreground image from the background image to extract the gray level range. Mrigana *et al.* [10] identifies an iris recognition using Circular Hough Transform. It includes methods like feature extraction, image segmentation, recognition and normalization. These features extraction are used to find the circular boundary of an iris; by this, we can find the radius of an iris.

Salam *et al.* [11] published a review of various glaucoma diagnostic techniques based on machine learning views. This paper emphasizes the importance of the functional and structural characteristics. It is mentioned that digital fundus and OCT pictures are used to identify glaucoma. It is explained well. When compared to functional features, structural features are more accurate for detecting previous glaucoma. More exact results can be gained by using hybrid features in training. Finally, the output of both fundus images and OCT images are correlated.

Shaaban *et al.* [12] proposed an algorithm to segment iris images of human eye which are captured in visible wavelength and under unconstrained environments. This algorithm reduces the error percentage of images along with iris obstructions and specular reflection. By using K means clustering algorithm they determined the expected region of the iris and finally they employed Circular Hough Transform (CHT) to find the radius and center.

Yousefi *et al.* [13] provided a multilevel technique for detecting glaucomatous field of visual impairment patterns and detecting glaucomatous development from field of vision data. The analytical pipeline is divided into three stages. They are clustering, glaucoma boundaries limit detection, and glaucoma progression detection testing. By degrading each cluster into multiple axes, the field of vision clusters were further assessed to recognize glaucomatous field of visual impairment patterns. The visual impairment variations of glaucoma sectors were then found at each axis. The proposed pipeline had clinical precision could be considered better when compared with the currently available approaches.

Most of the existing methodologies for glaucoma detection [14–17] is based on cup to disc ratio measurement on retinal fundus images. The continuous monitoring of glaucoma patients is difficult to do on fundus images. Hence, glaucoma detection based on frontal image is highly helpful and easy for diagnosis since ordinary camera can be used for capturing the frontal images.

The existing methodologies used deep learning for objects along with convolutional neural networks (CNN) in semantic segmentation. On considering the advantages of having Convolutional Neural Network (CNN), the fully convolutional network (FCN) structure, in a modified form is proposed and it comprises only convolutional layers for extracting features for glaucoma detection. Previously, IOP fundus images of the optic nerves were used widely in computer vision procedures. In this paper, the frontal eye images are used for the detection of glaucoma in human eyes.

11.3   Methodology

In the proposed methodology, the Fully Convolutional Network (FCN) system on the frontal eye photographs are used in the sclera and the iris segmentation. The advantage of the proposed method is that glaucoma detection can be performed using frontal images captured by ordinary camera. The proposed method is capable of segmenting iris, pupil and sclera regions; the individual regions of eye can be monitored continuously by the segmented image. This proposed work can be applied in an uncomplicated manner for telemedicine or remote monitoring since frontal

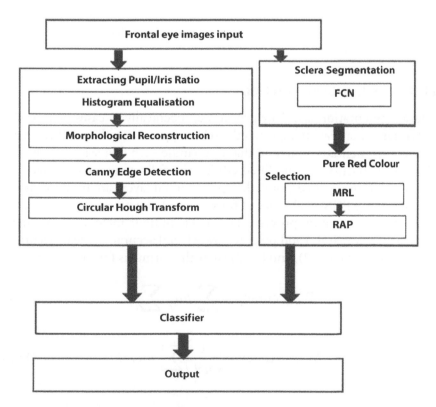

Figure 11.1 Block diagram of proposed work.

image based Glaucoma detection is proposed. The block representation of the proposed methodology is shown in Figure 11.1.

Instead of fully linked layers, the proposed network extracts features using convolutional layers and deconvolutional layers to restore the original size of the image. A Rectified Linear Unit (ReLU) activation function is included in each convolution layer. Maximum pooling is used to down sample the recovered images at the end of each phase. After the segmentation of the sclera, the pupil is extracted. The equalization of histogram method is utilized in order to increase the level of contrast of the pupil and iris area. The output image from the histogram equalization method is given as input to the morphological reconstruction technique, which removes the light reflection on the pupil. At last, Canny edge detection is used to discover the edges in the image at the preprocessing stage. After performing the above pre-processing, to determine the iris, the image is subjected to the Circular Hough Transform method. After that, the pupil is evaluated and the diameter or radius proportion is calculated.

After extracting sclera, the average level of redness and the red area percentage are calculated. Finally, by using SVM classifier, normal eye and glaucoma eye is detected. The software MATLAB 2018a is used for the implementation.

11.3.1   Sclera Segmentation

Sclera segmentation is a risky procedure, specifically in cases of excessive IOP, cataract, or glaucoma, when the sclera appears mostly red. As a result, a strong segmentation method that can handle such scenarios is required. This paper discusses, a modified edition the fully convolutional network (FCN) structure is incorporated. Convolutional layers are used to extract features in the FCN in absence of fully connected networks.

In the segmentation process, measurable outputs include region intersection of union(IOU) and pixel accuracy (total accuracy), mean accuracy, Equations (11.1), (11.2), and (11.3) show the formulas for these metrics.

$$\text{P\_Accuracy} = \sum_{i} nii \Big/ \sum_{i} ti \qquad (11.1)$$

$$\text{M\_Accuracy} = \left(\frac{1}{nci}\right) \sum_{i} nii \,/\, ti \qquad (11.2)$$

$$Mean\_IU = \left(\frac{1}{nci}\right)\sum_i nii \Big/ \left(ti + \sum_J nji - nii\right) \qquad (11.3)$$

While they are literally affiliated with class j, the pixel value is denoted by nii. exactly forecasted that occur to classi, and the pixel value is given by nij, accurately forecasted to appear in classi. nci stands for the number of forecasted classes. The number of pixels total associated with classj is tj = _inij.

11.3.1.1   Fully Convolutional Network

The proposed fully convolved neural network extracts features for glaucoma detection. Deconvolutional layers are used in the final stages of the networks to scale the image back to its original shape. Figure 11.2 depicts the network structure of the suggested network. To take advantage of boundary properties, each convolutional stage's outputs are merged to its former stages to improve segmentation edges. In the diagram below, every convolution step has an activation function called Rectified Linear Unit (ReLU), and pooling with maximum value is employed to downsample the recovered images at the end of each stage.

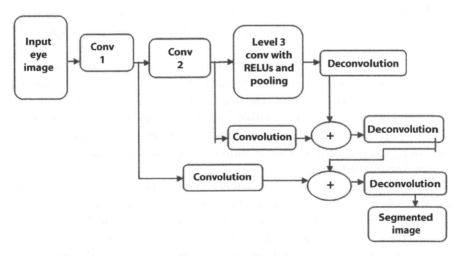

Figure 11.2 Fully convolutional neural network (FCN) structure.

Convolution Layers

The neurons in a convolutional layer connect to a few parts of the input images or the outcomes of the layer before it. While scanning through an image a convolutional layer acquires the features confined by the regions. The size of these regions are specified using the filter size as an input argument while initializing the layer. For each region, the multiplication operation of the weight and the inputs are performed by the network function which is then added by the bias terms. The regions are applied by the weight and these weights are named as filter. The filter moves in step size repeating the same computation in both parallel and perpendicular direction for each region along the input image. Stride is used to move the filter and this acts as the step size.

Feature Maps

By employing the same set of weights and bias for the convolution, the feature map is produced as a filter moves along the input. The count of feature maps will be the same as the filters used in the convolutional layer. Weights and bias are assigned to the respective feature map. So, in a convolutional layer, the total number of parameters is ((h*w*c + 1)*Number of Filters), where 1 is for the bias, and the heights of both the kernel size are represented by h, w, and c, correspondingly.

Striding

The each step moved by convolution filter is specified by stride. If the stride value is one, filters move on one pixel at a time.

Zero Padding

Padding is the method of assigning zeros towards the image's edge in rows or columns. Padding is used to regulate the display size of the image.

Size of Output

(Stride + 1)/(Input Size Filter Size + 2*Padding) has been used to compute the image output size from the convolutional layer. For the entire image to be entirely covered, this value must be an integer. With the increase of the network layer, more discriminative features are learnt by the network to describe the blood vessels. However, each stage has its own significance in providing the meaningful information required for segmentation.

Batch Normalization

Batch normalization layers as in [18] is generally used in network to speed up the training and it can also reduce network sensitivity. It is initialized between convolutional layers and nonlinearities such as ReLU layers. By dividing even by mini-batch standard deviation and removing the mini-batch mean, the batch normalization layer normalizes the activations used in each channel's network. The input is scaled and shifted by the scale factor, which is one of the network's learnable parameters. During network training, the offset and scaling factor are adjusted.

ReLU Layers

ReLU layer [19] works without affecting any significant difference to the accuracy and is able to train lot faster when compared to other layers of activation function. The size of the input is not affected by implementation of ReLU layer. The ReLu function is given by

$$f(x) = \begin{cases} x, x \geq 0 \\ 0, x < 0 \end{cases}$$

$$(11.4)$$

11.3.2   Pupil/Iris Ratio

Pupil/iris ratio is determined by reducing the dimensions of the pictures to 100 × 100. The red channel image is subsequently chosen since it eliminates duplicate data while simultaneously boosting the iris and, as a result, the pupil area. Applying these processes, the image is ready to apply the histogram equalization in order to increase the contrast rate of the Pupil and Iris area. The histogram is commonly employed to boost an image's overall contrast. Particularly when an image's useable data is represented by close contrast values. This is accomplished by successfully spreading out the most frequent intensity value, i.e., widening the image's intensity range without sacrificing image information. Thus, the intensities can be better disseminated. This makes the area with the lower local contrast to gain a high range of contrast and to better the details of the image that are over or under expose.

This method is very much used in images with background and foreground that are both bright and dark. The images produced may seems to be unrealistic but it is very useful for scientific purposes such as thermal imaging, getting a satellite image or x-ray images. This method works best when applied to an image with a higher color depth than palette size and 16-bit gray-scale images. In two ways, the histogram equalization can be implemented, one is image change and another is palette change. When the palette value is changed and the image is unchanged then it is known to be palette change histogram. If the palette remains unchanged and image changes then it is image change way of implementing the histogram equalization.

As the histogram increases and enhances the contrast of the image, we proceed to the next step called morphological reconstruction technique which removes the light reflection on the pupil. The morphological reconstruction is generally used for removing features from an image, without changing or altering the shape or structure of the object in the image. It is mostly used in removing shadows from images, segmenting MRI of structures inside the body, identifying language scripts and finding the connected path in a network or map.

This is based on the source image, marker image and marker point. There are four methods by which the morphological reconstruction can be done. They are reconstruction by dilation, reconstruction by erosion, grayscale morphological reconstruction and binary morphological reconstruction. Thus, an image with no reflection in pupil is obtained and is used for further process. The adaptive thresholding is applied to the obtained image of pupil from the morphological reconstruction so as to split the foreground from background for taking out the gray scale range that accommodates the Pupil and therefore the Iris. In adaptive thresholding method, the threshold value at every pixel place depends on the encircling pixels intensities. Finally, the image is subjected to a canny edge detection approach as a pre-processing phase. Canny edge detection uses multi-stage algorithm that's used to detect the edges in an image.

11.3.2.1   Canny Edge Detection

The Canny edge detection follows certain steps they are, to make the image less noisy the Gaussian filter is used which will smooth the image. Intensity gradients of the image are found. Non-maximum suppression is applied to remove the spurious response to edge detection. Double threshold is applied to determined potential edges. Hysteresis is applied to track the edges properly. In this process the edges are perfectly obtained as it contains the non-maximum suppression and hysteresis. After performing the above pre-processing, the Circular Hough Transform (CHT) technique is applied to the image in order to determine the Iris and then the Pupil. Then, the diameter ratio or radius ratio is detected and calculated. The MRL and RAP choices are determined once the sclera is extracted. The MRL heavily depends on the red pixel value.

Every visual element could be made up of thrice different values (Red(R), Green(G), and Blue(B)). Furthermore, there are numerous circumstances when assigning more values to the red section of the picture element will result in reddish colors. As a result, the value of the red pixel should be greater than the values of the green and blue components. To avoid the components from shifting to yellow(Y) or violet(V) colors, there shouldn't be too much of a disparity between the green and blue component values. To detect entirely diverse ranges of redness levels in the human eye, the nearest color to the pure red pixel value is applied.

11.3.2.2   Mean Redness Level (MRL)

Relative pupillary blockage causes the majority of these cases of primary angle closure glaucoma. Because aqueous humor passes via the iris-lens canal on its way from the posterior to the anterior chamber, it encounters more resistance in pupillary block. With a mid-dilated pupil, where there appears to be maximal contact with the iris and hence the lens, the likelihood of pupillary block becomes greatest. Other factors, such as the front lens surface being anterior to the plane of iris insertion into the membrane base, contribute to the blockage in eyes with angle closure. The peripheral iris bows forward and closes the appositional angle, due to the greater pressure gradient across the pupil. Iris angle crowding, which is caused by a thicker peripheral iris filling the gap between the TM and angle recess under dark conditions, is another mechanism thought to be important in primary angle closure. In primary open angle glaucoma, the IOP is assessed. Acute Angle-Closure glaucoma, a serious condition that makes the pressure inside the eye goes up suddenly. This pressure is normally referred to as Intraocular Pressure (IOP). It can increase within hours. It takes place when fluid within the eye can't drain that it drains usually. It's not quite as frequent as other varieties of glaucoma, which induce a much more gradual increase in pressure over time. It is caused by a rise in intraocular pressure, this is a fast or rapid increase in intraocular pressure (IOP). A series of canals drains the fluid from the eye. These canals are protected by a tissue mesh between the iris and the cornea. The angle between both the iris and the cornea is "closed" as the iris and the cornea move closer together. An acute attack is what happens whenever this happens.

It is excruciatingly uncomfortable. The canals are entirely blocked in acute angle closure glaucoma. It acts similarly to a piece of paper sliding over a sink drain in that it prevents fluid from flowing through them. The optic nerve is damaged due the pressure that builds up. If the problem is not treated quickly, complete loss of vision may occur. If the eyes dilate (pupil gets bigger) too much or too quickly, it leads to angle closure glaucoma.

As an outcome, assessing the sclera's redness using the average redness level is crucial for preventing either long-term and short-term IOP increases (MRL). Based on the redness pixel value ranges, the Mean Redness Level (MRL) will be evaluated using the equations below.

$$\text{Mean Redness Pixel } (MRP) = Mean(Red) = Mean(S(:,:,1)) = 1/m \sum\nolimits_{0}^{m} S(:,:,1)$$
$$(11.5)$$

$$\text{Mean Green Pixel}(MGP) = Mean(Green) = Mean(S(:,:,2)) = 1/m \sum\nolimits_{0}^{m} S(:,:,2)$$
$$(11.6)$$

$$MBP = Mean(Blue) = Mean(S(:,:,3)) = 1/m \sum\nolimits_{0}^{m} S(:,:,3) \quad (11.7)$$

$$\text{Mean Redness Level (MRL)} = (3 \times Mean\ (Red) - Mean\ (Green) - Mean\ (Blue)) / (3 \times 255) \qquad (11.8)$$

where Mean (Red) correlates to the mean of redness pixel value's which is calculated using equation (11.5), Mean (Green) is that the mean result of the pixel value of green is calculated using equation (11.6) and Mean (Blue) is that the pixel value of blue is calculated using Equation (11.7). Due to the reason that there are three channels, the coefficient value of three was chosen. The MRL ratio is determined using the color pixel values. The segmented sclera region is used to compute the MRL and RAP characteristics. This part is made by combining the retrieved sclera sections into a black image of the size which is identical. The color image is then analyzed pixel by pixel.

11.3.2.3 Red Area Percentage (RAP)

Every pixel that denotes a picture stored within a computer features a pixel value which describes the brightness of the pixel, and/or what color it should be. The pixel value in a grayscale image can be a single number that represents the pixel's brightness. The RAP is estimated using the sclera that has been removed from the equation. In our system, the RAP characteristics are measured as the mean redness pixel percentage within such a image in binary

$$\text{Red Area Percentage(RAP)} = 1/n \sum\nolimits_{i=0}^{n} p \qquad (11.9)$$

Pi indicates the red pixel values taken from the sclera inside the area of interest in this equation (11.9), while n is the total number of pixels in that region.

Frontal Images Used

Dataset of normal frontal eye images with its ground truth are collected from the Faculty of Computer and Information Science (University of Ljubljana). Here nearly 40 people's eyes are captured by seeing different directions of both left and right eyes. Each patient has nearly 170 images. Each image has the size of 3000 × 1700. Ground truth image dataset contains pupil, Iris and sclera portions separately with different colors. Red color images indicate the iris, Blue color images for pupil, and Green color images for sclera. Each image has the size of 3000 × 1700. Nearly 500 ground truth images is collected for each person. Glaucoma eye images are collected from the publically available website. Among them five glaucoma images are collected from Aravind Eye Hospital, Madurai.

11.4   Results and Discussion

From the collected dataset, the frontal eye images are given as input to the FCN network. Here sclera portion of the eye is extracted from the FCN network by the process of convolution and de convolution. At the end of

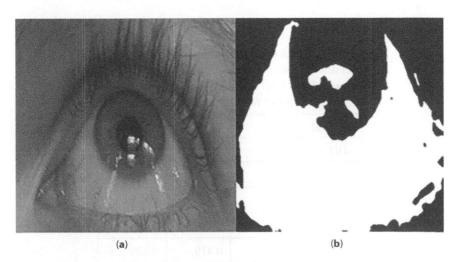

(a)   (b)

Figure 11.3 Sclera segmentation of frontal eye image. (a) Normal eye image; (b) extracted sclera image.

the system, de convolutional layers are utilized to reduce the photograph to its initial dimensions. The sclera segmented is shown in Figure 11.3.

11.4.1 Feature Extraction from Frontal Eye Images

11.4.1.1 Level of Mean Redness (MRL)

The Mean Redness Level was calculated using the span of red pixel values (MRL) Table 11.1 shows the relationship between normal and high pressure eye by calculating the MRL value clearly shows the difference of normal and glaucoma eye.

11.4.1.2 Percentage of Red Area (RAP)

The next feature is RAP calculated from the sclera that has been extracted. It is calculated by detecting the bi-level image's mean red pixel percentage. On adding the red pixel value in the colored image comparing it with the extracted portion of sclera image we get the RAP value. The extracted sclera potion contains MRL and RAP, which can be identified.

11.4.2 Images of the Frontal Eye Pupil/Iris Ratio

After extracting the features, iris/pupil ratio is determined by applying histogram equalization, morphological reconstruction, canny edge detection,

Table 11.1 For both normal and high blood pressure IOP scenarios, a collection of average/mean redness level (MRL) and percentage of red area/region (RAP) feature values is shown.

Normal		High	
MRL	RAP	MRL	RAP
0.343	0.323	0.379	0.645
0.213	0.297	0.383	0.477
0.107	0.186	0.399	0.555
0.291	0.35	0.419	0.609
0.285	0.322	0.427	0.659

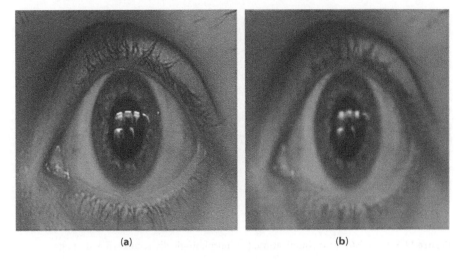

Figure 11.4 (a) Normal eye image, (b) histogram equalized image.

adaptive thresholding followed by circular Hough transform we find the iris/pupil ratio.

11.4.2.1   Histogram Equalization

Histogram equalization is applied to the normal frontal eye image as shown in Figure 11.4. This method is used to increase the disparity between the iris and pupil areas in a normal front eye image. Figure 11.4 represents the histogram equalized image which is obtained through histogram equalization.

11.4.2.2   Morphological Reconstruction

A morphological reconstruction method is applied on the pupil to eliminate the light reflection on it. The output image from the histogram equalization process which is shown within Figure 11.5a is given as the input to the morphological reconstruction process. The morphologically reconstructed image whose pupil doesn't have any light reflection is obtained as the output as shown in Figure 11.5b.

11.4.2.3   Canny Edge Detection

It is performed to recognize the pupil and iris boundaries since it includes Hysteresis thresholding and non-max suppression. Therefore morphologically

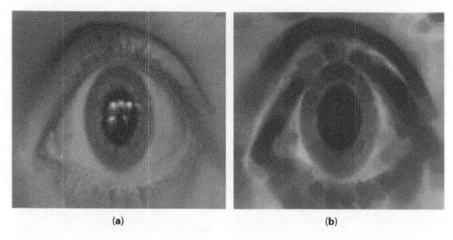

Figure 11.5 (a) Histogram equalization, (b) morphologically reconstructed image.

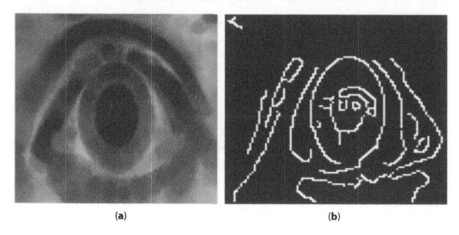

Figure 11.6 (a) Morphologically Reconstructed image, (b) canny edge detection of an image.

reconstructed image which is shown in Figure 11.6a is given as input to the canny edge detection method. Figure 11.6b gives the output of the canny edge detection method so as to determine the borders of pupil and iris.

11.4.2.4   Adaptive Thresholding

The gray scale range including the Iris and the Pupil is separated from the environment using Adaptive Thresholding. The output image from canny edge detection method which is shown in the Figure 11.7a is used as the

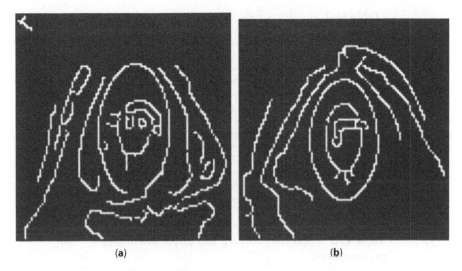

Figure 11.7 (a) Canny edge detection image, (b) adaptive thresholding image.

input to adaptive thresholding. Figure 11.7b is obtained as the output from the method adaptive thresholding.

11.4.2.5   Circular Hough Transform

The Circular Hough Transform (CHT) technique is applied to determine the pupil and the Iris region. Using the Hough transform output, Pupil or

Figure 11.8 Circular hough transformed image.

Table 11.2 Pupil/iris ratio, iris and pupil area of high-pressure eyes.

Pupil/iris ratio	Iris area	Pupil area
0.158253	1139.684	28.5424
0.183511	1444.87	48.65799
0.248787	2758.916	170.7626
0.289788	1617.61	135.8419
0.306853	1799.807	169.4675

Table 11.3 Pupil/iris ratio, iris and pupil area of high-pressure eyes.

Pupil/iris ratio	Iris area	Pupil area
0.199589	1064.84	52.70016
0.275586	4197.064	318.7571
0.301106	4592.585	416.3846
0.338495	3527.432	404.1696
0.41395	4637.487	794.6547

Iris region (or diameter) ratio is also calculated. Figure 11.8 represents the output of the Circular Hough Transform (CHT).

Table 11.2 shows the Pupil/Iris ratio, Iris area, and pupil area of normal eyes, whereas Table 11.3 shows the Pupil/Iris ratio, Iris, and pupil area of high-pressure eyes.

11.4.2.6   Classification

The frontal eye images were classified in order to identify glaucoma or normal eye the extracted five features are trained and tested using SVM classifier. There are 67 normal images and 19 glaucoma images are taken for classification. For training and testing these images are taken as two classes as normal and high pressure data. For that, the training data contain 50% of total images and testing data contain remaining 50 % of images. Likewise, it is classified in different proportions as 60% of training set and 40% of

Table 11.4 Training phase confusion matrix.

Output class	Normal pressure / high pressure	50% of training set		60% of training set		70% of training set		80% of training set	
		Normal	HP	Normal	HP	Normal	HP	Normal	HP
	Normal pressure	16	16	10	16	9	4	30	0
	high pressure	3	5	3	4	0	5	2	7

Table 11.5 Accuracy, sensitivity, and specificity of SVM training data.

Training data (%)	ACC (%)	SE (%)	SP (%)
50	52.5	50	62.5
60	42.4	38.4	57.14
70	77.7	69.2	100
80	94.8	100	77.8

testing set and 70% of training set and 30% of testing set. Table 11.4, lists the results obtained.

Table 11.5 shows an outcome of confusion matrices for the framework derived by Support Vector Machine classifiers. In this process, it is observed that increase in the training data leads to increase in the accuracy level also. By increasing the proportions of data such as 70% training and 30% testing, the maximum accuracy level is reached.

11.5   Conclusion and Future Work

This chapter presents an innovative automatic non-contact and non-invasive technique for analyzing frontal eye photographs to aid in the early detection of glaucoma threat is proposed in this chapter. Image processing and machine learning approaches based on vision are utilized to aid in the exposure to high eye pressure indications that can lead to Glaucoma. The fully convolutional network is used to segment sclera in this paper. Furthermore, employing Glaucoma diagnosis, data such as pupil or iris ratio, mean redness level (MRL), and red area (RAP) % are derived from frontal eye photos. The support vector machine classifier is used to determine whether a patient's eye is normal or has glaucoma. To use the SVM Classifier, the suggested framework has a general accuracy of above 70%.

Based on the statistics around the world about the glaucoma we are getting to know, it is causing a very serious effect on mankind. It is very important to diagnose this disease as early as possible in order to prevent the vision loss. Thus diagnosis plays a vital role in treating the disease. Glaucoma detection discussed in this chapter helps to diagnose the glaucoma within few minutes with a good accuracy. In turn it will increase the rate of testing and diagnosis of this disease.

References

1. Aloudat, M. and Faezipour, M., Histogram analysis for automatic blood vessels detection: First step of IOP, in: *Proc. IEEE Int. Conf. Electro/ Inf. Technol. (EIT)*, May 2015, pp. 146–151, 2015.
2. Aloudat, M. and Faezipour, M., Determining the thickness of the liquid on the cornea for open and closed angle glaucoma using haar filter, in: *Proc. IEEE Long Island Syst. Appl. Technol. Conf. (LISAT)*, May 2015, pp. 1–6, 2015.
3. Chen, J.J., Su, C.R., Grimson, W.E., Liu, L., Shiue, D.H., Object segmentation of database images by dual multiscale morphological reconstructions and retrieval applications. *IEEE Trans. Image Process.*, 21, 2, 828–843, Feb. 2012.
4. Chiou, J.C., *et al.*, Toward a wirelessly powered on-lens intraocular pressure monitoring system. *IEEE J. Biomed. Health Inform.*, 20, 5, 1216–1224, Sep. 2016.
5. Dutta, M.K., Mourya, A.K., Singh, A., Parthasarathi, M., Burget, R., Riha, K., Glaucoma detection by segmenting the super pixels from fundus colour retinal images, in: *Proc. Int. Conf. Med. Imag., m-Health Emerg. Commun. Syst. (Medcom)*, Greater Noida, India, Nov. 2014, pp. 86–90, 2014.
6. Popplewell, K., Roy, K., Ahmad, F., Shelton, J., Multispectral iris recognition utilizing hough transform and modified LBP. *IEEE. International Conference on Systems, Man, and Cybernetics*, San Diego, CA, USA, Oct 5–8, 2014, 2014.
7. Mansouri, K., Sommerhalder, J., Shaarawy, T., Prospective comparison of ultrasound bio microscopy and anterior segment optical coherence tomography for evaluation of anterior chamber dimensions in European eyes with primary angle closure. *Eye*, 24, 233–239, 2010.
8. Mariakakis, A., Wang, E., Patel, S., Wen, J.C., A smartphone-based system for assessing intraocular pressure, in: *Proc.38th Annu. Int. Conf. IEEE Eng. Med. Biol. Soc. (EMBC)*, Orlando FL, USA, Aug. 2016, pp. 4353–4356, 2016.
9. Mashhadi, M.B., Salarieh, N., Farahani, E.S., Marvasti, F., Level crossing speech sampling and its sparsity promoting reconstruction using an iterative method with adaptive thresholding. *IET Signal Process.*, 11, 6, 721–726, Aug. 2017.
10. Mrigana, W. and Jain, Dr. S., Iris recognition system using circular hough transforms. *Int. J. Adv. Res. Comput. Sci. Manage. Stud.*, 3, 7, 13–21, July 2015.
11. Salam, A.A., Akram, M.U., Wazir, K., Anwar, S.M., A review analysis on early glaucoma detection using structural features, in: *Proc. IEEE Int. Conf. Imag. Syst. Techn. (IST)*, Macau, China, Sep. 2015, pp. 1–6, 2015.
12. Sahmoud, S.A. and Abuhaiba, I.S., Efficient iris segmentation method in unconstrained environments. *Pattern Recognit.*, 46, 3174–3185, 2013.
13. Yousefi, S., *et al.*, Learning from data: Recognizing glaucomatous defect patterns and detecting progression from visual field measurements. *IEEE Trans. Biomed. Eng.*, 61, 7, 2112–2124, Jul. 2014.

14. Panda, R., Puhan, N.B., Rao, A., Padhy, D., Panda, G., Automated retinal nerve fiber layer defect detection using fundus imaging in glaucoma. *Comput. Med. Imaging Graph.*, 66, 56–65, 2018.
15. Kausu, T.R., Gopi, V.P., Wahid, K.A., Doma, W., Niwas, S. I., Combination of clinical and multiresolution features for glaucoma detection and its classification using fundus images. *Biocybern. Biomed. Eng.*, 38, 2, 329–341, 2018.
16. Issac, A. and Dutta, M.K., An adaptive threshold based image processing technique for improved glaucoma detection and classification. *Comput. Methods Programs Biomed.*, 122, 2, 229–244, 2015.
17. Pathan, S., Kumar, P., Pai, R.M., Bhandary, S.V., Automated segmentation and classification of retinal features for glaucoma diagnosis. *Biomed. Signal Process. Control*, 63, 102244, 2021.
18. https://www.mathworks.com/help/../ref/nnet.cnn.layer.maxpooling2dlayer.html
19. Nagi, J., Ducatelle, F., Di Caro, G.A., Ciresan, D., Meier, U., Giusti, A., Nagi, F., Schmidhuber, J., Gambardella, L.M., Max-pooling convolutional neural networks for vision-based hand gesture recognition. *IEEE International Conference on Signal and Image Processing Applications*, 2011.

12

State of Mental Health and Social Media: Analysis, Challenges, Advancements

**Atul Pankaj Patil[1], Kusum Lata Jain[1]*, Smaranika Mohapatra[2]
and Suyesha Singh[3]**

[1]*CCE, Manipal University Jaipur, Jaipur-Ajmer Express Highway, Dehmi Kalan,
Near GVK Toll Plaza, Jaipur, Rajasthan, India*
[2]*IT, Manipal University Jaipur, Jaipur-Ajmer Express Highway, Dehmi Kalan,
Near GVK Toll Plaza, Jaipur, Rajasthan, India*
[3]*Psychology, Manipal University Jaipur, Jaipur-Ajmer Express Highway,
Dehmi Kalan, Near GVK Toll Plaza, Jaipur, Rajasthan, India*

Abstract

Nowadays, mental illness is a burning study for the Healthcare Sector. Doctors, Experts, researchers, are keen to know exactly how to define what a mental disorder is when the person seems normal sometimes and is into a different state at some other. This is seen in social media, that the same person behaves differently as in person. The procedure we will use to analyze is simple; collect, process, and evaluate the person's personality profile with the help of a social media website which itself will generate a big dataset that will again be categorized using BigData Analytics. Many popular social media sites exist today, like Facebook, Snapchat, Twitter, etc. From the various social media platforms, Twitter was specifically chosen because the data from twitter of an individual can be effortlessly accessed, collected and viewed if the owner made his/her profile public. To analyze the personality traits a criterion was maintained for collecting the data, which chooses the age group between 18 and 25 years since this age group is a young age group that focuses greatly on social status and career growth. The chapter intends to:

1. Analyze what personality the person does have
2. Challenges faced during the collection of data from social media
3. What will be the future advancements to enhance the study of mental health, in the healthcare sector?

*Corresponding author: kusumlata.jain@jaipur.manipal.edu

D. Sumathi, T. Poongodi, B. Balamurugan and Lakshmana Kumar Ramasamy (eds.)
Cognitive Intelligence and Big Data in Healthcare, (327–348) © 2022 Scrivener Publishing LLC

Keywords: Healthcare, social media, big data, data mining, text classification, sentimental analysis

12.1   Introduction

Nowadays the users and people do share their emotions, opinions, suggestions, reviews, discussions, etc., on the social platform. Popular social media platforms today are Facebook, Twitter, Snapchat, etc., which provides a platform to share and to take advice from different persons on various topics where similar issues can have different perceptive of response and understanding [25]. Many researchers have started using these opinions and responses from the platform to discuss, predict, analyze, and evaluate the different personality traits, behavior, sentiments, etc., to understand the user's behavior and this can be used to get the status of their mental health. With very limited healthcare center [14] available in various cities, towns, or villages, where not always the doctors can diagnose the mental health of an individual unless the patient is not expressive, but the same person may share the conditions and opinions on how the patient is feeling inside on a social platform. The presence of polar facts which may be neglected can be determined or known by the healthcare workers to know the mental state of a patient.

The chapter focuses basically upon the various feeds and tweets collected from the Twitter platform to predict and analyze the issues raised by the people who share their opinions on an online platform and do seek advice from other users who had some earlier past experiences on similar topics and health issues. A case study has also been highlighted to understand the theme of the topic concerning mental health and social media platform.

12.2   Introduction to Big Data and Data Mining

Data and information have been always important factors for a better and growing organization and new developments. If the information we have is more in volume, the more optimally we can organize the system to provide better outcomes, and this is the reason that data collection is an integral part of every organization. This data can be used for predicting the recent trends of some parameters and due to which everyone is now producing and collecting more amount of data. A situation which everyone is facing that due to huge amount of data we are flooded with this amount on an everyday aspect of our lives like, social, work, health, etc. These technological developments have helped in generating a huge amount of data, which is unmanageable with the current techniques which have led to the term 'Big data'.

Concerning fulfilling present and future needs, we will develop new strategies and methods to manage the unmanageable data which will give meaningful information. This huge amount of data should have some characteristics and size is one of the considerations. The three dimensions of challenges are the three V's – Volume, velocity, and Variety where Volume refers to the magnitude of data, Velocity mentions as the rate at which data is produced and the speed at which it can be analyzed and can be treated upon and Variety refers to heterogeneity in a dataset used [4, 17]. To highlight this need socially, one such sector is social media.

Like any other industry, the social media industry is generating data at a very high speed that has some advantages and challenges. Each day, people around the globe working at different stakes generate a massive amount of data [16]. United State is raked first in use of Twitter with 62.55 Million used followed by Japan and India as on July 2020 with 49.1 and 17 million users, respectively [1]. This platform allows people to share their views and express comments and ideas about a specific subject or topic. Twitter [20] medium helps us to predict and analyze the state of mind of an individual on a certain topic [18]. People can be positive, negative, or optimistic on certain discussions and can share their views in that respect. Twitter has many advances like any other Social Media Platform like Facebook and LinkedIn such as messages on network, status, comments, views, feedbacks, surveys, experiences, etc.

Big data can be structured or unstructured which may include data video, audio, pictures, files, email information, etc. [2]. The development in Big Data trend from Social Media has brought new excitement among researchers in the field of Artificial Intelligence and data analytics. Analyze social media data using various traditional techniques of Data Mining [23] and Machine Learning [22] is still a hot topic and active domain for researchers [3].

There are various techniques to use this structured and unstructured data such as Text Analytics, Audio Analytics, Video Analytics, Social Media Analytics, and Predictive Analytics [4]. The Text Analytics technique is very useful for the topic we have chosen as it does use social media blogs, forums, etc., for the dataset and it uses machine learning, statistical analysis as the methodology. The user-generated data and the various relationships and interactions between the other network objects like people, products, institutions, etc., are the two basic sources of information in social media.

The collection of data and accumulation of it is done at every space, and to do the same many tools and techniques are being used to extract important and valid information from the huge volume of data [5]. Data Mining [15] includes different functionalities, methods, techniques, algorithms which are used to extract useful information from a large data repository. The stages for extracting the knowledge information from data are Data Pre-Processing, Data Warehouse, Selection, Final Dataset, Data Mining, Patterns to Analyze and Retrieve, and Analysis [6]. Various algorithms were developed like, Classification, Clustering, Cluster Analysis, Outlier Analysis, Characterization, etc. [7]. With an increase in usage of social media platforms, Facebook, Twitter, etc., are nowadays used to forecast results, opinions, mental state of a human, etc., at a very significant level. The challenges that the analysts do face in the social media platform are its large size, noise, and dimensionality of data. In social media platform, Text Mining is gaining popularity and is more successful than the other traditional mining techniques, like the information will be retrieved from document and that document will be pre-processed for a different group of symbols and character set and it will be analyzed to extract the information from the text [24].

12.3   Role of Sentimental Analysis in the Healthcare Sector

In the older days, people used to share their mental conditions with their friends and family to take advice from them, but with the advancements in technology and usage of social media nowadays people are sharing their mental health [13] related issues on an online platform and do take advice from other users. There are various blogs and healthcare centers that now opt for social media to help the patients that require attention or to guide and advise them related to health issues, symptoms, diseases, etc. The huge amount of data collected from thousands and millions of patients globally who have shared their opinions and illness over the twitter medium is a pathway for the development in hardware technologies and also has effectively volunteered to the use of Machine Learning techniques [11].

The term 'Sentiment' [19] means an opinion or feeling of emotional and physical sensation through an experience or perception. Discussing the Sentimental Analysis in the chapter is a type of textual mining or contextual mining of text, words, character which can identify and extract some important information and which can be analyzed using certain techniques and methodologies to understand the sentiment or opinion of a certain people, product, etc. With the availability and usage of the Internet, people do often share their stories and feeds on the social media platform, and they find it comfortable to share their experiences and emotions online.

The intense rise in blogging trend is also visible and seen in the healthcare organization in which the people do seek and share health-related problems and suggestions on a health forum so that the healthcare professionals, doctors, practitioners can suggest or give opinions for the feeds raised. The social-media platform considered here is Twitter which is a microblogging platform, and this platform helps to peek into the mental health of a person who does share the various feeds and opinions on the platform.

The Healthcare Organizations allow the Patients to share their problems and issues with other similar patients or doctors for support and consultation where a single query may be followed by multiple relies upon, tweets or comments which form a thread of tweets. This information that is generated from the thread is valuable data for the healthcare sector which reflects the sentiments of what the patients think and feel about their health. For example, patients that share their perception with other patients with similar health issue can share and get advice from the medical experience of the later ones, even the consultants can understand how the different patients have different symptoms and feeling in similar cases [8]. Sentiment analysis uses many computerized tools for automation, which allows comments and feeds to be analyzed easily and at a faster pace with a qualitative approach. The tools are based using machine learning or classifiers which can classify the texts and are focused, and objective oriented to extract and gather the information on a specific service. The tools and techniques used in sentiment analysis are responsible to work upon the unstructured and un-organized data and Twitter is more feasible than Facebook as Twitter allows easily to extract an opinion of a tweet from the text of a tweet [9].

There can be different ways to relate with the medical and mental health conditions in health-related feeds and tweets [10], which can be the following:

(i)   Health status – patients can have a different perception of a similar case of health which is one of the aspects.
(ii) The extent of the mental health of a person that may affect the mental health of a person.
(iii) The result of consultation over a social media platform can be positive or negative.

To explain the scenario, we can take a small example related to the tweets that are posted. Let's say, the user tweets more about the keywords like, feeling low, sick, ill, lazy, diet, fruits, vegetables [12], this may be compared as unhealthy and healthy mental health. The tweets or feeds can be collected and analyzed with the polarity of mental health. The healthcare people or Fitness gurus can suggest proper advice according to the state of mind and can prescribe the appropriate steps required to improve the state of mental health. The data that is collected from the tweets can also be useful to devise a proper system to perceive the proper medical attention that is required along with the Healthcare organizations can implement new methods and can devise new techniques to resolve such kind symptoms that may occur in certain situation. Different types of feeds or reviews have diverse effects on the usability of sentiment analysis. For example, "The *ZZZ Pharmaceuticals* do provide the best deals on medicines on *subsidized rates*". If this is being followed by a person and can get medicines at subsidized rates will go and check the Company. Similarly, if a person tweets," *PQR* is one of *the best multi-specialty hospitals* for a patient having *diabetes* and can *book at any time*", this will have multiple reactions as many people may have positive and negative experiences from the hospital, and from this, the hospital may also improvise their functionality areas [11].

12.4   Case Study: Analyzing Mental Health

12.4.1   Problem Statement

In this golden age of technology, humanity has found a new way of interaction through the internet using social media. We share messages, audio, pictures, and videos. It has become an essential part of our life from sharing our birth pictures to holiday/wedding pictures. We have been given a platform to showcase our views, opinions, channel our love for something/someone, write our thoughts, showcase our solidarity, or just keep up with the world. Predicting the behavior of an individual user has become instrumental to the commerce world and the healthcare world. Knowing how a user spends his time on the internet, one can show him relevant advertisements to his needs, show them content which they desire to watch, and sell them commodities which they desire to buy. In the healthcare world, correctly predicting the behavior of a user can help doctors and parents attend to the patient's utmost needs and possibly save their life, hence the enactment and essential need to predict behavior on social media.

During this research, the problem which is being discussed to show the correlation or difference in the behavior of a person [21] as people behave differently on Social Media Platform where the Big 5 Model [20] is used to compare the tweets posted and the real-life trait of the same person based on Big 5 personality prediction model.

12.4.2   Research Objectives

- To show whether the person acts true or not to the behavior he displays himself on social media vs. the person's behavior in real life.
- To show how much is the person acting true or not to the behaviors he displays himself on social media vs. the person's behavior in real life.
- To layout inferences on either the similarity or differences in his behavior with the outside world and with his behavior on the social media site, Twitter.
- To answer the question of, how true is the model and how effectively can it use for further use?

12.4.3   Methodology and Framework

12.4.3.1   Big 5 Personality Model

The Big 5 model of the personality of personality is the most widely accepted personality theory in the scientific community.

The Big 5 model shown in Figure 12.1 is so named because the model proposes that the human personality can be measured along 5 different dimensions called:

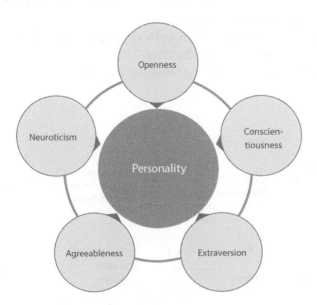

Figure 12.1 Big five model.

- Intellectual curiosity and creative imagination of a person described by the trait.

12.4.3.2 Openness to Explore

- Organization, productiveness, responsibility are given by **Conscientiousness**
- Sociability, assertiveness, responsibility are shown by **Extroversion**
- **Agreeableness** is accumulated by compassion, respectfulness, and trust in others
- A person's tendency towards anxiety and depression is accumulated by:

> **Neuroticism System Architecture:**
> The system architecture includes the Figure 12.2 as below:
> The given research project is carried in the following parts:

- Personality prediction of an individual of a person based on tweets on Twitter.

1. Twitter through which data set is created, cleaned, and then compared with keywords of the Big 5 model to predict the personality of the participant.
2. Microsoft Excel is used to store tweets gathered by hand-picking from twitter.com.
3. The environment to run python programming language is Visual Studio to clean the data.
4. Python is used as a programming language

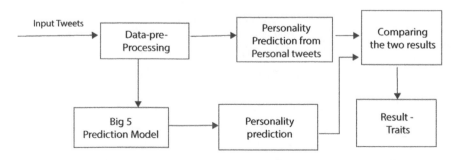

Figure 12.2 System architecture.

- Personality prediction of the same individual on the basics of Big 5 personality prediction. The selected participant is required to fill the Big 5 model prediction form. Compare the result and display.

12.4.3.3   Methodology

The given techniques are shown in parts:

- Data cleaning and pre-processing
- Tokenization: to convert tweets into tokens
- Comparative analysis to compare tokens with keywords of individual traits
- Prediction to obtain personality scores using the Big 5 model of the selected person in his real life.

Techniques used to input and clean data as shown in Figure 12.3 set in Microsoft Excel for pre-processing:

- **Main working:** The main working is shown in Figure 12.4.
- **Reading Data from Excel File**
  Data is stored in excel in form of rows and columns and the first task is to input the data into python for conversion as

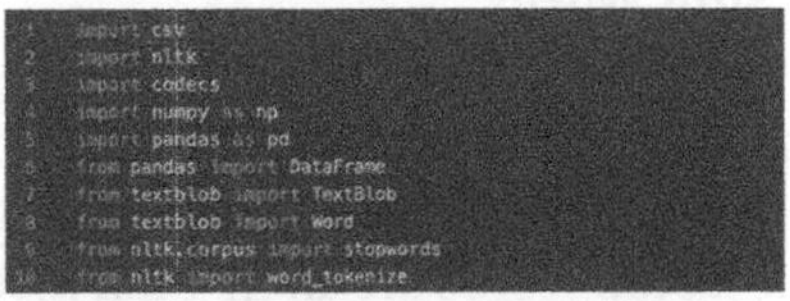

Figure 12.3 Import files.

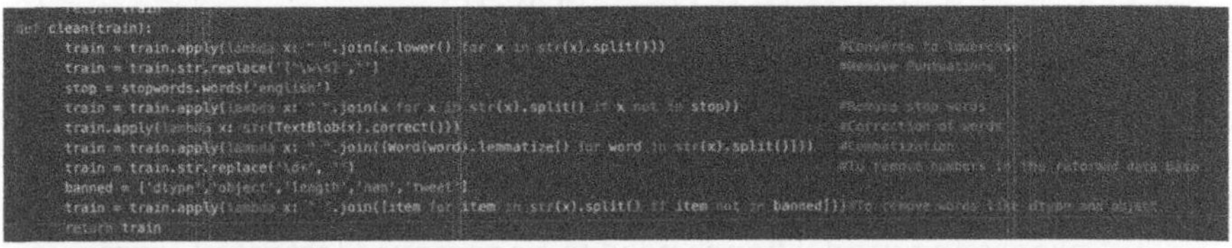

Figure 12.4 Data cleaning.

in Figure 12.5. The data is stored in a particular format for easier transition and computation of data. The given data is stored in a data frame format in python.

- **Conversion to Lowercase and Punctuations**
  The given data consists of uppercase and lowercase words and lots of punctuations. Since comparing it with keywords, it is desirable and easy if the words are in the same case thereby reducing the complexity of code and comparisons (refer to Figure 12.6).

```
def read():
    train = pd.read_csv('2TwitterDataBase.csv')  #To Read The Database
    return train
```

Figure 12.5 Train test.

```
def clean(train):
    train = train.apply(lambda x: " ".join(x.lower() for x in str(x).split()))  #Convert to Lowercase
    train = train.str.replace('[^\w\s]','')  #Remove Punctuations
```

Figure 12.6 Cleaning training data.

- **Correction of Words**
  Words used in today's social style misplace the letters in the same word either in a hurry to tweet, put it out there, or due to less knowledge. Nevertheless, I need the actual word from a broken word to categorize whether the word should go into a personality trait or just be used as a stock word (refer to Figure 12.7).
- **Removal of Stop Words**
  Words that are prepositions, the article serves no purpose for bringing out the personality of a person. Hence these words must be removed for easier processing of data (refer to Figure 12.8). Stop words are an in-built method that gathers all words of a particular language here English.
- **Lemmatization**
  Each word is used with different tenses to express the thoughts. For the analysis root word is required. This is done by Lemmatization (refer to Figure 12.9). This process is used to get root word. For example, playing becomes play. This will provide the same meaning for the different tense form of the word.
- **Removal of Figures from the Database**
  Numerical figures or numbers also serve no purpose in this processing model hence need to be removed (refer to Figure 12.10).

```
train.apply(lambda x: str(TextBlob(x).correct()))                    #Correction of words
```

Figure 12.7 Correction of words.

```
stop = stopwords.words('english')
train = train.apply(lambda x: " ".join(x for x in str(x).split() if x not in stop))    #Remove stop words
```

Figure 12.8 Remove stop words.

```
train = train.apply(lambda x: " ".join([Word(word).lemmatize() for word in str(x).split()]))    #Lemmatization
```

Figure 12.9 Lemmatization.

```
train = train.apply(lambda x: " ".join([Word(word).lemmatize() for word in str(x).split()]))    #Lemmatization
train = train.str.replace('\d+', '')                    #To remove numbers in the reformed data base
```

Figure 12.10 Removing numbers.

- **Removal of Words Like NaN, Type, and Object**
  Words like NaN occur if the tweet wasn't available in the database; words like type and object occur when the data is cleaned by implementing functions such as removal of numbers (refer to Figure 12.11).
- **Writing Data to Excel File**
  The data needs to be stored in another excel file so that we do not need to process the data again and again when we implement our prediction model (refer to Figure 12.12).
- **Techniques Used to Convert Tweets into Tokens** (refer to Figure 12.13)
  Lists are giving easier work than data frame. Individual lists in collected data belonging to a specific person and make

```
banned = ['dtype','object','length','nan','tweet']
train = train.apply(lambda x: ' '.join([item for item in str(x).split() if item not in banned]))#To remove words like dtype and object
return train
```

Figure 12.11 Removal of numbers.

```
#To write the cleaned data back to the csv file
def write(train):
        train.to_csv('3ReformedDataBase.csv')
```

Figure 12.12 Prediction model.

```
tweetsinlist = dataframetolist(train)        #To convert dataframe into list
for tweet in tweetsinlist:
    personaltokens = personaltokenization(tweet)
    analysis(personaltokens)
#write(train)
```

Figure 12.13 To convert dataframe into list.

it easier for tokenization and compare. A built-in method word tokenize is used to convert words into tokens from nltk package (refer to Figure 12.14).

- **Techniques for comparison tokens with keywords based on personality prediction:** refer Figure 12.15.
- An example of agreeableness.txt and conscientious.txt (refer to Figure 12.16).

```
def dataframetolist(train):
    tweetsinlist = train.values.tolist()
    return tweetsinlist
def tokenization(tweets):
    words = word_tokenize(tweets)
    return words
def personaltokenization(tweet):
    tokens = tokenization(tweet)        #Tokenization
    return tokens
```

Figure 12.14 Tokenization.

```
agreeableness = open("agreeableness.txt").read().split()
conscientious = open("conscientious.txt").read().split()
extraversion = open("extraversion.txt").read().split()
openness = open("openness.txt").read().split()
neuroticism = open("neuroticism.txt").read().split()
```

Figure 12.15 Personality traits.

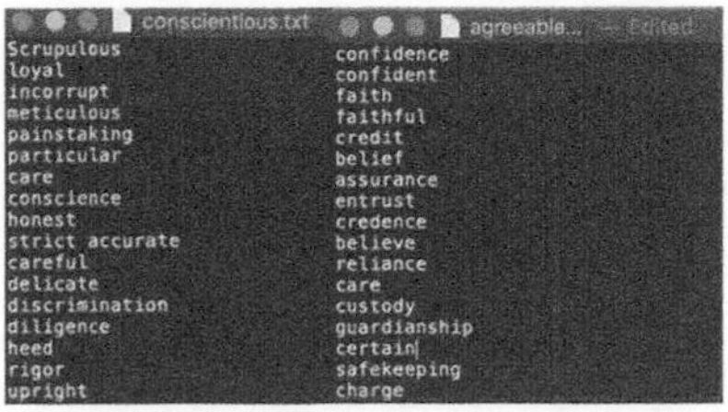

Figure 12.16 Generated words.

The method is named analysis for comparing tokens with keywords stored in separate files, this improves our clarity of what we are doing (refer to Figure 12.17).

A technique used to obtain personality scores using the Big 5 model of the selected person in his real life.

The selected participant is required to fill this form of 50 questions and evaluate himself based on the question (refer Figure 12.18) he felt most comfortable with.

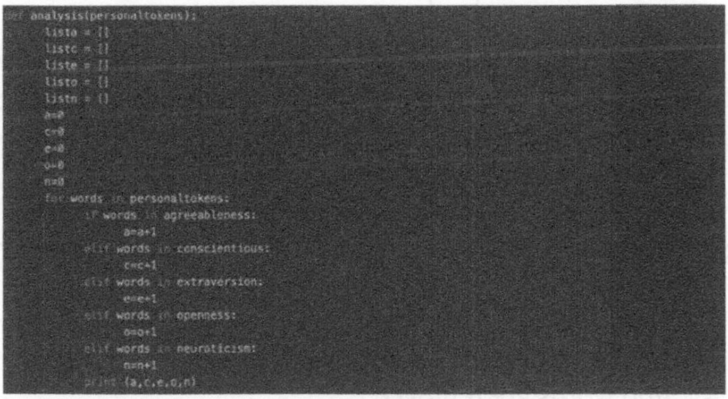

```
def analysis(personaltokens):
    lista = []
    listc = []
    liste = []
    listo = []
    listn = []
    a=0
    c=0
    e=0
    o=0
    n=0
    for words in personaltokens:
        if words in agreeableness:
            a=a+1
        elif words in conscientious:
            c=c+1
        elif words in extraversion:
            e=e+1
        elif words in openness:
            o=o+1
        elif words in neuroticism:
            n=n+1
        print (a,c,e,o,n)
```

Figure 12.17 Analysis.

$E = 20 +$ (1)___ - (6)___ + (11)___ - (16)___ + (21)___ - (26)___ + (31)___ - (36)___ + (41)___ - (46)___ = ___

$A = 14 -$ (2)___ + (7)___ - (12)___ + (17)___ - (22)___ + (27)___ - (32)___ + (37)___ + (42)___ + (47)___ = ___

$C = 14 +$ (3)___ - (8)___ + (13)___ - (18)___ + (23)___ - (28)___ + (33)___ - (38)___ + (43)___ + (48)___ - ___

$N = 38 -$ (4)___ + (9)___ - (14)___ + (19)___ - (24)___ - (29)___ - (34)___ - (39)___ - (44)___ - (49)___ = ___

$O = 8 +$ (5)___ - (10)___ + (15)___ - (20)___ + (25)___ - (30)___ + (35)___ + (40)___ + (45)___ + (50)___ = ___

The scores you calculate should be between zero and forty. Below is a description of each trait.

- **Extroversion (E)** is the personality trait of seeking fulfillment from sources outside the self or in community. High scorers tend to be very social while low scorers prefer to work on their projects alone.

- **Agreeableness (A)** reflects much individuals adjust their behavior to suit others. High scorers are typically polite and like people. Low scorers tend to 'tell it like it is'.

- **Conscientiousness (C)** is the personality trait of being honest and hardworking. High scorers tend to follow rules and prefer clean homes. Low scorers may be messy and cheat others.

- **Neuroticism (N)** is the personality trait of being emotional.

- **Openness to Experience (O)** is the personality trait of seeking new experience and intellectual pursuits. High scores may day dream a lot. Low scorers may be very down to earth.

Figure 12.18 Description of each trait.

12.4.3.4   Detailed Design Methodologies

1. Data is collected for 60 people, 25 tweets each created a collection of 1500 tweets for the analysis. Data is collected on individual basis as APIs can not be used to collect data as per the legal norms given on Twitter as well as it is not possible to give restriction for age group targeted. Some of the parameters on which tweets can be extracted using APIs are geographical position, name, keywords, tendencies, etc.

2. After preprocessing, python is used to refine data to implement Natural Language Processing function. The given data set's values are preprocessed in the following way:

- Only small case is used.
- Stop words are removed
- Special characters are removed
- Spelling correction is done
- Removal of tense/identification of root word/lemmatization
- Removal of facts, figures, and emoticons
- Extra works like type, object, and NaN need to be removed
- Tokenization

3. Comparison of the tokenized word forms the individual traits from the Big 5 model.

4. To conclude the analysis in percentage based upon the personality traits for individuals on social media using tokenized words.

5. Send a Big 5 form to the selected participant and derive his personality traits from the input the participant fills in.

6. Comparison of personality traits derived through tweets and physical psychological test for Big 5 model form.

7. Draw out the desired conclusion and comply with the given in the research objective.

12.4.3.5   Work Done Details as Required

- Raw unprocessed data (refer to Figure 12.19)
- Clean processed database (refer to Figure 12.20)
- Comparison (refer to Figure 12.21)
- Individual tokenization (refer Figure 12.22)
- Individual's tweets mapped with keywords of Big 5 model (refer to Figure 12.23)

Figure 12.19 Raw unprocessed data.

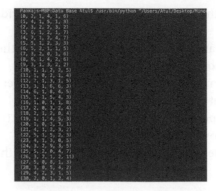

Figure 12.20 Clean processed data.

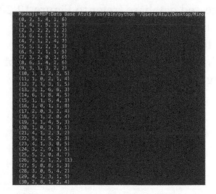

Figure 12.21 Comparision.

Figure 12.22 Individual tokenization.

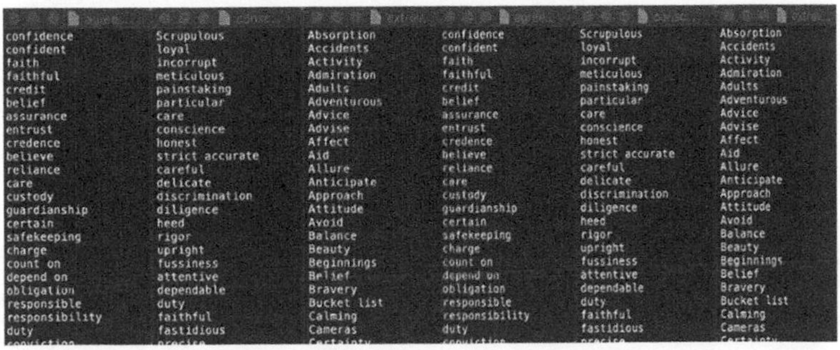

Figure 12.23

12.5 Results and Discussion

1-Analysis of the first selected participant in reference to Figure 12.24:
Participant 1. The Table 12.1 shows the analysis of Participant 1.

$$E = 20 + 4 - 2 + 5 - 2 + 2 - 2 + 4 - 2 + 4 - 3 = 28$$

$$A = 14 - 5 + 4 - 1 + 5 - 1 + 4 - 1 + 4 + 5 + 4 = 32$$

$$C = 14 + 4 - 2 + 4 - 2 + 3 - 2 + 4 - 2 + 3 + 2 = 26$$

$$N = 38 - 2 + 2 - 3 + 5 - 2 - 1 - 3 - 1 - 1 - 1 = 32$$

$$O = 8 + 3 - 2 + 4 - 2 + 3 - 1 + 4 + 3 + 3 + 4 = 27$$

Figure 12.24 Analysis of Participant 1.

Table 12.1 Analysis for participant 1.

Personality trait	Result in percentage for psychological test	Result in percentage with social media
Extraversion:	9.3%	2%
Agreeableness:	23%	7%
Consciousness:	22.62%	40%
Openness:	22.99%	20%
Neuroticism:	17.62%	40%

The inferences made from the following table can be said as follows:

- The participant seems to display more consciousness and neuroticism on social media platform then in real world.
- The participant's feed of 25 tweets felt lacks words that could be related to extraversion and agreeableness.
- The participant scores roughly the same in the area of Openness.
- The bar graph for first participant is shown in Figure 12.25.

2-Analysis of the second selected participant in reference to Figure 12.26:
Participant 2 The Table 12.2 shows the analysis of Participant 2.
The inferences made from the following table can be said as follows:

- The participant also shows different behaviors in real and social life.
- The participant displays an equal amount in consciousness and Openness.
- The participant bar graph is shown in Figure 12.27.

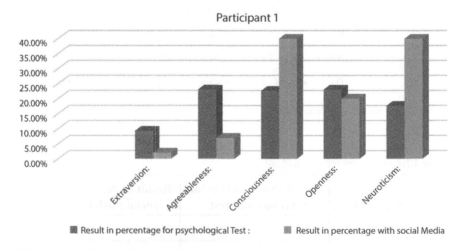

Figure 12.25 Result of test.

$$E = 20 + _{(1)}\underline{2} - _{(6)}\underline{4} + _{(11)}\underline{2} - _{(16)}\underline{2} + _{(21)}\underline{3} - _{(26)}\underline{3} + _{(31)}\underline{3} - _{(36)}\underline{5} + _{(41)}\underline{5} - _{(46)}\underline{5} = \underline{21}$$
$$A = 14 - _{(2)}\underline{2} + _{(7)}\underline{3} - _{(12)}\underline{3} + _{(17)}\underline{4} - _{(22)}\underline{1} + _{(27)}\underline{5} - _{(32)}\underline{2} + _{(37)}\underline{2} + _{(42)}\underline{4} + _{(47)}\underline{3} = \underline{27}$$
$$C = 14 + _{(3)}\underline{3} - _{(8)}\underline{1} + _{(13)}\underline{5} - _{(18)}\underline{3} + _{(23)}\underline{3} - _{(28)}\underline{1} + _{(35)}\underline{5} - _{(38)}\underline{2} + _{(43)}\underline{4} + _{(48)}\underline{3} = \underline{30}$$
$$N = 38 - _{(4)}\underline{2} + _{(9)}\underline{4} - _{(14)}\underline{5} + _{(19)}\underline{3} - _{(24)}\underline{2} - _{(29)}\underline{2} - _{(34)}\underline{1} - _{(39)}\underline{2} - _{(44)}\underline{3} - _{(49)}\underline{1} = \underline{27}$$
$$O = 8 + _{(5)}\underline{3} - _{(10)}\underline{1} + _{(15)}\underline{5} - _{(20)}\underline{1} + _{(25)}\underline{4} - _{(30)}\underline{1} + _{(35)}\underline{2} + _{(40)}\underline{2} + _{(45)}\underline{5} + _{(50)}\underline{5} = \underline{31}$$

Figure 12.26 Different behavior of participant 2.

Table 12.2 Analysis for second participant.

Personality trait	Result in percentage for psychological test	Result in percentage with social media
Extraversion:	17.10%	7%
Agreeableness:	18.36%	2%
Consciousness:	22.98%	40%
Openness:	16.97%	40%
Neuroticism:	18.62%	24%

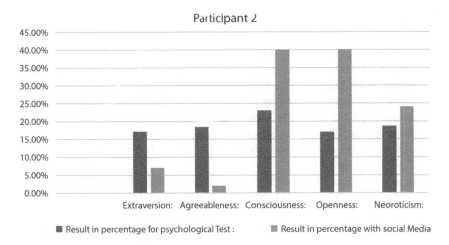

Figure 12.27 Result of test for participant 2.

12.6   Conclusion and Future

The study gives and inference that young adults are living different lives in real and online world. They show difference more then 80% of time. The analysis is only done with one psychological test but can be extended to more and specific one for the traits if required. Data is small and match was found only for two instances. A bigger data can also be used to create a prototype. With the various studies and surveys, it can be concluded that

Sentiment Analysis is playing a bigger role in Healthcare Sector and, this analysis was only possible and evolved due to the social media platforms. The people feel free to post anonymously and do ask for recommendations and advice from healthcare professionals or from people who had similar issues and experiences earlier. Sentiment Analysis uses various methods and techniques which help to extract the personal mental health of individuals. The use of scientific knowledge in helping people with issues gets easily identified with the social media platform. There are also many challenges faced by this Sentiment analysis technique implemented on checking up with Mental health. For instance, the complex nature in which the users or patients express their sentiments, feeds or opinions, implication, etc. supervised techniques with higher precision can be used for more accurate and precise findings which may uncover bigger issues of mental state/health.

References

1. https://www.statista.com/statistics/
2. Sehgal, D. and Agarwal, A.K., Sentiment analysis of big data applications using twitter Data with the help of HADOOP framework. *2016 International Conference System Modeling & Advancement in Research Trends (SMART)*, Moradabad, pp. 251–255, 2016.
3. Zhao, J., Liu, K., Xu, L., *Sentiment Analysis: Mining Opinions, Sentiments, and Emotions*, B. Liu (Ed.), Cambridge University Press, MIT Press Direct, Cambridge, US, 2015.
4. Gandomi, A. and Haider, M., Beyond the hype: Big data concepts, methods, and analytics. *Int. J. Inf. Manage.*, 35, 2, 137–144, April 2015.
5. Gupta, M.K. and Chandra, P., A comprehensive survey of data mining. *Int. J. Inf. Technol.*, 12, 1243–1257, 2020. https://doi.org/10.1007/s41870-020-00427-7.
6. Colak, I., Sagiroglu, S., Yesilbudak, M., Data mining and wind power prediction: A literature review. *Renew. Energy*, 46, 241–247, October 2012.
7. Han, J. and Kamber, M., *Data Mining Concepts and Techniques*, pp. 21–27, Elsevier Inc., San Francisco, 2006.
8. Yang, F., Lee, A.J., Kuo, S., Mining health social media with sentiment analysis. *J. Med. Syst.*, 40, 236, 2016. https://doi.org/10.1007/s10916-016-0604-4.
9. Gohil, S., Vuik, S., Darzi, A., Sentiment analysis of healthcare tweets: Review of the methods used. *JMIR Public Health Surveill.*, 4, 2, e43, PMID: 29685871 PMCID: 5938573, 2018.
10. Yadav, S., Ekbal, A., Saha, S., Bhattacharyya, P., Medical sentiment analysis using social media: Towards building a patient assisted system. *LREC*, 2018.

11. Khan, T. and Khalid, S., Sentiment analysis for healthcare. *IJPHIM*, 3, 78–91, 2015.
12. Kashyap, R. and Nahapetian, A., Tweet analysis for user health monitoring. *ICST*, 2014.
13. Diorio, C., *et al.*, A world of competing sorrows': A mixed methods analysis of media reports of children with cancer abandoning conventional treatment. *PloS One*, 13, 12, e0209738, Dec. 21 2018.
14. Khan, M.T. and Khalid, S., Sentiment analysis for healthcare. *IJPHIM*, 3, 2, 78–91, 2015Nov. 7 2020.
15. Martin, N., De Weerdt, J., Fernández-Llatas, C., Gal, A., Gatta, R., Ibáñez, G., Johnson, O., Mannhardt, F., Marco-Ruiz, L., Mertens, S., Munoz-Gama, J., Seoane, F., Vanthienen, J., Wynn, M.T., Boilève, D.B., Bergs, J., Joosten-Melis, M., Schretlen, S., Acker, B.V., Recommendations for enhancing the usability and understandability of process mining in healthcare. *Artif. Intell. Med.*, 109, 101962, 2020. https://doi.org/10.1016/j.artmed.2020.101962.
16. Agrawal, R. and Prahakaran, S., Big data in digital healthcare: lessons learnt and recommendations for general practice. *Heredity*, 124, 525–534, 2020. https://doi.org/10.1038/s41437-020-0303-2.
17. Wang, J., Yang, Y., Wang, T., Sherratt, R.S., Zhang, J., Big data service architecture: a survey. *J. Internet Technol.*, 21, 2, 393–405, Mar. 2020.
18. Sharma, A. and Ghose, U., Sentimental analysis of twitter data with respect to general elections in India. *Procedia Comput. Sci.*, 173, 325–334, 2020. https://doi.org/10.1016/j.procs.2020.06.038.
19. Chakraborty, K., Bhattacharyya, S., Bag, R., A survey of sentiment analysis from social media data. *IEEE Trans. Comput. Soc. Syst.*, 7, 2, 450–464, April 2020.
20. Robinson, E., Hull, L., Petrides, K.V., Big five model and trait emotional intelligence in camouflaging behaviors in autism. *Pers. Individ. Differ.*, 152, 109565, 2020. https://doi.org/10.1016/j.paid.2019.109565.
21. Gallo, F.R., Simari, G., II, Martinez, M.V., Falappa, M.A., Predicting user reactions to twitter feed content based on personality type and social cues. *Future Gener. Comp. Sy.*, 110, 918–930, 2020. https://doi.org/10.1016/j.future.2019.10.044.
22. Nandal, N., Tanwar, R., Pruthi, J., Machine learning based aspect level sentiment analysis for amazon products. *Spat. Inf. Res.*, 28, 601–607, 2020. https://doi.org/10.1007/s41324-020-00320-2.
23. Jiawei, H., Kamber, M., Pei, J., *Data Mining: Concepts and Techniques*, Third Edition, Morgan Kaufmann, Waltham MA, 2012.
24. Mihuandayani, Utami, E., Luthfi, E.T., Text mining based on tax comments as big data analysis using SVM and feature selection. *2018 International Conference on Information and Communications Technology (ICOIACT)*, 2018.
25. Tandera, T., Hendro, Suhartono, D., Wongso, R., Prasetio, Y.L., Personality prediction system from facebook users. *2nd International Conference on Computer Science and Computational Intelligence 2017, ICCSCI 2017*, Bali, Indonesia, October 13–14 2017, 2017.

13

Applications of Artificial Intelligence, Blockchain, and Internet-of-Things in Management of Chronic Disease

Geetanjali[1], Rishabha Malviya[1*], Rajendra Awasthi[2†], Pramod Kumar Sharma[1], Nidhi Kala[3], Vinod Kumar[4] and Sanjay Kumar Yadav[5]

[1]*Department of Pharmacy, School of Medical and Allied Sciences, Galgotias University, Greater Noida, Gautam Buddha Nagar, Uttar Pradesh, India*
[2]*Department of Pharmaceutical Sciences, School of Health Sciences and Technology, University of Petroleum and Energy Studies (UPES), Energy Acres, Bidholi, Via - Prem Nagar, Dehradun, Uttarakhand, India*
[3]*Saraswati College of Pharmacy, Pilkhuwa, Hapur, Uttar Pradesh, India*
[4]*College of Pharmacy, Fatehullapur, Ghazipur, Uttar Pradesh, India*
[5]*Seth Vishambhar Nath Institute of Pharmaceutical Sciences, Barabanki, Uttar Pradesh, India*

Abstract

Healthcare cost of chronic disease management can be reduced using several advanced technologies. Wearable technology and mobile applications (apps) are widely available for health monitoring. These technologies are used by doctors, patients, and researchers for checking the health status. These devices can help in the development of telemedicine and telehealth via the use of Internet-of-Things, blockchain, and Artificial Intelligence (AI). AI has important applications in healthcare management. Diseases such as cardiac disorders, lung and heart problems, stroke and neurological disorders can be easily identified using AI systems. The AI system collects information and transfers them to analyst and help in reducing healthcare risks. Self-control and self-monitoring devices are useful for the elder people and those who cannot meet doctors frequently. It develops a

---

Corresponding author: rishabhamalviya19@gmail.com
†*Corresponding author*: awasthi02@gmail.com

D. Sumathi, T. Poongodi, B. Balamurugan and Lakshmana Kumar Ramasamy (eds.)
Cognitive Intelligence and Big Data in Healthcare, (349–366) © 2022 Scrivener Publishing LLC

secure, private, and trustable relationship between patients and healthcare providers. Blockchain technology helps in analysis of big data in healthcare, protect it, and maintain data transparency. Rapid progress of analytics techniques can control healthcare data and improve overall lifestyle.

Keywords: Artificial intelligence, disease management, healthcare, Internet-of-Things, mobile applications, telemedicine

13.1   Introduction

The advanced technologies used by medical specialists, patients, researchers and large organizations, such as hospitals and healthcare research institutions, include machine learning, blockchain, the Internet-of-Things (IoT) and cloud services, and deep learning. With its origin in the mid-1900s, today, the healthcare industry was an asset for AI [1, 2]. It was among the most advanced markets in the world. The AI market should reach US$150 billion by 2026. Several AI based healthcare application are available commercially. The main purpose of Medical AI was to detect, predict, treat and manage various diseases. The AI was also used in the patient monitoring and drug development [3]. AI was used in patient management with multi-organ involvement, erratic acute events and expectations for disease progression [4]. The blockchain technology was acquiring popularity in healthcare services due to its unique properties like security and operation of distributed database without an administrator or a central authority. Block chain utilizes peeve network to prepare a file of ordering documentation called blocks to form a digital ledger. Block chain helps to ameliorate the lucidity or legitimate of health sector data [5]. Blockchain technology has different models for chronic disease management and prevention. These models can predict the risk of chronic disease and helps the patient to minimize the chances of risk. This ultimately leads to reduce the cost of healthcare [6]. IoT plays a key role in patient health improvement. It minimizes the costs of treatment and travelling needs of both the patients and doctors. The IoT utilizes networked biosensors to simultaneously collect the data for clinical analysis. In IoT, the continuous monitoring of chronic illnesses including diabetes, obesity, hypertension, heart failure, hyperlipidemia, asthma, support for elderly care, depression and preventive care were performed [7]. The below sections will describe the applications, challenges and prospects of these new technologies used in healthcare system.

13.2   Artificial Intelligence and Management of Chronic Diseases

There are currently numerous AI tools and methods used to treat medical illnesses including diabetes, congestive heart failure and high blood pressure. It is used in data assignment and analysis, managing health related complications, estimating treatment success and in pathology and health research [1]. Bayesian AI algorithms can be used to reduce treatment cost and improve patient outcome. Vemulapalli *et al.* reported non-obvious, clinically relevant relationships which are potential in improving patient care quality. Medical informatics is the sub-discipline of health informatics that provides the information needed by the patient as well as doctors. Information exchange related issues can be solved using medical informatics. It also helps in understanding the needs of a patient to construct an effective program using state-of-the-art AI technologies to create an inter active interpretation system. Unlike many other knowledge-based systems, it is also working on the basis of empirical data related to actual patient information [8, 9].

AI provides an easy and accessible online data for predictive, preventive and personalized medicine for heart failure paradigm shift records. The expected outcomes are created by data analysis, thus provide an advance and personalized self-care. It reduces the cost per patient and allows long-term sustainability of cardiac procedures and surgeries [10]. The AI was also tested to assess pancreatitis-related liver fibrosis and pancreatic cancer. Based on multiple factors, it can be used in determining patient prognoses or foresee their response to treatments. Rong *et al.* reported biomedical applications of AI in diagnosis and research. Telemedicine provides novel solutions for healthcare [11, 12]. AI is applied in the diagnosis and prognosis of diseases, management of treatment, prediction of outcomes, and drug development. It increases the learning capacity and provides decision making support systems that can help to transform healthcare in the future. AI helps in healthcare through machine learning algorithms and also plays an important role in privacy management, data sharing, and storage of genetic information [13, 14].

The AI tools are better for individual performance, manage workload and reduce the chances of human errors. It can be used in single disease management to improve quality and efficiency of a clinical practice [15]. Different chronic diseases like cardiac disorders, hypertension, obesity, respiratory problems, hyperlipidemia and digestive-tract diseases can be better managed using AI applications in mobile phones. Due to the hectic lifestyle, elderly patients cannot interact with doctors and physiotherapists to maintain their health status. The mobile Apps or wearable devices can help to maintain the adequate medical services for a healthy life. Patients from rural areas do not receive proper medical attention. Thus, AI based techniques can be utilized to improve the healthcare needs of such patients at minimum healthcare costs [16].

Jiang *et al.* summarized applications of AI tools in the management of diseases like cancer, stroke, neurological disorders, and cardiovascular disease. AI is helpful in the diagnosis and identification of skin cancer subtypes. Controlled movement of a patient's diagnosis in neurological disorders and spinal motor neurons discharge time can be recorded using AI tools. Another healthcare application use of AI is the diagnosis of cardiac patient utilizing cardiac magnetic resonance imaging (MRI) images. Better results from the investigations like detection, diagnosis, treatment and prediction of stroke have been reported using AI technologies [17]. Figure 13.1 illustrates the schematic diagram of healthcare application in these areas.

AI was used to accumulate the personal data for constant health monitoring and evaluate healthcare. It is used to collect the deeper information about a patient, which can transfer the data translated from simple facial pictures and videos [18]. AI has been widely used in diagnostic tests, such as pulmonary function test and computed tomography for obstructive lung diseases. AI tools can collect the accurate data and their automated interpretation to detect the disease state. The computed tomography imaging helps to recognize the neural network state of diseases. AI was therefore

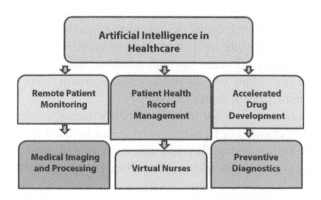

Figure 13.1 Schematic presentation of applications of AI in healthcare.

used for an early diagnosis with machine learning for obstructive lung disease [19].

A timely diagnosis, ongoing medical care and patient education were also essential for the diabetic patient in order to minimize long-term complication risks and prevent acute complications. In addition to the medication, other preventive measures for the management of diabetes requires adherence to self-care of patients which includes carefully counting carbohydrates, scheduling meals, monitoring blood glucose levels, and exercise. AI can effectively measure and control such parameters. AI can predict, prevent and handle diabetic complications. The collection of information from the patients using AI also helps to minimize healthcare risks. AI tools can provide personalized treatment of diabetes and it can be a most promising tool towards the best healthcare in near future [20].

AI has played potential role in various fields of medicine like radiology, dermatology, pulmonology, cardiology, neurology, internal medicine, ophthalmology and oncology. It collects a large number of patient data, maintain and assist it properly for health management. AI has been widely investigated in ophthalmology. This helps the physicians to provide more effective and better patient care with early diagnosis and effective treatment at reduce cost [21, 22]. Visual assessment of liver images has been utilized for diagnosis, characterization and monitoring of liver diseases. The medical imaging approach uses deep machine learning algorithms. It reduces the load of physicians and generates an effective and accurate report [23].

A study recruited 295 participants to examine the link between chronical and depressive tiredness syndrome by using AI instruments. In candidate biomarkers of chronic fatigue syndrome and depressive diseases with the same biomarkers and different biomarkers of both diseases, age and gender differences were recorded. However, the investigated AI method *i.e.* principal components analysis reflected that either depressive disorder or chronic fatigue syndrome were differentiate thoroughly in plasma metabolite [24].

The analysis of data from hundred serum samples from healthy subjects and arthritic patient is done using a machine-learning algorithm in a survey. The study involved standard immunoassays tests to detect and analyze glycan markers for rheumatoid arthritis. Glycan analysis was carried out using whole serum samples. The results were compared to enzyme-linked lectin-binding assay plates with adsorbed protein. The combining rheumatoid arthritis markers with glycan analysis resulted in better discrimination accuracy. However, the immunoassays could not identify seronegative arthritic patients without autoantibodies [25]. Singh *et al.* designed a system for diagnosing Arthritis using a fuzzy logic controller based on the application of Zadeh's fuzzy set theory. Risk conditions are more in case of undiagnosed patients. The AI application can help to detect the locomotry abnormalities, diagnosis and treatment of osteoarthritis and rheumatoid arthritis [26].

Computer system applications for stroke management have been also reported. It helps to improve diagnosis, analysis and management of data related to stroke using stroke imaging approach. The deep learning technique can be used based on artificial neural network of the human brain. Telemedicine provides healthcare management for chronic diseases like diabetes, lung and heart disease [27].

A robotic system can facilitate the surgery, but for the movement and control the system still it requires a surgeon. AI could be used in breast cancer screening and lymphatic metastasis identification. The histopathology data evaluation can improve the quality of care for cancer patients. Wearable devices can detect the heart rate, calories burn and skin temperature. The device sensors can also detect the symptoms of Parkinson's disease like posture, speech patterns and impaired hand movement [28]. Alzheimer's disease (AD) is a neurological disorder and its progression may cause death of brain tissues. In a study Farooq *et al.* attempted early-stage detection of AD using deep learning depend chassis for analyzing structural MRI scans. The study was based on the collection of MRI scans, extraction of grey matter from the scans, grey matter slice from axial scans (each volume is converted into approximately 166 2D slices) followed by deep learning and diagnosis of AD its mild cognitive impairment, the crucial moment of mild cognitive impairment, or normal cognitive. These models are free of factors that normally cause errors in human diagnosis. These models are confident and can be diagnosed much more quickly [29].

AI shares the medical data that provide transparency and secure big data. It can work using online healthcare or telemedicine followed by consulting the data with physicians. It gives safety to the patient and increases productivity. It develops collaboration between patient, physician and data scientist [30]. Thus, based on the available literature, AI is recommended for various healthcare applications such as diagnosis and treatment of various diseases and population health management.

13.3   Blockchain and Healthcare

Blockchain is a digital repository in the chronological and public recording of transactions in Bitcoin and in another cryptocurrency. Webopedia has defined block chain as a kind of data structure that allows transactions to be digitally identified and tracked and shared across a distributed computer network to develop a spread network. Block chain's distributed ledger technology offers a transparent and secure way to monitor ownership and transfer of assets. The blockchain provides safe and protected medical care in healthcare and research sectors, especially regarding data privacy [31].

13.3.1 Blockchain and Healthcare Management of Chronic Disease

Blockchains are used for the collection of big data of patients in a secure form for future utilization. It can be used to avoid the encryption by third-party and to secure the digital transitions related to the healthcare data. Blockchain also protect data from cryptographic harsh in healthcare areas. The mobile applications are used to collect the health data and assist treatment individually [32]. Figure 13.2 illustrates applications of the blockchain in management of various chronic diseases.

Blockchain technology is used by stakeholders to deceases the transactional costs, ensure transparency, and to maintain the record of transaction history. It provides a better platform for low-income people for the prevention and better management of chronic diseases. More attention is needed to ascertain how a blockchain model can be applied correctly (identification of selected chronic diseases, allocation of alternative currencies, calculation of risk scores, tracking of healthcare costs, and position of various stakeholders) to improve health behavior, decrease the risk

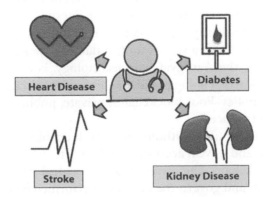

Figure 13.2 Schematic illustration of applications of Blockchain in the management of various chronic diseases.

scores of chronic disease and reduces financial burden on the healthcare system [33].

Ethereum protocol based blockchain facilitates data transitions and transparency during treatment. It can monitor patient safely, publicly verifiable and unfalsifiable environment for proper workflow during treatment of diseases [34]. Nichol and Brandt integrated the applications of blockchain and conception of co-creation of trust for healthcare. The study recommended that the investigated concept had a positive impact on patient satisfaction, healthcare outcomes, fraud, and reduced security risks related to the interoperability. In healthcare management, the blockchain has successfully rebuilt the trust of a patient by ensuring security and treatment satisfaction [35].

Blockchain technology is used to care elderly patients or in chronic disease management. The number of media disruptions involved during the treatment of diseases could lead to consume time and require resource-intensive authentication. Blockchain technology provides treatment information to healthcare providers involved in medical practice such as general partitions, medical specialists and therapists [36]. Blockchain technology can analyze and store the healthcare data and maintain privacy. The pseudonymous nature and privacy of blockchain technology help to record personal health as a digital asset and as a digital currency on the blockchain. Persons can also provide medical records to doctors, hospitals, insurance companies and others by accessing the health records using their private keys [37].

In various areas of health, such as clinical studies, personal medicine, and the sharing of patient medical data, Blockchain can operate. Blockchain systems keep patients' health data safe and secure. The Blockchain system allows the recording and distribution of data (public and easy to confirm in non-affiliated provider organisms). A hacker doesn't have a central owner or hub to corrupt or disrupt data. Data from different sources were always updated, while data from a single, unified database was collected [6]. The Indian ecosystem, the AarogyaChain technology, is a technology based blockchain solution that is suggested for eliminating hi-cups in implementation of health policy. Four blockchains, private, public, hybrid and consortium, were introduced.

The blockchain is public without property. It enables the participants to join the network and leave it according to their interests. There's one owner on a private blockchain. The owner acts as a control layer, which runs on top of blockchain and govern the activities performed by the participants. A permissioned blockchain is recommended for better output. It lies in between the public and private. This could provide several benefits in the healthcare sector because small units kept lots of data related to the diseases. Blockchain technology is not a medical environment panacea, but a reliable and effective solution [38].

The blockchain network is a larger and secure network, reducing the absence of trust between healthcare organizations. Fast Healthcare Interoperability Resources (FHIR) and Chain-based DApp (decentered app) show that blockchain is able to facilitate successful healthcare data sharing and to keep the confidentiality of original data sources confidential. The blockchain keeps patient records of physicians and clinical data analysts that create confidence between the digital healthcare systems. Manual maintenance of patients' large data is a complicated process, so that it is secure and safe to handle such data [39, 40].

Globally Blockchain is used, with US$500 million expected to be passed in 2022. Patient services, population health system and pharmaceutical supply chains can be automatically monitored. However, although blockchain techniques have several advantages, they must improve their health, health and health education services [41]. Blockchain techniques prepare a prototype framework for data management and patient care for oncological investigations. From the day when treatment started to completion of treatment, every data can be uploaded by the doctor and the access can be public/private depending on patient consent [42].

Electronic record of healthcare data is difficult to maintain security. Blockchain technology provides accountable, immutable, and trustable in transactions and transparent mode for data protection. Patient data can be maintained using a blockchain network system and can be collaborated with the patient, researchers, health providers and data management systems. Therefore, the goal of blockchain in upcoming future is to connect health and medical research data so it can enhance healthcare data management [43]. Blockchain is a pool of data in which a patient, researcher and healthcare provider have access of information. The patients can feed health-related data in the blockchain platform. It helps to improve the condition and treatments of patient health. The wearable devices generate the data which can be controlled by patients. The privacy of patient health data was maintained properly using blockchain technique and also developed the third party trust [44].

Blockchain technology is a network umbrella that enhances confidence and transparency in privacy, security, and security. Under the HIPAA Regulation, privacy shall be maintained for individual health information transmitted or maintained in all or all forms, and it shall be provided in accordance with the HIPAA (Health Insurance Transportability Act

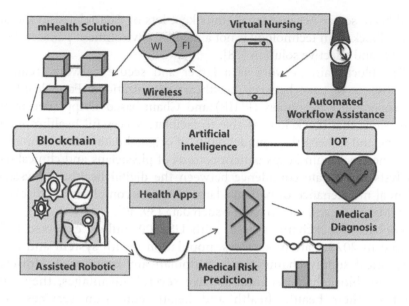

Figure 13.3 Schematic presentation of healthcare management using advanced technologies (AI, Blockchain, and IoT).

1996) [45]. Figure 13.3 illustrates a schematic diagram of healthcare management using AI, Blockchain and IoT.

13.4   Internet-of-Things and Healthcare Management of Chronic Disease

The follow-up data of a diabetic patient can be maintained using IoT. The advance system of IoT monitors routine workout and food habit of the patient. The IoT provides patient information to the doctors. The IoT connect directly to the internet and provide disease related record to the physician which is totally secure. It has both the open and private excess, which improves the security of the data of the patient [46].

The IoT technology integrates into the management of chronic disease. The idea of 'health' or 'smart health' is initiated by the IoT. E-Health interventions are thought to be successful in simplifying the process and facilitating resource utilization by enhancing the exchange of information between patients and various medical service providers [47]. Regular health monitoring and monitoring can reduce the risk of chronic conditions developing. It can help prevent chronic sudden attacks and increase the likelihood that disease is detected early. A remote health surveillance system can be used for continuous health surveillance. However, it needs to be optimized in terms of power utilization and data quality. It also clarifies the needs and targets of an efficient patient remote monitoring system [48].

IoT was used in the measurement of disease heart rate and blood pressure. IoT is primarily used by doctors when the patient is taken off hospital for a certain period of time to monitor patient health data [49]. IoT, cloud computing and big data analysis can all technologically provide data so-called intelligent healthcare. It can assist the patient and the doctor in automating the complete data on health. In order to immediately transit their condition, patients can use various devices. Moreover, intelligent healthcare helps the patient to control their care more effectively [50]. IoT provides a patient monitoring sensor connected to the internet. It can collect and store critical data from the patient. The recorded data are discussed with the doctor for the appropriate treatment of the disease for further analyses. Data interchanged among linked devices comprise textual information, numeric values, images, video data including sonography, endoscopy, etc. [51].

The IoT can be connected consistently by all subjects and healthcare professionals. They analyze safety and privacy characteristics in connection with authentication, power, energy, resource service quality, and wireless health monitoring in real time. However, there is poorly defined system architecture of IoT; data restriction and its preservation of integrity are still difficult [52].

In the resolution of heart disease problems, IoT techniques have a tremendous superiority. It can change the mode of service and instigation the healthcare system depends on the patient's physical status rather than feelings. For the implementation of the universal health service, a remote monitoring program is necessary. Li *et al.* Proposed an overarching monitoring system capable of sending patient physical signals to provide real-time medical applications. The system included two components: (i) transfer of data and (ii) acquisition of data [53].

The uses of advanced technology in the health sector were increasing day by day. E-Health was a part of advance technology in which the mobile applications are used for healthcare. IoT can provide the data of disease and related treatment for the mobile application of patient for easy handling of the diseased condition [54]. The rising costs of medical care show a major impact on the quality of life and these costs are even higher in the case of chronic diseases. Healthcare providers can collect data from remote monitoring devices like glucometer, pulse oximeter, *etc.* Devices like XBOX Kinect sensor are used in the smart intensive care units to protect a patient from the risk of disease [55].

13.5   Conclusions

Technologies such as AI, blockchain and the IoT hold an unprecedented potential in the healthcare system when used individually or integrated for a specific diseased condition. The blockchain helps to maintain and analyze big data. The IoT communicates patient data in an easier way with the doctors. The healthcare providers can provide better results for the diagnosis and therapies using such smart healthcare techniques. The real-time data management devices provide an early diagnosis and prevention of chronic diseases. Using these advanced technologies, health can be monitored on a personal basis to get adequate medical services and prompt healthy life. This chapter describes different roles of these technologies in the healthcare sector. These technologies can decrease expenses and time consumption during medication and thus expected to introduce new vistas for better health services by discovering mobile applications, wearable devices and diagnostic systems.

References

1. Becker, A., Artificial intelligence in medicine: What is it doing for us today? *Health Policy Technol.*, 8, 2, 198–205, 2019. https://doi.org/10.1016/j.hlpt.2019.03.004.
2. Tian, S., Yang, W., Le Grange, J.M., Wang, P., Huang, W., Ye, Z., Smart healthcare: Making medical care more intelligent. *GHJ*, 3, 3, 62–65, 2019.
3. Malviya, R. and Sharma, A., Applications of computational methods and modelling in drug delivery, in: *Machine Learning and Analytics in Healthcare Systems*, 1, H. Bansal, B. Balusamy, T. Poongodi, K. Firoz Khan, (Eds.), p. 28, CRC Press, Boca Raton, FL, 2021, https://doi.org/10.1201/9781003185246.
4. Miller, D.D. and Brown, E.W., Artificial intelligence in medical practice: The question to the answer? *Am. J. Med.*, 131, 2, 129–133, 2018. https://doi.org/10.1016/j.amjmed.2017.10.035.
5. Angraal, S., Krumholz, H.M., Schulz, W.L., Blockchain technology: Applications in healthcare. *Circ. Cardiovasc. Qual. Outcomes*, 10, 9, e003800, 2017. https://doi.org/10.1161/CIRCOUTCOMES.117.003800.
6. Paglialonga, A. and Keshavjee, K., Use of alternative currencies, blockchain technology, and predictive analytics for chronic disease prevention:

A conceptual model. *Stud. Health Technol. Inform.*, 264, 1872–1873, 2019. https://doi.org/10.3233/SHTI190690.

7. Ravi, P. and Kumar, N., Internet of things (IoT): A revolutionary approach towards healthcare surveillance, in: *Proceedings of the 3rd National Conference on Image Processing, Computing, Communication, Networking and Data Analytics*, Karnataka, India, pp. 257–262, 2018, https://doi.org/10.21467/proceedings.

8. Vemulapalli, V., Qu, J., Garren, J.M., Rodrigues, L.O., Kiebish, M.A., Sarangarajan, R., Narain, N.R., Akmaev, V.R., Non-obvious correlations to disease management unraveled by Bayesian artificial intelligence analyses of CMS data. *Artif. Intell. Med.*, 74, 1–8, 2016. https://doi.org/10.1016/j.artmed.2016.11.001.

9. Buchanan, B.G., Moore, J.D., Forsythe, D.E., Carenini, G., Ohlsson, S., Banks, G., An intelligent interactive system for delivering individualized information to patients. *Artif. Intell. Med.*, 7, 2, 117–154, 1995. https://doi.org/10.1016/0933-3657(94)00029-R.

10. Barrett, M., Boyne, J., Brandts, J., Brunner-La Rocca, H.P., De Maesschalck, L., De Wit, K., Dixon, L., Eurlings, C., Fitzsimons, D., Golubnitschaja, O., Hageman, A., Artificial intelligence supported patient self care in chronic heart failure: A paradigm shift from reactive to predictive, preventive and personalised care. *EPMA J.*, 10, 445–464, 2019. https://doi.org/10.1007/s13167-019-00188-9.

11. Le Berre, C., Sandborn, W.J., Aridhi, S., Devignes, M.D., Fournier, L., Smail-Tabbone, M., Danese, S., Peyrin-Biroulet, L., Application of artificial intelligence to gastroenterology and hepatology. *Gastroenterology*, 158, 1, 76–94, 2020.

12. Rong, G., Mendez, A., Assi, E.B., Zhao, B., Sawan, M., Artificial intelligence in healthcare: Review and prediction case studies. *Engineering*, 6, 3, 291–301, 2020. https://doi.org/10.1016/j.eng.2019.08.015.

13. Le Page, M., Meet your digital doctor. *New Sci.*, 242, 3236, 20–21, 2019. https://doi.org/10.1016/S0262-4079(19)31171-6.

14. Noorbakhsh-Sabet, N., Zand, R., Zhang, Y., Abedi, V., Artificial intelligence transforms the future of healthcare. *Am. J. Med.*, 132, 7, 795–801, 2019. https://doi.org/10.1016/j.amjmed.2019.01.017.

15. Ho, C.W., Soon, D., Caals, K., Kapur, J., Governance of automated image analysis and artificial intelligence analytics in healthcare. *Clin. Radiol.*, 74, 5, 329–337, 2019. https://doi.org/10.1016/j.crad.2019.02.005.

16. Sharma, A., Malviya, R., Awasthi, R., Sharma, P.K., Artificial intelligence, blockchain, and internet of medical things: New technologies in detecting, preventing, and controlling of emergent diseases, in: *Advances in Multidisciplinary Medical Technologies-Engineering, Modeling and Findings*, A. Khelassi, and V.V. Estrela, (Eds.), pp. 127–154, Springer, Cham, 2021, https://doi.org/10.1007/978-3-030-57552-6_10.

17. Jiang, F., Jiang, Y., Zhi, H., Dong, Y., Li, H., Ma, S., Wang, Y., Dong, Q., Shen, H., Wang, Y., Artificial intelligence in healthcare: Past, present and

future. *Stroke Vasc. Neurol.*, 2, 4, 230–243, 2017. https://doi.org/10.1136/svn-2017-000101.

18. Mamoshina, P., Ojomoko, L., Yanovich, Y., Ostrovski, A., Botezatu, A., Prikhodko, P., Izumchenko, E., Aliper, A., Romantsov, K., Zhebrak, A., Ogu, I.O., Zhavoronkov, A., Converging blockchain and next-generation artificial intelligence technologies to decentralize and accelerate biomedical research and healthcare. *Oncotarget*, 9, 5, 5665–5690, 2018. https://doi.org/10.18632%2Foncotarget.22345.

19. Das, N., Topalovic, M., Janssens, W., Artificial intelligence in diagnosis of obstructive lung disease: Current status and future potential. *Curr. Opin. Pulmon. Med.*, 24, 2, 117–123, 2018. https://doi.org/10.1097/MCP.0000000000000459.

20. Contreras, I. and Vehi, J., Artificial intelligence for diabetes management and decision support: Literature review. *J. Med. Internet Res.*, 20, 5, e10775, 2018. https://doi.org/10.2196/10775.

21. Kapoor, R., Walters, S.P., Al-Aswad, L.A., The current state of artificial intelligence in ophthalmology. *Surv. Ophthalmol.*, 64, 2, 233–240, 2019. https://doi.org/10.1016/j.survophthal.2018.09.002.

22. Hogarty, D.T., Mackey, D.A., Hewitt, A.W., Current state and future prospects of artificial intelligence in ophthalmology: A review. *Clin. Experiment. Ophthalmol.*, 47, 1, 128–139, 2019. http://dx.doi.org/10.1111/ceo.13381.

23. Zhou, L.Q., Wang, J.Y., Yu, S.Y., Wu, G.G., Wei, Q., Deng, Y.B., Wu, X.L., Cui, X.W., Dietrich, C.F., Artificial intelligence in medical imaging of the liver. *World J. Gastroenterol.*, 25, 6, 672–682, 2019. https://doi.org/10.3748%2Fwjg.v25.i6.672.

24. Zhang, F., Wu, C., Jia, C., Gao, K., Wang, J., Zhao, H., Wang, W., Chen, J., Artificial intelligence based discovery of the association between depression and chronic fatigue syndrome. *J. Affect. Disord.*, 25, 380–390, 2019. https://doi.org/10.1016/j.jad.2019.03.011.

25. Chocholova, E., Bertok, T., Jane, E., Lorencova, L., Holazova, A., Belicka, L., Belicky, S., Mislovicova, D., Vikartovska, A., Imrich, R., Kasak, P., Glycomics meets artificial intelligence–potential of glycan analysis for identification of seropositive and seronegative rheumatoid arthritis patients revealed. *Clin. Chim. Acta*, 481, 49–55, 2018. https://doi.org/10.1016/j.cca.2018.02.031.

26. Singh, S., Kumar, A., Panneerselvam, K., Vennila, J.J., Diagnosis of arthritis through fuzzy inference system. *J. Med. Syst.*, 36, 3, 1459–1468, 2012. https://doi.org/10.1007/s10916-010-9606-9.

27. Lee, E.J., Kim, Y.H., Kim, N., Kang, D.W., Deep into the brain: Artificial intelligence in stroke imaging. *J. Stroke*, 19, 3, 277, 2017. https://dx.doi.org/10.5853%2Fjos.2017.02054.

28. Yu, K.H., Beam, A.L., Kohane, I.S., Artificial intelligence in healthcare. *Nat. Biomed. Eng.*, 2, 10, 719–731, 2018. https://doi.org/10.1038/s41551-018-0305-z.

29. Farooq, A., Anwar, S., Awais, M., Alnowami, M., Artificial intelligence based smart diagnosis of Alzheimer's disease and mild cognitive impairment. *International Smart Cities Conference (ISC2)*, IEEE, pp. 1–4, September 2017, https://doi.org/10.1109/ISC2.2017.8090871.

30. He, J., Baxter, S.L., Xu, J., Xu, J., Zhou, X., Zhang, K., The practical implementation of artificial intelligence technologies in medicine. *Nat. Med.*, 25, 1, 30–36, 2019. https://doi.org/10.1038/s41591-018-0307-0.

31. Atlam, H.F. and Wills, G.B., Technical aspects of blockchain and IoT, in: *Advances in Computers*, vol. 115, pp. 1–39, 2019, https://doi.org/10.1016/bs.adcom.2018.10.006.

32. Clim, A., Zota, R.D., Constantinescu, R., Data exchanges based on blockchain in m-Health applications. *Procedia Comput. Sci.*, 160, 281–288, 2019. https://doi.org/10.1016/j.procs.2019.11.088.

33. Siyal, A.A., Junejo, A.Z., Zawish, M., Ahmed, K., Khalil, A., Soursou, G., Applications of blockchain technology in medicine and healthcare: Challenges and future perspectives. *Cryptography*, 3, 1, 3, 2019. https://doi.org/10.3390/cryptography3010003.

34. Nichol, P.B. and Brandt, J., Co-creation of trust for healthcare: The cryptocitizen framework for interoperability with blockchain. *Res. Proposal*, 1–10, 2016. https://doi.org/10.13140/RG.2.1.1545.4963.

35. Mettler, M., Block chain technology in healthcare: The revolution starts here. *IEEE 18th International Conference on e-Health Networking, Applications and Services, Healthcom*, pp. 1–3, 2016, https://doi.org/10.1109/HealthCom.2016.7749510.

36. Swan, M., Blockchain for business: Next-generation enterprise artificial intelligence systems, in: *Advances in Computers*, vol. 111, pp. 121–162, 2018, https://doi.org/10.1016/bs.adcom.2018.03.013.

37. Casino, F., Dasaklis, T.K., Patsakis, C., A systematic literature review of blockchain-based applications: Current status, classification and open issues. *Telemat. Inform.*, 36, 55–81, 2019. https://doi.org/10.1016/j.tele.2018.11.006.

38. Pandey, P. and Litoriya, R., Implementing healthcare services on a large scale: Challenges and remedies based on blockchain technology. *Health Policy Technol.*, 9, 1, 69–78, 2020. https://doi.org/10.1016/j.hlpt.2020.01.004.

39. Zhang, P., White, J., Schmidt, D.C., Lenz, G., Rosenbloom, S.T., FHIRChain: Applying blockchain to securely and scalably share clinical data. *Comput. Struct. Biotechnol. J.*, 16, 267–278, 2018. https://doi.org/10.1016/j.csbj.2018.07.004.

40. Onik, M.M., Aich, S., Yang, J., Kim, C.S., Kim, H.C., Blockchain in healthcare: Challenges and solutions, in: *Big Data Analytics for Intelligent Healthcare Management*, pp. 197–226, 2019, https://doi.org/10.1016/B978-0-12-818146-1.00008-8.

41. Hasselgren, A., Kralevska, K., Gligoroski, D., Pedersen, S.A., Faxvaag, A., Blockchain in healthcare and health sciences–a scoping review. *Int. J. Med. Inform.*, 134, 104040, 2019. https://doi.org/10.1016/j.ijmedinf.2019.104040.

42. Dubovitskaya, A., Xu, Z., Ryu, S., Schumacher, M., Wang, F., How blockchain could empower ehealth: An application for radiation oncology, in: *VLDB Workshop on Data Management and Analytics for Medicine and Healthcare,* pp. 3–6, 2017, https://doi.org/10.1007/978-3-319-67186-4_1.

43. Dubovitskaya, A., Xu, Z., Ryu, S., Schumacher, M., Wang, F., Secure and trustable electronic medical records sharing using blockchain, in: *AMIA Annual Symposium Proceedings,* vol. 650, American Medical Informatics Association, 2017.

44. Cichosz, S.L., Stausholm, M.N., Kronborg, T., Vestergaard, P., Hejlesen, O., How to use blockchain for diabetes healthcare data and access management: An operational concept. *J. Diabetes Sci. Technol.,* 13, 2, 248–253, 2019. https://doi.org/10.1177%2F1932296818790281.

45. Daniel, J., Sargolzaei, A., Abdelghani, M., Sargolzaei, S., Amaba, B., Blockchain technology, cognitive computing, and healthcare innovations. *J. Adv. Inf. Technol.,* 8, 3, 194–198, 2017. https://doi.org/10.12720/jait.8.3.194–198.

46. Gomez, J., Oviedo, B., Zhuma, E., Patient monitoring system based on internet of things. *Procedia Comput. Sci.,* 83, 90–97, 2016. https://doi.org/10.1016/j.procs.2016.04.103.

47. Yuehong, Y.I., Zeng, Y., Chen, X., Fan, Y., The internet of things in healthcare: An overview. *J. Ind. Inf. Integr.,* 1, 3–13, 2016. https://doi.org/10.1016/j.jii.2016.03.004.

48. Anzanpour, A., Rashid, H., Rahmani, A.M., Jantsch, A., Dutt, N., Liljeberg, P., Energy-efficient and reliable wearable internet-of-things through fog-assisted dynamic goal management. *Procedia Comput. Sci.,* 151, 493–500, 2019. https://doi.org/10.1016/j.procs.2019.04.067.

49. Alansari, Z., Anuar, N.B., Kamsin, A., Soomro, S., Belgaum, M.R., The internet of things adoption in healthcare applications. *IEEE 3rd International Conference on Engineering Technologies and Social Sciences (ICETSS),* pp. 1–5, 2017, https://doi.org/10.1109/ICETSS.2017.8324138.

50. Dash, S., Shakyawar, S.K., Sharma, M., Kaushik, S., Big data in healthcare: Management, analysis and future prospects. *J. Big Data,* 6, 54, 2019. https://doi.org/10.1186/s40537-019-0217-0.

51. Pramanik, P.K., Upadhyaya, B.K., Pal, S., Pal, T., Internet of things, smart sensors, and pervasive systems: Enabling connected and pervasive healthcare, in: *Healthcare Data Analytics and Management,* pp. 1–58, 2019, https://doi.org/10.1016/B978-0-12-815368-0.00001-4.

52. Dhanvijay, M.M. and Patil, S.C., Internet of things: A survey of enabling technologies in healthcare and its application. *Comput. Netw.,* 15, 113–131, 2019. https://doi.org/10.1016/j.comnet.2019.03.006.

53. Li, C., Hu, X., Zhang, L., The IoT-based heart disease monitoring system for pervasive healthcare service. *Procedia Comput. Sci.,* 112, 2328–2334, 2017. https://doi.org/10.1016/j.procs.2017.08.265.

54. Dimitrov, D.V., Medical internet of things and big data in healthcare. *Healthc. Inform. Res.,* 22, 3, 156, 2016. https://doi.org/10.4258/hir.2016.22.3.156.

55. Chiuchisan, I., Costin, H.N., Geman, O., Adopting the internet of things technologies in healthcare systems, in: *2014 International Conference and Exposition on Electrical and Power Engineering (EPE)*, IEEE, pp. 532–535, 2014. https//doi.org/10.1016/j.procs.2016.04.103.

14

Research Challenges and Future Directions in Applying Cognitive Computing in the Healthcare Domain

BKSP Kumar Raju Alluri

SCOPE, VIT-AP University, AP, Amaravati, India

Abstract

Prevention is better than cure' is the most common saying over the decades, and we could not completely accomplish this in the context of Healthcare. The application of cognitive computing gave a lot of hope to identify and cure the diseases at early stages. Many healthcare-based cognitive applications are currently in place like, Smart Monitoring of various health parameters, assessing the health risk, and prescribing the diet and daily routine. Human touch cannot be replaced by cognitive computing-based assistants, but the research should move in that direction such that collaborative workforce can be deployed in emergency situations. In this chapter, we discuss applications, challenges, and future directions of using cognitive assisted technology in healthcare management.

Keywords: Healthcare, cognitive services, deep learning, decision making

14.1 Introduction

Healthcare is one of the key domains with regards to Data Analytics. Evaluating this in 2020 alone, 20.5 billion dollars was the portion of the Healthcare and it is relied upon to increment to 77.5 billion in next 5 years. The tremendous ascent in the market request is because of the utilization of Information Centric Technologies (ICT) like Natural Language Processing, Machine Learning, Deep Learning, and Artificial Intelligence. Implanting a

Email: bksp.kumar@vitap.ac.in

D. Sumathi, T. Poongodi, B. Balamurugan and Lakshmana Kumar Ramasamy (eds.)
Cognitive Intelligence and Big Data in Healthcare, (367–390) © 2022 Scrivener Publishing LLC

few of these innovations to imitate the human manner of thinking with viability and productivity is the objective of Cognitive Computing [1].

Chronic diseases are increasing extensively due to habitual differences in the human lifestyle. The technological improvements shed lights on addressing various domain-based issues and it is not exception to Healthcare. In recent times, the application of ICTs solved various Healthcare predictive and reactive issues [2]. The objective of cognitive computing is to automatically solve the problems without much intervention of the humans. For example, personalized monitoring of the patients is difficult for the hospitals and the cognitive services can have friendly interaction and assist them in basic medical needs after the treatment.

Cognitive systems can talk and hear content to infer the objective angle. The thinking offered by the frameworks is probabilistic in nature and would aid the working experts to take viable business choices. Healthcare Cognitive Assistive Technology (CAT) for the most part centers on data analysis to give an intelligent and circumstance-mindful arrangements by imitating human perspective. Content in Electronic Health Records is targeting the usage of big data analytics and we require devoted CAT specialists to channel and measure the dynamic decision making process [3].

Would AI be able to supplant the Humans? A similar inquiry can be reworded for the clinical field as, "Can Cognitive Computing supplant Doctors?" The appropriate response is an unmistakable No. The cognitive agents are being created to work inseparably with people for improving the nature of therapy in clinical proactive and responsive circumstances. Likewise, human touch can't be totally supplanted, and the Doctors can rather work more on this viewpoint and leave the weight of minor biological processes to the cognitive agents.

In the recent past, the utilizations of healthcare based cognitive computing expanded at very high pace and some of them are referenced below:

1. IBM Watson is used by different German emergency clinics to identify and fix different uncommon illnesses.
2. NLP is utilized for programmed examination of the best-in-class oncology work and its archetypes.
3. Man-made intelligence empowered stages are accessible to help clinical imaging and analysis.
4. Scientists utilized progressed language models to distinguish the connection of manifestations across different patients with regard to an objective infection.

5. Electronic Health Records content was standardized, filtered, and analyzed to support the AI recommendation engines.

Cognitive Inference Engine (CIE) takes any kind of information i.e., organized/semi-organized and unstructured (Figure 14.1). Understanding the information is the initial step performed by non-CAT agents which is accomplished through visual examination and descriptive statistics. CIE deployed in target CAT specialist would begin getting essential inductions from the information followed by the model building utilizing different ICTs which are then tried on the genuine test data. The choices projected by the CAT specialists can't be taken as final for executing on critical health situations and this would require human impedance. To make the forecasts

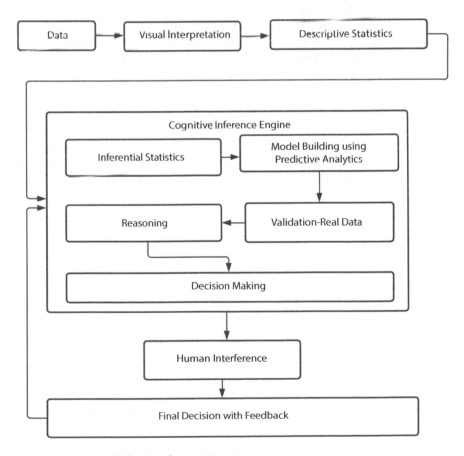

Figure 14.1 General lifecycle of a cognitive agent.

more legitimate, the new CAT specialists are embedded with sensible thinking capabilities utilizing Explainable AI. At last, as of now we can't disregard human interference for taking an official choice and the machine justifiable input is then sent back for support learning [4]. Note that every learning module is not mandatory for each CAT specialist, and it depends upon the business necessities.

Cognitive Computing with regards to medical services gathers information from numerous sources like ecological and clinical information alongside individual and diagnostic reports for better view of the hidden circumstance/illness (Figure 14.2). Effective decision making is impossible by examining the information from single source and it should correlate the data from different organized/semi and unstructured information sources [5].

Healthcare management (HCM) objective is to decrease the expenses of the essential and progressed therapies with the end goal that productivity is profoundly improved. It is obvious that, patients' HCM affected by Government, Healthcare Providers and Researchers (Figure 14.3). Government bodies ought to ceaselessly screen the people's wellbeing and affordable status through different immediate and backhanded sources. The status would then as given as one of the inputs to the scientists using which the target of innovation will be characterized with strong motivation [4]. Medical care Providers are the direct point of contact with patients and the ideal service given is beyond value. The "ideal" administration making a back stride because of the commercialization, and this can be taken care by presenting CAT agents for circumstance-mindful fields like Healthcare.

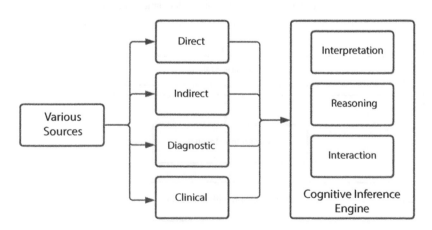

Figure 14.2 Various sources of information for CIE.

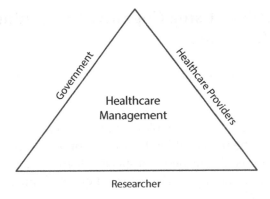

Figure 14.3 Various stakeholders in healthcare management.

14.2 Cognitive Computing Framework in Healthcare

Cognitive Computing services are offered in various categories and more than one aspect can also be considered for enhancing the user experience (Figure 14.4).

- Hardware or Software
- Technology being used: NLP, Deep Learning, Machine Learning, and Artificial IntelligenceUse cases (like, AI assistant for Surgeries, Error Reduction and administrative workflow management)
- Beneficiary: Patient, Doctor, Nursing Assistant, Non-Medical Staff, etc.

A few different applications are additionally important for the Cognitive Health Management, and they became mainstream in various viewpoints like Hardware/Software focused, Technology, End User, and Place. The end client is the main partner dependent on which the directions of outlining the objectives and fostering the application would totally change. Additionally, setting mindfulness and situational awareness empowered in the CAT agents would make them more successful while serving the patients [5].

14.3   Benefits of Using Cognitive Computing for Healthcare

There are numerous benefits of utilizing cognitive assistance for healthcare management.

1. **Decrease in Cost**: A couple of clinical benefits are exorbitant and can't be managed by the lower economy populace. This burden was diminished to a specific degree and yet advancing without taking off the nature of quality human intercession [6–9].
2. **Speed and Accuracy**: Individual Data assortment and connection investigation of different genes, protein arrangements, and illnesses would make the clinical staff to take exact prescient ends [10, 11].
3. **Process Optimization**: The AI enabled Cognitive Computing would optimize the daily operational and clinical activities and thus ensures the improved caring and diagnosis of the patients [12–14].
4. **Training**: The CAT agents can be utilized for preparing the para clinical staff and training the clinical staff [11, 12].
5. **Improved Support**: Using Cognitive empowered auto-specialists would decrease the manual exertion in tackling the client/patient issues and increase the subsequent fulfillment [10, 11].
6. **Preparing Electronic Health Records**: Maintaining the patient clinical history in digital form would permit the Healthcare Provider to effectively send the information to CAT agents. Additionally, Optical Character Recognition is utilized to try and change the Handwritten content over to the cognitive assistant [12, 15–17].
7. **Improved Diagnosis**: Patient's clinical reports were examined utilizing intellectual tools with less human intercession and this further saved the time and improved viability [18, 19].
8. **Customized Treatment**: Analyzing the clinical history of patient and recognizing comparable history of patients and correlating their treatments and outcomes is troublesome

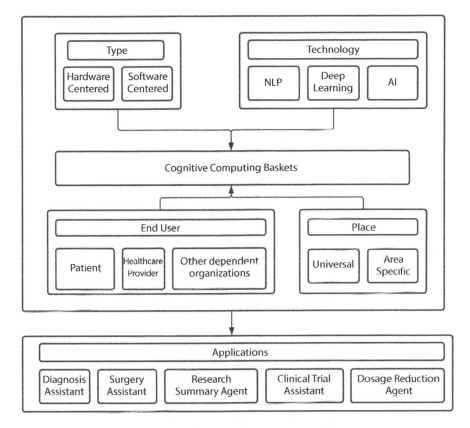

Figure 14.4 Aspects for deploying cognitive services across various applications.

and tedious work. This is currently addressed by CAT agents through Cognitive Inference Engine [20, 21].

9. **Information Recording**: There are numerous portable applications which would record different estimations like Blood Pressure, Heart rate, Oximetry, Actigraphy, and Pulse Wave Velocity. These boundaries are investigated on ceaseless premise and alarm the client for beginning remedial activities [22, 23].

These benefits are weighted based on the number of research papers cited highlighting various aspects of cognitive healthcare management (Figure 14.5 and Figure 14.6).

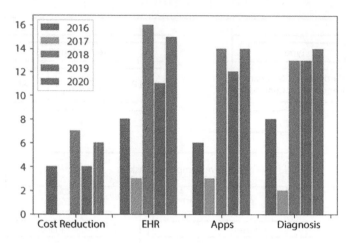

Figure 14.5 Aspect importance for effective cognitive healthcare management.

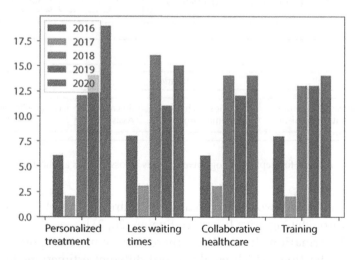

Figure 14.6 Aspect importance for effective cognitive healthcare management.

14.4   Applications of Deploying Cognitive Assisted Technology in Healthcare Management

Various individuals in healthcare management are:

1. Patient – gives data about the indications and history of clinical issues.
2. Medical services providers – this gathering will offer clinical types of assistance needed for relieving the patient infection.

3. Drug companies – conducts best in class examination to decrease the time taken to control the infections without side effects.

4. Insurance agencies – these organizations would take patient's past clinical information to suggest the right strategy such that it benefits the client in long run by balancing their business strategy.

5. Government bodies – all exploration and business medical care associations should act as per the policies of the government and the different bodies comprise to update the rules at periodical time frames dependent on the medical service circumstances in the society.

6. Information services – various third-party organizations conduct several surveys to collect health status of individuals or regions/areas. This information would be additionally utilized by the examination establishments and government bodies to start likely arrangement for improvement of the public health.

We have divided Cognitive Services currently into two groups – Patients and Healthcare Providers. Below, we discuss the applications in the context of these two buckets.

14.4.1   Using Cognitive Services for a Patient's Healthcare Management

1. **Decision Making**: Patients might want to find out about the illness/disease dependent on the manifestations signaled by the CAT agents. For instance, portable specialist agent would give customized rules in dealing with heart related issues [35]. On the opposite side, Diagnostic Reports ought to be surveyed and assessed with utmost precision and the enormous lift toward this path is achieved through CAT. For instance, time utilization to finish radiologist every day exercises can be radically decreased with semi-computerized frameworks like MedicalSieve [36].

2. **Patient Awareness**: An interactive natural language system is required for creating awareness about the symptoms, disease, and daily activities for pre- and post-treatments.

3. **Giving Companionship**: Aged individuals need help for doing their day-by-day proactive tasks and this is feasible to a limited degree with CAT specialists.

4. **Daily Activity Assistant Agents**: Reminding the patient to take the meds as per the remedy and answering client different routine inquiries independent of patient clinical history is possible with cognitive services. Likewise, observing capacities of psychological specialists can be conveyed to any PC and they can evaluate and suggest small scale sitting activities [37].

5. **CAT for Physically challenged**: A savvy and tweaked route framework to help visually challenged people is possible. Not just this, Prosthetic organs like Hands, Legs were being utilized and they increased client solace in the recent occasions with a decrease in cost.

14.4.2   Using Cognitive Services for Healthcare Providers

1. **Decision Support System**: Sometimes Doctors would confuse for taking the right choice and this happens much of the time during crisis situations. The cognitive services would investigate comparative cases all throughout the globe and can give effective recommendations.

2. **Diagnosis Assistant System**: Humans will in general commit mistakes, and this can happen when the indicative reports from various specializations need to be correlated to take conclusion. Cognitive services can check and sum up the reports adequately by which the right treatment can be initiated.

3. **Psychometric Analysis**: The psychological capacities are precisely measured, assessed and this aides in treating mental inabilities at the beginning stages.

4. **Monitoring**: It would be hard for nursing assistants to persistently screen and dissect the information and all these aspects considered, the CAT agents can successfully screen, record, and caution the anomalies [38]. For instance, tracking the client for treatment adherence is manual and wasteful and this exertion is diminished with the aid of cognitive assistants.

5. **Document Analysis**: Some of the symptomatic reports can be dissected by the CAT specialists and alongside this, EHRs of patient clinical history ought to likewise be examined for evaluating the current circumstance and its criticality.

6. **Customized Treatment**: Patients with comparable side effects can't be endorsed with same medicine and the therapy will fluctuate dependent on the patient's clinical history.

7. **Patient Info Extractor**: The specialist should lead a meeting with patient to find out more about the issue and sum up the difficult portrayal to Healthcare Provider.

8. **Auto-Documentation**: Manual documentation of the expert doctors' procedures is time taking and inclined to mistakes. This can be decreased by CAT specialists imagining, deciphering the treatment and produce the documentation naturally. For instance, in [39], the authors fostered a specialist where it can screen the surgical process, recognize the activities, and record them as documentation adhering to the guidelines.

9. **Tele-Medication**: Assisting the patient through phone turned out to be normal of late and this ought to be supplanted by CAT specialist and when the client was not fulfilled, it tends to be diverted to the expert's recommendation.

10. **Training**: Training Healthcare Providers is repetitive task for the management and the training workforce can be reduced with the deployment of CAT agents. This is conceivable in the circumstances with not much specialized ability requirement like training para clinical staff. Broadening it further, the capability in surgical process can be surveyed and scored utilizing CAT specialists and the same was discussed in [40, 41].

14.5 Challenges in Using the Cognitive Assistive Technology in Healthcare Management

Ineptness of the mechanical complexities in medical care would depart numerous difficulties in Cognitive Computing and some of them are briefed below:

1. **Information Privacy**: Patient's information is extremely sensitive and not taking care of in a right manner would penetrate the information security systems and thus would affect the hidden trust of the medical clinic personnel or the association [24, 25].

2. **Taking care of Heterogeneity**: To foster an all-encompassing assistance empowered with intellectual processing, the application would need smoothed out help across various partners [26, 27].

3. **Customized Solutions**: Cognitive Computing utilized general frameworks to foster answers for the target domain. Yet, there is a requirement for custom fitted models which would decrease the development time and expands the ease of use of the intellectual administrations [28, 29].

4. **Volume and Variety**: Healthcare information produced in business and non-business purposes is tremendous and heterogeneous in nature and handling it is tedious. For instance, because of the wearable gadgets and hand-held devices, the individual information being gathered is huge and it would be roughly 1 million GB in an individual's lifetime because of which handling and creating significant ends is time consuming [30, 31].

5. **Prevention**: "Prevention is better than cure" is a typical saying from ages and it isn't even almost accomplished with our general symptomatic diagnostic framework. Because of the wearable gadgets and the knowledge incorporated into it, an individual can forestall certain infections and surprisingly in the most pessimistic scenario, the indications are recognized at beginning phases. However, the intellectual administrations are still at the starting stages as far as tremendous expectations from the technical and non-technical community. To additionally dominate, redid calculations should be yet evolved to connect the information from different sources like, prescriptions, manifestations, lab reports, social history, and family ancestry [5].

6. **Updates**: Another gap at present being stressed by cognitive computing is to give reasonable bits of knowledge of the exploration work occurring all throughout the world by which the nature of clinical consideration would improve. Many research papers were being published in the worldwide market and no individual can process those to deploy them in its entirety. Utilizing the cognitive services for this issue would truly make the healthcare suppliers to stay updated [8].

7. **Thorough Data Availability** [22]: The Healthcare information is abundant however every bit of it was not effectively used in computerized stages. This is creating difficulties for the medical care specialists to mimic human comprehension.

8. **Decreasing Deployment Costs**: Reducing the processing time of CAT agents requires huge infrastructure and this would bring out significant expenses. In addition, different associations are yet wondering whether to move medical services information to cloud or not because

of absence of straightforwardness in information stockpiling and calculations [22].

9. **Heterogeneous Treatments**: Knowledge transfer from Healthcare Providers to CAT agents isn't simple concerning a similar ailment and indications. Additionally, various recommendations can be given and recognizing the right path in critical situation still needs to be explored [33].

10. **Increased Participation**: In all developing countries, lot of small, medium and large-scale hospitals still need to be digitalized and a large number of them are a long way from utilizing CAT specialists for viable Healthcare Management [32].

11. **Correlations**: The information across numerous sources should be correlated under one cohesive strategy and this is time consuming. For instance, patient information gathered from diagnostic reports, electronic health records and wearable gadgets all together need to be analyzed in the global context [34].

From last few years, these challenges of Cognitive Healthcare are highly cited, and they are summarized in Figure 14.7 and Figure 14.8.

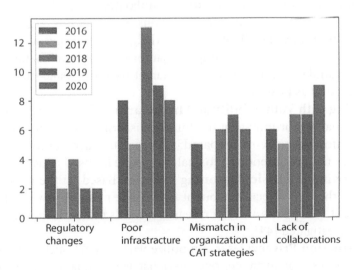

Figure 14.7 Challenges most cited for deploying cognitive assisted healthcare services.

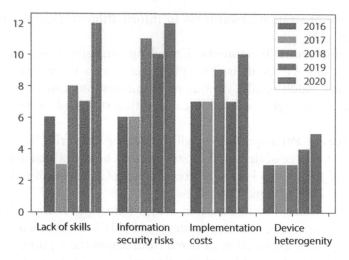

Figure 14.8 Other challenges most cited for deploying cognitive assisted healthcare services.

14.6   Future Directions for Extending Heathcare Services Using CATs

1. **Communication at Different Granularities**: The CAT specialists should show the distinction in discussions based on the target user. For instance, assuming the client isn't knowledgeable, the specialist ought to convey the content without using any jargons. It ought to change the discussion granularity dependent on the target user and make the conversation as natural as possible.

2. **Dealing with Vulnerability and Irregularities**: The CAT specialists use the information for imitating the human discernment. On the off chance that the information being prepared is uproarious, current intellectual specialists are not robust enough to deal with these kinds of issues [42, 43].

3. **Improving the Basic Reasoning Abilities**: Based on the patient basic situation, the CAT specialists ought to help the medical service providers in different viewpoints and the research towards this path should be thoroughly investigated [44].

4. **Information Privacy**: User can utilize various CAT specialists for various purposes. For instance, one specialist would quantify physiological activities of the client, and this would act like additional input for Meal guide agent to customize the diet recommendations effectively. In any case, these inquiries raise the issue of information protection while sharing the data.

5. **Conflict Resolution**: When numerous CAT specialists are attempting to assist a solitary patient then it may sometimes mislead and end up in adverse guidance. For instance, consider a wellbeing application which prescribes everyday food routine to keep heart healthy and the opposite side, if the same patient is utilizing an alternate application for getting ideas to improve protein content, then these two headings endure with clashing goals [45–47].

6. **Improving the Friendly Experience**: Patients/Healthcare suppliers utilizing VR/AR specialists should wear the gadgets and it is awkward to the client and it may not be comfortable in all conditions.

7. **Flexibility**: Patient experiencing certain sicknesses would change voice and looks. For instance, throat disease patient would have changes in the vocal attributes and the separate CAT specialists ought to be adaptable to these kinds of circumstances [48].

8. **Stay Away From Multi-Client Clashes**: Certain CAT specialists like home pods will be utilized by entire housemates and the recommendations can be additionally customized to enhance client experience without ignoring the privacy.

9. **Reduce Costs**: Certain applications require organization of various specialists which would bring about immense expense [49].

10. **Improving the Analytic Exactness**: Many AI models which would show high correctness during simulation can't project the same performance with real data. To address this, the models should well capture the data which is comprehensive and diversified [50–52].

11. **Resource Constrained Environments**: CAT specialists working with restricted assets like battery and memory ought to be advanced to perform complex handling tasks [53, 54]. For instance, in [55], the authors fostered a mechanical partner for object location utilizing the cloud assets and by optimizing the neighborhood calculations.

12. **Emergency Health Records (EMR)**: The content in EMR is filled with short forms and distinctive jargons in relation to Electronic Health Records (EHR). Altered ML approaches should be intended to handle EMR data [47, 53].

13. **Anticipated Performance from CAT Specialists**: Response time, reliability, cost, explainability, and scalability. All these performance metrics may not be fulfilled by each kind of CAT specialist and a compromise between the exhibition measurements ought to be appropriately settled.

14. **Mental Capacities**: Mentally challenged users ought to be trained with CAT specialists to improve their psychological capacities [56, 57]. For instance, in [58], VR based game has been created to improve Parkinson's

patients. Likewise, different applications for improving concentration and memory were accessible but limited in exceeding human expectations.

15. **Improved Learning**: Healthcare Providers can be trained on a simulation environment utilizing VR/AR headsets and this establishes a sensible realistic environment [4, 41].

16. **Reduce the Errors in the Documentation**: Manual recoding of the medical procedures in critical and non-critical situations is time consuming and error prone. The CAT agents can observe and document the process in efficient and effective manner [59, 60].

17. **Ensure the Right Diagnosis**: Many ML models are analyzing the diagnostic reports with high accuracies but mostly in simulation environments. The models can be further improved to suit for diversified diagnosis without compromising on cost.

18. **Customized Monitoring**: Healthcare suppliers ought to have the option to screen the patients for adjustable contentions dependent on the circumstance of the patient. Yet, current CAT specialists were not totally customizable to these kinds of prerequisites [61].

19. **Connecting with Patients**: Patients experiencing infections would have some physical and mental insecurities. The CAT specialists should connect with them considering personalized interests and this would straightforwardly or in a roundabout way assists the patients with showing the wellbeing progress [62].

20. **Graphical Representation**: The fast method of understanding the pattern in the clinical records is to envision both organized and unstructured information. This visual examination ought to likewise be displayed at numerous granularities to make it interpretable for different individuals associated with Healthcare Management which is challenging in realistic scenarios.

21. **Right Dose Treatment**: In most of the cases, the medication which worked for a patient may not work with same viability for the other patient with similar symptoms. To address this challenge, progressed examination should be performed during the clinical treatment to recognize the distinctive elements for the noticed contrasts.

22. **Prevention**: Many illnesses would begin with less serious indications and on the off chance that the patient is analyzed at the ideal time, the seriousness can be diminished in most of the cases. This can be accomplished when the basic illness symptomatic diagnostic abilities were deployed to handheld gadgets.

23. **Controlling the Pandemic**: Pandemic affects millions of individuals and the same was proved with COVID19. It's more than a year that the first case of COVID19 was reported and still it is not controlled completely.

This shows the directions to excel the cognitive stream to handle similar challenges in the future.

24. **Drug Releases**: Without the intercession of Data Analytics, the drug discovery was profoundly tedious interaction, and it can keep going for a long time. This time has been reduced with the intellectual administrations to specific degree and still considerably more savvy CAT specialists should be used for faster drug deployment.

25. **Broadened Features**: The CAT specialists ought not restrict the applications to Healthcare and the patients need deep rooted help and the initial move towards this is virtual mentors [60, 61]. This isn't yet intelligent and shrewd to be abused in the enormous populace spaces.

26. **Training Challenges**: CAT specialists would require extensive training for conveying to the outer world. For instance, assuming a CAT specialist need to help the target client, specialist ought to be provided with different inquiry noting sets and this is troublesome especially when addressing the issue on account of comprehensiveness [34].

27. **Filling the Gap in Terminology**: Two kinds of individuals work on creating CAT specialists, i.e., Clinical area specialists and non-medical personnel. For non-clinical analysts, understanding the ideas about the human functioning is troublesome and time taking process. On the opposite side, for clinical experts, debugging software engineering-based specialists requires additional effort [32, 33].

28. **For ICU**: Mistakes by the CAT specialists in the ordinary circumstances would not be extreme and a similar pattern observed with ICU would cost a whole life and this isn't at all permissible. Current CAT specialists should be altered for crisis conditions and reenacting this for exploratory designs is time taking process [63]. For instance, scientists are utilizing Reinforcement Learning to decrease the odds of over finding and over treatment [60].

29. **Computerization**: Certain CAT specialists could automate the decision making for few medical services applications but in some cases, the choices should be mediated by the human specialists.

30. **Physical Disabilities**: CAT specialists need to discover the core explanations behind different actual inabilities and assuming this done at the beginning phases of pregnancy, it can take be life saver for both parents and kid.

31. **Noisy Environments**: The CAT specialists' efficiency is decreased in loud conditions, and this can severely affect a patient's life that is relying on the agents for enhanced monitoring and care.

32. **Network Issues**: Healthcare specialists' sense, send and measure the data in the cloud. The justification doing this is save the restricted assets of

specialists and furthermore to have quick response time. However, in specific circumstances, like network failures, the greater part of the specialist modules can't work, and this thus would influence the cognitive services. This motivates the development and deployment of cognitive assistants with edge computing capabilities.

14.7   Addressing CAT Challenges in Healthcare as a General Framework

All the prospects of enabling cognitive services in healthcare can be deployed to real workforce when each of the above-mentioned challenges is handled in their own way. But summarizing all of them, we list three general guidelines that can be considered as viable alternatives in using cognitive services for healthcare.

1. **Identify the Business Strategy**: Business vision and mission should be in sync with the objective of using cognitive services in the decision making. If they differ apart, the cost and effort would be increased and thus reduces the mileage of the organization.
2. **Stable and Safe Infrastructure**: The products embedded with cognition would require a secure and reliable service environment by ensuring privacy.
3. **Improve the Expertise**: Collecting and maintaining data is one aspect and the other issue is, the underlying applications which are currently being developed should be properly designed to facilitate the cognitive services and this requires extensive thought process to get a holistic solution.

14.8   Conclusion

Health is the most important aspect that an individual considers and spends beyond his/her capabilities especially during critical illness. Smart healthcare management uses various cognitive services to proactively diagnose the diseases at early stages and reduce the severity in the consequences. These services are not limited to proactive analysis and would aid during the treatment lifecycle across several stakeholders. Cognitive agents are underutilized because of several challenges and myths in health-care community, and all of these are discussed in this chapter by mentioning possible directions in addressing the issues. We strongly believe that the perspectives to solve current health issues will be completely changed and many of them will end up at holistic individual controlled healthcare management.

References

1. Gudivada, V.N., Pankanti, S., Seetharaman, G., Zhang, Y., Cognitive computing systems: Their potential and the future. *Computer*, 52, 5, 13–18, 2019.

2. Zhao, S., *et al.*, *Edge-Based Wearable Systems for Cognitive Assistance: Design Challenges, Solution Framework, and Application to Emergency Healthcare*, CMU, Pennsylvania, 2020.

3. Zhu, Rongbo, *et al.*, Cognitive-inspired computing: Advances and novel applications. *Future Gener. Comp. Sy.*, 109, 706–709, 2020.

4. Cui, J., *et al.*, Pairwise comparison learning based bearing health quantitative modeling and its application in service life prediction. *Future Gener. Comp. Sy.*, 97, 578–586, 2019.

5. Deepak Kumar, J., *et al.*, An intelligent cognitive-inspired computing with big data analytics framework for sentiment analysis and classification. *Inf. Process. Manage.*, 59,1, 102758, 2022.

6. Munzer, B.W., Khan, M.M., Shipman, B., Mahajan, P., Augmented reality in emergency medicine: A scoping review. *J. Med. Internet Res.*, 21, 4, e12368, 2019.

7. Amato, F., Marrone, S., Moscato, V., Piantadosi, G., Picariello, A., Sansone, C., HOLMeS: eHealth in the big data and deep learning era. *Information*, 10, 2, 34–54, 2019.

8. Albesher, A.A., IoT in healthcare: Recent advances in the development of smart cyber-physical ubiquitous environments. *IJCSNS*, 19, 2, 181–186, 2019.

9. Onasanya, A. and Elshakankiri, M., Smart integrated IoT healthcare system for cancer care. *Wirel. Netw.*, 27, 6, 4297–4312, 2021.

10. Pace, P., Aloi, G., Gravina, R., Caliciuri, G., Fortino, G., Liotta, A., An edge-based architecture to support efficient applications for healthcare industry 4.0. *IEEE Trans. Industr. Inform.*, 15, 1, 481–489, 2019.

11. Munzer, B.W., Khan, M.M., Shipman, B., Mahajan, P., Augmented reality in emergency medicine: A scoping review. *J. Med. Internet Res.*, 21, 4, e12368, 2019.

12. Sannino, G., De Falco, I., De Pietro, G., A continuous noninvasive arterial pressure (CNAP) approach for health 4.0 systems. *IEEE Trans. Industr. Inform.*, 15, 1, 498–506, 2019.

13. Almulhim, M., Islam, N., Zaman, N., A lightweight and secure authentication scheme for IoT based e-health applications. *IJCSNS*, 19, 1, 107–120, 2019.

14. Hassan, M.K., El Desouky, A., II, Elghamrawy, S.M., Sarhan, A.M., A hybrid real-time remote monitoring framework with NB-WOA algorithm for patients with chronic diseases. *Future Gener. Comp. Sy.*, 93, 77–95, 2019.

15. Khan, Khalid S., *et al.*, *Undertaking systematic reviews of research on effectiveness: CRD's guidance for carrying out or commissioning reviews.* No. 4, 2n, NHS Centre for Reviews and Dissemination, 2001.

16. Onasanya, A., Lakkis, S., Elshakankiri, M., Implementing IoT/ WSN based smart saskatchewan healthcare system. *Wirel. Netw.*, 25, 7, 3999, 2019.

17. Mutlag, A.A., Ghani, M.K.A., Arunkumar, N., Mohammed, M.A., Mohd, O., Enabling technologies for fog computing in healthcare IoT systems. *Future Gener. Comp. Sy.*, 90, 62–78, 2019.

18. Kang, M., Park, E., Cho, B.H., Lee, K.S., Recent patient health monitoring platforms incorporating internet of things-enabled smart devices. *Int. Neurourol. J.*, 22, Suppl 2, S76, 2018.

19. Chen, M., Li, W., Hao, Y., Qian, Y., Humar, I., Edge cognitive computing based smart healthcare system. *Future Gener. Comp. Sy.*, 86, 403–411, 2018.

20. Ali, O., Shrestha, A., Soar, J., Wamba, S., Cloud computing-enabled healthcare opportunities, issues, and applications: A systematic review. *Int. J. Inf. Manage.*, 43, 146–158, 2018.

21. Garai, A., Pentek, I., Adamko, A., Nemeth, A., A clinical system integration methodology for bio-sensory technology with cloud architecture. *Acta Cybern.*, 23, 2, 513–536, 2017.

22. Almulhim, M., Islam, N., Zaman, N., A lightweight and secure authentication scheme for IoT based e-health applications. *IJCSNS*, 19, 1, 107–120, 2019.

23. Wang, G., Lu, R., Guan, Y.L., Achieve privacy-preserving priority classification on patient health data in remote ehealthcare system. *IEEE Access*, 7, 33565–33576, 2019.

24. Elhoseny, M., Abdelaziz, A., Salama, A.S., Riad, A.M., Muhammad, K., Sangaiah, A.K., A hybrid model of internet of things and cloud computing to manage big data in health services applications. *Future Gener. Comp. Sy.*, 86, 1383–1394, 2018.

25. Jeong, J.S., Han, O., You, Y.Y., A design characteristics of smart healthcare system as the IoT application. *Indian J. Sci. Technol.*, 9, 37, 52, 2016.

26. Saxena, D. and Raychoudhury, V., Design and verification of an NDN-based safety-critical application: A case study with smart healthcare. *IEEE Trans. Syst. Man Cybern.: Syst.*, 49, 5, 991–1005, 2017.

27. Abdellatif, A.A., Mohamed, A., Chiasserini, C.F., Tlili, M., Erbad, A., Edge computing for smart health: Context-aware approaches, opportunities, and challenges. *IEEE Netw.*, 33, 3, 196, 2019.
28. Din, S. and Paul, A., Smart health monitoring and management system: Toward autonomous wearable sensing for internet of things using big data analytics. *Future Gener. Comp. Sy.*, 91, 611–619, 2019.
29. Hsu, W.C. and Li, J.H., Visualising and mapping the intellectual structure of medical big data. *J. Inf. Sci.*, 45, 2, 239–258, 2019.
30. Aceto, G., Persico, V., Pescape, A., The role of information and communication technologies in healthcare: Taxonomies, perspectives, and challenges. *J. Netw. Comput. Appl.*, 107, 125–154, 2018.
31. Sakr, S. and Elgammal, A., Towards a comprehensive data analytics framework for smart healthcare services. *Big Data Res.*, 4, 44–58, 2016.
32. Sheth, A., Yip, H.Y., Shekarpour, S., Extending patient-chatbot experience with internet-of-things and background knowledge: Case studies with healthcare applications. *IEEE Intell. Syst.*, 34, 4, 24–30, 2019.
33. Amin, S.U., Hussain, M.S., Muhammad, G., Alhussein, M., Rahman, M.A., Cognitive smart healthcare for pathology detection and monitoring. *IEEE Access*, 7, 10745–10753, 2019.
34. Shahid, A. H. and Singh, M. P., Computational intelligence techniques for medical diagnosis and prognosis: Problems and current developments. *Biocybern. Biomed. Eng.*, 39, 3, 638–672, 2019.
35. Schizas, C.N., Cognitive computing for supporting eHealth. *Health Technol.*, 7, 1, 11–12, 2017.
36. Syeda-Mahmood, T., *et al.*, Medical sieve: A cognitive assistant for radiologists and cardiologists. *International Society for Optics and Photonics Medical Imaging 2016: Computer-Aided Diagnosis*, vol. 9785, 2016.
37. González-Ortega, D., Díaz-Pernas, F.J., Martínez-Zarzuela, M., Antón-Rodríguez, M., A kinect-based system for cognitive rehabilitation exercises monitoring. *Comput. Methods Programs Biomed.*, 113, 2, 620–631, 20142014.
38. Ruminski, C.M., Clark, M.T., Lake, D.E., Kitzmiller, R.R., Keim-Malpass, J., Robertson, M.P., Simons, T.R., Moorman, J.R., Calland, J.F., Impact of predictive analytics based on continuous cardiorespiratory monitoring in a surgical and trauma intensive care unit. *J. Clin. Monit. Comput.*, 332019, 4, 703–711, 2019.
39. Padoy, N., Blum, T., Ahmadi, S.-A., Feussner, H., Berger, M.-O., Navab, N., Statistical modeling and recognition of surgical workflow. *Med. Image Anal.*, 16, 3, 632–641, 20122012.
40. Miller, K. and Curet, M., Intuitive surgical: An overview. *Robot.-Assist. Minim. Invasive Surg.*, 3–11, 2019.
41. Perrenot, C., Perez, M., Tran, N., Jehl, J. P., Felblinger, J., Bresler, L., Hubert, J., The virtual reality simulator dV-Trainer® is a valid assessment tool for robotic surgical skills. *Surg. Endosc.*, 26, 9, 2587–2593, 2012.

42. Hoque, E., Dickerson, R.F., Preum, S.M., Hanson, M., Barth, A., Stankovic, J.A., Holmes: A comprehensive anomaly detection system for daily in-home activities, in: *2015 International Conference on Distributed Computing in Sensor Systems*, IEEE, pp. 40–51, 2015.

43. Preum, S.M., Stankovic, J.A., Qi, Y., MAPer: A multi-scale adaptive personalized model for temporal human behavior prediction, in: *Proceedings of the 24th ACM International on Conference on Information and Knowledge Management*, pp. 433–442, 2015.

44. Grudin, J., Human-computer interaction. *Annu. Rev. Inf. Sci. Technol.*, 45, 1, 367–430, 2011.

45. Ma, M., Preum, S.M., Stankovic, J.A., Cityguard: A watchdog for safety-aware conflict detection in smart cities, in: *Proceedings of the Second International Conference on Internet-of-Things Design and Implementation*, pp. 259–270, 2017.

46. Preum, S.M., Mondol, A.S., Ma, M., Wang, H., Stankovic, J.A., Preclude: Conflict detection in textual health advice, in: *2017 IEEE International Conference on Pervasive Computing and Communications (PerCom)*, IEEE, pp. 286–296, 2017.

47. Alam, R., Dugan, J., Homdee, N., Gandhi, N., Ghaemmaghami, B., Meda, H., Lach, J., BESI: Reliable and heterogeneous sensing and intervention for in-home health applications. in: *2017 IEEE/ACM International Conference on Connected Health: Applications, Systems and Engineering Technologies (CHASE)*, pp. 147–156, IEEE, 2017, July.

48. Kumar, A., Using cognition to resolve duplicacy issues in socially connected healthcare for smart cities. *Comput. Commun.*, 152, 272–281, 2020.

49. Sato, D., Oh, U., Naito, K., Takagi, H., Kitani, K., Asakawa, C., Navcog3: An evaluation of a smartphone-based blind indoor navigation assistant with semantic features in a large-scale environment, in: *Proceedings of the 19th International ACM SIGACCESS Conference on Computers and Accessibility*, ACM, pp. 270–279, 2017.

50. Obermeyer, Z., Powers, B., Vogeli, C., Mullainathan, S., Dissecting racial bias in an algorithm used to manage the health of populations. *Science*, 366, 6464, 447–453, 2019.

51. Reddy, S., Allan, S., Coghlan, S., Cooper, P., A governance model for the application of AI in healthcare. *J. Am. Med. Inform. Assoc.*, 273, 491–497, 2020.

52. Strickland, E., IBM watson, heal thyself: How IBM overpromised and under-delivered on AI healthcare. *IEEE Spectr.*, 56, 4, 24–31, 2019.

53. Preum, S., Shu, S., Hotaki, M., Williams, R., Stankovic, J., Alemzadeh, H., CognitiveEMS: A cognitive assistant system for emergency medical services. *ACM SIGBED Rev.*, 16, 2, 51–60, 2019.

54. Musliner, D.J., Hendler, J.A., Agrawala, A.K., Durfee, E.H., Strosnider, J.K., Paul, C.J., The challenges of real-time AI. *Computer*, 28, 1, 58–66, 1995.

55. Vorobieva, H., Soury, M., Hède, P., Leroux, C., Morignot, P., Object recognition and ontology for manipulation with an assistant robot, in: *International Conference on Smart Homes and Health Telematics*, Springer, pp. 178–185, 2010.
56. Chang, Y.-J., Kang, Y.-S., Huang, P.-C., An augmented reality (AR)-based vocational task prompting system for people with cognitive impairments. *Res. Dev. Disabil.*, 34, 10, 3049–3056, 2013.
57. Van de Laar, B., Nijholt, A., Zwiers, J., Monitoring user's brain activity for a virtual coach, in: *International Conference on Entertainment Computing*, Springer, pp. 511–513, 2010.
58. dos Santos Mendes, F.A., Pompeu, J.E., Lobo, A.M., da Silva, K.G., de Paula Oliveira, T., Zomignani, A.P., Piemonte, M.E.P., Motor learning, retention and transfer after virtual-reality-based training in Parkinson's disease–effect of motor and cognitive demands of games: A longitudinal, controlled clinical study. *Physiotherapy*, 98, 3, 217–223, 2012.
59. Croatti, A., Montagna, S., Ricci, A., A personal medical digital assistant agent for supporting human operators in emergency scenarios. in: *Agents and multi agent systems for healthcare*, pp. 59–75, Springer, Cham., 2017.
60. Croatti, A., Montagna, S., Ricci, A., Gamberini, E., Albarello, V., Agnoletti, V., BDI personal medical assistant agents: The case of trauma tracking and alerting. *Artif. Intell. Med.*, 96, 187–197, 2019.
61. Ruminski, C.M., Clark, M.T., Lake, D.E., Kitzmiller, R.R., Keim-Malpass, J., Robertson, M.P., Simons, T.R., Moorman, J.R., Calland, J.F., Impact of predictive analytics based on continuous cardiorespiratory monitoring in a surgical and trauma intensive care unit. *J. Clin. Monit. Comput.*, 33, 4, 703–711, 2019.
62. Mostajeran, F., Katzakis, N., Ariza, O., Freiwald, J.P., Steinicke, F., Welcoming a holographic virtual coach for balance training at home: Two focus groups with older adults, in: *2019 IEEE Conference on Virtual Reality and 3D User Interfaces (VR)*, IEEE, pp. 1465–1470, 2019.
63. Komorowski, M., Celi, L.A., Badawi, O., Gordon, A.C., Faisal, A.A., The artificial intelligence clinician learns optimal treatment strategies for sepsis in intensive care. *Nat. Med.*, 24, 11, 1716–1720, 2018.

Index

Printed and bound by CPI Group (UK) Ltd, Croydon, CR0 4YY

27/10/2024

14580133-0002